DOCUMENTING
TRANSNATIONAL MIGRATION

General Editor: **Jacqueline Waldren**, *Institute of Social Anthropology,*
University of Oxford

DOCUMENTING
TRANSNATIONAL MIGRATION

Jordanian Men Working and Studying
in Europe, Asia and North America

Richard T. Antoun

Berghahn Books
New York • Oxford

First published in 2005 by

Berghahn Books

www.berghahnbooks.com

Library of Congress Cataloging-in-Publication Data

Antoun, Richard T.
   Documenting transnational migration : Jordanian men working and studying in Europe,
Asia, and North America / Richard T. Antoun.
      p. cm. — (New directions in anthropology ; v. 25)
   Includes bibliographical references and index.
   ISBN 1-84545-037-X (hardback : alk. paper)
      1. Jordan—Emigration and immigration. 2. Alien labor, Jordanian—Foreign countries.
   3. Jordanian students—Foreign countries. I. Title. II. Series.

JV8749.5.A58 2005
04.8'095695—dc23   2004062349

British Library Cataloguing in Publication Data

A catalogue record for this book is available from
the British Library.

Printed in the United States on acid-free paper

ISBN 1-84545-037-X hardback

CONTENTS

Key to Transliteration of Arabic Letters and Symbols

CONSONANTS

ا	a	د	d	ط	ṭ	م	m
ب	b	ذ	dh	ظ	TH	ن	n
ت	t	ر	r	ع	ʾ	ه	h
ث	th	ز	z	غ	gh	و	w
ج	j	س	s	ف	f	ى	y
ح	ḥ	ش	sh	ق	q		
خ	kh	ص	ṣ	ك	k		
		ض	ḍ	ل	l		

VOWELS

ـَ	a
ـِ	i
ـُ	u

OTHER SYMBOLS

- • indicated by the doubling of the letter

- ـ indicated by the doubling of the letter
  followed by a vowel

Place names will be spelled according to the most common usage found on maps.

LIST OF TABLES, CHART, DIAGRAM, MAP, KEY

⚜

Chapter 2

Chapter 4

Chapter 5

Chapter 6

Chapter 7

Chapter 8

PREFACE

The reader of any book has the right to know how it came to be. My interest in the study of transnational migration as a major sociocultural process connecting the global society and the local community did not begin until 1986 when I went for the seventh time in twenty-seven years to conduct field research in the peasant village of Kufr al-Ma, Jordan. I had collected data on migration for work from Kufr al-Ma to the Arabian Peninsula in 1979 during a brief field trip and previously in 1966, when I noted that a number of villagers had traveled to Beirut in the previous decade to seek work mainly as manual laborers. In my first field trip in 1959–60 I had even noted that the middle-aged generation of villagers had worked temporarily as construction laborers and fishermen in British mandated Palestine in the 1930s; and that a number of elders had been drafted into the Ottoman army and sent to the Balkans, Anatolia, and Egypt during World War I! But these facts created no serious interest on my part in pursuing the study of transnational migration.

My decision to pursue the subject in earnest began only in 1986 when I began conversing with returned migrants regarding their experiences abroad after long-time residence in Arabia, Europe, North America, and Asia as workers, army trainees, and, above all, students pursuing higher education. I became familiar with their long exposure to radically different cultures, and the processes by which they coped, adapted, and preserved their own ethnic identities and, in the process, transformed them. As I questioned them about their attitudes towards current social questions such as the unemployment problem in Jordan, birth control, women's work outside the home, the continuing pertinence of tribal law, and their views about the value of their own village upbringing, traditions, and way of life, I realized that a case study of transnational migration could illuminate the relationship between individual and social change and between the dominant demographic, economic, and social development at the end of the twentieth century—transnational migration—and the historic anchor of social life and culture—the local community.

Two other observations moved me to continue my study as I began reading books on the subject in academic libraries, continued interviewing migrants in Jordan as well as in the diaspora (United States and Greece), and, not least important, began to read more regularly press reports on transnational migration in the United States. The first was that although the writing on transnational migration was massive, it focused mainly on its economic and demographic aspects (on "labor migration," shortage of labor, remittances, inflation, and dependence on foreign labor) and neglected its humanistic aspects—the impact it had on the migrants themselves: their style of life, their worldviews, and their attitudes towards current social questions. In particular, it neglected transnational migration for higher education—the dominant stream of migration from Kufr al-Ma and, perhaps, Jordan.

Second, I noted that both American academic and journalistic writing about migration emphasized its negative implications: its association with oppression, fragmentation, disjunction, anomie, crime, illegality, racism, and the attempts of states to control migration in a punitive fashion. This writing did not emphasize migration's positive and transformative aspects, the aspects that impressed me in my own research: modes of controlled acculturation, living in two worlds, "living on the border," the reinterpretation of tradition and through such reinterpretation the accommodation of transnational migrants to a local (origin) community of continued resilience.

My previous field work of over thirty years in Kufr al-Ma involving substantial participant observation had acquainted me with many of the fathers and grandfathers of current migrants, most of whom had never met me but had heard about me, if only because I had deposited a copy of the ethnographic monograph I had written about the community in the local school library.[1] With one exception all migrants cooperated with me in my stated endeavor to write a book about the impact of transnational migration on them and on the village.[2] My knowledge of the village community and the individual families within it, including genealogical data, and occupational and interpersonal histories, has undoubtedly aided me in the interpretation of the impact of the migration experience not only on the sons but on their fathers, and has provided an in-depth view of migration synchronically and diachronically. One chapter is specifically devoted to the question of the intergenerational reinterpretation of traditions and emphasizes that this problem is best handled by an analysis at the family (rather than some higher) level.

The detailed ethnography that follows is contextually situated through the lives of human beings within the framework of a particular society, culture, and time. The society is Jordan, the culture is tribal, post-peasant, and Middle Eastern, and the time is the explosion of transnational migration as a result of OPEC oil prices in the 1970s and 1980s, which makes the setting global. The best way for outsiders to understand a culture/society is to work through a problem or process (here transnational migration) by appreciating how it affects the lives of flesh-and-blood people. This detailed ethnography, contextualized in time and place and traced through the lives of individuals, is the choice new direction of anthropology at the beginning of a new century. However, this study does have comparative implications. At this point in history as the United States, Europe, and the Middle East become more involved with one another (economically, politically, and, unfortunately, militarily) and stereotypes proliferate, descriptive accounts that include (rather than exclude) the Middle Eastern people will become more important. Jordan's tribal culture is in some respects like Iraq's. My description of Jordanian tribal norms and their adjustment to the ever-changing transnational world will be useful for Americans and Europeans trying to understand Iraqis as they react to the intrusion of another radically different culture into their society.

I wish to record my thanks to all those individuals and institutions who have supported my current research, including the State University of New York at Binghamton for awarding me two sabbatical research leaves, one to conduct the field research and another to write the manuscript, and the New York State United University Professions Committee for awarding me an Experienced Faculty Travel Award in 1990 that enabled me to interview migrants in Texas and Seattle, Washington in 1991. I wish to thank the American Center for Oriental Research and its former director, David McCreery, for allowing me to use its accommodations and research facilities in Amman in 1986 and again in 1989. I would like to thank the Institute of Archeology and Anthropology of Yarmouk University and its former director, Moawiyah Ibrahim, and in particular, my colleague, Seteny Shami of the same institution, for their cooperation and support during my intensive period of field work in northern Jordan in 1986. I also wish to thank Raslan Ahmed Beni Yasin, former director of the Center for Jordanian Studies, at the same university for his help in providing me office space to process my research results.

Thanks are also due to graphic artist Stan Kauffman in Educational Communications and to Kathleen Stanley of the Department of Anthropology for their professional help in preparing maps, diagrams, and tables.

Specific thanks is due to my friends, colleagues, and graduate students, those at other universities as well as those at the State University of New York at Binghamton, for taking the time out of busy schedules to read parts of the manuscript and to offer helpful comments and criticisms. In particular I would like to thank Hastings Donnan, Ilyas BaYunus, Barbara Metcalf, Peter Dodd, Nicolas Gavrielides, Iftikhar Ahmed, Fran Abrahamer Rothstein, Andrew Shryock, Helen Rivlin, Robert Latowsky, Bill Young, Muneera Murdock, Robert Cunningham, Rukhsana Hasan, Vinnie Melomo, Spyros Spyrou, Howard Rosing, Dick Moench, Randy McGuire, Fuad Khuri, Sam Chianis, and Mary Hegland.

Finally, I wish to thank my wife, who supported me through the whole enterprise, and the people of Kufr al-Ma who have put up with my constant intrusions into their lives over the years, particularly the migrants who were hospitable to me both in Jordan and in the diaspora. I hope that this book by recording a signifi-cant process of change as well as continuity in their lives, and by documenting a worldwide process of migration in specific and human terms, will contribute to a greater understanding of their world and ours.

Notes

1. The title of the monograph is *Arab Village: A Social Structural Study of a Transjordanian Peasant Community,* 1972. One migrant whom I met at the Seattle airport in 1991 said that he remem-bered me from his childhood in the village—I knew his father but did not remember him—because I passed out candy to the children when I got off the bus at the village entrance. I have no recollection of such an event but assume it occurred.

2. This is not to say that all migrants trusted me or surveyed my activities with complete approval. In fact, as a result of my field work in 1986 I became aware of considerable ambivalence about my presence, particularly by the younger generation of village men, who set out to convert me to Islam. The village's changing perception of me and its significance for my field research is an important subject pertinent to critical anthropology and its emphasis on the dialogical charac-ter of field inquiry, questions of identity, and the existence of power differentials. I have written about this problem in other places. See Antoun, "Civil Society, Tribal Process, and Change in Jordan: An Anthropological View," *International Journal of Middle East Studies,* Vol. 32, 2000, 441–463; *Understanding Fundamentalism: Christian, Islamic and Jewish Movements,* AltaMira Press, Walnut Creek, California, 2001; and "Fundamentalism and the Bureaucratization of Religion: A Jordanian Case Study" (unpublished manuscript).

INTRODUCTION
Transnational Migration, the Themes Pursued in Its Analysis, and the Jordanian Background of the Case Study

Goals of the Research and Its Methodology

This book is an in-depth anthropological case study of the experience of transnational migration of villagers from one community, the village of Kufr al-Ma, in one country in the Middle East, Jordan. It is in-depth not only in its combination of standard research techniques (questionnaires, interviews and surveys) with participant observation to provide greater contextualization for the individuals and families studied, but also in drawing on the data gathered in nine research trips over a period of thirty-nine years, often dealing with several generations of the same family in the same community. By recording the experiences of these migrants the book provides a valuable historical record of a single case. This book, then, is intended as a contribution to oral micro-social history as well as social anthropology.

But the case reflects a process that is worldwide, and the implications of the study are comparative. The terms, "transnational" and "community" are important here. The migration described is not just over national borders, it is across them in a contraventional sense: the migration establishes social networks, acculturative trends and images, and aspirations that cannot be contained by nations. In many cases these images and aspirations are triggered by residence in not just one country but several. The establishment of a new journal entitled, *Diaspora*, in 1991 is a belated recognition of the necessity to deal with "the world as a 'space' continually reshaped by forces—cultural, political, technological, demographic, and above all economic...." And the necessity to recognize that "the nation-state ... imagine[d] and represent[ed] ... as a land, a territory, a place that functions as the site of homogeneity, equilibrium, integration" no longer captures the reality of day-to-day living or imagining of millions of current and former migrants in a transnational world.[1]

On the other hand, the village from which this migration flows was and still is a "community" in the sense of a discrete settlement that continues to provide a focus for the interests and the imagination of migrants, if not their residence.[2] Ninety percent of all migrants who have left Kufr al-Ma have returned to Jordan. The great majority still live in the village, though they work outside it. Those who do not live in it maintain contact through frequent visitation of their immediate families, kinfolk, affines, lands, or enterprises. This paradox/tension between the transnational world and the weakening but persistent community is a focus of description and analysis.

Documentation, then, is a primary goal of this book. It aims to provide a record of both change and continuity—to record the variety of visions of the village past, the role of father/son, and that of the law/state as well as the acculturative trends and/or the process of "living in two worlds." The book also provides descriptive statistics on migrants: their age, sex, and occupation, their countries of destination, institutional foci (university campus vs. military classroom and barracks vs. mosque), number of years lived/worked in the diaspora, incomes, educational levels, and number of home visits.

A second goal is humanistic: to provide an account of the migration experience from the migrant's perspective. "To present the insider's view of a culture has long been one of the stated goals of the profession of anthropology."[3] To that end I have attempted to include the verbatim statements of as many migrants as possible, however infelicitous or repetitive.

Besides providing a multivocal account of the migrant's experience, the study aims to record migrants' attitudes towards important social questions, e.g., unemployment, birth control, tribal law, women's work, i.e., towards social change; and it aims to analyze them in terms of concepts such as the reinterpretation of tradition, the pluralization of belief, compartmentalization, the decline of multiplexity, antagonistic acculturation, the encapsulation of migrants in the diaspora, preadaptive experience before the diaspora, and the internalization/rejection of paternal models. At a more general theoretical level, the aim of the book is to capture both social action and meaning, i.e., to describe what people do and also what reasons they give for doing it.

The methodology applied follows from the goals of the research and my previous field work experience in the village. Since I had earned the trust of the older generation of village members through my previous research in the community over a number of years, I was able to conduct a number of conversation-interviews with their sons, brothers, grandsons, and nephews in the village in 1986, when the bulk of data for the book was collected.[4] I label these "conversation-interviews" because although I had a set number of questions that I asked each migrant,[5] at each point the individual was allowed to elaborate on what they thought was important, i.e., to tell their own stories. Often, I interjected questions that led informants to elaborate *their* stories. These stories are essential for allowing multivocality in the study. As the recent work in critical anthropology has affirmed, it is necessary for the anthropologist to allow voices other than his/her own to speak.[6]

Initial conversation-interviews with returned migrants in Kufr al-Ma in 1986 were followed by four interviews with migrants and their spouses in Texas and one in Seattle in 1990 and an interview with a migrant couple in Greece in 1993. In addition to participant observation and conversation-interviews, the author collected descriptive statistics from village informants on transnational migration from the village first in 1979 and again in 1986. On three short one-week field trips in 1984, 1989, and 1998 supplementary qualitative and quantitative data were gathered in the village and in Irbid and Amman.

Quite apart from the techniques of research, the well-documented case study has been selected as the method of research. The validity of the case study's conclusions rests upon the internal coherence of the argument, the detailed synchronic and diachronic data that provides the evidence, and the close fit between the evidence and the concepts used.

Themes Pursued and Concepts Used

Following the introduction, this book is divided into eight chapters. All eight chapters describe an aspect of transnational migration through migrant accounts, with the last examining these accounts in a comparative perspective to highlight their crosscultural significance. Four of the chapters, 3, 4, 5, and 6, describe a much neglected aspect, migration in pursuit of higher education (to Greece, Pakistan, the United States, and western Europe); one, the second, describes migration for work (to the Arabian Peninsula); one, the first, describes migration through military channels (to the U.S.A., Great Britain, France, and Pakistan); and the seventh chapter weighs the impact of migration, both internal and transnational, on the village community, in particular on the attitudes of family members towards one another.

We start with migration through the army because the Jordanian army antedated the Jordanian state, was instrumental in its creation, and along with other public sector institutions continues to provide the main field of employment for Jordanians. Chapter One focuses on the Jordanian army as a vehicle for economic, social, and attitudinal change and as a vehicle for multinational and multicultural exposure on the one hand, and as an institution that merges into society (due to liberal home-leave policy, recognition of bureaucratic levels, and promotion through the ranks), and is at one with society's conservative aims and values, on the other. Army men sent on military missions abroad, frequently to several countries, were encapsulated in classrooms and barracks on army bases, and met natives of the countries they visited, usually in limited milieus such as discos, hospitals, and embassies. The chapter describes the continuum of multicultural exposure and its implications for change/conservatism and poses the question of whether the army is a disseminator of practical skills useful to retired veterans and whether the status of those veterans has an impact on village life.

The second chapter provides an illuminating glimpse of the society and culture of the Arabian Peninsula from the migrant perspective. It is dominated by the attempt to make sense out of the substantial instrumental, circulatory (as well as chain) migration of Jordanian villagers to Saudi Arabia and the Gulf following the rise of OPEC oil prices in 1973. This migration was without the hope or desire of assimilation and without the possibility of integration into Arabian society. The chapter documents the amazingly diverse white collar and blue collar occupational structure with sharply contrasting daily, weekly, and monthly work rhythms in diverse geographical settings and ecological niches. A major aim of the analysis is to explain the counter-intuitive fact that the great majority of migrants from Kufr al-Ma were encapsulated in residence, work, and leisure activities from Saudis and native Gulf residents while at the same time they had a wide exposure to Europeans and North Americans on the one hand and non-Arabian Arabs (Syrians, Lebanese, Sudanese, Egyptians, Palestinians) and Asians on the other. These issues are explored in excerpts from seven conversation-interviews with migrants. The chapter records descriptive statistics for migrants, the wide variety of experiences they enjoyed/endured, and the ethnic stratification that frequently constrained their living circumstances. It introduces the concept of the reinterpretation of tradition as an adaptive cultural mechanism in relation to attitudes towards tribal and Islamic law.

Chapter Three describes in capsule fashion the migration of two young students for higher education to Germany and Egypt/England. It treats transnational migration as a stress-point in a life history and raises the question of the consequences for the individual migrant of a prolonged exposure to alien cultural and political systems and radically different living circumstances. It points to the counter-intuitive fact that the pursuit of secular education for professional skills has religious dimensions and examines the possibility of the survival of the religious persona in a secular society. The chapter introduces the concepts of pre-adaptation, controlled acculturation, "living on the border," and patrifilial identification to explain how Jordanian students were able to maintain their ethnic identity over many years in societies that in some respects they admired and were fascinated with, but that they regarded as morally, deeply flawed.

Chapter Four sets out to explain two outstanding puzzling facts about Jordanian migration to Greece. Despite the wide gap in religion between Jordan and Greece (Islam vs. Greek Orthodox Christianity) and the completely different languages spoken, migrants to Greece in pursuit of higher education (almost entirely medicine, veterinary medicine, and engineering) had the highest rate of exogamous marriage (six of eight to Greek women) and the lowest rate of return to Jordan after finishing their education (three of eight). The chapter describes and analyzes the surprising fit between Jordanian men of tribal background and Greek women of northern rural background and considers the importance of the Greek consanguine family and the Greek ethos of openness to strangers and lively after-hours family and friend-oriented public life. The chapter also explores the mechanisms by which Jordanian men preserved their ethnic identity in an open society that permitted them to work with, court, and marry Greeks. Concepts such as impression management, dissimulation (*taqiyya*), symbolic ethnicity, reidentification by alter, as well as the importance of naming children and the Muslim marriage contract are introduced to understand the preservation of ethnic identity despite longtime residence (from seven to fourteen years) and integration into Greek society. The concept of the reinterpretation of tradition also is reintroduced and elaborated with respect to the Jordanian code of modesty and honor as it operates in Greece.

Chapter Five describes the chain migration to Pakistan, by far the most popular target for the pursuit of higher education (twenty-seven students) and contrasts it with the chain migration to Greece with a dispersion (rather than a concentration as in Greece) of migrants, geographically, institutionally, and occupationally over the country and its universities. In Pakistan Jordanians experienced diverse multicultural exposure, fraternizing with students from different nations and traveling to different areas of Pakistan (as a result of prolonged student strikes and government closure), and observing a variety of its ethnic groups. Unlike in Greece, however, students in Pakistan were encapsulated residentially, linguistically, and commensally (in separate dining facilities) with only one of the twenty-seven marrying a Pakistani, and all returning to Jordan. The chapter explores the factors working against acculturation and assimilation in Pakistan, including the status incongruence of Jordanian students and Pakistani professors, the linguistic situation in Pakistan, and the lack of fit between the relatively egalitarian Jordanian tribal ethos and the class/caste system of Pakistan[7] as well as the extremes of wealth and poverty. The chapter also emphasizes the varying experiences of migrants, often little related to the pursuit of higher education, e.g., with Arabian businessmen and Afghan rebels who are the products of transnational migration and a truly global society.

Chapter Six returns to the theme of the reaction of migrants to prolonged exposure to an open society and an alien culture and political system and weighs the possibilities for the development of three forms of sociocultural transformation—assimilation, acculturation, and "living on the border"—in six indepth conversation-interviews with migrants to Texas and their wives. It explores the key role of the mentor (good friend, girlfriend/wife, affine, ethnic family) in the transformative process and explores the varied mechanisms of controlled acculturation (e.g., Sunday dinner-soiree, basketball group), that allowed migrants who did not choose to assimilate not only to maintain their ethnic identity, but also to transform its cultural content, while "living on the border." The chapter returns to concepts/themes previously discussed such as programmed decision-making, the pluralization of belief, and the relativization of public value to understand how new cultural content related to new demographic, technological, and social structural circumstances is accommodated to Jordanian mores concerning the sexual division of labor, work and marriage, and the honor code. It also introduces the concept of misadaptation to complement the concept of preadaptation to understand why some migrants readily opt for assimilation and others do not. The chapter also contrasts the exposure of Jordanian students in the United States with those in Greece and Pakistan by emphasizing the constant change the former experienced/endured whether in home, school, work, or social environments.

Chapter Seven returns to the theme/concept of the reinterpretation of tradition as a significant process in coping with change and explores this theme at the family level, documenting and analyzing the various views/evaluations held by a number of brothers toward their father, and by implication toward the past and their own village community. It also documents both the supportive and the conflictive aspects of father-son relations as well as the persistence of some joint family corporations (groups of brothers) acting to afford mutual sibling support for higher professional education and marriage over a number of years. The chapter emphasizes the multivocality of tradition even within a single family and yet the continued normative resonance of the moral (village) society in spite of the decline of multiplexity and the egalitarian ethos and the strain developing between close kinsmen as a result of geographical mobility, occupational differentiation, wealth differences, and the development of different styles of life and attitudes.

The last chapter takes the data on transnational migration from Kufr al-Ma, and explores its comparative theoretical implications, pointing out the relevance of the Jordanian case for other cases of migration in the global society. It analyzes the attempt of migrants to achieve socioeconomic integration as well as cultural (cognitive) integration in the diaspora in terms of three quite different though sometimes overlapping styles of adjustment and adaptation: assimilator, sojourner, and exile. It discusses the various factors working for or against assimilation. And it states the rationale for the author's more positive view of the experience of transnational migration in the postmodern world than those who view it negatively in terms of exploitation, fragmentation, alienation, and anomie.

Migration and the Middle East

Migration is a phenomenon of great antiquity and of universal scope, and it has occurred due to a variety of particular circumstances or some combination of them: poor geographic or climatic conditions, conquest, pursuit of higher social and economic status, and religious reasons (pilgrimage, persecution).[8] At the beginning of the century one school of anthropological thought with its home in Vienna, termed the *kulturkreislehre* or culture circle doctrine, explained the diffusion of all culture in terms of the successive mass migrations of peoples across continents and the deposit of their cultural traditions/artifacts in layerlike strata over long periods of time.[9] A well-known anthropogeographer, Ratzel, writing at the end of the nineteenth century, stated that the earth must have been traversed many, many times by primitive groups dating back to early times, accounting for the constant spread of culture. He is remembered for his aphorism, "The world is small." More recently, anthropologists have drawn attention to the important social psychological factors that make the current experience of transnational migration a very different one for different migrants in the same place, or even for the same migrant at different times during the stay in the diaspora, by referring to "the crazy space between exile and migration."[10]

Some scholars of migration question the very use of the term, "migration," to describe the current movement of people between the Middle East, North Africa, and Europe, suggesting the phrases, "shift of manpower" or "labor migration" as more appropriate to emphasize the temporary (though perhaps long-term) character of the phenomenon and its exploitative (as well as beneficial) economic and political consequences for labor-exporting and labor-importing countries.[11]

In the Middle East large-scale movements of people by states for reasons of real politik and in the twentieth century, nationalism, have not been infrequent, e.g., in the sixteenth century the Safavid shahs, Tahmasp and Abbas, forcibly removed Kurds from border areas in western Iran and resettled them more than one thousand miles away in border areas in eastern Iran and Afghanistan.[12] And after World War I there was a large-scale exchange of ethnic populations between Greece and Turkey. Indeed, Janet Abu-Lughod has argued that war and politics are the underlying factors accounting for migrations in the Arab World.[13] She points out that wars have led to the relocation of Egyptians both internally and externally (to Kuwait and Saudi Arabia) in 1967, the migration of Syrians from the Golan to Damascus, the removal of western businessmen from Beirut to Athens and Amman (in both 1967 and 1982), and the migration of Lebanese from southern Lebanon to Beirut. She emphasizes that such migrations are unpredictable, depending on the sudden outbreaks of war or their reversals, as with the sudden 1975 Egyptian-Israeli peace treaty (and the sudden 1993 Palestinian-Israeli accord).

The 1991 Gulf War is another example of war and international politics' unpredictable impact on migration in the Middle East.[14] Television screens and newspapers were filled with images of bedraggled refugees standing or camping at international border crossings. In August 1990, months before the Gulf War began, there was an exodus of a million Arab and Asian workers and an additional 460,000 Kuwaitis from Iraq and Kuwait. One million Yemenis were also forced to leave Saudi Arabia during the following autumn. And after the civil war in Iraq early in 1991, 1½ million Kurds fled to Turkey or Iran, or were displaced in Iraq itself along with Shi'a Muslims.[15]

Refugees and ethnic minorities have long been a major component of Middle Eastern and, indeed, world migration. In 1991 "11.2 million of the world's total of 16.7 million refugees originated in the region, ranging from Afghanistan to Morocco and Turkey to the Horn of Africa."[16] See Table 1 in appendix following chapter for a breakdown of the sources of refugees in the Middle East and their countries of asylum. These descriptive statistics, provided by the sociologist Humphrey, emphasize not only the importance of forced migration in the Middle East and North Africa, but also the fragility of the integration of migrants in the place of migration. The sudden reversal of migrant fortunes by war and international politics is well illustrated by the Yemeni case in the Gulf War. The Yemenis had an elite status in Saudi Arabia. They entered the country without work permits or the necessity of a sponsor/guarantor (*kafil*), and they could obtain a visa at any port of entry and without a passport. They were the only migrant group in Saudi Arabia allowed to own businesses. Because of the refusal of the Yemeni government to condemn the August Iraqi invasion of Kuwait, on 19 September, 1990 all Yemenis in Saudi Arabia were given thirty days to find a Saudi sponsor or majority owner for their businesses and to obtain a residence permit.[17] A massive exodus of a million Yemenis back to Yemen occurred, with huge refugee camps and a general polarization of Yemeni society as a result.

Another enormous flow of labor migration complements the unpredictable flow of forced migration discussed above. This flow is instrumental and economic in motivation, directed at Europe and the Arabian Peninsula, and is a matter of family decision-making and individual choice; though that decision-making is constrained by the dependent relationship of certain polities and economies in the world economic system. One flow is that of Turks to Germany (1.5 million in 1984) with smaller numbers to France, the Netherlands, and Belgium.[18] Initially in the 1950s and 1960s these were young, skilled single males and later, in the 1970s and 1980s, unskilled married men who brought their wives and children.[19] Although their initial aim was to emigrate for a certain amount of time to earn a certain amount of money for a certain purpose, as time passed more and more migrants tended to stay in Germany and take up a new way of life permitting them to earn nonagricultural income on a long-term basis. In 1980 almost 20 percent had been in Germany ten to fifteen years, and another 30 percent between six and ten years.[20] The second flow from North Africa to France and secondarily Belgium and the Netherlands, reached more than five million by 1995. The last flow, triggered by the 1973 oil-pricing revolution, led to a quantum leap of transnational migration in the Middle East to the Arabian Peninsula and Libya. By 1975, 3.5 million migrants were living in these Middle Eastern countries, and it was estimated that 5.5 million were living there by 1985.[21] Tables 2 and 3 (appendix) record the flow of migrant workers into the labor-importing countries of the Middle East in 1975 and 1985. The oil-producing countries relied so much on imported workers because of their low population, their young age profile, and low female participation in the (extramural) workforce, the lack of education, literacy, and training of that workforce, and a tribal ethos unfriendly to manual work.[22] This migrant manpower was predominantly of males, largely without their families, with recruitment by firms located within the host country, by local agents, by unofficial middlemen, or as part of a "package deal" by a number of multinational corporations, sometimes through advertising. However, as the migration cycle continues, the tendency is for family members to accompany the migrant worker. Work and residence permits are often strictly confined to times stipulated in work contracts, and change of work is possible only through written permission. Unless migrant workers belong to highly skilled professional groups, they are not formally granted permission to settle in a host country for an indefinite period unless they are accompanied by their families.[23] That is, Middle Eastern migrants in the oil countries are classified as nonpermanent noncitizens. This last wave of migration to Arabia was probably not primarily a response to economic and political crises at home, but to the opportunity to enhance income abroad and raise the standard of living of the family.[24] There is some evidence that in the rural sector it was not the poorest but rather the somewhat better-off peasants who migrated.[25]

The flow of migrants from the non–oil exporting countries of the Middle East (Egypt, Yemen, Jordan, Syria, Lebanon, Sudan) and increasingly South and Southeast Asia (Pakistan, India, Thailand) into the oil-exporting states of the Arabian Peninsula (Saudi Arabia, Kuwait, Qatar, United Arab Emirates, Bahrain, Oman) has led to problems and concerns on the part of both labor-supplying and labor-receiving countries. For the former, concern has arisen over shortage of labor, inflation, shift in consumption patterns away from domestically produced products, abandonment of marginal agricultural land, and a decline of family cohesion.

The impact of transnational migration in critical social matters such as fertility reduction, population control, and rural-urban migration can be quite unpredictable, having little effect in Egypt but considerable effect in Morocco, where fertility declined and rural-urban migration increased.[26] For the labor-receiving countries concern has arisen over the increasing dependence on foreign labor, overpopulation imbalance (the nationals of Kuwait, Qatar, and the United Arab Emirates were already a minority in their own countries by 1975), and exposure of their population to ideas and styles of life that are not welcome. The labor-supplying countries have greatly benefited from remittances, mainly spent on consumer durables, but also on construction, repayment of debts, and purchase of land. The labor-receiving countries have benefited from a relatively cheap and efficient workforce that has played an indispensable role in building their infrastructures and running their bureaucracies.[27]

As the Jordanian experience discussed in this book will indicate, the oil states of the Arabian Peninsula have not accepted migrant nationals from other Arab states as status equals (not to speak of culturally diverse migrants from South and Southeast Asia). Ethnic stratification and not cultural pluralism is the prevailing pattern on the peninsula, and although multiplex relations have occasionally developed between migrants and indigenes, the norm is the segregation of migrants physically and socially.

It is remarkable that the literature on transnational migration in the Middle East almost entirely ignores migration for higher education. It also gives a very poor sense of the variety of experiences migrants have enjoyed/endured/reflected on in the diaspora, the variety of attitudes they have entertained, and the impact they have had on social and cultural change in their home communities. This neglect reflects the literature's dominant focus on demographic and economic factors, and its defining migration in terms of "labor migration" and "shift of manpower" rather than in terms of a wider cultural and humanistic framework. This Jordanian case study addresses such neglected concerns and describes and analyzes the significance of the powerful stream of migration for higher education. The study indicates the impossibility of reducing migrant experience to a series of generalities about migrants whether within single countries like Saudi Arabia, Pakistan, or the United States, within institutional foci like universities, armies, or business offices, or within occupational categories such as teacher, student, manager, construction worker, housewife, soldier, doctor, or clerk.

The Jordanian Context of Migration

The Village in 1960 and Before[28]

Today Kufr al-Ma is a municipality located in the eastern foothills of the Jordan Valley characterized by transnational migration to seventeen different countries. In 1960 it was one of the cereal-growing villages that constituted the Ajlun district of northeastern Jordan. The Al-Kura subdistrict of northwestern Jordan in which the village lay is a badly eroded area. In modern times its climate and low rainfall have precluded a majority of villagers from tilling the land, though in 1960 dry cereal-farming was still an important activity in Kufr al-Ma, and, together with shepherding, occupied about 40 percent of the workforce.[29] Its population of two thousand was composed entirely of Sunni Muslims.

In 1960 the village was divided into three named patrilineal descent groups or clans ('ashiras) and a number of smaller independent families. Each one of these groups tended to cluster in its own quarter of the village. More important was the fact that approximately 80 percent of all men and women whose marriages were recorded, married within the village. The whole village constituted a web of kinship in which any person could usually discover a link, however distant, with any other if he looked hard enough (and could thereby address him/her by the appropriate kinship term). On the other hand, rivalries existed between the component lineages of the larger patrilineal descent groups, and these lineages combined and recombined in a kaleidoscopic fashion behind the two village mayors (*mukhtars*), each of whom represented his own clan as well as the village.[30] Thus in 1960 the community could be regarded at any single point in time as congeries of separate families and allied or estranged lineages or as a unified group linked by descent, marriage, and ties of propinquity and by a historical tradition of unity. The villagers referred to themselves as "the peoples of Tibne," a nearby village that they claimed as their ancestral home (along with ten other villages) in the last century. Of significance is the fact that villagers preferred to refer to themselves in the idiom of unity (i.e., in terms of propinquity and matri-laterality or *makhwal*) rather than in terms of division (i.e., marriage ties or *nasab,* which stressed separation). The religious structure of the community was also a unitary one. Since 1952 a permanent religious leader recruited from the village itself had combined the role of prayer-leader (*imam*) and preacher (*khatib*).

Although a diversified occupational structure (discussed below) and the resul-tant economic differentiation prevented classification of all the residents of the village as "peasants" (*fellahin*), this is so only if the peasantry is defined in terms of economic criteria (occupation and income). If the criterion is cultural rather than economic, that is, if style of life is the main referent (including clothing, di-alect, diet, recreation, education, and outstanding personality traits), then all the residents of Kufr al-Ma were "peasants" in 1960. They wore the shawl and head-band (and did not walk in public bareheaded), assembled in their own guest houses (and not the coffee shops in town), and negotiated marriages and dis-cussed crop conditions (and not national politics). In town circles the *fellahin* achieved a kind of notoriety for their rudeness, naivete, and duplicity (rather than their knowledge or sophistication).

The occupational structure of the village in 1960 had an agricultural, a mili-tary, and a commercial-artisanal-semiprofessional component. The terms, *fellah* (owner of land or sharecropper for ½ the crop), *harrath* (sharecropper for ¼ of the crop), *qatruz* (agricultural pieceworker), *'amil yawmi* (daily agricultural la-borer), and *fellawti* (landless laborer) designated degrees of economic status based on land tenure. However, the single most important fact about the occu-pational structure of the village was that less than 40 percent of the employed men were engaged in subsistence agriculture. Of the 200 households censused, 92 possessed no land whatsoever. The consequences of such an occupational structure for mobility were plain. A certain number of men (34) found employ-ment in the village as shopkeepers, artisans, and stonecutters; many others (39) worked outside of the village but in the locality, as masons, peddlers, and local la-borers; the remainder (141) found employment as clerks and ushers in local or regional government offices, as soldiers, and as laborers in distant towns, army camps, and the capital, Amman. In addition, many peasants, particularly share-croppers, were forced to hire out their labor in surrounding villages or in the Jor-dan Valley.

Kufr al-Ma has been characterized by long-distance mobility since the establishment of the British Mandate in Palestine (1920). A large majority of the villagers worked in Palestine on three or more separate occasions. Many used to leave after the harvest or during drought seasons to spend three or more months in Haifa or Tel Aviv, where they worked as fishermen, construction laborers, factory hands, gardeners, and harvesters. Many villagers spent long periods of time in Palestine, worked under Jews and Englishmen, participated in the Palestinian national struggle, and returned to the village in their middle years to marry and take up their former occupations.

With the end of the Palestinian War in 1949 and the closing of the western border of Jordan to the new state of Israel, the towns that had provided an outlet for such migration—Haifa, Acre, Jaffa, and Tel Aviv—were suddenly cut off. Long-distance migration was now, to some degree at least, directed toward the north (Beirut and Damascus) and, more important, the east (Amman). But migratory labor toward these cities remained a trickle as compared with the former pattern of migration to Palestine.

It was the expansion of the Jordanian Army at the time of, and following, the first Arab-Israeli War that counterbalanced the economic opportunities that had been lost by the partition of Palestine. Indeed, the new economic opportunities were far better than the old. Competition for entrance into the Jordanian Army became so intense that bribery was often the only sure means of enlistment. Only forty years earlier men had given away their lands (and cut off their fingers) to avoid service in the Ottoman Turkish army!

The labor migration to Palestine had been largely sporadic. Men would leave after the harvest, only to return two or three months later. They might not go again for several years if agricultural production proved sufficient. The monetary returns varied, but they were, in general, small. After three months a man might return to the village with the equivalent of twelve dollars saved, at most twenty-five. Moreover, the daily returns in the fishing industry were unpredictable, and it was in fishing that the great majority of migrants were engaged. A day's wage would depend on the catch and would vary between nothing and one pound sterling. As political disturbances increased, the better-paid jobs within the Jewish section of the economy disappeared, particularly after the decision of the Jewish Agency in Zurich in 1929 to exclude Arab labor from all Jewish enterprises.

Employment in the Jordanian army, on the other hand, guaranteed a young recruit a monthly salary. With each additional child the soldier received an additional stipend. In 1960, of fourteen lineages examined in Kufr al-Ma, seven had a soldier as the highest salaried man, while in four, the highest salaried man was a government employee working outside the village. The richest farmers in Kufr al-Ma were not, therefore, able to match the income of the salaried employees of the village even in 1960. In general a gap of $275 or more separated them, at that time a considerable amount. The same gap existed between prosperous village grocers and salaried employees. Table 4 (appendix) records the progressive advancement of occupational mobility in three generations of two families in Kufr al-Ma spanning the period from 1930 to 1960. The first family records mobility for a father, his six sons, and their twenty-eight sons; the second records mobility for three brothers, their ten sons and three daughters, and the latter's fifty-two sons.

After World War II another change occurred that drew Kufr al-Ma, politically, economically, and ideologically, within the bounds of a larger framework. The region of Al-Kura, in which Kufr al-Ma lies, was elevated to the status of a subdistrict or *qada'*. As a result a number of government offices were established in Deir Abu Said, a neighboring village. Deir Abu Said became the administrative center of the subdistrict, and access to government offices became easier for the peasants of Kufr al-Ma. A subdistrict officer in charge of government wheat distributions, water allocations, and school improvements resided in Deir Abu Said. The chief forest ranger, who guarded the woodlands from depredation by peasants searching for firewood and from foraging animals, established his office there, as did the inspectors of agriculture and health. A civil court which heard all cases of crop damage, a land registry office which handled all cases involving land title and sale, a dispensary, and a tax office were also established there. Finally, in 1953, a religious court was set up in Deir Abu Said to hear cases involving marriage, inheritance, divorce, and endowments.

The Wider Jordanian Context

At this point it is necessary to consider in capsule fashion the wider Jordanian social, economic, and historical context and its impact on the life-paths of Jordanians— a context which frames the saga of recent transnational migration from Kufr al-Ma. A geographer, Wahlin, has observed on the basis of his study of the 'Allan district of Jordan, just south of Al-Kura, that over the course of the last hundred years changes in the national economy and labor market have led to change in mode of living, and occupational pursuits, and to a leap in education.[31] He argues that where agriculture accounts for only 11 percent of employment, as it did in Jordan in 1979, "life ... will ... become impossible or at least hazardous and full of hardship [for the individual], unless he is not only literate but also capable of assimilating new knowledge and adapting himself to new conditions."[32]

A hundred years ago Transjordanians were peasants growing grain or fruit, or pastoral nomads who provided meat and milk products together with a few merchants. By 1980 farming had decreased dramatically and military, professional, and service occupations had proliferated. As Wahlin observed, "new livelihood strategies" emerged "with risk-spreading as a keynote."[33] Rather than peasants and nomads, Jordanians became fresh fruit and vegetable growers for the market, i.e., farmers, chicken and egg-raisers for urban markets, soldiers, police, government employees, merchants, service workers such as truck and taxi drivers, or some combination of the above. Before the introduction of the capitalist system in Jordan, land had been held to produce food for its owners/cultivators or to build and extend a tribal territory. Today, it is used for one other purpose—to earn money either by speculation or by producing cash crops. The significance of land changed when agriculture or animal husbandry ceased to be the only way of earning a living; land became a commodity with a price that could be sold to educate one's children or used as security for loans.[34]

The leap in education has been perhaps the most spectacular change. From a system of peripatetic education based upon Islamic instruction (quite often in a one-on-one situation in the student's or the teacher's home), Jordanians rapidly accepted a formal, secular system of education that was alien to them, and recognized its importance.[35] Wahlin observes that two new and significant educational norms were quickly accepted in the 'Allan area: all children should go to school, and there should be a school in each community.[36] This acceptance was remarkable in a country where there was no high school in Amman, the capital city, or Irbid, the second largest city, till 1950. Formal classroom education, and intrastate and subsequently transnational migration became a standard part of a "life-path" for most Jordanian families, i.e., a "sequence of activities and living places which together describe a person's [family's] life."[37] It is notable that the establishment of a village school had to be at the initiative of village residents themselves; it was they who had to supply a place to hold school before the government would provide a teacher. As Seecombe has observed in his case study of Sammu' village in the Al-Kura district in 1985, quite apart from transnational migration, there has been a wider pattern of extra-village employment for some time.[38] Of active male heads of households in his sample, 32 percent were serving in the Jordanian armed services, the majority returning once a week or once every two weeks to the village as "weekend husbands." Other absentee workers commuted from jobs in various parts of Jordan including Irbid, Amman, Zarqa, and Aqaba daily or weekly, with less than 25 percent of those interviewed owning agricultural land.[39] Table 5 records the occupational distribution of the Jordanian population in 1961 and 1979.

As pronounced as change was in mode of living, occupation, migration, and education, Wahlin detected a remarkable social structural and cultural continuity among the rural people of the 'Allan district, an observation compatible with both my own work and that of other researchers in Jordan. For instance, with respect to land ownership (as opposed to land use), Wahlin reported a notable continuity of "tribal plates." That is, compact territories continued to be owned and jealously preserved by members of one tribe (or sometimes two allied tribes) who continued to live on and cultivate them from one generation to the next. "According to the prevailing tribal ethos, land in these 'plates' should not be alienated to members of other tribes, and opportunities to extend one's 'plate' are probably generally welcomed."[40] A notable continuity marked village territories as well. Though egalitarian inheritance rules, both civil and Islamic, worked to fragment land parcels between siblings, marriage, exchange of land parcels, and purchase of them constantly worked to reconsolidate land in family and tribal domains.[41]

Even the most recent household strategies to diversify income referred to above are probably new extensions of an old strategy to spread risks: the strategy originally combined various modes of cultivation and pastoral nomadic life simultaneously or seasonally in the late nineteenth and early twentieth centuries; more recently in the 1950s and 1960s, the strategy combined agricultural, military, manual laboring, and commercial occupations within a single household.

When migrants did begin leaving their villages in large numbers in the 1960s (and that movement accelerated in the 1970s and 1980s), they did not lose touch with their families. Wahlin reports for 'Allan, "... many of those who at some stage lived outside their native area, or even outside Jordan, later moved back to their village. This goes for persons of all degrees of education."[42] This finding is consistent with the results of my own research and with Seecombe, who reports of the migration from the village of Sammu' to Arabia, "despite their absence for an average of six or more years, emigrants retain strong links with their village of origin ... with a third of current migrants visiting the village more than once a year." Even migrants who took their dependents with them to Arabia visited once a year. Often, these visits (certainly for teachers but also for others) were quite long, lasting sometimes the whole summer.[43] Seecombe also comments on the pattern of spending a high proportion of remittances on either upgrading, expansion of, or new village housing as a demonstration of the commitment of migrants to their home village. This observation is again consistent with my own findings in Kufr al-Ma. Rubay'ah, who has written a detailed monograph on intrastate migration from the Jordan Valley to Irbid, has also commented on the frequency of visits of urban migrants back to their rural home communities. Forty-one percent of his sample returned once a month, 20 percent once a week, and another 18 percent at least once every three months.[44]

Even when permanent migration does take place, its results tend to be conservative. A demographer, Samha, has pointed out that the prevailing pattern of internal (intrastate) migration in Jordan has been family rather than individual migration. "This sudden and direct relocation of entire families" from rural to urban areas, he states, "has prevented rapid social integration and adaptation to urban life," and also resulted in the retention of [rural] customs and traditions.[45] Seecombe points out that even in Arabia "few emigrants are isolated from the village milieu," with ¾ reporting a contact with a friend, neighbor, or relative from the village during their residence abroad. Most migrants, in fact, received help in the migration process from villagers and relatives already abroad in arranging residence permits and finding accommodation and work.[46]

Apart from continued attachment to the village community and continued contact with relatives and co-villagers in the diaspora, there are two demographic facts regarding migration in Jordan that must be remembered. The first is that the extensive emigration for work abroad that began in the 1970s (by the early

1980s 40 percent of all actively employed Jordanians worked outside the country) must be seen against the background of the massive influx of Palestinian refugees into Jordan in the 1940s, '50s and '60s and the inflow of foreign workers in the 1980s. The second demographic fact is the volatility of migration in Jordan. There were heavy population outflows in 1976 (83,000) and 1977 (104,000), but a net return of Jordanians to the East Bank of a few thousand in 1978, 17,000 in 1979, and then down to 1,000 in 1980. The number of work permits issued to non-Jordanians escalated: 19,000 in 1978, 26,000 in 1979, and 80,000 in 1980.[47] The sudden influx of Jordanians back into Jordan just before and following the Gulf War in 1990–91 is just the latest instance of volatility.

There is also a clear difference between the pre-1948 migration, which was temporary, irregular, unskilled, poorly paid, and keyed to agricultural crises; the internal and external migration of the 1950s and 1960s and the early 1990s, which was keyed to political crises and war; and the transnational emigration that occurred in the 1970s and 1980s, which was keyed to the opening up of work opportunities in Arabia as a result of the 1973 OPEC pricing revolution. As indicated above, this latter emigration has become preferred and "a step in life planning."[48]

Rubay'ah reports that the motive for the rural-urban migration from the Jordan Valley to Irbid in the late 1960s was, on the face of it, the war and unsettled conditions following clashes between Palestinians and Israelis in the Valley. But he concludes that the main motivation was neither war, the pull of the city (i.e., its social services, public utilities, and superior educational facilities), nor the desire to raise social status (although he gave evidence of this result), but rather the necessity to meet "basic needs," i.e., food, clothing, and adequate housing.[49] The transnational migration from Kufr al-Ma, however, though motivated by such basic needs on the part of some migrants, particularly to Arabia, was primarily motivated by the desire for upward mobility and higher socioeconomic status.

Despite the different motivations for migration, the attributes of Jordanian emigrants working in the Arab region are consistent, according to a 1980 survey, and they are as follows: dominantly male (95 percent), between the prime working ages of 20–39 (80 percent), married (66 percent), and educated (⅓ had been to university). Over 40 percent of the current migrants in the survey had professional or technical positions, with a large number of teachers and soldiers being seconded by the Jordanian government to various states in the Arabian peninsula.[50] Rubay'ah's study of rural-urban migration also indicated a dominantly male (85 percent) and married (93 percent) migrant population. The study reported that these migrants were older (65 percent between 30 and 60), with a large majority (88 percent) having taken their families with them to the city.[51]

The migration from Kufr al-Ma to Arabia was also composed of a dominantly male (over 90 percent), married, and relatively well-educated population (90 percent had high school equivalency). However, its age range tended to be a much wider age range including older migrants. Emigrants from the village in 1979 tended to be younger and composed of more single men as compared with 1986. In 1979, ¾ of male migrants left their spouses in Jordan whereas by 1986 almost half had brought them to Arabia. (See chapter two following, tables 1–8 for descriptive statistics on work migration.) On the other hand, the transnational migration for higher education from Kufr al-Ma was overwhelmingly of single, young men in their twenties, as will be discussed in later chapters.

All those who have commented on the economic impact of transnational migration for work in Jordan have highlighted the volume of remittances. By 1984 remittances had become "the largest single component of the Jordan[ian] Gross National Product."[52] See Table 6. For Jordanian villagers the impact of remittances is magnified. Seecombe reports that in Sammu' among current migrant households "income from abroad was the major, and in most cases, the only reported source of household income."[53] The majority received remittances on a regular monthly basis. Keely and Saket's survey reports that in addition to remittances, migrants often brought back durable goods, 75 percent brought gifts, and 90 percent reported bringing back cash on their return.[54] As discussed above, remittances changed the face of the village of Sammu' as a result of construction activity.

Remittances have had the same dramatic effect in Kufr al-Ma. There, remittances have produced cement rather than stone and adobe houses, glass windows with painted grilles rather than empty window apertures blocked with stone in the winter to keep out the cold, and through household tax contributions to the new municipality of Kufr al-Ma, paved roads, streetlights, curbs, trash collection, and a mortuary. As noted below, remittances also produced a hum of commercial and artisanal activity in the village.

The Migration Revolution: The Village Before and After

Social and economic change, as suggested above, did not arise suddenly in Kufr al-Ma after the 1973 OPEC oil-pricing revolution and the leap of transnational migration. Change had already permeated the village with economic differentiation and occupational mobility and the impact of external roles and resources such as teacher, subdistrict officer, policeman, forest ranger, land registry officer, civil court judge, Islamic court judge, and village improvement officer.[55] However, it was the oil-pricing revolution that led to a quantum leap in migration, a quantum leap in resources flowing back to the village, and a change in its legal status (it became a municipality in 1981) and its public face. Even those who did not migrate benefited from the migration not just through remittances to migrant families, but also through the general rise in real income for most occupational categories due to the shortage of labor, even in spite of inflation. For most occupational categories annual income quadrupled and for some such as masons, stonecutters, and peasants with ample land it rose even more sharply. Table 7 records the difference in incomes for occupational categories in Kufr al-Ma between 1960 and 1986.

By June 1986, 72 individuals from the village (67 males and 5 females) from a total population of 4,500 had worked on the Arabian peninsula with 63 currently working there in occupations that included the following: teachers, soldiers, health specialists, business managers, accountants, engineers, clerks, surveyors, translators, telephone operators, automobile mechanics, masons, construction workers, and drivers. More interesting, perhaps, was the fact that 36 men had returned from studying abroad and 35 were currently pursuing higher education abroad in 14 different countries: Pakistan, Egypt, Greece, Lebanon, Syria, Turkey, Romania, Yugoslavia, Russia, Germany, England, Saudi Arabia, Abu Dhabi, and the United States. (See Table 8.) Their studies focused on the professions and on semiprofessional crafts (55), the humanities, religion, and social sciences (31), and to a lesser degree the physical sciences (14). They ranged from engineering, medicine, agriculture, journalism and law, to English language and literature, Arabic language and literature, and Islamic studies, and from political science to psychology, naval science, veterinary medicine, and linguistics. Table 9 lists the four-year specializations and the numbers of students. The time these Jordanian students spent abroad, whether for education or work, was usually five or more years and sometimes significantly longer. After graduation they were employed in 18 different occupations, 68 categorized as professionals (white collar, high salary occupations requiring a professional education), 17 as military, and 12 as bureaucrats. Table 10 records the numbers.

An additional thirty-five students pursued/were pursuing two-year study programs in Jordan, focusing on semiprofessional skills such as accountancy, nutrition, pharmacy, and health. Others were studying the physical sciences (7) and the Islamic and social sciences (7), mainly with a view to teaching these subjects at the elementary or middle school level. Table 11 records their numbers.

To indicate the extended lengths of time spent in foreign countries, one-third of those working on the Arabian peninsula in 1986 had spent from 7 to 9 years there; another 12 percent, 10 to 12 years; and another 12 percent, 12 to 18 years. Of the five young men from Kufr al-Ma pursuing higher education and/or work in the United States interviewed by me in 1991, one had spent 13 years and three 11 years in the country.

Although women had not yet left the country to pursue higher education abroad in 1986, 36 women from the village had pursued or were pursuing tertiary education elsewhere in Jordan, 28 in junior colleges and 8 in four-year colleges. Twelve of these women were currently employed as teachers and 2 as headmistresses in middle schools. Eleven were single and still studying, 8 were married with children and working (teaching), and 6 were married and teaching. Table 12 records their numbers, specializations, and occupations.

To appreciate the significance of these facts regarding migration for education and work, one must understand the material, social, and cultural circumstances of the village in 1960, twenty-five years before. At that time all houses were built of clay and stone (as opposed to cement today). The village roads were narrow lanes with numerous rock outcrops. Refuse (the mark of civilization) was non-existent, since no one could afford to purchase food in glass or plastic containers, and the only canned goods available in the meager village stores were tuna fish and sardines. Only one man in the whole village purchased a newspaper—so there was no paper! The winter rains were collected in cisterns which usually ran dry in July, after which time water had to be purchased from the next village, which had a spring. Today, all houses have piped water. In 1960 there was no electricity, and on moonless nights one stumbled along narrow paths (now paved) with a flashlight or a Coleman lamp. Today all homes are electrified and almost every family has a television, and some have two.

In 1967 there was one automobile and one telephone in the village post office. By 1986, there were thirty telephones (and a long waiting-list for installation) and 123 automobiles and trucks. In 1960 one bus a day went to Irbid, the nearest market town, early in the morning and returned late in the afternoon. In 1986 buses and service taxis began running at 6 a.m. and continued throughout the day and early evening. In 1960 approximately ⅔ of the working male population worked in and around the village. In 1986 more than ¾ worked outside it. In 1960 eleven tiny grocery shops existed, stocking sugar, tea, one brand of plain packaged biscuits, matches, native Nablus soap, pencils, canned sardines and tuna fish, kerosene wicks, rock candy, and rubber plough shoes, among other things; peasants often paid the shopkeeper in kind with sacks of grain harvested in June. In 1960 no fresh vegetables or fruits or plastic goods of any kind were sold in the shops.

By 1986 there were 52 commercial establishments in the village, including 20 grocery shops, 8 greengrocers, 6 chicken-sellers, 4 building block workshops, 4 electrical supply shops, 3 builders' suppliers, 2 tile-making workshops, 2 petrol stations, 1 plate-glass seller, 1 aluminum seller, and 1 auto garage. No payments in kind were accepted in these establishments as had been common in 1960. In any case little grain was grown on village lands any longer; most land had been converted to olive growing or to housing plots for an expanding village (incipient town) which had begun to assume a homestead pattern in certain areas (rather than a nucleated village).

Throughout the twentieth century the village had been represented to the outside world by a mayor/mayors (*mukhtars*) selected largely on the basis of clan affiliation, up till 1972 when a village council was selected.[56] But the real change in the local political structure occurred in 1981 with the establishment of the municipality of Kufr al-Ma. For the first time the village was empowered to borrow money (from the City and Village Development Bank) to execute plans for village improvement and development. The critical enabling factor here was the rise of incomes in the village, which allowed the collection of the local taxes needed to complement the loans to fund the projects. Within five years the main roads of the village were paved, electricity was extended to the whole village, water was extended to all houses within the village proper and to some houses outside it, and a small health center was built as well as a school with sixty rooms. In addition, street lamps were put in place along the main road, and in 1986 plans were being made to build a slaughterhouse and a wall around the cemetery. By then Kufr al-Ma had the legal status and appearance of a town.

Most important, for our purposes, in 1960 two one-room schools had existed in the village, one for boys through the sixth grade and one for girls through the third grade. Only one man had left the village for higher education abroad (to Germany) in 1960, and only one other was in high school (in the nearby market town of Irbid). In 1986 there were 670 female students in Kufr al-Ma and 777 male students through the ninth grade, and approximately 200 additional students attended high school in adjoining Deir Abu Said. In 1960 it would have been unimaginable for anyone to suggest that large numbers of young men would leave the village and the country for higher education abroad on four continents, and even more ridiculous to suggest that any women in the village would leave it to pursue a high school education, not to speak of higher education.[57] These men and women not only imagined such migration, they realized it. The remaining chapters of this book describe how they did it, and with what consequences for themselves, their families, and their community.

Notes

1. See "The Nation-State, and its Others: In Lieu of a Preface," by Kachig Tololyan, *Diaspora*, 1:1, Spring 1991, p. 6.
2. For a description and analysis of the village in 1960 as a multiplex, corporate community see Antoun, *Arab Village*, pp. 103–113. For a reflection on some aspects of community life in the 1980s see chapter 7 below. For a discussion of changes taking place in the 1990s and the decline, though not the disappearance, of the moral community see Antoun, "Civil Society, Tribal Process, and Change in Jordan: An Anthropological View," *International Journal of Middle East Studies*, Vol. 32, 2000.
3. See L.L. Langness and Gelya Frank's *Lives: An Anthropological Approach to Biography*, p. 29.
4. In this account women's voices are mainly (though not entirely) missing. As a young, single, foreign, non-Muslim, male observer and researcher in a tribal culture with a strong modesty code it was not possible for me to interview women. This situation changed to some degree by 1986 when some women, mainly educated, remained in the room (watching) television when I entered the guest room. Formerly, they had always left. Although I chatted with a few, I was only able to interview one. It should be remembered that by the 1980s Islamic fundamentalism had become a very influential religious movement in this part of Jordan, and its impact was to enforce the modesty code, albeit in a modified form. See Antoun, "On the Modesty of Women in Arab Muslim Villages: A Study in the Accommodation of Traditions," *American Anthropologist* (70: 671–697) 1968, for a detailed description and analysis of the modesty code in the 1960s.
5. The questionnaire differed somewhat, depending on whether the migrant had left Jordan in the pursuit of higher education, in the pursuit of work, or as a member of a military training mission.
6. Among many, one sole-authored and two edited volumes have emphasized critical anthropology's attention to two primary issues in field work, description, and analysis: the issue of the

anthropologist's voice in relation to the voices of the people studied and the issue of the power of the anthropologist in relation to the power of the people studied. For elaboration of the issues and varying positions taken on them see James Clifford and George Marcus, editors, *Writing Culture: The Poetics and Politics of Ethnography*, 1986, James Clifford, *The Predicament of Culture: Twentieth Century Ethnography, Literature, and Art*, 1988, and Roger Sanjek, editor, *Fieldnotes: The Makings of Anthropology*, 1990.

7. I am defining caste here in terms of an absolute bar to marriage between different social categories rather than in terms of concepts of ritual pollution (as in Hinduism).

8. See M.K. Masud's essay, "The Obligation to Migrate: the Doctrine of *hijra* in Islamic Law," in Dale Eickelman and James Piscatori, *Muslim Travelers: Pilgrimage, Migration, and the Religious Imagination*, 1990.

9. See Clyde Kluckhohn, "Some Reflections on the Method and Theory of the Kulturkreislehre," *American Anthropologist*, Vol. 30, No. 2, 1936.

10. See M. Fischer's and M. Abedi's analysis of Muslims in Houston in their book, *Debating Muslims: Cultural Dialogues in Postmodernity and Tradition*, 1990.

11. See N. Abadan-Unat's essay on "Turkish Migration to Europe and the Middle East: Its Impact on Social Structure and Social Legislation," in Social Legislation in the Contemporary Middle East, L.O. Michalak and J.W. Salacuse, editors, 1986. See also F. Halliday's "Labor Migration in the Arab World," *MERIP Reports*, Vol. 14, No. 4, May 1984; Michael Humphrey's "Migrants, Workers and Refugees, *Middle East Report*, vol. 23, No. 2, March–April 1993; and Caglar Keyder's and Ayhan Aksu-Koc's *External Labour Migration from Turkey and its Impact: an Evaluation of the Literature*, 1988.

12. See M. Izady, *A Concise Handbook of Kurds*, 1992 for details.

13. J. Abu-Lughod, "Recent Migrations in the Arab World," in *Arab Society: Social Science Perspectives*, N. Hopkins and S. Ibrahim, editors, 1977.

14. The spring 2003 war by the United States and Great Britain against Iraq is another example of this unpredictable impact. It was thought that massive dislocation and proliferation of transnational refugees would occur as it had in the 1991 Gulf War. It did not.

15. See Humphrey, *opis cit.* p. 2.

16. Ibid.

17. See Thomas Stevenson, "Yemeni Workers Come Home: Reabsorbing One Million Migrants," in *Middle East Report*, Vol. 23, No. 2, March–April 1993.

18. N. Abadan-unat, *opis. cit.*, p. 327.

19. See Keyder and Aksu-Koc, pp. 28 ff.

20. *Opis. cit.* pp. 46–47.

21. Abadan-Unat, p. 345.

22. See James Socknat, Stace Birks, and Ismail Serageldin, "International Labor Migration in the Middle East and North Africa: Current and Prospective Dimensions, 1975–1985," in Michalak and Salacuse, 1986 pp. 287 ff.

23. *Opis. cit.*, pp. 301 and 347.

24. See I. Seecombe's "Labour Migration and the Transformation of a Village Economy: A Case Study from Northwest Jordan," in R. Lawless, *The Middle Eastern Village: Changing Economic and Social Relations*, 1987; R. Latowsky, "Egyptian Labor Abroad: Mass Participation and Modest Returns," *MERIP Reports*, Vol. 14, No. 4, May 1984; T. Stevenson, "Yemeni Workers Come Home: Reabsorbing One Million Migrants," *Middle East Report*, Vol. 23, No. 2, March–April 1993.

25. See F. Khafagy, "Women and Labor Migration: One Village in Egypt," *MERIP Reports*, Vol. 14, No. 4, May 1984.

26. See Youssef Courbage, "Demographic Change in the Arab World: The Impact of Migration, Education and Taxes in Egypt and Morocco," *Middle East Report*, Vol. 24, No. 5, September–October, 1994.

27. See Socknet, Birks, and Serageldin for a good discussion of the costs and benefits of transnational migration in the Middle East for labor exporters and labor importers. Some countries like Jordan are both.

28. I have chosen 1960 as the baseline for tracing change because my own field work in Kufr al-Ma began then and allowed me to construct a detailed social structural, cultural, spatial, and demographic picture of the village at that time. See Antoun, *Arab Village: A Social Structural Study of a Transjordanian Peasant Community,* Indiana University Press, 1972.

29. For the ecological and historical background of the village see Antoun, *Arab Village,* Chapter 1.

30. For a detailed analysis of local-level politics, the principles of coalition-formation, and the process of socioeconomic and political change involving the competition between clans and mayors over such issues as the building of the village school, the establishment of the village council, and the resort by villagers to external resources and roles such as the subdistrict officer, the police, political parties, tribal leaders, and migrant labor in towns see Antoun, *Low-Key Politics: Local-Level Leadership and Change in the Middle East,* 1979.

31. See Lars Wahlin, "Diffusion and Acceptance of Modern Schooling in Rural Jordan," in Lawless, 1987, pp. 166 and 172.

32. Opis. cit. p. 72.

33. Wahlin, "Back to Settled Life? Rural Change in the 'Allan Area of Jordan, 1867–1980," 1994, p. 17.

34. See Wahlin, "Inheritance of Land in the Jordanian Hill Country," *British Journal of Middle Eastern Studies,* Vol. 21, No. 1, Summer 1994, pp. 9, 17, and 21.

35. See Antoun, *Muslim Preacher in the Modern World: A Jordanian Case Study in Comparative Perspective,* 1989, particularly chapters 3 and 9 for an in-depth description and analysis of Islamic education and preaching in Kufr al-Ma.

36. Wahlin, 1987, p. 146.

37. See Wahlin, 1987, pp. 166 ff. for details.

38. Ian Seecombe, "Labour Migration and the Transformation of a Village Economy," in *The Middle Eastern Village,* 1987, p. 123.

39. Seecombe, pp. 121 and 123.

40. See Wahlin, BJMES, 1994, pp. 20 and 23.

41. Opis. cit. p. 24.

42. Wahlin, 1987, p. 169.

43. Seecombe, p. 129.

44. See Ahmed Rubay'ah, *hijrat al-rifiyyin min al-aghwar al-shimaliyya ila madinat irbid: dawafi'iha, mashakiliha, atharaha 'ala khatat al-tanmiyya* (in Arabic) (Rural Migration from the Northern Jordan Valley to Irbid City: Its Impact, Its Problems, Its Consequences for Development Plans, 1982, p. 124.

45. Mousa Samha, "The Impact of Migration on the Population Changes in Jordan," paper written at the Center for Demographic Studies, Duke University, and presented at a conference sponsored by the Southwest Asian and North African Program at the State University of New York in Binghamton, April, 1987.

46. Seecombe, p. 131.

47. See Socknet, Birks, and Serageldin, 1986, p. 301.

48. Basson as quoted in Seecombe, p. 121. Rubay'ah reports the same economic and planned motivation for intrastate migration in the late 1960s. See Rubay'ah, pp. 102 ff.

49. See Rubay'ah, p. 132.

50. For details see B. Keely and B. Saket, "Jordanian Migrant Workers in the Arab Region: A Case Study of Consequences for Labor Supplying Countries," *The Middle East Journal,* Vol. 30, No. 4, Autumn 1984, pp. 89 ff.

51. See Rubay'ah, pp. 31–35.

52. Samha, p. 12.

53. Seecombe, p. 133.
54. Keely and Saket, p. 694.
55. See Antoun, *Low-Key Politics,* 1979, chapter 5 for an analysis of the impact of external roles and resources on the village well before the leap of transnational migration, and also for the factors constraining change and working against villagers utilizing the external arena.
56. For a description and analysis of the long struggle to establish a village council in Kufr al-Ma and its implications for peasant social structure and culture see Antoun, *Low-Key Politics,* chapter 6.
57. The strongest cultural barrier to the prospect of women leaving the community to pursue education was the code of modesty. For a detailed analysis of the modesty code and its behavioral implications see Antoun, "On the Modesty of Women in Arab Muslim Villages: A Study in the Accommodation of Traditions," *American Anthropologist,* Vol. 70, No. 4, 1968.

APPENDIX

TABLE 1 • *The Middle East: Source of Most of the World's Refugees*

Refugees and Asylum Seekers: Where Do They Come From?

	1984	1991	Sept. 30, 1992
Afghanistan	3,656,000*	6,600,800*	4,639,800
Palestinians	2,017,000	2,525,000	2,654,207
Ethiopia/Eritrea	1,209,000	752,400*	495,600
Iraq	60,000	217,500*	217,500
Iran	27,000*	50,000	50,000
Somalia	**	717,600	1,036,400
Sudan	39,000	202,500	228,500
Western Sahara	165,000	165,000*	165,000
Middle East Total	7,173,000	11,230,800	9,487,007
World Total	9,091,000	16,647,550	

*Estimates vary.
**Not available or less than 25,000.

Source: US Committee for Refugees. These figures do not include people who left their countries as refugees, or refugee-like circumstances, but who have been granted permanent resettlement in another country, such as the Ethiopian and Russian Jews who have settled in Israel.

"Refugees" at Home: Internally Displaced Civilians

Displaced people are those who have been forced out of their homes by violent conflict, drought, famine and other natural or human-made disasters, but have not crossed international borders, and thus or not officially "refugees."

Afghanistan	2,000,000
Cyprus	268,000
Ethiopia/Eritrea	1,000,000
Lebanon	750,000
Iraq	700,000
Turkey	30,000
Somalia	500,000–1,000,000
Sudan	4,750,000

Source: US Committee for Refugees. As of December 31, 1991.

Refugees in All but Name ...

Many people "fear prosecution or harm if returned to their home countries," and may thus be refugees, but are not recognized as such by governments. Estimates of their numbers vary widely because many are undocumented.

Host Country	Origin	Number
Egypt	Palestinians	100,000
Iran	Iraq	500,000
Jordan	Palestinians	740,000
Kuwait	Palestinians	80,000
Lebanon	Palestinians	40,000
Turkey	Iran	100,000

Source: US Committee for Refugees. As of December 31, 1991.

Refugees and Asylum Seekers: Where Do They Go?

Asylum Country	Subtotal by Source Country	Total
Afghanistan		87,500
Tajikstan	87,500**	
Algeria		204,000
W. Sahara	165,000	
Mali	35,000	
Others	4,000*	
Djibouti		110,000
Somalia	105,000	
Ethiopia/Eritrea	5,000	
Egypt		7,750
Ethiopia/Eritrea	600	
Palestinians	5,500	
Somalia	1,300	
Others	350*	
Ethiopia/Eritrea		415,000
Somalia	400,000	
Sudan	15,000	
Gaza Strip		560,207
Palestinians	560,207	
Iran		3,050,000*
Afghanistan	2,900,000	
Iraq	150,000*	
Iraq		48,000
Iran	48,000	
Jordan		1,010,719
Palestinians	1,010,719	
Lebanon		323,027
Palestinians	319,427	
Others	3,600*	
Morocco		800*

Asylum Country	Subtotal by Source Country	Total
Pakistan		1,703,000
Afghanistan	1,700,000	
Others	3,000*	
Saudi Arabia		184,000
Iraq	34,000	
Somalia	150,000	
Somalia		5,000
Ethiopia/Eritrea	5,000	
Sudan		427,000
Ethiopia/Eritrea	400,000	
Other	27,000	
Syria		303,207
Palestinians	299,207	
Iraq	4,000	
Tunisia		50*
Turkey		31,500
Iraq	29,500	
Iran	2,000	
West Bank		459,147
Palestinians	459,147	
Yemen		50,000
Somalia	50,000	

*As of December 31, 1992
**According to the International Red Cross estimates (Washington Post, February 5, 1993).

Source: US Committee for Refugees. As of September 30, 1992, except where indicated. There are also Afghan refugees in India (9,800) and Tajikstan (30,000); Ethiopian/Eritrean refugees in Kenya (85,000); Somali refugees in Central African Republic (10,000), Kenya (18,000), Uganda (75,500) and Zaire (110,000).

TABLE 2 • *Migrant Workers in the Arab Middle East, 1975*

From / To	EGYPT	YEMEN A.R.	JORDAN/PALESTINE	YEMEN D.R.	SYRIAN A.R.	LEBANON	SUDAN	TUNISIA	OMAN	IRAQ	SOMALIA	ALGERIA/MOROCCO	PAKISTAN	INDIA	OTHER ASIANS	EUROPE & AMERICA	AFRICA & OTHERS	TURKEY	IRAN	TOTAL
SAUDI ARABIA	95,000	280,400	175,000	55,000	15,000	20,000	35,000	—	17,500	2,000	5,000	—	15,000	15,000	8,000	15,000	10,000	500	10,000	773,400
LIBYAN ARAB JAMAHIRIYA	229,500	—	14,150	—	13,000	5,700	7,000	38,500	—	—	—	2,500	4,500	500	500	7,000	500	9,000	—	332,350
UNITED ARAB EMIRATES	12,500	4,500	14,500	4,500	4,500	1,500	—	14,000	—	500	1,000	—	100,000	61,500	2,000	5,000	—	—	21,000	251,500
KUWAIT	37,558	2,757	47,653	8,658	16,547	7,232	873	49	3,660	17,999	247	47	11,038	21,475	1,103	2,028	107	37	28,933	208,001
OMAN	4,600	100	1,600	100	400	1,100	500	100	—	—	300	—	32,500	26,000	200	2,800	400	—	400	70,700
IRAQ	7,000	—	5,000	—	—	3,000	200	—	—	—	—	—	5,000	5,000	—	500	—	—	40,000	65,700
QATAR	2,850	1,250	6,000	1,250	750	500	400	—	1,870	—	—	—	16,000	16,000	2,000	846	—	—	4,000	53,716
JORDAN	5,300	—	—	—	20,000	7,500	—	—	—	—	—	—	—	—	—	100	—	—	—	32,900
BAHRAIN	1,237	1,121	614	1,122	68	129	400	—	1,383	126	—	—	6,680	8,943	981	4,442	57	—	1,982	29,285

Source: *Third World Quarterly* based on J S Birks & C A Sinclair, *International Migration and Development in The Arab Region*, Geneva: ILO, 1980. This data, based on official government sources, probably understates the extent of migration in 1975.

TABLE 3 • *Migrant Workers in the Labor-Importing Countries by Country of Origin (thousands)*

Country of origin	1975		1985	
	Number	%	Number	%
Egypt	353.7	22.0	616.9	18.2
Iran	70.0	4.3	98.1	2.9
Iraq	18.7	1.2	11.6	0.3
Jordan	139.0	8.6	267.0	7.9
Lebanon	28.5	1.8	71.7	2.1
Morocco	2.2	0.1	9.8	0.3
Oman	30.8	1.9	44.6	1.3
Sudan	26.0	1.6	80.0	2.4
Syria	38.1	2.4	91.8	2.7
Tunisia	29.8	1.8	62.2	1.8
YAR	328.5	20.4	381.0	11.2
PDRY	45.8	2.8	80.9	2.4
India	141.9	8.8	291.2	8.6
Pakistan	205.7	12.8	446.0	13.1
East Asia	20.5	1.3	369.9	10.9
Rest of the world	130.8	8.2	472.8	13.9
Total	1,610.0	100.0	3,395.5	100.0

Note: Labor-importing countries are Algeria, Bahrain, Iraq, Kuwait, Libya, Oman, Qatar, Saudi Arabia and the UAE.

Source: Ismail Serageldin, James Socknat, Stace Birks, Bob Li and Clive Sinclair, *Manpower and International Labor Migration in the Middle East and North Africa* (Washington: Oxford University Press for the World Bank, 1983), p. 46, table 5-1.

TABLE 4 • *Occupational Mobility in Three Generations of Two Families*

Family #1

1st Generation	1 Cultivator (own land)

2nd Generation (6 brothers)	4 Cultivators 1 Preacher 1 Policeman

3rd Generation (28 1st cousins)	14 Students	2 Primary, 6 Middle, 6 High School
	5 Army	1 Regular, 4 Draft
	2 Police	
	1 Professor	
	1 Municipal Clerk	
	1 Asst. Shopkeeper (Acct.)	
	1 Auto Mechanic	
	1 Smith	
3rd Generation:	1 Mason	
14 Students, 7 Army	1 Laborer	

	Inside/Outside Kufr Al-Ma	
1st Gen.	1	0
2nd Gen.	5	1
3rd Gen.*	12	16

Family #2

1st Generation (3 brothers)	3 Cultivators

2nd Generation (13 1st cousins)	2 Cultivators	(Retired Army)
	2 Truck Drivers	(Retired Army)
	3 House wives	
	1 Shopkeeper	
	1 Post Office Employee	
	1 Regular Army	
	1 Watchman	
	1 Baker	

3rd Generation (52 2nd cousins)	23 Students	12 Primary, 6 Middle, 2 High School, 3 Univ.
	15 Army	10 Regular, 5 Draft
	4 Truck Drivers/Shopkeeper's Asst.	
	1 Shopkeeper	
	1 Preacher	
	1 Teacher	
	1 Surveyor	
	1 Electrician	
	1 Business Manager (Newspaper)	
	1 Construction Laborer	* 3rd Generation:
	1 Unemployed	23 Students, 14 Army

	Inside/Outside Kufr Al-Ma	
1st Gen.	3	0
2nd Gen.	7	5
3rd Gen.*	23	29

TABLE 5 • *Percentage Distribution of Economically Active Population by Occupation 1961 and 1979 in the East Bank (Percentages)*

Occupation	1961	1979
Professionals	4.1	12.47
Managers & Administrators	0.6	1.67
Clerical Workers	4.1	6.23
Sales Workers	6.8	7.63
Service Workers	5.9	6.71
Agricultural Workers	35.4	11.45
Production Workers	36.2	53.82
Other	6.9	—
TOTAL	100.0	100.0

Source: Jordanian Department of Statistics, 1979 and 1961 Census

TABLE 6 • *Volume of Jordanian Remittances Abroad and Ratio of Remittances to GNP 1971–1984*

Year	Remittances in JD million	% of GNP
1971	4.97	2.5
1972	7.41	3.4
1973	14.7	6.1
1974	24.13	8.9
1975	53.25	15.5
1976	136.41	25.1
1977	154.75	24.8
1978	159.38	22.0
1979	180.42	20.5
1980	236.68	22.0
1981	340.89	23.3
1982	381.9	25.0
1983	402.9	26.7
1984	475.0	30.4

Source: Haddad, 1986; Saket, 1983.

	1981	1983	1986
Jordan Dinar (JD) =	US $3.07	US $2.84	US $2.64
US Dollar =	JD .326	JD .352	JD .350

TABLE 7 • *Annual Income for Selected Occupations in Kufr Al-Ma: 1960 vs. 1986*

1960		1986	
Agriculture	$225–630	$1,755	Sharecropper ¾ crop
Army	$476–1,624	$3,240	Army Corporal (6 years service)
		$4,032	Air Force (25 years service)
		$4,320	Police
		$3,060	Retired Army
		$6,552	Army Sergeant (25 years service)
		$2,678	Army (4 year enlistment)
Government	$1,000–1,946	$3,960	Lower-Echelon Inspector (Irbid)
		$3,060	Municipality Tax Collector (KM)
Shopkeeper	$200–470	$2,160	Assistant-Shopkeeper (Irbid)
		$3,168	Green-Grocer (KM)
		$4,500	Shopkeeper/Chicken-Seller
Builder	$300	$2,100	Stone Cutter
		$2,880	Plasterer
		$2,678	Assistant-Builder
		$3,240	Contract Pick-up Driver
		$3,348	Municipality Driver
		$4,380	International Truck Driver

TABLE 8 • *Number Studied or Studying Abroad 1986*

Countries	Studied	Studying
Pakistan	10	13
USA	1	5
Yugoslavia	1	4
Greece	5	3
Egypt	2	3
Lebanon	1	2
Saudi Arabia	4	2
Syria	2	1
Rumania	1	1
Russia	2	1
Turkey	2	1
Germany	2	0
Abu Dhabi	1	0
England	1	0
Total	35	36

TABLE 9 • *Four-Year Student Specializations 1986*
(all categories past and present excluding women)

Engineering	16.5
English Language and Literature	14
Medicine	12
Agriculture	7
Law	6
Arabic Language and Literature	6
Biology	6
Islamic Studies	5
Mathematics	3.5
Veterinary Medicine	3
Journalism	3
Physics	2
Geology	2
Physical Education	2
History	2
Political Science	2
Chemistry	1
Science and Technology	1
Health Services	1
Naval Science	1
Business	1
Design	1
Teaching Methods	1
Linguistics	1
Psychology	1
Geography	1
Unknown	11
Total	83

TABLE 10 • *Occupations of Graduated Students 1986 (all categories including men and women, and 2-year and 4-year programs)*

Teacher	35
Army	17
Doctor	8
Government Employee	6
Clerk	6
Preacher	5
Translator	4
Engineer	4
Veterinarian	3
Accountant	2
Hospital Technician	2
University Researcher	2
Headmistress	2
Shop Keeper	2
Professor	1
Army Officer	1
Nurse	1
Radio Technician	1
Unemployed	8
Unknown	9
Total	119

Professionals	68	(white collar, high salary, professional education)
Army	17	
Bureaucrats	12	(government, white collar, low salary)
Other	5	

TABLE 11 • *Two-year Student Specializations 1986 (all categories past and present excluding women)*

Semi-Professional Skills	Accounting	4
	Business	1
	Business Admin.	1
	Agriculture	2
	Food Technology	1
	Nutrition	1
	Lab Technology	1
	Industrial Arts	1
	Mechanics	1
	Pharmacy	1
	Health Studies	2
	Primary Education	2
	General Education	1
	Physical Education	1
	Design	1
	Total	21
Science	Sciences	2
	Science and Math	3
	Total	7
Religious and Social Science	Islamic Studies	4
	Geography	3
	Total	7
	Grand Total	35

TABLE 12 • *Women's Higher Education 1986 (Studied or Studying, including 2-year and 4-year programs)*

Marital Status		Employment Status	
Single	19	Still Studying	14
Married	17	Working	17
		Unemployed	3
		Unknown	2

Employment/Marital Status	
Single Still Studying	11
Married, Working with Children	8
Married, Working	6
Single, Unemployed	3
Single, Working	1
Married Still Studying	1
Married Unemployed	0

Number of Years Specialized	
Two-Years	28
Four-Years	8

Occupations	
Teachers	12
Housewives	4
Head Mistresses	2
Unemployed	3

Specializations of Women		
Arabic Literature	7	[5]*
Primary School Education	6	
Mathematics	4	[1]
Sciences	4	[1]
Secretarial	2	
Political Science/Edu.	2	
Religion	2	
English	2	
Physical Education	1	
Art	1	
Engineering	1	
Accounting	1	
Health Studies	1	[1]

* brackets indicate 4-Year Education

1

THE ARMY AS AN EXTENSION OF SOCIETY AND A VEHICLE FOR MULTICULTURAL EXPOSURE AND ATTITUDINAL CHANGE

If one powerful stream of migrants has sought work across adjoining international borders (Arabia) and another has crossed the seas and continental land masses for higher education, a third has reached foreign lands and cultures through the Jordanian army. This third stream is the subject of this chapter. The Jordanian army has played a key role in the development of the Jordanian state and society. The Jordanian royal family has based its support on the tribes of Jordan, on ethnic minorities such as Christians, Chechens, and Circassians, on a segment of the Palestinian population, and, most important, on the armed forces on which it has lavished patronage.[1] Indeed, the Jordanian army (Arab Legion) antedated the state of Jordan. Moreover, from the very beginning of the foundation of the state in 1921, the public sector has always played the primary role in the economic system (hiring the most people). The public sector, including the bureaucracy and public companies, continues to this day to play the dominant economic role in the economy. The army is a major component of that public sector.

Studies of the Jordanian army generally have emphasized its stabilizing role: either internally in terms of integrating its multiethnic population (e.g., Palestinians and Bedouin), solidifying the state, crushing dissident political movements, and defending the Hashemite monarchy; or externally, in terms of providing a reliable force against radical regimes, abetting U.S. foreign policy aims (particularly the quest for peace between Palestinians and Israelis), and generally aiding Jordan in becoming an island of relative political stability and economic prosperity in an "unstable region" beset by wars, revolutions, and radical economic fluctuations.[2] In this predilection for political and geopolitical analysis, almost always viewed from the standpoint of the United States, Europe, or Israel, the significance of the army for social and cultural change has been largely neglected.

The Jordanian army has been an agent of change since its inception. Jureidini and McLaurin (1984) make the argument explicit:

> ... throughout the Middle East, government has been the sponsor and mediator of change, at least in its initial phases.[3] From the time of Abdullah's arrival in the "area east of the Jordan" in 1920 one of his principal objectives was to build a state and construct a national—and personal—allegiance where none had been. For this reason, it may be argued that planned social change has been a constant feature of Jordanian national policy. The struggle to create loyalties to Transjordan (or, later, Jordan) or even to create narrower loyalties to its Hashemite rulers, ... meant the eventual superimposition of national loyalties on tribal loyalties.[4]

Jureidini and McLaurin identify sedentarization, education, and mass communication as the "three major factors [that] have contributed to change in the traditional tribal structure of Jordanian society."[5] One does not have to agree with the authors' narrow evolutionary perspective or with the way they define and analyze tribalism and its relation to nationalism to agree with them when they suggest that "the army was a powerful agent of social change" (pp. 49–50), and that the army pioneered in two of the three above-mentioned sociocultural processes: sedentarization and education.

Vatikiotis (1967) has emphasized the role of the army early on as a shaper of the political destiny of the peoples east of the Jordan River:

> While Jordan has been an independent sovereign state only since 1946, its army dates back in one form or another to 1921. The army ... preceded the emergence of a sovereign independent state in Jordan. In fact, one could argue in this case that the army created the state.... the army was a vehicle and an instrument for the pacification and integration of a predominantly tribal society into a state to whose central authority the tribes became responsive and to whose administrative control they became subjected.[6]

The close connection between the founding of the state, the development of the army, and the change of tribal social structure is spelled out by Vatikiotis:

> If restraint, both social and individual, is a mark of civilization, then the army civilized the tribesman towards a measure of modernity by diverting his sense of tribal collectivity and *esprit de corps* into a sense of loyalty and a feeling of allegiance for a paramount chief—the monarch. From an occasional raider of other tribes or of settled agricultural communities for pillage and plunder, the tribesman has been transformed in the Legion into an expert professional in the organized and disciplined use of force for purposes determined and ordered by a central government.[7]

Vatikiotis states as a fact without substantiating evidence what is a hypothesis, namely that the tribesmen have evolved from what he terms a "tribal collectivity" to "modernity" (without defining either concept). This chapter will question the simplistic evolutionary view of the progression of Jordanians from "tribalism" to "professionalism" and "modernity" while at the same time exploring the diverse attitudes and reactions of rural Jordanians from Kufr al-Ma to their experiences both as army men and sojourners abroad. One aim of the chapter is to let Jordanians speak for themselves on these matters rather than being spoken for.[8] Out of this discussion will emerge the complexity of treating such matters as tribalism, social change, modernity, honor, nationalism, professionalism, multiculturalism, migration, and the contribution of the army experience itself to sociocultural change.

To appreciate the comments of army men and army migrants about their experience it is first necessary to emphasize a few historical facts about Jordan itself and the political and social context in which the state arose. Before its designation by the British as the Emirate of Transjordan in 1923 the area east of the Jordan River had no fixed name. It was simply referred to as *sharq al-urdunn*, "(the lands) east of the Jordan," i.e., it had only a vague geographical identity.[9] Indeed, as Vatikiotis has pointed out, "this territory in its entirety had never been a separate, or independent, political entity.[10]

> ... for some 400 years [the Ottomans] considered it no more than an area lying astride the pilgrimage route from Syria to Mecca—both a west–east and a north–south highway. They therefore paid the tribes roaming its vast expanses in order not to attack the caravans or molest travelers. They also built some forts and water reservoirs across it to secure the safety of these caravans. They did not however set up any government or administrative apparatus for the area.[11]

Vatikiotis continues his capsule history by saying that in the sixteenth century "a vast migration of tribes from the interior of Arabia took place.... Their rivalries and frequent wars dominated events in that area until the nineteenth century."[12] And again:

> Throughout the seventeenth and eighteenth centuries the Turks could protect the pilgrimage road to Mecca and other routes of communication only by subsidizing the tribal shaykhs. This however did not always guarantee the passivity of the beduin, for he could still act wantonly and violently against travelers and settled communities.[13] ... in the mid-nineteenth century, the Turks made a concerted effort to restore order. They sent out administrative officers, governors (*qaimaqam*), accompanied by small garrison forces, to various districts in the area.[14]

At the beginning of the twentieth century tribal rebellions against attempts by Turkish authorities to carry out censuses, register lands, conscript soldiers, and collect taxes were not uncommon in Transjordan. Such was the situation until and after the establishment of the Emirate of Transjordan in 1923. At that time security forces were reorganized under the British officer Frederick Peake, with a subsidy from Great Britain with the mission of searching out and punishing rebels and dealing with tribal uprisings and other challenges to the authority of the newly-created Emirate with its headquarters in Amman. This new "Mobile Force" merged with local gendarmes under Peake's command and was named, *al-jaysh al-'arabi*, literally, "the Arab Army," anglicized into "the Arab Legion."

Jureidini and McLaurin have pointed out that the development of Jordanian nationalism in the twentieth century has been impeded by several factors, among them, "the lack of differentiation by border: northern Jordan might as well be southern Syria; southern Jordan, northern Arabia; eastern Jordan, western Iraq."[15] What is implied but not stated here is that Transjordan is not only a geographical-topographical but also a cultural extension of the lands that surround it.

The authors amplify the lack of distinctiveness of Transjordan in its historical dimension by saying:

> The other major Arab states, however weak their national identities, have all had some political tradition on which to draw in attempting to develop modern nationalistic support: Iraqis could look back to the Abbasids, Syrians to the Umayyads. If Saudi Arabia is a relatively new political entity, there is still a Saudi pride in their role as guardians of the holy cities and as the fount of much original Arab culture. Egypt, alone among the Arab states, can point to thousands of years of a distinctly Egyptian heritage. Algeria, Morocco, and Tunisia have all had extensive traditions as separate identities with clear histories. Only Libya challenges Jordan in its absence of a quasi-national tradition, the various parts of the country being unified only after World War II.[16]

After 1950, Jordanian nationalism, such as it was, developed in one dimension, interactively and reactively to the influx of 750,000 Palestinian refugees, fleeing Palestine as a result of the first Arab–Israeli War. At that point and still today, as Jureidini and McLaurin phrase it, "What Jordanians (East Bankers) know is that they are not Palestinians, Syrians, Saudis or Iraqis."[17]

Without elaborating on the theme, the authors call attention to two separate and simultaneous processes that are ongoing in Jordan, holding that the implication of these two processes on the Jordanian Army is still open. The two processes are Palestinianization and Jordanianization:

> It is too early to determine whether these changes will "Palestinianize" the army or "Jordanianize" the Palestinians.[18]

Jureidini and McLaurin also emphasize the degree to which Jordanian identity is implicated not in a dynasty (as in Saudi Arabia) but in the person of the monarch:

> … to the extent that Jordan is a meaningful concept, it is difficult for many Jordanians to understand that meaning without reference to the king. King Hussein symbolizes the state in a way quite unlike other rulers in the Middle East.[19]

Aside from the complex question of how the Palestinianization of Jordan will affect the character of change including that of the Jordanian Army, one must emphasize the complicated relationship of urban, rural, and pastoral groups to one another and their overall relationship to the "tribal society" of Jordan to understand the discussion of "tradition" and change that follows. Vatikiotis has mentioned the implication of the Arabic term *hadari,* used by Jordanians to refer to the nontribal half of the social dichotomy, tribal—nontribal, without fully explaining it.[20] *Hadari* literally means "pertaining to settlement," and its antonym would therefore be "pertaining to nomadism," or *badawi.* But in Jordan *hadari* is used to contrast with *'asha'iri,* i.e., "tribal." In Jordan "tribal" refers to a set of values emphasizing honor, generosity, and manliness inclusive of such attributes as wisdom, diplomacy, patience, and magnanimity. As such, the term could be applied to much of the population of Jordan including many urbanites and Palestinians. More narrowly, however, it refers to the segmentary character of tribal groups[21] (that chronically fissure and fuse depending on the presence or absence of crises), to the flexible situational character of leadership, and in the Arab World to a certain mode of conflict resolution defined by "tribal law": an unwritten (until very recently) code of procedures emphasizing intermediaries and mediation (*wasta*), delegations (*jaha*), dyadic diplomacy (*mulaqa*), truce (*'atwa*), compensation (*diyya*), and final reconciliation and peacemaking (*sulha*). The process of tribal conflict resolution assumes the principle of collective responsibility on the part of a stipulated and limited set of patrilineal kinsmen who must either take revenge or seek/receive compensation (if victimized) or seek protection (*dakhl*), truce and mediation, and pay compensation (if defined as offender).[22]

The problem with the equation of *hadari* with the settled people of Jordan is that the villagers of Jordan are dominantly "tribal" in their adherence to the distinctive mode of conflict resolution outlined above. In terms of politico-legal culture, then, the dichotomy is more properly between civil law on the one hand and tribal law on the other. These dichotomous classifications are confused further by the fact that many urbanites, and most townsmen including some Palestinians trace their descent to "tribes." The genealogical definition of tribalism, then, overlaps the legal definition in terms of reference to social groups, and both crosscut the classification of settlement types: urban, village, nomadic.

With the sedentarization of tribal nomads in Jordan in the 1930s, '40s, and '50s, the ethos and customs of many settled people have approximated those of many pastoralists—who, in any case by 1977 made up no more than 3 percent of the population.[23] When, therefore, Jureidini and McLaurin discuss the "behavioral manifestations" of the "decline of the tribe" in the last half of the twentieth century, including as indicators physical mobility without reference to tribal areas, the opening up of avenues of mobility in government and the professions, and the resort to extratribal allies for resolution of intratribal conflict resolution, they are obscuring the fact that the social type, ethos, and culture which they describe as declining was never confined to pastoralists (the nomad-settled dichotomy is not useful, culturally) and continues resilient in many of its aspects, and is in fact the focus of continuing reinterpretation, as the work of Linda Layne and Andrew Shryock demonstrates.[24]

This discussion of tribalism and its relationship to the three social types—urban, village, nomadic—is directly relevant to the development of the Jordanian Army and its policies of recruitment and promotion. Frederick Peake, the first head of the Arab Legion and John B. Glubb, its second English commander, in fact followed very different recruitment and promotion policies with their sources in different social types. Vatikiotis contrasts their policies by quoting the two commanders at length and interpreting their policies:

> "My policy," Peake stated once, "was to raise a Force from the sedentary, or village, Arabs, which would gradually be able to check the Beduin and allow an Arab government to rule the country without fear or interference from the tribal chiefs."[25]

Vatikiotis observes that Peake's policy of recruiting the new "Mobile Force" from peasants and some townsmen was abetted by the Beduins' own reluctance to join the Legion, "for they saw it strengthened the hand of a central ruler [Emir Abdullah, against them]."[26]

Glubb, on the other hand, explained his very different policy of recruitment and promotion this way:

> … Arab and Muslim armies never had a system of officers and men because they did not have a corresponding division into [feudal] social classes…. The system of appointing officers from high school or university direct to commissions as officers or cadets has the disadvantage that in the Arab countries 'tribesmen,' whether *fellahin* (peasants) or beduins, have strong warrior traditions, … whereas the city dwellers have no military traditions, particularly in Palestine…. promotion from the ranks which I favoured was in strict Arab and Islamic tradition, whereas direct commissions for college boys, which the "effendi" and official classes supported, was a slavish imitation of unsuitable European methods, which Europe itself is now discarding…. Thus, of the two sources of recruitment of officers, I and Muslim and Arab tradition favoured no class distinctions, but the choice of officers from communities with fighting traditions.[27]

Glubb goes on to specify his rationale of recruiting Beduins, expressed in his euphemism, "communities with fighting traditions," and excluding town-dwellers in terms of the very small numbers of urbanites and the likelihood that they would come from families producing politicians and civil officials who would not have the country's best interests at heart:

> In Arab countries where family loyalties are much stronger than national loyalties, this means that every such officer has some connection with a politician or political party…. In so small a country as Jordan, it is most important *not* to recruit officers

from important and powerful families. This applies as much to the sons of tribal chiefs as to those of cabinet ministers.[28]

The continuing importance of these "tribal" army units recruited in the 1930s, '40s, and early '50s is attested to by Vatikiotis' reference in the early 1960s to the

> ... overwhelming beduin-tribal and peasant composition of Infantry and Armour units on the one hand and the 80 per cent over 20 per cent predomination of *haḍari* personnel in the technical branches (Maintenance, Signals, Medical Corps) and Engineer arm on the other.[29]

And also, by the fact that these same tribal units were instrumental in the victory of the Jordanian Army over the PLO forces during the critical struggle of Black September, 1970. A later (1983) study continues to refer to the tribal backgrounds of the Jordanian officer corps, though now many officers "are university graduates from urban families with tribal backgrounds." In the enlisted ranks, on the other hand,"the mechanized infantry units remain almost exclusively composed of Bedouin volunteers" (national conscription had been introduced in Jordan in 1976).[30]

In any case, the close link of the army to the survival of the state did not change after the granting of independence to Transjordan in 1946. From 1950 to 1957 the largest item in the budget was for the Arab Legion, its spending being more than for all other government departments combined.[31] In the middle 1960s the army composed ci. 12 percent of the economically active population.[32]

The Jordanian Army: Professionals, Intelligensia, or Tribesmen?

A number of social scientists have discussed the development of modern armies in the nineteenth and twentieth centuries in terms of their development of military "professionalism" and in the Middle East in the twentieth century in terms of the development of the "intelligensia," all the discussion assuming that the world, including the third world, here the Arab world, is modernizing and in the process of doing so, embracing "modernity." A brief discussion of the attributes of modernity, professionalism, and the intelligensia follows to inform our later discussion of army migrants' experiences and attitudes and to assess the role of the army in social change.

By referring to modernity, following Manning Nash, I distinguish between two aspects of change. The first, "modernization," focuses on the "historically chancey" process of economic growth and its "different routes, timetables and strategies" together with the political and social changes that are its concomitants. On the other hand, for Nash, "Modernity is the social, cultural and psychological framework which facilitates the application of tested knowledge to all phases and branches of production. Modernization is the process of transformation toward the establishment and institutionalization of the framework of modernity."[33] Modernity focuses on the values which are its prerequisites such as the relatively unhampered search for new knowledge, a positive stance toward innovation, a fostering of social mobility, and an achievement ethic which channels rewards to high performers.[34]

Be'eri defines the intelligensia as an intellectual elite whose education is distinguished by its western orientation; in general, they are considered the best educated group in society. By definition, the category excludes religious savants and functionaries and assumes a secular orientation and a modern view of social change. Indeed, there is an assumption that the intelligensia will form the cadre of social ferment, and even revolutionary activity, should it take place. In terms of occupations, the free professions—teachers, doctors, lawyers, and engineers—form the core of the intelligensia as well as government officials with the stipulated education and orientation.[35]

In the Arab World, Be'eri argues, the intelligensia has developed other attributes: It is not just activist, but highly politicized and deeply ambivalent about the "assimilation of the values and way of life of the enemy [the west]."[36] Be'eri elaborates on this ambivalence:

> The intellectual is torn between the desire to learn and imitate the values and way of life of the foreigners and the will to protect himself against foreign principles and to reinforce his national values.... calling for acceptance of the west culturally but its rejection politically.... should he try to rouse the public at large, he will find that their reaction derives from tradition [Islamic zeal] rather than from the new spirit.[37]

As a result Arab intellectuals are left "irresolute" in their struggle against western colonial powers on the one hand and in their commitment to and application of westernization on the other.[38] Be'eri argues that in Turkey, Egypt, and other Arab countries the officer corps has occupied a central position in the intelligensia:

> Army officers were not the first to be touched by the winds of modernization, but the officer class was the first social group which as an entire group and as a group of recognized social and political standing was influenced by the new spirit of modernism.[39]

Be'eri has pointed out that since army men can't be pioneers in the strict intellectual aspect of reformist movements (as researchers, literateurs, or teachers) because of the nature of their profession (the management and application of violence) they tended to greater politicization. This tendency was accentuated in the Middle East by the hostile relationship of the leadership of modernized armies with the autocratic/monarchical/colonial rulers of their polities, e.g., Sultan Abd al-Hamid, the Hashemite kings of Iraq and Jordan, and the French and British colonial governors and supervisors.[40] The self-image of the military intelligensia (officers) in the Middle East, Be'eri continues, often stresses their roles as saviours of the country, its standard-bearers, and its guardians.[41]

Another way of thinking about army men in the nineteenth and twentieth centuries is to view them as developing "professionals." Barber stipulates the attributes of "the professions" as a high degree of systematic knowledge, a primary orientation towards the community (and not self) interest, a high degree of self-control of behavior through codes of ethics and voluntary associations, and a system of rewards, monetary and honorary (titles, medals, prizes, offices) that is mainly a symbol of work achievement and not an end in itself.[42]

Huntington, on the other hand, stipulates the attributes of professionalism as three: expertise (specific knowledge judged by universalistic standards); responsibility (involving performing a service essential to society—the concept of a "higher calling" is implied here); and corporateness (professionals consciously form discrete groups set apart from laymen with the group developing standardized norms of conduct with appropriate monitoring); membership in such groups is itself the criterion of professional status. The expertise of the military professional (officer) is the management of violence, "a complex intellectual skill requiring comprehensive study and training"; the responsibility of the military officer is to his client, society. Enlisted men lack intellectual skills and professional responsibility: "They are specialists in the application of violence not the management of violence."[43] Huntington also holds that because the military view of man is that he is selfish and weak, the chief needs of army life are organization, discipline, and leadership, and the highest military virtues are loyalty and obedience.[44]

Blau and Scott, on the other hand, stress the equivalence of professional and bureaucratic attributes in defining the professions as well as bureaucracies: decisions are governed by universal standards (rules); expertise is specific to the position occupied; affective neutrality is the dominant ethos pursued with clients; and in both professions and bureaucracies achieved status governs recruitment and promotion. However, the social control mechanisms in bureaucracies and professions are quite different: hierarchical control in bureaucracies with directives from above, whereas in the professions self-control is inculcated, with surveillance of conduct by peers.[45] The sociologist Max Weber also regarded the modern army as essentially "bureaucratic," as defined by rationality in decision-making, impersonality in social relations, and centralization of authority through superordinate-subordinate relationships. The final critical attribute of bureaucracies was the "routinization of tasks" through rules, roles, and files. Weber regarded the development of professional standing armies as impossible without the development of a bureaucratic structure and ethos.[46]

Jones has argued, against Huntington, that it is the "bureaucratic" rather than the "professional" attributes that define the modern military, that the ethic of public service and self-control is an ideal and not a behavioral reality, and that "military professionals" are in fact for much of the time engaged in administration. Furthermore, this bureaucratic attitude leads military men to despise the politicians and makes it difficult for them to simply act as "passive obedient neutral instrument[s]" in their hands.[47]

In discussing "Arab officer politicians" and their general tendency to be "nationalists favoring social reforms, zealous supporters of the state's independence and prestige, and indifferent to the values of individual freedom," Be'eri regards this general ideological orientation to be a "projection of their habits as soldiers—persons who are constantly seeking technical and organizational improvement and who are used to issuing orders; 'the art of persuasion' is not their particular proficiency."[48] In spite of their tendency to politicization, then, Be'eri regards Arab military officers as possessing key professional and bureaucratic attributes.

In two articles Khuri has challenged the view that modern Arab armies are best viewed as professional organizations. In the first (with Obermeyer, 1974) he has outlined a much more complex view of such armies. With the independence of the Arab nations after World War II these armies have developed "the triple character of a profession, a model of development and a microcosm of the state with tentacles reaching, through compulsory military service, to all groups in society."[49] Modern Arab armies are models of development not only because they develop technology much earlier than in industry or agriculture, but also, and for Khuri perhaps more important, because they develop literacy, standardized patterns of work, and a model welfare system: security of employment insurance against death, sickness, and accidents, family benefits and allowances, and pensions.[50]

In a second (1981) article Khuri develops the theme, begun in the first, of the army as a microcosm of the state.[51] This aspect of army life has three dimensions: (1) military officials become instruments of integration in local communities, e.g., they displace village notables as council heads and as mediators exercising the important *ḥakam* (wise arbitrator) role, and in doing so link these communities to the state; (2) the military bureaucracy (like the civilian) becomes a vehicle for social mobility (encouraging literacy, travel, and contacts with outsiders); and (3) it also becomes a main avenue by which public services like those mentioned above filter down to citizens, i.e., it becomes an informal bureaucracy subject to demands for intermediation (*wasta*) for more services including employment in the army itself. Conversely, viewed from above, "officers become leaders, linking local and relatively isolated peasant communities with the central administration and government."[52] But by virtue of the two important functions mentioned above (local mediation and bureaucratic mediation) army men remain/become deeply implicated in ties of kinship, marriage, and sectarian and home-town allegiance that shape their informal alliances and cliques within the army as well.[53] Khuri also argues that the sharp distinction between classes characteristic of peasant societies in the Middle East is reinforced in the army by virtue of the fact that officers received salaries 3–6 times those of soldiers and a "multitude of privileges" including housing allowances, educational facilities for children, cars, drivers, and cooks.[54]

Summing up, Khuri argues that "the military is no more nor less modernistic than structurally similar groups," [e.g.,] "elementary and secondary school teach-

44

ers, skilled technicians, university students, clerks, salaried labor, political parties (or) labor unions…;"[55] that the norms of Middle Eastern armies are the norms of their societies, generally, e.g., manliness, honor, dignity, generosity, self-respect, toughness, revengefulness, anger, and support of the weak—and not professional norms.[56] And that military officers are deeply implicated in the social structural cleavages of their societies, restricting their capacity to act as instruments of social development, even when they emphasize that goal (which is not always).

What evidence is there that the Jordanian army reflects a professional orientation or that it is either composed of or influenced by an intelligensia? Jureidini and McLaurin, writing in the early 1980s, state that the Jordanian army has maintained an "apolitical professionalism," has excelled in "fighting qualities" (in World War II, during the first Arab-Israeli War of 1948–49, and during Black September, 1970), and has maintained discipline.[57] Be'eri, as mentioned, views Arab officers' orientation to national independence and social reform as a product, in part, of their professions as soldiers. And Vatikiotis points out that until 1956 "promotion, whether to NCO ranks or officer grades, remained a traditional Legion procedure, characterized by a series of examinations, performance ratings by unit commanders and other military qualifications, and conduct criteria.[58] This procedure was in line with Glubb's view that the Arab Legion was to be "a highly trained, mobile corps d'elite."[59]

At the same time Vatikiotis points out that until around 1960 the officer corps of the Jordanian army could not be considered an elite as distinguished from enlisted personnel. There were no special educational qualifications for officers and no military academy. Prior to the 1960s "all Legion officers were selected from NCO ranks for special training in the Cadet School," which was itself only organized in 1950.[60] Before the 1950s the bulk of the enlisted ranks, whether in the infantry and armor or technical wing of the army, had an education that ranged from semiliterate to fourth primary school with the educational level of senior noncommissioned officers ranging from fourth year primary to first year secondary school.[61] Until 1956 there were no direct commissions into the army for those holding high school diplomas or university degrees.[62] And yet Vatikiotis states that the noncommissioned officers "represented perhaps the most professional element in the Legion; at least in terms of expertise, discipline and *esprit de corps*."[63] The top NCOs had at least ten years' service and it was unlikely, says Vatikiotis, that they would shed their professional neutrality and engage in political "conspiracies" because "they had attained high NCO rank after long and exacting service."[64]

Retirement, Village Life, and Modernity

Several men from the village of Kufr al-Ma, some only recently retired, reflect this process of regular promotion through enlisted ranks and frequent promotion from the ranks to officership that was the mark of the Jordanian army as a long-service volunteer force until 1956. National conscription was not introduced in Jordan until 1976, and observers writing in 1983 state, "the draft remains highly selective, so that the army contains only 10% conscripts."[65] It is worthwhile briefly recounting pertinent facts in the careers of these men and plumbing their implications for the issues raised above. The men are listed in Table 1.1 following.

A, age twenty-nine at retirement in 1981, served nineteen years in the Jordanian army, starting as a private, all the while serving in the artillery; he retired as a master sergeant. He said that he would have become an officer had he remained in the army, but the army of Abu Dhabi, where he intended to serve after retirement, did not recruit or keep foreign nationals after age thirty-five. He served with the signal corps in Abu Dhabi from 1981 to 1987, being promoted to corporal at the time he left. "A" had studied through the fourth grade in public school and became a grocer in the adjoining district center of Deir Abu Said after his retirement. We shall note below his reflections on his army experience at home and abroad. Although he did not pick up any practical skills to apply to civilian life while in the army, as did other enlisted men in the infantry and artillery, he did parlay his Jordanian army experience into six years of military service on the Gulf at a salary that was initially four times his Jordanian army salary at retirement and later more than twelve times that salary.

One of the other men who after longtime army service (twenty-two years) and retirement served in the Gulf was F, age fifty at the time of his enlistment in the army of Bahrain in 1984. F had served in the infantry during his entire Jordanian army service, had four years of primary school education, and was only a private first class at retirement. But his experience as drillmaster in the army allowed him to get a promotion to sergeant in Bahrain, where he was put in charge of training infantry. His salary in Bahrain was four times his Jordanian army pension.

B, age forty-nine at retirement, joined the army as a private in 1954 after finishing six years of primary school education (all there was at the local level at the time). He served twenty-one years in the infantry and later intelligence service, having been promoted to master sergeant at retirement in 1975. He joined the army of Abu Dhabi in 1976 as an intelligence specialist, serving nine years and retiring from that service in 1985. Several years after his retirement he was elected head of the municipality of Kufr al-Ma; he had served many years earlier as mayor (*mukhtar*) of the village for two years. After retirement he opened up a construction materials store at the village entrance. When B was interviewed in 1986, one of his sons was studying business management in the United States and another was studying avionics at an institute in Karachi, Pakistan. A third son had received a bachelor of nursing degree from Tripoli, Lebanon in 1977 and was studying for a bachelor of laws by correspondence from the Arab University in Beirut.

C, age thirty-nine at retirement, joined the Jordanian army in 1953, serving twenty years in the infantry. He was promoted through the ranks from private to

46

TABLE 1.1 • *Soldiers Promoted Through the Ranks and Retired*

Migrant's Designation in Book	Age	Year Entered Army	Year Left Army	No. of Years Served	Rank When Left	Army Bureau & Specialties	Education	Countries/Cities in Which Stationed	Present Occupation	Village Offices Held	No. of Sons Studied/Studying Abroad	Country in Which Sons Studied/Studying
A	34	1972 (Jordan) 1981 (Abu Dhabi)	1981 (J) 1987 (AD)	19 (J) 7 (AD)	Master Sergeant Corporal	Artillery Signal Corps	4th Primary	Abu Dhabi	Grocer			
B	60	1954 (J) 1976 (AD)	1975 (J) 1985 (AD)	21 (J) 9 (AD)	Master Sergeant	Infantry & Intelligence	6th Primary	Abu Dhabi	Construction Materials Storekeeper	Village Mayor Municipality Head	3	USA Pakistan Lebanon
C	52	1953	1973	20	1st Lieutenant	Infantry: Clerk, Bookkeeper, Quartermaster	9th Junior High School/ High School School-learning Certificate/Law School by Correspondence, Arab Univ of Beirut		Shopkeeper	Head of Village Council; Head of the Municipality		
D	56	1945	1968	23	Captain	Infantry; Transport, Radio	Kuttab/ 5th Primary	Jerusalem (12 Years)	Retired/Mgr of Farmland	Head of Village Council; Member, Municipality Council	3	Pakistan
E	53	1952	1981	29	Captain	Dental Technician	6th Primary	Jerusalem Ramallah Amman	Dental Technician		2	Pakistan England
F	50	1961	1983	22 (J) 2 (AD)	Private 1st Class Sergeant	Infantry Infantry Drillmaster	4th Primary	Bahrain	Infantry Drillmaster (Bahrain)		1	Greece

47

NCO and then to first lieutenant. After retirement he became president of the village council, a position he occupied for nine years while earning his living as a grocer in the adjoining district center. He subsequently served as head of the municipality of Kufr al-Ma for two years. When he entered the army he had finished junior high school (nine years). After retirement he earned his high school degree, and at the time he was interviewed in 1986 he had been studying two years for a law degree by correspondence at the Arab University in Beirut.

D, age thirty-eight at retirement in 1968, entered the army in 1945, serving twenty-three years; he was promoted through the ranks to captain. He served in the transport section of the infantry. He had finished five years of primary school (all that was available) preceded by two years of religious schooling (*kuttab*) when he enlisted. He served in Palestine for approximately half of his military service and married a Palestinian woman from Jerusalem. After leaving the army he served as president of the village council (an unpaid position) for five years while earning his living from a village grocery to supplement his army pension. Later he worked for four years as a shipping supervisor in the port of Aqaba till his son graduated from a university in Pakistan; then he returned to the village and served for two years as a member of the municipality council. At the time of the interview in 1986, he was managing his investments, mainly land in Kufr al-Ma and the Jordan valley. One of his sons, a graduate of Hyderabad University in Pakistan with a B.A. in English, was working as a successful business manager in Saudi Arabia, and another was studying for an M.A. in English at Sind University in Pakistan.

After finishing six years of primary school, E served twenty-nine years in the army, nearly all of it as a dental technician, retiring in 1981. He spent nearly all of his army service in cities and towns, one year in Jerusalem, one year in Ramallah, Palestine, and the remainder in Amman. He was promoted from private to NCO and thence to captain. One of his sons had earned a degree in veterinary medicine from Pakistan and thereafter a M. Sc. in Animal Health from the Royal Veterinary College in London. His son was the head of the local department of agriculture office in Deir Abu Said. In 1986 a second son had just returned with a degree in animal husbandry from Pakistan and had secured a position as laboratory supervisor at Jordan University. A third son was still in Pakistan studying for a degree in food technology. In 1986 E was working in a part-time private practice three days a week as a dental technician in Amman.

All of these enlisted men promoted through the ranks reflect the aspect of modernity which "channels rewards to high performers." Their professional expertise and competence was ostensibly recognized and rewarded by promotion and its perquisites. What is particularly interesting is that some of these men, B, C, and E, not themselves highly educated—though as sons of peasants they had gone as far as they could in the local public school system at the time—pursued education in the army in the fields of dentistry, intelligence, and accountancy, with C continuing his studies with higher education after retirement. B and C, in addition, pursued religious learning on their own, purchasing and perusing various commentaries of the Quran. Furthermore, four of these men had sent their sons abroad for a higher education to Pakistan, Lebanon, England, Greece, and the United States in such varied fields as medicine, veterinary medicine, avionics, business management, English, and nursing, reflecting "the relatively unhampered search for new knowledge" characteristic of modernity. Although none of these men had been educated abroad, three had served in the Gulf states where they were exposed to a multiethnic society, and two had spent long periods in Palestine in towns or urban centers where they came into contact with a much more highly educated population oriented towards modernity, perhaps partially as a result of their long exposure to and conflict with British colonial rule on the one hand and Jewish settlement on the other.

Indeed, there is evidence that these men after retirement consciously sought to solidify their similar worldviews through a social network by the marriage of their children and siblings. There were four marriages between the children of D and E, the two men who had achieved the status of captain from that of private and educated five of their sons abroad, and a marriage between C's sister and F. In 1986 F's son had just returned from Greece with a medical degree and was serving as a doctor in an army hospital. This son had received a seven year army scholarship for study abroad for which he qualified by virtue of his father's long army service and his own high scholastic average.

Thus, a number of army men who received extended army training, after their retirement from it, sent their sons for "comprehensive study and training" abroad. One could argue, then, that these men completed their "professionalism" after retirement and vicariously became one of the "intelligensia" through their sons.

There is one respect, however, in which viewing these army men as professionals is clearly unwarranted—that is the view that emphasizes the separate "corporate" character of professionals. These NCOs who became officers clearly breached the bounds of any officer class, on the one hand, since they were promoted through the ranks, and on the other, as Khuri suggests, they remained integrated in their local communities, and, in fact, solidified their positions in them by occupying leadership positions after retirement. There is a spatial and institutional aspect to this integration relating to army policy: the Jordanian army pursued a very liberal daily and weekend leave policy, particularly after officers and NCOs advanced in service. Some soldiers finished work in the midafternoon and were permitted to leave base for their homes and families to stay overnight. Since Jordan was a small country, and Kufr al-Ma was only two hours distant from some army bases, this was feasible, particularly if one possessed a car, or, if not, availed oneself of the regular "service" taxis. Moreover, some soldiers were given long weekends beginning on Thursday afternoon and ending on Monday morning.

Though they had a commitment to work achievement, work discipline, organization and planning, and the development of professional expertise either for themselves or their children, or both, they remained integrated in their local community and partial to many of its values, e.g., honor, generosity, and dignity, and to the social relations implied by them—loyalty to kin, tribal mediation, and the modesty of men and women in all public places/endeavors. They could hardly conduct their social relations in terms of some bureaucratic ideal of impersonality or affective neutrality, and did not demonstrate any propensity to do so. On the other hand, this continued social integration with their home community as well as their commitment to many of its norms did not, as Khuri suggests, prevent them from actively pursuing in their own lives or vicariously pursuing through their sons, whom they supported and encouraged, financially, morally, and humanistically, pioneering ventures in the fields of occupational expertise and higher education; these ventures were a hallmark of both professionalism and modernity.

C is perhaps, the outstanding example of this commitment in his own inveterate continuation of his studies after retirement. When I asked him in 1986 why he chose to continue studying (he had retired in 1973), he replied that the aim was "to raise the standard (of knowledge) and to be an informed citizen" (*al-hadaf an yarfa' al-mustawa wa tkunn muwaṭin mafhum*). The aim was not material (*maddi*). Then he quoted a Tradition of the Prophet on learning: "Seek learning from the cradle to the grave" (*utlab al-'ilm min al-mahad ila al-lahad*). He said that he had a younger brother who failed his exams and he kept pushing him till he went back and took his school exams and passed. I asked him if he would support his five children to get an education and, if so, how far? He replied that he would support them, including his four daughters, as far as they could go. One of his daughters was then in the second year of high school. He then quoted a proverb: "The mother is a school (in herself); if you educate her, you have educated a folk, noble and high-born."

C was no doubt exceptional in his commitment to education, but E, the dental technician, was also remarkable in his commitment to proficiency. He took four courses in the army, all on dentistry, to improve his dental skills, and took an examination in the Ministry of Health after retirement that qualified him to take up a private practice as a dental technician. He was a prime example of technological modernization. When I was interviewing his son who had just returned from Pakistan in 1986, I posed the question of whether the latter favored birth control. The son replied negatively, saying that it violated religious precepts. E disagreed with his son and said that the religious scholars (*'ulema*) did not forbid it now. And that he had begun practicing it fifteen years ago after the birth of his ninth child. He had not had children since then. Certainly, for his fellow villagers this was innovative behavior at the time. Neither E nor his son wore headdresses, and they wore western pants and jackets. E had both a sitting room (*diwan*) furnished with soft chairs, a carpet, and fancy decorated glass tables, as well as a small traditional guest room (*maḍafa*) where we ate a tray of rice and chicken, but with spoons and separate dishes for each guest. I saw no religious symbols in E's home. There were, however, pictures of his family decorating the walls.

After B finished his primary school in the nearby subdistrict center in 1944, he became at the age of seventeen the *mukhtar* (mayor) of the village and was instrumental in getting the first school established in Kufr al-Ma. Two years later he joined the army. In 1986 during the course of an interview we began to discuss the work of the municipality of Kufr al-Ma which had been established in 1981. One of its first projects for which it raised money was the paving of the rough, zigzag dirt roads inside the village. B said that there was "trafficking" on the part of the municipality and that straightforwardness was the essence of dignity (*karama*). He said that there were still 14–20 houses in the lower quarter where he lived and near the center of the village that had no electricity and several that had no paved access roads; whereas, a road had been built to the northern edge of the village to access a single house (in which lived the son of an influential relative of the head of the municipality). B commented further on the work of the municipality. He said that the paved roads inside the village were crooked, weaving back and forth, left and right (to accommodate the whims of individual villagers). Then he recited a poem reflecting his criticism of the head of the municipality and the serious flaws in his leadership:

> The capable enemy you'll swear by (respect).
> Satisfying the people is an end you'll never attain.
> The messengers of the people lean towards the person (leader) who has
> no tilting.
> And he who has no tilting (concern for the people,
> commitment),
> Away from him the people lean.

In the poem B was stating the necessity for leaders to use their reason; to maintain universalistic standards of fairness in building the village roads; while at the same time maintaining firmness in the public interest in the execution of that reasonable standard. Later B ran for and won the position as head of the municipality.

My interview with D in 1986, on the other hand, illustrates how many of these retired army men, whatever attributes of modernity and professionalism they had assumed, remained grounded in the norms of their own religious culture. It also illustrates the complex mix of attributes one is likely to find when such ideal types as "the professional" and "the intelligensia" are applied to flesh and blood people. Ventilating the problems of high white-collar unemployment and overpopulation in Jordan, I asked D, "What are your views on birth control?" Our dialogue proceeded as follows:

> "It has its (appropriate) circumstances in Islam" (*fi ilha THuruf fi al-islam*). He then quoted the Quran, "There is not a creature on earth except that God provides for it." Then he quoted another Quranic verse, "Don't kill your children fearing want

(hunger), we will provide for them and you too" (*wa la taqtalu awladakum khashyata imlaq; nahnu narziquhum wa iyyakum*). "But," he continued, "from a human point of view, if the mother is ill or has given birth to many offspring and it harms the mother's life, then you can use birth control." "Where will the jobs for future graduates come?" I asked. He replied that religion did not contradict itself; Jordan still didn't have overpopulation. "But," he said, "our income is restricted. One is perplexed as between (the demands of) religion and the demands of modern life." "But," he said finally, returning to his earlier theme, "God's earth is wide" (*arḍ allah wasi'a*); "one doesn't have to stay in Kufr al-Ma (to pursue a livelihood)." He added that the constitution of Jordan supports birth control in emergencies. I then recounted to D the story of my poor cousins in rural Lebanon who had seized the opportunities that had opened up in the backwaters and peripheries of the country in the 1970s as a result of the Lebanese civil war and the investment of Beirut, to point out the role of economic opportunity in economic success. D's comment after hearing the story was, "There, you see, God provides," (*allah yarzaq*); "God opened up a path," (*allah fatah tariq*).

D's suggested resolution to the problems of overpopulation and unemployment are grounded firmly in a religious worldview: God would provide for additional bodies and souls—he was compassionate and merciful—and my stress on economic opportunity as the key to my cousins' success in Lebanon, D interpreted as God's omniscience and compassion.

But in another respect, D's replies were reasoned and thoughtful, weighing options, alternatives, and possibilities of interpretation that reflected an appreciation of a complex modern world. Immediately after pronouncing the Quranic passage with an air of finality, "Don't kill your children fearing want," he said, "From a human point of view if the mother is ill or has given birth to many offspring ... you can use birth control." Shortly after, he said, emphasizing the compelling but competing standards, "One is perplexed between (the demands of) religion and the demands of modern life." In his appreciation of the complexity of the modern world and his willingness to reflect upon and wrestle with the dilemmas it posed, D was a leading member of the intelligensia of the village.

But as a member of the local-level intelligensia he was not ambivalent about the West in any of its political or social representations, as Be'eri suggests. He had no "hang-ups" about accepting innovation, even in the sensitive field of male-female relations: When I visited his house and found him absent, his wife came and talked to me on the veranda, and other women from the household came and sat down on the veranda. His Pakistani daughter-in-law was called in to shake hands with me, and his son's wife sat with us for a short time at mealtime. While we waited for D to return, I was asked whether I would like to come and watch television with the women; all of this was highly unusual social behavior for the village, which had changed in many respects since 1959 when I first entered it, but not in its basic expectation of modesty for men and women. D was ambivalent, but it was not an ambivalence directed against the West and expressing itself in political opposition or cultural exclusiveness. Rather, his ambivalence was about the modern world, generally, and the predicaments it presented to him and the many others like him who had, themselves, or vicariously through their sons, ventured out into the world, and wished to incorporate its benefits and at the same time remain faithful to their own proven traditions and fundamental beliefs.

Adaptations and Evaluations

It is now appropriate, first, to describe the continuum of post-retirement adaptations of Jordanian soldiers from Kufr al-Ma in terms of the concept of the army as a "technical college of society," implying a double accent on professionalism and modernity.[66] And second, to describe the range of their evaluations of the army experience and its impact on society.

We will proceed from the most to the least adaptive cases. E, the dental technician, is the clearest case of a successful, immediate, straight-line postretirement life based on skills learned in the army. E took four successive training courses in dentistry, qualified as a dental technician (he could put in false teeth and bridges but not drill or fill cavities), then qualified as a dental technician in civilian life, and as a result of his income was able to send three sons for higher education overseas. C's post-retirement adaptation is less dramatic, but nevertheless clear and persuasive. During his army career he took courses in clerical skills, administration, accountancy, and warehousing. All of these skills are useful to him in pursuing his current occupation of general grocer, and, undoubtedly, were also useful in his service as president of the village council and head of the municipality. B's training in intelligence allowed him to gain a similar position in Abu Dhabi at higher pay, thereby providing the savings to educate his three sons abroad. As a result of his nine years of service in that army, his son qualified for a four-year university scholarship in the United States. F's long service in the infantry also provided the experience to qualify for a higher-paying position in the army of Bahrain. His long service in the Jordanian army resulted in an army scholarship for his son to Greece. It is questionable whether B's or F's army training is or will be of practical use in their post-army careers.

J (see Table 1.3) is a first lieutenant with seventeen years' service in the mechanical section of the air force. He has taken specialized courses in diesel engines, electric generators, control switch gears, and motor generator sets as well as management, first aid, and firefighting. Although many of these courses were extremely specialized, some will undoubtedly help him on retirement when he actively attends to an electric appliance repair shop in the village for which he has already purchased the land and built the building.

Another villager was forced to retire early from the infantry at a sergeant's rank in 1973 as a result of a wound received in the 1967 Arab–Israeli War which affected his eyesight. While in the army he enrolled in training programs in light arms, anti-aircraft guns, machine guns, mortars, chemical warfare, and firefighting. He said that while drivers, mechanics, and electricians benefited from army training courses, he himself never did in terms of preparing him for his post-retirement occupation as an owner and manager of a cinder-block workshop, a tile workshop, and an aluminum goods store. Although the army did not prepare him for his career in commerce, like J and others, part of his successful adaptation is a result of the fact that he began his post-retirement occupation two years before he retired; his brother managed the cinder-block workshop till he retired. This overlap in pre and postretirement occupations was encouraged by the army's liberal furlough and weekend leave policies referred to above.

A contrasting case of rough adaptation is that of A's elder brother, who retired from the air force in 1978 at age thirty-six after serving sixteen years. After working two years as a typist in a local government office he opened up a grocery shop in the provincial capital of Irbid in 1980. He said that he was quite unprepared to work as a merchant. Neither he nor his father nor grandfather had shopkeeping experience from which he could benefit, nor did his army training help him. He made many mistakes, and during his first two years his shop made no profit because he bought so many goods that had low-turnover value.

A, himself, became a grocer in the nearby subdistrict center in 1988. While he was still serving with the army of Abu Dhabi I discussed the possibilities of his future employment with his elder brother, the grocer, and a younger brother who worked as an assistant to his elder brother in the Irbid grocery, taking a truck loaded with goods out to the surrounding villages and selling off the truck. They both agreed that A had no useful economic skills as a result of his infantry service, and that the only thing they could do was set him up in a grocery shop where he would be guided—and partially bankrolled—by his brothers. This they did. A named the shop, "The Shop of Compassion," reflecting his religious orientation.

Another soldier from the village, M, entered the army at the age of sixteen in 1964, serving in the artillery. From 1971 to 1977 he entered into various sports competitions while in the army including broad jumping, high jumping, pole vaulting, and hurdles, all the while serving in the artillery. He won a variety of medals in these competitions, which he showed me, and had often competed in the presence of the king. But he developed back trouble in the army, and after an unsuccessful operation in 1979 he was forced to retire at age thirty-one. He now walks with a limp. While in the army he took two training courses, one for artillery and the other for sports competition. His adaptation has been rougher and more unstable than that of A's brother, continually shifting from one short-term gain venture to another: he opened a village grocery shop two months after retiring in 1981 which he kept for three years. He also bought a Datsun pickup truck in which he bought vegetables from the Jordan Valley and Irbid to sell in the village; he sold it the same year. In 1983 he bought a Volkswagen bus for $2,500 and sold groceries from it in the surrounding villages, making an annual income of $2,500–$3,100. His aim was always to make a quick profit. He sold the Volkswagen bus at a profit of $2,000 and bought a 1985 diesel Nissan pickup. In 1986 he sold the pickup at a profit of $450. In 1986 at the time I interviewed him he had just bought $8,000 worth of shoes, sandals, and slippers which he was selling in a rented shop in the village. Before he went into the army he ploughed on his father's land; he has never ploughed since his army service.

Our last retiree, L, opened a secondhand clothing shop immediately after his retirement in 1985. He had finished four years of primary school before entering the infantry, in which he served twenty-one years. He sells women's dresses manufactured in Europe and the United States which he purchased from a Jordanian company that imports used clothing from abroad. His shop opened with a capital of $1,000. He served as a Jordanian embassy guard for two years in Baghdad, Iraq and developed no economic skills while in the army. I asked him whether he had any experience in shopkeeping before. He replied that he had none. "I took a chance," he said. "I opened up my shop and trusted in God, Lord of the worlds. I had no experience whatsoever." I asked,"Why did you pick clothes to sell?" He replied, "I take pleasure in laying out clothes.... It is a clean restful job." He earns $250 a month from his shop. L is a soldier emerging from the army with no skills and without beginning his enterprise in a testing period before retirement. That is, he is a soldier with virtually no preadaptation to post-retirement life. Nevertheless, he immediately took up employment, saying, "otherwise, I'll get lazy," and trusted in Providence to see him through an enterprise that chance began.

How do these soldiers, those mentioned above and others, evaluate their army experience? There is substantial agreement and also considerable variety in their evaluations. The following evaluations are arranged in a continuum, generally from the most positive to those which weigh the pros and cons or hedge their evaluations to those that are clearly negative. It should be understood that the following evaluations were selected by the author to reflect the variety of opinions. The great majority of men interviewed evaluated their army experience in a positive way. Considering the tribal background of the villagers and the long association of the tribes with the army referred to above, that fact is not surprising. That makes the negative evaluations below all the more interesting. Generally, as the responses moved from the positive to the negative end of the continuum, they became more elaborate and complex.

Our first informant, G, age thirty-three at the time of the interview, is a master sergeant and a fitter mechanic in the air force who has been sent on missions to Great Britain, France, and the United States. In the army he studied gyroscope systems, navigation, and American English. I asked him, "What is your view of the impact of the army on society?" He replied:

"You take a pension—it will stay with you till you die; if you die it stays with your son. In the army you find more occupations (trades) that you can't find in civilian life. You also mix with more than one kind of human being (*ta'ashshur min akthar min jins bashari*), from the north (of Jordan), from the south." He said that if he retired he could work with an airline company or a phosphate company, since they used electrical apparatus. "Those who pick up a trade benefit," he said. As an example he cited the fact that he could be a driver after retirement—he could drive a big trailer.

G in short order, then, ticked off four benefits of army service: a pension, learning a skill, cultural exposure, and getting a job on retirement.

A, who served seven years in Abu Dhabi after nineteen in the Jordanian army in the artillery, replied when I asked him, "What is your view of the army?":

> "The widest door (of opportunity) for young men is the army; it will exterminate unemployment. Anyone unemployed (who joins the army) will reap health, lower prices for goods, and a pension. Three quarters of the Jordanians were in the army. The people support it. All (families) have members in it. Even people in the university will go into the army and get a position."

A stipulates five separate benefits of the army, three being economic. He is the first to introduce the theme of the army as a national institution, stressing its populist character.

C, the retired director of army clerks, prioritized the patriotic theme in his reply to my question, "Did you like your army service?" "Yes," he said. "First, you serve your country; second, you make a living; and third, you get training in skills." And he proceeded to tick off the training courses he took while in the army.

When I asked L, the retired owner of the secondhand clothing store, "What's your view of the army's effect in society?" he deemphasized the economic benefits emphasized by A, C, and G, and stressed a nationalistic theme, saying, "I went into the service as a citizen (*watani*) not to benefit myself in my postarmy employment." Later in the interview, as we were discussing possible economic ramifications of army service, he repeated, "The army didn't benefit me (occupationally)."

A's younger brother had been conscripted into the army and served two years in the tank corps, leaving in 1984 at the age of twenty-six to work as an assistant shopkeeper with his elder brother. When I asked him, "How do you evaluate service in the army?" he said, "Army service is something excellent. It is the badge of the human being (*shu'ar al-insan*). Man relishes (life in) the army because he is a protection for his country (*al-insan byilizz bil jaysh li an huwa himaya lil balad*)."

J, the air force lieutenant who had seventeen years' service and had been sent on three missions abroad (including the U.S.A.), regarded the army as a boon to education and the model welfare system. In reply to my question, he gives the most elaborate rendition of the army's benefits:

> "Today there are no illiterates. What I used to see in the United States, I see it in Jordan. Technicians get the benefit (of army training), and soldiers benefit materially. Your rights (*huquq*) are preserved (in the army). If you die after one day in the army your

family has a monthly pension, and your life is insured. They provide homes cheaply if you want to bring your family inside the army camp. They give loans up to $12,000 from private to NCO, and officers qualify for loans up to $40,000." He said that the training he gets in electrical engineering in the army is better than he could have got in civilian life. I said that it seemed at some periods that half the village was in the army. He said that they took the uneducated and tried to teach them a skill. I said, "But not everyone goes into the technical side of the army." He replied, "They give you three chances to pick up a vocation (*mihna*); there are three exams." He said that in the army the least educated go into the infantry and the artillery.

The owner of the cinder-block workshop who had to take an early retirement due to his injury in the 1967 war also gave a short but unqualified positive view of the army when I asked, "Do soldiers benefit from the army?" He replied that drivers, mechanics, and electricians benefited after they got out and added, "The army is the best institute in Jordan as far as salary and livelihood go (*al-jaysh aḥsan muʾassasa fil urdun bi-nisbat al-rawatib wal maʾisha*)." He said that he would encourage his son to go into the army.

In contrast to these unqualified positive evaluations of army experience are others also positive, but more immediately pragmatic. The migrant who worked as a plasterer in Saudi Arabia and had served in the army stressed the material benefits of staying, and low income (in comparison with what one could earn from migration) as a reason for leaving when I asked, "What is the impact of the army on society?"

"It's sweet: a good salary, good clothing, good food." "Why did you leave, then?" I asked. He replied that he wasn't making enough income. He was in the infantry. There were no training programs (for skills); they used to dig trenches. But he said he was in the infantry in name only; he spent most of his time repairing houses. He said he didn't want to be a mason in the army; there was a chance to become a mason in civilian life and get an increase in income. But he said he did not want to (leave the army); (in fact) he saw himself short-changing the army (by leaving).

The migrant who was serving as an educational administrator in southern Arabia and who had been previously conscripted into the army for two years (see next chapter) also had a positive pragmatic view of the army, but he hedged it by introducing the differential benefit for people of different economic status when I asked, "What is your view of the impact of the army on society?" He replied:

"People were poor. He who had material possessions (*madda*) taught his children. The man without material possessions sends his children to the army and (they) stay on to get a pension. Do they benefit (by army service)? He can be a clerk, an accountant or typist (in the army), and now he has a steady income after retirement. If he goes into the tank corps, he can still go to the Gulf (to serve as a soldier there afterwards) and find work. When I was small all my efforts were to avoid the army. I always wanted to have a university degree. But I had to serve in the army, and they didn't allow me to leave the country, and we only had a few institutes (of learning at the time).

A similar hedged, but much more negative reply, indicating class-distinction, was given by the son of D, who was a very successful business manager in Saudi Arabia after getting his B.A. degree in English from Pakistan. He had never served in the army. Our interview on the subject in 1986 proceeded as follows:

> I asked, "What is your view of army service?" He replied, "These people aren't there by their own choice: one who can't study, he has no way except by joining the army. The army will teach a certain kind of strict life and finally exert an influence. The government pays more attention to the city—there are clubs (there). Most of the people from the army are from villages. They can't come to Amman for a few hours (to attend clubs and become knowledgeable and refined). There is an athletic club in Kufr al-Ma. People (in the village) think only lousy boys go there—most of the people won't want their sons there. A club—like libraries, lectures."

D's son quickly shifts the dialogue from one on the benefits of army service to one specifying the dichotomous roads to modernity. He associates the army with the non-modern, the uneducated, the unprogressive, the (backward) villages. They provide a contrast set with the capital city and its voluntary associations (clubs) and libraries and lectures. Nevertheless, D's son views the army as a necessary institution, providing remedial education and discipline for the bulk of the population that cannot get access to higher education and a more enlightened way of life.

H, a thirty-five-year-old major in the infantry who had been sent on two educational and training missions to Great Britain and the United States, gave a very different kind of appraisal stressing the positive aspect of enculturation and identity reformation for those who undergo officer training as well as the lack of preparation for civilian life. In reply to my question, "What is your view of the army as a profession?" he said:

> "You have to do it (in army training) and don't expect your subordinates to argue. You are expected to be subject to harsh conditions (as opposed to civilian life). You are expected to be physically fit. They (the army) try to make you forget everything and be a different person; and be able to survive in difficult circumstances; to do much and expect little. I interjected, "How about adaptation after the army?" He replied, "There is no preparation for civilian life. That is one reason I am pursuing studies while in the army (he was working for a B.A. in English at a nearby university)—to cope with the demands of life when I become a civilian. If I leave (the army) in two or three years perhaps I'll get an M.A. or Ph.D., or I may get a scholarship from the army or at Yarmouk University. If I get a scholarship from the army, I'll be assigned to Mu'ta (a military academy) to teach in Kerak. Graduates of Mu'ta serve in the army or police, or I'll go to Yarmouk to teach." He said that he wanted a teaching job. This was his aim, whether at Yarmouk University, in the army or on his own (privately).

Two respondents, both migrants, and neither with army service, gave negative evaluations. The first was the son of B, the intelligence officer who served in Abu

Dhabi. He had been studying computer science in Houston, Texas (see interview with "Zayd" in chapter 6 below) at the time I interviewed him on a visit home in Kufr al-Ma in 1986. I asked him, "What is the effect of the army on society?" He answered in the following way:

> "The army is good, but it should give more to individuals. They take his (the soldier's) youth and don't give him much in return. The salary is minimal. It isn't good enough. Conscription? I'm not for it. I think people should become acquainted with it (the army) for three months. I don't see any reason to take two years of my life and give me only 20 dinars (ci. $50) a month. I don't think that's good. And once again I'll have to be dependent on my father for money. I'll feel awkward."

What is striking about this reply is its extreme (by Jordanian standards) and conscious individualism—its concern for the rights of the individual and for self-interest. In 1991 I interviewed B's son, now age thirty, this time in Houston when he had just finished a four-year degree in business management and was driving a limousine to earn money. He was talking about buying his way out of military service by paying $6,000, as the government, in economic need, allowed. He said that this system of buying out was unfair and shameful, but he would avail himself of it. He said that he had had enough hardships in the United States, and didn't want more in the army. Earlier in the interview he had told me that his father constantly encouraged him when he was a child to study hard, and when he slacked off, his father threatened, "If you don't study, you'll be eating dust; you'll go into the army." His father, a twenty-one-year veteran and NCO, clearly implanted the negative view of the army from childhood. What is notably absent from his son's comments on army service is any reference to patriotism.

By far the most negative view of the army is held by N, another brother of A (not the assistant-shopkeeper). I asked N, "What do you think of the army as a profession?" He gave me a long answer, beginning with the statement, "Soldiering is charity (*ṣadaqa*) from the state." N's indictment of the army was much more sweeping than that of B's son. The army didn't simply give you a meager salary and take your youth away. It wasted men and resources and molded fearful conformists who were incapable of contributing to society upon the termination of their army service, and taught them to deal with their families in an authoritarian rather than a humane manner.

The great majority of our informants, then, evaluated the army experience in a positive manner with an emphasis on its economic benefits, particularly its excellent welfare system, and to a lesser extent on its teaching of skills that might be useful later in life, though there was a less positive evaluation for the infantry and artillery in this respect. For some, the army was "the technical college of society" and a vanguard, but for others it was no such thing.

Only a few men cited patriotic motives for army service and none reflected the "warrior ethos" that one might have anticipated in a tribal society (and explicitly vouched for by Peake and Glubb and, at second hand, by Vatikiotis), though these men were the offspring of sedentary peasants and not nomadic pastoralists. On the other hand, this finding accommodates the analysis of Vatikiotis and Jureidini and McLaurin, who stress Transjordan's lack of nationalist tradition, historically, politically, or even geographically.

A minor but important theme, reflected by three former soldiers but implied by others, is that the army was and is the home for the less fortunate, the less educated, the less progressive—the home for the parts of society that were becoming obsolete and not those that would be leading the country into modernity. This is an interesting conclusion in view of the fact that in 1986 there was no evidence that Kufr al-Ma or other surrounding villages were becoming obsolete. The population had more than doubled since 1960; rural-urban migration had been, if anything, reversed—most villagers were now commuters to towns. The roads had been paved; the village had been electrified; nearly every house had piped water; a building boom was under way. And, most important, over 130 young men had left the village to seek higher education abroad, and the overwhelming majority had returned to Jordan, most finding jobs in the towns and cities, where if possible, they commuted to the village where their families were located on a daily or weekly basis. Or, if not possible, they lived in towns but kept their domiciles in the village and anticipated returning there at least at retirement, if not earlier. Why there should be this discrepancy on the part of many between cognitive constructions and behavioral patterns will be examined in succeeding chapters.

Migration and the Army: Training Missions and Military Employment Abroad

After having reviewed the growth of the Jordanian army in its social, historical, and political setting, and described the adaptations of soldiers and the evaluations of their army experience, it is now appropriate to return to the central theme of transnational migration. Army men have spent substantial periods abroad either in the service of Arab Gulf armies after retirement or on training missions abroad, mainly but not exclusively to the United States and Europe. We have already referred to three men, A, B, and F, who served in the Gulf after retirement. They and two others, about whom much less information was gathered, are listed in Table 1.2, which also lists some of their important social and military attributes as well as pertinent facts of migration.

In the last thirty years the Jordanian army has selected many officers to continue specialized military education and training abroad after receiving commissions, particularly in the United States and Great Britain. NCOs and some enlisted men have also been sent abroad to get training in certain specialties or to serve as security personnel. The twelve men from Kufr al-Ma (about whom I have information) who have served on training missions abroad are listed in Table 1.3.

TABLE 1.2 • *Retired Soldiers in Gulf Armies*

Migrant's Designation in Book	Age	Marital Status	Children	Year Entered Army	Year Left Army	No. of Years Served	Retired/Current Rank	Army Branch & Specialties	Countries Stationed/Time Spent	Gulf Military Income	Yrs of Formal Schooling	Present Occupation	Monthly Income from Retirement & Current Civilian Occupation	Kinship-Residence Pattern
A	34	M	Yes, 7	1962 (J)* 1981 (AD)*	1981 (J) 1987 (AD)	19 7	Master Serg (J) Corporal (AD)	Artillery Signal Corps (J)	Abu Dhabi 7 years	450 Dinars/ Mon. (1981) 1800 Dinars/ Mon. (1987)	9	Grocer	Pension, 70D Shop, 150-200	Co-Jordanians
B	60	M	Yes, 5	1954 (J) 1976 (AD)	1975 (J) 1985 (AD)	21 9	Master Serg	Infantry & Intelligence	Abu Dhabi 9 years	300 DM (1976) 550 DM (1985)	6	Construction Materials Storeowner		
F	50	M	Yes	1961 (J) 1984 (Bahrain)	1983	22 3	Master Serg	Infantry Drillmaster	Bahrain 3 years	400 DM	4	Army Drillmaster	Pension 100D	Co-Villagers
	35	M	Yes	1983 (Bahrain)		7 (J) 3 (B)*			Bahrain 4 years	200 DM		Soldier		Co-Villagers
	35	M	Yes	1983 (Bahrain)		8 (J) 4 (B)	Private		Bahrain 4 years	200 DM		Soldier		Co-Villagers

*J = Jordanian Army; AD = Army of Abu Dhabi; B = Army of Bahrain

61

TABLE 1.3 • *Soldiers Sent on Missions Abroad*

Migrant's Designation in Book	Age	Marital Status	Children	Yrs of Formal Sch	Year Entered Army & Status	Rank	Branch	Yrs Svd	Monthly Military Income	Country/s Visited	Time Spent	City/Town Resided	Present Occupation	Income from 1986 Occupation	Army Specializations/ Courses
G	33	M	Yes	12	1972 Active	Master Sergeant	Air Force	14	140	England 1974 / France 1981 / USA 1984	18 mo. / 4 mo. / 8 mo.	Town near Birmingham / Rance/Vallance / Vicksburg, MI	Air Force Fitter Mechanic	1,680 D/year	Fitter Mechanic/ Gyroscope systems/ Navigation/American English
H	35	M	No	15	1971 Active	Major	Infantry	16		England 1972 / England 1975 / USA 1982-83	1 yr / 3 mo. / 7 mo.	Sandhurst / Columbus, GA	Infantry Officer		Infantry Command/ Intelligence/Guided Weapons/Division Headquarters/Officer's Military Academy
I	30	M	Yes	8	1970 Active	Sergeant	Security police	16	4 (1970) 108 (1986) 470 (USA)	USA	9 mo.	Washington, DC / Alexandria, VA			Special Diplomatic Security
J	35	M	Yes	12	1969 Active	First Lieutenant	Air Force	17		USA 1977 / USA 1980	2 mo. / 2 mo.	Los Angeles, CA / Los Angeles, CA			Electrical Engineering/ First Aid/Fire Fighting Apparatuses/Management/Diesel Engines/ Central Switch Gears/ Motor Generator Sets
K	42	M	No		Retired		Signal Corps		70 (Army Pension)	Qatar / England	1 yr / 1 mo.	London (J. Embassy)	Unemployed		Radio
L	40	M	Yes, 7	4	1964 Retired	Enlisted Man	Infantry	21	90 (Army Pension)	Iraq	2 yrs	Baghdad	2nd Hand Clother		Embassy Guard
O	33	M	Yes	12 SLC	1970 Civilian	Corporal	Marines	8	15 (1970) 50 (1977)	Pakistan	1 yr	Karachi	Business Manager (Saudi Arabia)	600D/ mo.	Diving

Age	Marital Status	Children	Yrs of Formal Sch	Army Status	Rank	Branch		Countries Visited	Time Spent	Cities Resided	Occupation	Salary	Main Specialties / Training
43	D	No.	20	1965 Civilian	Captain	Tank Corps Security	120 (1970) 320 England (1977)	Pakistan 1970 Europe 1976 England 1977	1 yr 1 yr 1 yr	Karachi Various cities London	Night Auditor, Dallas-Fort Worth Airport	18,000 Dollars/yr	Naval School/Airport Security/Embassy Guard/Officer's Military Academy
33	M	Yes	16	1970 Active	Sergeant	Air Force	182	USA	5 mo.	Danville, Ill (Chanute Air Force Base)			Life Saving Equipment/Parachute Rigging
				Active	Major	Air Force		USA	3 mo.	El Paso, TX			Air Defense
								USA	3 mo.	El Paso, TX			
								France	7 mo.				
28				1978 Active				Australia 1983 — 1 yr Australia 1985 — 1 yr					
				Active	Major			USA	2 yr	Instructor Army General Staff College			

Totals

No. of Migrants	Age	Marital Status	Children	Yrs of Formal Sch	Army Status	Rank	Branch	Yrs Svd	Countries Visited	Time Spent (Months, All Missions)	American Cities Resided (No. of Missions)	Main Specialties (Technical are Asterisked)
12	20's – 1	M – 8	Yes – 6	6 – 1	Active – 8	Major – 3	Air Force – 4	Less 10 – 1	USA – 7	1-3 – 16	Los Angeles, CA – 2	Radio*
	30's – 6	D – 1	No – 3	6-8 – 1	Retired – 2	Captain – 1	Infantry – 2	10-15 – 1	England – 4	4-6 – 2	El Paso, TX – 2	Life-Saving Equip*
	40's – 3	UN – 4	UN – 3	9-12 – 3	Civilian – 2	Lieut – 1	Signal – 1	15-20 – 4	Pakistan – 2	7-9 – 4	Washington, DC – 1	Air Defense*
	**UN – 3			13-15 – 1		Serg – 3	Security – 1	20+ – 1	France – 2	10-11 – 0	Columbus, GA – 1	Security (Airport & Embassy)
				15+ – 1		Corps – 1	Tank – 1	UN – 5	Australia – 1	12 – 8	Vicksburg, MI – 1	Electrical Engineering*
				UN – 4		Priv – 1	Marines – 1		Iraq – 1	18 – 1		Diving
						UN – 2	UN – 2		Qatar – 1	24 – 2		Intelligence
									Europe – 1			Guided Weapons*
												Navigation*
												Mechanisms*

Eight were active (in 1986) and four were retired. All but one of these men is married and almost all are in their thirties and forties. Five of the seven (for whom I have information) have had at least a high school education. Five are officers; the majority entered the army after 1969; all have served at least six years and five have served at least sixteen years. The United States, Great Britain, France, and Pakistan have been the countries most visited for training in order of numbers; the largest number spent one to three months on their missions abroad and the next largest number spent one year. The specialties they studied ranged from air defense and electrical engineering to life-saving equipment and underwater diving. Table 1.3 summarizes significant social/military/migration attributes of the army missions of these twelve men.

The list of men in tables 1.1, 1.2, and 1.3 is not a sample, but rather all the men about whom I have pertinent information (there may be others) in the given category of migration.

The conversations/interviews with seven of these men focused on two matters: (1) their degree of multicultural exposure and (2) the possible impact of this exposure on the men's attitudes towards current social issues and their general worldview. The conversations are divided into two categories: the first four men are those who went on training missions to Europe or the United States; and the last three those who went on missions or sought military employment in Arab countries. Multicultural exposure was determined by three factors: the number of countries in which they trained/served/worked; the amount of time they spent on each mission; and the number of missions.

Analysis

Before describing the continuum of multicultural exposure abroad and exploring its implications for these soldiers' views of current social issues and for modernity, one must not overestimate the degree of that exposure. Many Jordanian men in and out of the army were encapsulated in migrant host societies for long periods, witness the migrant to England (chapter three) who worked in London for several years and studied in Leeds for several more. Of the twenty-three army missions abroad about which I have information (see Table 1.3) more than $\frac{1}{3}$ were for six months or less and more than $\frac{1}{2}$ were for nine months or less. Most men lived and studied on base and spent their weeknight leisure activity at the base club, with weekends spent in pan-cultural cities such as London and Washington, D.C. The men from other cultures whom they met abroad, they interacted with mainly in class or in the army barracks. Often their barracks-mates included fellow Jordanians. Foreign women were usually met in restricted and defined settings like embassies, discos, and hospitals. There were some exceptions to this pattern of encapsulation in time and space, as, for instance, G, who in one of his three missions formed a friendship with an American sergeant whose home he visited many times and whose car he borrowed often; and J, whose work/class time was only from Monday to Thursday and who was invited to American homes on ten to fifteen different occasions during two, two-month tours to Los Angeles.

G had by far the greatest multicultural exposure of those who went to Europe and the United States, spending thirty months and visiting three different countries. In addition to cultivating his American friend in Mississippi, he was invited out by French acquaintances to dinner and a nightclub, and he reciprocated by inviting them to a homemade dinner; and he spent ten days in the home of a Scottish couple, as well as meeting English families at pubs.

G developed very positive views of both English personality traits (they were "good people" and "friendly") and English military education/training, particularly in their superiority in the teaching of the application of the principles learned. He stated that there was no discrimination by the English against foreign trainees; on the contrary, the foreign trainees had more options (e.g., in food, changing the bed sheets every day) than Englishmen. He even liked English food! He was also very positive in his evaluation of France (its beauty) and the French (everybody worked), though he criticized their military instruction. He was also positive about the United States and Americans. He admired the freedom, the right of the younger generation to live their own life (exactly what the migrant to London-Leeds criticized), and the amenities everywhere available. But on the negative side he cited the problems of drugs, crime, and drunkenness.

On the one hand, one might argue that G's positive evaluation of all three cultures to which he was exposed was the result of his longer exposure to them, and the result of more frequent and intensive interaction. Or one could argue that it was simply a reflection of his inquiring nature and his gregarious personality. But one could also argue that it was the result of the structure of the military sojourn abroad. All of the Jordanian men sent for military training abroad were part of formal government-to-government missions and as such were privileged visitors—by definition they were an elite—and unlikely targets of discrimination. On the contrary, their hosts were usually preselected; they were the targets of favor.

H places second on the continuum of exposure, spending twenty-two months in two different English-speaking countries. Largely on the basis of his experience in military training but also as a result of his brief glimpses of life outside the camp, he was persuaded of the general superiority of English life and culture, and when I asked him to evaluate the strengths and weaknesses of the British system of (military) education, he could think of no weaknesses. He was particularly impressed with the English public's continuous preoccupation with reading, even on the journey back and forth to work. He regarded British military instruction as superior, their attitude more serious, their discipline more strict, and their application more thorough than in American military instruction. He also credited the British military training as inculcating cooperation and esprit de corps as compared with the American. His own high evaluation of British society, largely on the basis of its cultural focus on education, accorded very much with his own high personal evaluation of education in his own life cycle: his early disappointment at not going to university and his present determination to finish a B.A. degree before army retirement. In both England and the United States he had only the briefest of contact with family culture—no such contact in Britain and only a weekend with American families in Washington, D.C. In England he spent much time in bookstores, nightclubs, and restaurants. Although he went on a two-week training exercise to Germany with soldiers from many different countries, he had little contact with Germans, although he regarded them as more conservative and miserly. It is perhaps important to note that before he ever went to England he had spent six months in a highly modernized (in terms of material culture) Arab society, that of Kuwait. Interestingly, after the first month, he alone of the soldiers traveling to Europe and the United States expressed little surprise or concern over what others regarded as gross violations of the Middle Eastern code of modesty: cross-sex public hugging and kissing in public conveyances, streets, and parks.

Although J spent only a total of four months in two missions to Los Angeles, his eight-hour day, four-day week schedule allowed him ample time to observe both public and some private life in different settings in the Los Angeles area. He also traveled widely in California while his mates were preoccupied with girlfriends or drinking. However, some of this leisure time was spent with fellow Jordanians, other Arabs, or Iranians. Note, however, that on his way back to Jordan he chose to spend a month in Italy, and he visited Vienna.

But his multicultural exposure began long before he got to California, and was largely a result of his own father's occupational mobility and exposure to town life within Jordan, and his two elder brothers' education and work in foreign countries in and out of the Arab world (Saudi Arabia, Egypt, Turkey, and England). In fact, J specifically makes a causal link between his father's and his own early life "outside" (the village) and his father's and his brothers' economic success. It may also be the major factor in explaining his own powerful identification with certain aspects of modernity such as education and the organization of work (described below).[67]

I, the diplomatic security guard, spent nine months in Washington, D.C., though he traveled a good deal with the ambassador, time enough to become acquainted with a narrow segment of the American population—the girlfriends he met in discos and bars and whom he took out on dates on weekends, though some of these girlfriends did take him to their homes. The women he met at the Jordanian embassy were implicitly regarded as off limits for socializing. "I" reacted positively to American life, particularly its sexual freedom; indeed, one could say he was seduced by this aspect of American life as well as by all of its creature comforts, since he said that he wished to return and acquire a green (residence) card. He was the only soldier who expressed such a wish. "I" also expressed admiration for the organization (*niTHam*) of American life and the general honesty and trustworthiness found in public municipal and commercial arenas. He complained only about the high cost of living. Thus I, in some ways one of the most privileged of the soldiers abroad and one of the most traveled within the United States, was at the same time one of the most encapsulated in time and space: weekdays with the ambassador, weekends with dates to military base clubs, nightclubs, athletic events, and beaches.

K is the army migrant who spread-eagles and connects our two categories of soldiers: those who went to Europe/U.S.A. and those who went elsewhere in the Arab world. K spent the least amount of time in Europe, only one month, and that month shuttling between the hospital and the embassy; this, after he spent one year in Qatar, one of the multiethnic Gulf societies. His observations about Qataris were always implicitly by contrast with Jordanians. He admired their patriotism but not their tribalism, which was abridged: their hospitality to strangers was lacking, and they did not have a full-fledged system of tribal conflict-resolution. He commented adversely on the flouting of sexual morality as a result of multiethnic liaisons (between Yemeni men and Indian women), but very favorably about religious culture and the availability of Muslim worship places.

In London he commented on English trustworthiness, honesty, and particularly cleanliness, but not their hospitality. He also was disturbed in London by sexual immorality, and the open soliciting in the streets, comparing such behavior to that of animals. It seems that almost all of his insight into English life was based on his contacts, mainly with older women, presumably patients and nurses in the hospital where he was treated, some of whom, it seems, later met him socially outside the hospital.

A, the artilleryman serving in Abu Dhabi, had the longest exposure to a multiethnic society in the Arab world, spending seven years there. However, he too was encapsulated, meeting members of other cultures mainly in the barracks. He said that he had interactions with other Jordanians and Pakistanis but not with Europeans or "Asians," i.e., non-Muslims from Asia like Thais, Filipinos, and Indians. Still, early in the conversation A depicts with sensitivity the problems of acculturation in a multiethnic society: many Arab men take Indian and Pakistani wives, and the children born of these marriages are reared by non-Arab mothers and taught a language other than Arabic as their truly "mother" tongue. Words from such languages had crept into Gulf Arabic. Although in this Gulf society soldiers from a panoply of cultures lived cheek by jowl together in the barracks (Yemenis, Egyptians, Sudanis, Omanis, Pakistanis, Palestinians, Indians, Jordanians), there was a strong tendency for separate socializing and an ethnic division of labor, e.g., the Indians were servants. A himself roomed with an Egyptian for two years after he left the barracks and subsequently with Jordanians and Palestinians. Thus, during his six year stay he gradually moved back culturally, in stages, to interaction first with his own cultural mates (other Arabs) and then with his own Jordanian countrymen. Interestingly, in this mix of cultures and nationalities in the army barracks and related complexes, examples of contact with the natives of the country, the Abu Dhabians, were very few! As in Saudi Arabia with migrants for work, the army migrants on the gulf saw surprisingly little of the indigenous inhabitants of the host country and never visited them in their homes. Thus, although Abu Dhabi city was close by and highly modernized technologically (with air-conditioning, electricity, and high-rise buildings) and Abu Dhabians were eager to embrace the latest innovations and entertainments, A felt a sense of psychological deprivation there due to boredom and worry over separation from his family as well as the encapsulated/segmented character of this multiethnic society.

A commented favorably on the Abu Dhabians' attempt to preserve their tribal culture—their food, the giving of first fruits to the tribal chief (though their tribal culture was clearly weaker than Jordan's)—and on their enlightened political leadership. On the other hand, he criticized the corruption (*fasad*) of a society where drinking and fornication accompanied rapid riches, as he did the laziness and by implication the arrogance of the indigenes. The Pakistanis, the non-Arab ethnic group with whom there was the most interaction presumably on the basis of their common religion, were commented on for their capacity to work, their obedience, and their peculiar habit of rubbing themselves all over with smelly oils and jellies.

Apparently A did develop some significant friendships with soldiers from the Arab emirates, Pakistan, and the Sudan since they corresponded with him for a time, a correspondence that lapsed when he failed to reply.

It is appropriate that we end by describing the experience of L, the embassy guard to Iraq, because in many respects Iraq is closer to Jordan culturally than any of the other Arab countries mentioned above. It is a society with a tribal background like Jordan, modernizing rapidly like Jordan, both technologically and socially, and with a secular political regime, albeit dictatorial and drawn from a dominant nationalist political movement, rather than monarchical and based on a combination of inherited charisma, tribalism, and Arab nationalism.

L had a strong positive view of Iraqis as "cultivated people," as intelligent and honest. He admired the prominent role of women in public life—as market sellers, shopkeepers, and bus drivers—and he commented on their kind and gentle behavior. He regarded Iraqis as extremely enlightened and by implication, forward-looking, and linked this present condition with their historic role as a fount of civilization. But all of his contact with Iraqis was in the general public arenas mentioned above—he was never invited into an Iraqi home. Of course, it is possible that this highly positive view of Iraqis is in part a result of the fact that L moved around Baghdad in uniform in a country at war (with Iran) and that it was his uniform and not his foreign status that elicited the favorable treatment.

Migration and Modernity

Now let us return to the theme introduced earlier in this chapter, the theme of the possible connections between migration and modernity. Modernity is defined as the social, cultural, and psychological framework which facilitates the application of tested knowledge to all phases of production: the unhampered search for knowledge, a positive stance toward innovation, a fostering of social mobility, and an achievement ethic that channels rewards to high performers. The constant seeking of technological and educational self-improvement is an implication of modernity. In addition, modernity is associated with professionalization and bureaucratization and the values they represent: universalistic standards of expertise, recruitment and promotion, an ethical system of self-control associated with a corporate body, rewards for work achievement associated with a "higher calling," the routinization of tasks through rules, roles, and files, implying planning and discipline; and impartiality and affective neutrality in dealing with the public.

To what degree do the Jordanian soldiers from Kufr al-Ma reflect attributes of modernity in relation to their experiences abroad? Below follows a brief attempt to answer this question based on the conversations with each soldier and my knowledge of the general community and family structure of Kufr al-Ma from 1959 to 1986. The soldiers are analyzed in the order in which they evince such attributes, beginning with the most "modern," J (see table 1.3), and ending with the least, A (see tables 1.1 and 1.2).

J, a lieutenant and air force technician sent twice for short-term missions to Los Angeles, is staunchly modern in his views. He favors "family planning" (*tan-THim al-nasl*) and strongly advocates self-improvement through education, condemning his patrilineal kinsmen for not educating their sons. He sees education as an elixir of progress and as a means of freeing villagers from the domination of an old tribal elite (the Pasha). Of all the soldiers interviewed, he had excelled in educational self-improvement in Jordan, having taken six separate courses in subjects ranging from "new apparatuses" to firefighting and first aid. His ambivalence about tribal law was in part a result of the fact that "It was not based on knowledge (*'ilm*)." His eagerness to know "new" facts reflects his interest in innovation.

In the United States J admires "the organization of work" and the clear separation of work and leisure time ("their always being there at the right time"), clearly an aspect of "the routinization of tasks"; and he likes the flexibility of an educational process that allows for and answers all questions, though it does not "reveal all facts"—for which he criticized it. The army itself is praised for its fostering technological modernization and education. J is explicit about the fact that part of the value of education is that it rewards high performance, and he praises the army for offering numerous opportunities to take courses and pass exams (judged according to universalistic standards).

69

The other pillar of J's modern orientation is his strong advocacy of sociogeographic mobility. He spent much of the interview describing his father's occupational and geographic mobility as well as his two brothers' odysseys in pursuit of an education and contrasted this going/living/working/studying "outside" with the narrow worldview of those "acclimatized" to the village. He made an explicit causal connection between those living on the outside—he had been the only villager to go to kindergarten and to Los Angeles—and his father's, his brothers', and his own economic success.

It is interesting that in his visits to American families in the Los Angeles area, J viewed favorably the American conjugal family's (composed of mother, father, and children) structure and behavior; on a given issue the husband and wife expressed different points of view, discussed them, and came to a joint decision. He did not contrast the conjugal family pejoratively with the consanguine (large extended) family, as, for instance, H and A did (see below). It is the conjugal (rather than the consanguine) family that is the essential social component of a modern society based on high mobility.

Not all of J's evaluations of modern life in Los Angeles were positive. He condemned the freedom that was leading to the dissolution of the family, allowing children after age sixteen to proceed without parental supervision, e.g., to sleep away from home without parents' knowledge of their whereabouts or activities. He avoided nightclubs and prostitutes as well as alcohol, and quoted the Quran ("God will provide sustenance") when I asked him about how one might solve the unemployment problem in Jordan. And he specifically contrasted this religious orientation with the American "who plans for everything." His disapproval of tribal law was in part based on its discrepant relation to religious law. As strong as his commitment to education was, when I asked him if he would educate his daughter, he made his answer conditional, "I will if there is scope, and circumstances don't prevent it." He would in any case educate her through high school (not a given in the village at the time).

G, the fitter mechanic sent to three countries for the longest period, thirty months, also championed certain values keyed to modernity, chief among them the independence of the individual, particularly the younger generation and within that category, the child. He spoke, referring to his own childhood, of the oppression of the child in the village, of corporal punishment, e.g., because one had asked for money for school supplies. More generally, he referred to the older generation's treatment of women and children as based on the economic and sex/age division of labor: the male heads of households only thought about how their sons could help them in ploughing or shepherding or earning money—not about their education; and the father arranged the marriage of his sons to women who could make a substantial economic contribution to the household. He contrasted this attitude with what he observed in England, where the English forced the younger generation to live their own life, not the life the father wanted for them. He said, "I'm not going to force my son to become a doctor. Let the child select the road he wants."

G's description of the oppression of his childhood and his championing of independence is interesting in a number of respects. First, he was one of only two villagers who ever described their childhood upbringing in these terms. All others described their childhood in favorable and usually nostalgic terms, stressing the love and care they received from their families, and the simplicity and basic security of life in a small multiplex village despite its material poverty. I myself over the course of nine field trips over thirty-five years never witnessed harsh corporal punishment of a child; on the contrary, my impression was that generally, villagers spoiled their children, particularly boys. Second, the migrant to England referred to in chapter 3 below (Yusuf) condemned the very individuality and independence of English life that G praised, finding the fact that the sons and daughters were expected to leave the parental house after age eighteen as bizarre and undermining the family and societal morals. Third, it is notable that both G and his brother, a supervisor in Saudi Arabia, married the sisters of J, that is, into a family whose members were noted for their living much of their lives "on the outside." Finally, in his evaluation of army life, G was the only one to mention its cultural value—of exposing soldiers to people from other cultures and subcultures, as he said, "You mix with more than one kind of human being" in the army.

On the other hand, G's embracing individualism and independence was limited by religious law and ethics and village custom that rejected drugs, alcoholism, and illicit sexual relations, and in general imposed a modesty code on the public behavior of men and women. Unlike H, he did not with time take such immodest public behavior in his stride; on the contrary, he condemned it in the strongest terms: "I hated it; I don't accept it; it's a terrible matter." When I asked him what his view of women working outside the house was, he said that he was against it—the husband was the breadwinner and the wife was born to bring up her children, not to become a government worker. He also remained bound by tribal law, seeing it as more effective, in many matters, than state law. Still, he staunchly defended family planning against his cousin's assault, reasoning in terms of matching income with mouths to feed and minds to educate rather than discussing the matter in terms of Quranic verses and God's benevolence and omniscience.

For H, the infantry major sent to England and the United States, like for G, there is a close connection between the attribute of modernity embraced, indeed championed, and his own personal history. With G, individual choice and independence were focused on as an expression of a childhood perceived to be too oppressive. H, on the other hand, focused on education as the be-all and end-all of his childhood and his army life; he went on three educational training missions abroad through 1986, and I was told, on a fourth subsequently. And education was to be the focus of his future civilian life. When I asked H what his view of his own childhood and family upbringing was, he spent almost the entire time discussing his early school life, school peers, and his failure to get a university education, and the circumstances that surrounded that failure. Significantly, he divided his life between a pre and a post 1965 period. Before that time his large consanguine family comprised a single household of a number of brothers and their families; and with one brother helping another, he was assured that he would be sent to the university. With the breakup of the consanguine household, his hopes disappeared. Thus for H, unlike J, the consanguine family was the preferred form, and not the conjugal that characterized the modern world, because the former offered the chance for an education. His personal commitment to education was significant in H's rating English culture so highly: England was a country of readers.

The other respect in which H was clearly modern was in his professionalism. He emphasized, time and again, the superior discipline of English military training, and stipulated the expectation of sacrifice—"to do much and expect little"—born of a commitment to a higher calling, the officer's profession. He admired English training for the cooperative work activity involved in solving a problem (rather than an every-man-for-himself attitude), indicating a corporate body with an esprit de corps. The discipline, cooperative work activity, and sacrifice also indicated the existence of an ethical system of self-control and peer respect characteristic of a "profession" as opposed to an occupational or a kinship group. H explicitly referred to the rigorous enculturation process of professional army officer training that "make[s] you forget everything and be a different person."

Moving outside his own army experience and the field of education and into family and social matters, H's modern credentials were lacking. When I asked him his view of birth control, he responded quickly that his religion didn't allow it. But on asking him other more specific questions, he admitted certain contingencies in which it might be allowed. When I asked him, "What is your view of women working outside the home?" he began his answer by endorsing the idea, saying that women were half the population. However, he quickly followed the endorsement by saying, "But women in our society aren't mature enough; they don't understand their position in society. If they are outside the house they forget their responsibility back home."

Although K spent only one month in England, his experience at the London hospital impressed him with the cleanliness, honesty, and trustworthiness of the English, although like G he was repelled by the sexual license there, as he was previously in Qatar. Three of his comments specifically relate to modernity. First, his "love [of] people who have ambition," mentioned in connection with praise of the entrepreneur who went to North Africa to sell houses, indicates his strong support of the achievement ethic. Second, his commitment to innovation was implicitly reflected in his condemnation of its opposite, blind modernization, i.e., imitation—"one person buys a tractor and succeeds; then you get twenty buying tractors." Third, like the medical student to Germany (Ali) referred to in chapter 3, there is a definite evolutionary implication with a reverse twist in K's remark, "the old (English) generation built the civilization and the new generation is tearing it down." The natural course of progress was being reversed by an irresponsible and immoral younger generation.

Beneath the ambassadorial security guard's seduction with the comparative sexual freedom of life in the Washington, D.C. area—there was no condemnation of that life at all in our conversation with him—there was an appreciation of other more fundamental values related to modernity. Order/disorder (*niTHam/fawda*) and deceit (*ghish*) are key words in his discourse. The fact that people lined up in an orderly manner whether in shops or in traffic made a great impression on him, as opposed to the disorder/anarchy (*fawda*) that by implication prevailed in urban Jordan.

Significantly, "I" reiterates the theme stressed most strongly by K, the honesty of the local population in the public arena. "If you go to someone and he can help you, he'll help; if not he'll tell you." "I" and K are perhaps contrasting this frank and straightforward approach of Americans to questions and problems posed by others, to "the art of pleasing (*musayara*) that prevails in many situations in Jordan, i.e., the individual from whom help is sought, but who may not be in a position to give it, seeks to please the questioner/seeker of help by telling him what he/she wants to hear. There is also an evolutionary implication here in the remarks of "I" and K: honesty, frankness, and fulfilling one's promises are the marks of civilized societies.

The other side of I's seduction by the glamorous surface of life in Washington, D.C. is the apologetic attitude he took toward his mother's traditional village folk dress. Although many Jordanians were attracted by the life they witnessed in Europe or the United States, few regarded it as superior in an overall sense as attested to by the fact that about 90 percent of the migrants about whom I have data returned to Jordan at the end of their educational-work stays. Even "I," who joked about village manners and who indicated that he would like to return to the United States and secure a green (residence) card—but not citizenship—is still drawn back to his native village as a place of residence (rather than Amman where his father lives) by the fact that it is his birthplace, it is quiet, and there is fresh air there.

A, the artilleryman who served seven years in Abu Dhabi and was in the best position to describe how the multiethnic societies of the Arab Gulf operated, was also the strongest advocate/representative of the values of his Jordanian peasant/tribal society. He regarded the countryside as more attractive than the city because its air was pure, its social life fuller and more satisfying, the mixing of the sexes absent, and the people more "guarding of custom." The extension of water, electricity, and town-style housing (of cement or smooth stone rather than rough stone and adobe) to the countryside had added to its inherent superiority. He supports tribal law because "it preserves the ties of people with one another," and he regards the army as an unmixed blessing—"the widest door of opportunity" from which one reaps employment, health, and economic security. But television had penetrated the village and "spoiled our social life; people can't sit with one another (any more as they used to do in the guest houses of the village)."

A went on for some time describing the struggle of his consanguine family, first led by his older brother and him, and subsequently by his younger brother who received employment in Saudi Arabia, to bankroll his still younger brothers in their higher education in Pakistan. This large family also cooperated economically in marrying off one of the younger brothers after he returned with his degree from abroad. For A, then, the large consanguine family, not the conjugal family, was the social basis for education and economic advancement. A also had a different and much more favorable view of his father than his brother, N (see chapter 7 below). He said that his father (as mayor, arbitrator, troubleshooter, and generous host) left the family with a "sweet reputation."

A, by intent, gave his children, both male and female, names with religious connotations: epithets of the prophets, attributes of God, names found in Quranic verses, or prominent figures in the early religious history of Islam. His father, before him, had named several of his sons after prominent military heroes and martyrs.

A's worldview, then, while it allowed for achievement and education, indeed encouraged them, and accommodated to a six-year sojourn "on the outside," reflected a village perspective whose markers of status were for males, an educational degree, government employment/position, marriage, the building of a new-style house in the village, and the raising of a family there.[68] The assumption behind A's residence and work in the diaspora, like many other migrants, was that he would return to his family and live out the days of his life in the village. He was clearly uncomfortable during his stay on the Gulf and longed to return to his family and community. All along, whether in the army or in the diaspora, it was the collective consanguine family enterprise that framed his endeavors. And culturally, it was religious and tribal values, essentially those of his father, that shaped the way he looked at the world, his family, and himself. This worldview was, to be sure, amended by and accommodated to values reflecting modernity. A had left the comfort of his village and lived in a multicultural society for seven years. He staunchly supported education and family planning, and sacrificed considerably to advance the former for his brothers.[69] He kept one room in his house free of furniture and with only mattresses and pillows along the walls for those who wished to recline on the floor in the style of the old *maḍafa* (guest house); as well as a new-style *diwan* with a sofa, lounge chairs, and a long coffee table.

But his residence in the diaspora had not, like for those who had gone to Europe or the United States, exposed him to a radically different society and way of life. Moreover, although Arab Gulf societies were multiethnic and composed of Europeans and Asians as well as Arabs from different parts of the Middle East, they were segmented and encapsulated societies in which significant social interaction across ethnic boundaries was restricted.

The impact of the migration experience abroad, then, on the attitudes and worldviews of migrants is unpredictable and determined by a complex set of factors including the length of time spent abroad, the language, religion, and class structure of the host country, the structure of the receiving educational-military institutions, the ethnic status of the host group as opposed to the migrant group, the policies of receiving governments toward migrants, the ideologies dominating host governments (e.g., socialist, capitalist, Islamic), and not least, the personalities of the migrants themselves. An illustration of the complexity of this process is the fact that the full brothers, A and N, both of whom spent long periods abroad within the Arab world (in Abu Dhabi and in Cairo and Saudi Arabia) came back to the village with completely different views of such matters as the value of army service, the value of tribal law, the value of their own village upbringing, and the worth of their own father.

Notes

1. See Curtis R. Ryan, *Jordan in Transition: From Hussein to Abdullah,* Lynne Reiner, 2002, for a description and analysis of the social support elements of the Jordanian state and royal family.
2. Although many of these studies are perceptive and useful, they foster many of the stereotypes current regarding the Arab world, particularly those that regard nomads and peasants in an evolutionary perspective with "tribalism" at one end, the obviously retarded end, of the continuum and modernity-urbanism-professionalism at the other, obviously advanced end. See, for instance, P.J. Vatikiotis, *Politics and the Military in Jordan: A Study of the Arab Legion 1921–1957,* 1967; Eliezer Be'eri, *Army Officers in Arab Politics and Society,* 1970; Robert B. Satloff, *Troubles on the East Bank: Challenges to the Domestic Stability of Jordan,* 1986; Arthur D. Day, *East Bank/West Bank: Jordan and the Prospects of Peace,* 1986; and Richard Gabriel and Alan S. MacDougall, "Jordan" in *Fighting Armies: Antagonists in the Middle East, A Combat Assessment,* Richard A. Gabriel, editor, 1983. Only Paul A. Jureidini's and R.D. McLaurin's *Jordan: The Impact of Social Change on the Role of the Tribes* has emphasized the importance of the army as a vehicle of change, though they too have been concerned with "Jordanian Stability" (a chapter heading) and the geopolitical rather than the cultural implications of the army's role. However, they do call attention to the social changes in the tribal structure introduced in part by the army.
3. Jureidini and McLaurin, p. 30.
4. Jureidini and McLaurin, p. 27.
5. Jureidini and McLaurin, pp. 29–30.
6. Vatikiotis, p. 5.
7. Ibid.
8. Although I did have a set list of questions to pose to returned migrants, the communication between me and them often took the form of a conversation, since I was interested in probing their conceptions, views, and framings of issues, problems, and events, as far as they would develop them. The communication between me and them, then, moves back and forth between the form of an interview and that of a conversation.
9. See Vatikiotis, p. 33.
10. Ibid.
11. Vatikiotis, p. 34.
12. Ibid.

13. Ibid.
14. Vatikiotis, p. 35.
15. Jureidini and McLaurin, p. 53.
16. *Op. cit.,* p. 27.
17. *Op. cit.,* p. 55. This statement is an oversimplification since many Palestinians have now lived in Jordan for over forty years, many have been born in Jordan, all have Jordanian citizenship, and many have served in the Jordanian army and bureaucracy. The identity, "Jordanian/Palestinian" is a complex one and not straightforward as the authors suggest. It may be more useful to look at Jordanian/Palestinian identity in terms of ethnic boundaries and the situational crossing and recrossing of these boundaries when it is useful to do so on the part of any given individual. See Fredrik Barth, *Ethnic Groups and Boundaries,* for a discussion of this approach to ethnicity. See also Linda Layne's perceptive analysis of Jordanian/Palestinian identity in *Home and Homeland: The Dialogics of Tribal and National Identities in Jordan.*
18. *Op. cit.,* p. 58.
19. *Op. cit.,* p. 55. The wide national and international attendance of King Hussein's funeral in Amman in 1999 and the emotional outpouring of tribute on this occasion testifies to this conclusion.
20. See Vatikiotis' brief discussion of this issue, mainly in a footnote, p. 20.
21. A large social anthropological literature exists on the subject of segmentary tribal systems. See, for instance, Edward E. Evans-Pritchard, *The Nuer,* 1940, Meyer Fortes, *The Dynamics of Clanship among the Tallensi,* 1945 and *The Web of Kinship among the Tallensi,* 1949, and Ian Lewis, *A Pastoral Democracy,* 1961. On applications of the concept to the Middle East see William Irons, "Nomadism as a Political Adaptation: The Case of the Yomut Turkmen," *American Ethnologist,* Vol. 1, No. 4, November 1974, Philip Salzman, "Does Complementary Opposition Exist," *American Anthropologist,* Vol. 80, No. 1, March 1978 and, most important, Emrys Peters, *The Bedouin of Cyrenaica: Studies in Personal and Corporate Power,* edited by Jack Goody and Emmanuel Marx, 1990.
22. See Antoun, "Institutionalized Deconfrontation: A Case Study of Conflict Resolution among Tribal Peasants in Jordan, in *Conflict Resolution in the Arab World,* edited by Paul Salem, American University of Beirut and Syracuse University Presses, 1997. This essay gives a detailed description and analysis of a single case of tribal conflict resolution in the Ajlun district of Jordan in 1960 and describes the changes that have occurred since that time in the process of local conflict resolution, particularly with respect to its accommodation with state law and administration and socioeconomic change. For recent changes (as well as continuities) in Jordanian attitudes toward tribal law see Antoun, "Civil Society, Tribal Process, and Change in Jordan: An Anthropological View," *International Journal of Middle East Studies,* 32 (November 2000): 441–463.
23. Jureidini and McLaurin, p. 31.
24. See Jureidini and McLaurin's discussion, pp. 45–48; for recent discussion and analysis of the lively reinterpretation of tribalism by Jordanian urban intellectuals with tribal roots and by sedentarized tribal peasants see Linda Layne's "Tribesmen as Citizens: Primordial Ties and Democracy in Rural Jordan," in Layne, editor, *Elections in the Middle East: Implications of Recent Trends,* 1987 and Layne, "The Dialogics of Tribal Self-Representation in Jordan," *American Ethnologist,* Vol. 16, No. 1, February 1989. See also Andrew Shryock's "House Politics in Tribal Jordan: Reflections on Honor, Family, and Nation in the Hashemite Kingdom," in *Tribu, Parentele et Etat en Pays d'Islam,* edited by Edouard Conte, Paul Dresch, and Lucette Valensi (Paris: Laboratoire d'Anthropologie Sociale, College de France, 2000).
25. As quoted in Vatikiotis, p. 69. The original quotation is from C.S. Jarvis, *The Arab Command,* 1943. See Frederick G. Peake, *The History of East Jordan,* 1935 and *A History of Jordan and its Tribes,* 1958 for Peake's point of view on historical matters.
26. Ibid.
27. Glubb as quoted in a private communication to Vatikiotis, pp. 76–77.

28. *Op. cit.,* pp. 77–78.
29. *Op. cit.,* p. 92.
30. See Richard A. Gabriel and Alan S. MacDougall, "Jordan," in Richard Gabriel, editor, *Fighting Armies: Antagonists in the Middle East, A Combat Assessment,* 1983, pp. 34–35.
31. Vatikiotis, p. 10.
32. Figured on the basis of information provided by Vatikiotis, p. 12.
33. Nash, p. 21. See Manning Nash, "Modernization: Cultural Meanings—The Widening Gap Between the Intellectuals and the Process," *Economic Development and Cultural Change,* Vol. 25, Supplement 1977.
34. *Op. cit.,* p. 20.
35. See Eliezer Be'eri's discussion in *Army Officers in Arab Politics and Society,* 1970, p. 352.
36. *Op. cit.,* pp. 354–55.
37. *Op. cit.,* p. 354.
38. Ibid.
39. *Op. cit.,* p. 357.
40. *Op. cit.,* p. 358.
41. *Op. cit.,* pp. 358–59.
42. See Bernard Barber, "Toward a Definition of the Professions," in Amos Perlmutter and Valerie P. Bennett, editors, *The Political Influence of the Military: A Comparative Reader,* 1980, pp. 31–32.
43. Huntington, p. 45. See Samuel P. Huntington, "Officership as a Profession," in *The Political Influence of the Military,* pp. 37–45.
44. See Huntington, "The Professional Military Ethic," in *The Political Influence of the Military,* pp. 47–51.
45. See Peter Blau and W.R. Scott, "Professional and Bureaucratic Orientation," in *The Political Influence of the Military,* pp. 34–37.
46. See Perlmutter and Bennett, pp. 71–72, for a summary of Weber's views.
47. See W.H. Morris Jones, "Armed Forces and the State," in Perlmutter and Bennett, pp. 54–55.
48. Be'eri, p. 360.
49. See Fuad Khuri and Gerald Obermeyer, "The Social Bases for Military Intervention in the Middle East," in Catherine M. Kelleher, editor, *Political-Military Systems: Comparative Perspectives,* 1976, p. 62.
50. *Op. cit.,* p. 63.
51. See Fuad Khuri, "Modernizing societies in the Middle East," in Morris Janowitz, editor, *Civil-Military Relations: Regional Perspectives,* 1981, pp. 160–82.
52. *Op. cit.,* p. 177. See also Khuri and Obermeyer, p. 74.
53. *Op. cit.,* 176.
54. See Khuri, 1981, pp. 176–77.
55. *Op. cit.,* p. 172.
56. *Op. cit.,* p. 165.
57. See Jureidini and McLaurin, pp. 64–65.
58. Vatikiotis, p. 92.
59. *Op. cit.,* p. 91.
60. *Op. cit.,* p. 21.
61. *Op. cit.,* p. 91.
62. *Op. cit.,* p. 26.
63. *Op. cit.,* p. 146.
64. Ibid.
65. Gabriel and MacDougall in Gabriel, editor, p. 34.
66. Murad, as quoted in Khuri and Obermeyer, p. 63.
67. Eight years after this interview, J continued his penchant for multicultural exposure and occupational mobility by volunteering in 1994 for the United Nations Peacekeeping Force in the

former Yugoslavia. He served as a generator engineer in Zagreb for three months, in Skopje, Macedonia for a year, and in Split, Croatia for six months.

68. A world-view is the picture people hold of the way things are; their concepts of nature, self, and society; their most comprehensive ideas of order. I have drawn on Clifford Geertz's concepts of world view and ethos as elaborated in his article, "Ethos, World View and the Analysis of Sacred Symbols," 1st published in *The Antioch Review*, Vol. 17, No. 4, 1957 and reprinted in *The Interpretation of Cultures*, 1973.

69. In an interview in 1998, A informed me that his son was studying dentistry in the Ukraine.

2

THE JORDANIAN DIASPORA IN ARABIA: INSTRUMENTAL CIRCULATORY MIGRATION, CULTURAL DIVERSITY, AND ETHNIC STRATIFICATION

The first person now working abroad to leave the village of Kufr al-Ma for an extended period for the purpose of obtaining a higher education was the son of an army officer who went to Egypt in 1957 for his last year of high school. In the following year he left for West Germany where he spent eleven years studying medicine in Heidelberg, thereafter opening a practice in Mannheim, Germany where he now lives. In 1963 two other young men left the village for an extended period abroad. One was the son of the clerk of the local civil court, who left to study medicine in Turkey after finishing high school in Nablus, Palestine. He finished his medical studies in 1970 and after a year working as an unpaid intern in an Amman hospital went to Medina, Saudi Arabia in 1972 to work as a doctor for the Red Crescent Society. After four years he established a private practice there which he maintains to this day. One other student, the son of the clerk-usher of the local Islamic court, went abroad to study medicine in West Germany, graduating in 1971, but pursuing medical specializations in Germany and returning to Jordan only in 1980 to practice medicine in the nearby market town. No other person left the village to pursue higher education abroad till 1970. The three young men to pursue medical educations abroad in the late 1950s and early 1960s were harbingers of the stream of unmarried young village men to leave the country for higher education for many years in the seventies and eighties. But they were atypical of those that followed in the profession they chose, the countries in which they chose to study, the economic rewards they reaped, and the decision

79

(two of three) to remain abroad. No other students from Kufr al-Ma chose medicine (some chose veterinary medicine), none went to Germany, the overwhelming majority returned to live and work in Jordan, and although most subsequently became professionals and secured jobs, their incomes were not nearly equivalent to those of the three pioneers.

The first person to leave directly from Kufr al-Ma to pursue work in the Arabian Peninsula was the son of a Palestinian refugee living in the village who went to Kuwait in 1959 and obtained a job as a clerk typist in the Sudanese embassy in Kuwait City.[1] In 1960 a native villager obtained a job as hospital attendant in the Kuwaiti Department of Health. In 1961 two other villagers left for Kuwait and obtained much less rewarding jobs, one as carpenter's helper. In 1963 and 1964 four other villagers left for Kuwait and received employment as gardener, telephone company watchman, taxi driver, and carpenter's assistant. In 1965 another villager obtained employment in a furniture factory. Four of the seven villagers living in Kuwait City in 1966 were rooming together and two others were brothers.

The first person to leave directly from Kufr al-Ma to pursue work in Saudi Arabia was the son of a cultivator, who left in 1963 after spending four years as a nurse at an American hospital in Jerusalem. He went to Riyadh, where he obtained a job as translator/clerk/typist in the Ministry of Works, and thereafter, in the civil court of the Ministry of Justice where he worked until 1992. Each of the three migrants leaving the village in 1963 for Germany, Turkey, and Saudi Arabia are exceptional and pioneers: only one other villager went to Germany for education; no other villager practices medicine in Saudi Arabia and no other has stayed close to the twenty-two years of the doctor trained in Turkey; a number of villagers went to work in Riyadh, subsequently, but none secured a regular job in the Saudi bureaucracy.

In one other significant respect, however, these three men were already indicative of a pattern of migration and cultural exposure: they stayed for long periods in foreign countries, and they were exposed to multiple, frequently very different, cultures. The clerk/typist practiced his English for four years with Americans in the Jerusalem hospital before he went to Arabia. The medical student in Turkey spent his last year of high school in Nablus, Palestine, a hotbed of Arab nationalism, and his first two years in Turkey in the cosmopolitan city of Istanbul, a city, as he said, "where you can find anything you want." And the medical student in Germany spent his first year abroad in Cairo.

Although one teacher from the village left to work in Arabia, in Abu Dhabi in 1971, the migration for work to Arabia did not begin in earnest in Kufr al-Ma until 1974 when seven men left and 1975 when eleven left the village (see Table 2.1 in chapter appendix). Four of the eleven men who left in 1975 exemplify the range of occupations, workplaces, and occupational trajectories in this period: the first found a job as an auto mechanic in the inland oasis of Al-Ayn in Abu Dhabi; a second, a retired Jordanian army officer, took a position as an artillery range-finder and intelligence officer in the army of Abu Dhabi; a third a job as a surveyor for several English companies in Riyadh; and the fourth secured employment as a plasterer in Al-Medina. The latter first worked for an Arab company, then for a Dutch-Saudi company, and finally as an independent contractor, moving from the inland oasis of Al-Ha'il to the holy city of Medina. With each change he secured a substantial increase in income. For nonprofessionals in Arabia this progression to employment by foreigner to independent contractor status was much to be desired though seldom achieved. For such men frequent occupational mobility was not uncommon and, indeed, striven for; these were the true twentieth century raiders in Arabia who sought to make the most of their opportunities in an uncertain economic climate.

On the other hand, white collar professionals from the start established another mode of living in Arabia—as teachers and soldiers on long-term (and in a few cases open-ended) contracts in given locales. A Jordanian teacher's contract was usually for five years, but a few men who early on took up administrative positions in the local educational hierarchy stayed much longer—till the 1991 Gulf War.

Even though the migration for work to Arabia from Kufr al-Ma had just begun in earnest in 1974–75, the occupational migration pattern was emerging clearly (see Table 2.2, appendix): health specialists, translators, business managers and accountants joining teachers and soldiers as professionals and semiprofessionals; construction workers, drivers, and oil drillers joining plasterers, masons, and mechanics in the ranks of the semiskilled; with clerks, typists, and telephone operators occupying lower-echelon white collar positions.

By 1975 the geographical and spatial contours of migration to Arabia had already emerged with migration spread-eagling the peninsula from coastal entrepôts to capital cities to inland oases to highland borderlands to movable desert oil rigs. By the middle of the 1980s migrants to Saudi Arabia worked in twenty-two separate locations (see Table 2.3, appendix) in all kinds of settlements from large cities, to towns, to villages, to Bedouin camps in all parts of Arabia: The Gulf, upper, middle, and lower; the Saudi side of the Yemen border; Oman, the Hijaz, the Saudi side of the northern border with Iraq–Jordan, the Tihama, Asir, the Nejd, and the Nefud (see map).

At two points in time, in the winter of 1979 and the spring of 1986, I collected a convenience sample of migrants from the village to Arabia. In the earlier period in a week's visit and before I was aware of the importance of migration in the recent life of the village, I asked the village preacher, who had an excellent memory and had proved accurate on many other matters of local import, to list the migrants who were presently working on the Arabian peninsula. He listed fifty-three persons including two women. In 1986 during more than five months of field work I often sat in the various guest rooms in which many village men were gathered in the evening and solicited data from various clans and families about migrants to Arabia. I gathered data on sixty-three villagers, including five

81

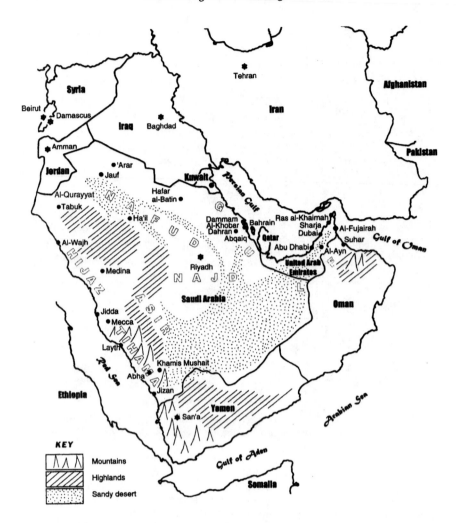

MIGRANT LOCATIONS IN ARABIA

women who were currently working in Arabia and eleven men who had spent considerable periods there and had returned to the village. During this period, I also interviewed many migrants who had returned to the village on holidays or during the course of circular migration. Table 2.1 on years of initial departure for the Arabian peninsula indicates the buildup of migration from the middle seventies through the early eighties on the one hand and the volatility of migration on the other. For instance, although the years 1974, 1975, 1976, 1977, 1978, 1981, and 1983 were years when a number of men left for work there, during the years immediately preceding or following, 1973, 1979, and 1982, few men left. In 1985 for the first time no one left the village for Arabia.

Table 2.3 indicates that in 1979 a large number of migrants concentrated on the middle Gulf and the economic activity near the oil fields at Dhammam and Dhahran whereas in 1986 there was a concentration on Riyadh and the inland oasis of Al-Ayn in Abu Dhabi. In both periods the number going to Saudi Arabia was approximately three times as many as those going to Abu Dhabi (see Table 2.4) and in both periods Riyadh and Al-Ayn were the locations that drew the most migrants. However, migrants went to all parts of Arabia and this pattern of geographical dispersion was evident even in the earlier period.

The overwhelming dominance of males in the migration is continuous, but the ages of such migrants differ somewhat in the two periods, although over 50 percent in both are between the ages of 26 and 35 (see Table 2.5). The paucity of migrants under age 25 in both periods relates to the proliferation of white collar positions such as teachers which require post–high school education and some teaching experience in Jordan before qualifying for teaching missions abroad.

The dominance of married migrants is evident in both periods, though more pronounced in the later period (see Table 2.6). In 1986, 67 migrants were married, and only 2 were single with one of the latter betrothed; in 1979, 42 migrants were married and 11 were single. There is a significant difference in the number of spouses (principally wives) accompanying working partners to Arabia in the two periods: there were 10 wives in Arabia in 1979 as opposed to 33 remaining in the village; in 1986, 29 spouses lived in Arabia, almost 50 percent, and 33 remained in the village. Regarding income, in 1979, the largest number (17) or 33 percent made between $600 and $900 a month or $7,200–10,800 a year with another 25 percent (13) making $1,200–1,500 a month or $18,400–21,600 a year (see Table 2.8). In 1986 the largest number (18) or 35 percent made between $14,400–18,000 a year and 42 of 52 or 81 percent between $7,200 and $18,000 a year.

In 1979 the largest occupational categories were clerks (7) and teachers (7) followed by masons (5), with telephone operators, auto mechanics, and surveyors as the only other occupations with at least three individuals represented (see Table 2.2). In 1986 the largest number were teachers (12), followed by managers and soldiers and then translators. In both years white collar employees dominated, divided between professionals and office workers in 1979 and professionals and business managers and accountants in 1986. In both periods manual laborers were present, but a distinct minority. More common, particularly in 1979, were blue collar employees associated with construction, e.g., masons, surveyors, and plasterers. By 1986 a proliferation of white collar specializations, some dealing with health matters, was evident.

I collected a limited amount of data in 1979 on interpersonal kinship relations in the diaspora on twelve migrants (see Table 2.9): seven lived with or close to their brothers; another four lived with close clansmen, and one with a co-villager. The data on interpersonal kinship relations in the diaspora was fuller for 1986 and confirmed the surprising number of brothers and first cousins who lived together, nine or 39 percent, with another three or 13 percent living with or close to clansmen or villagers and another 7 (30 percent) living with or close to co-Jordanians; only four (18 percent) lived in Saudi Arabia without regular contact with fellow nationals. In 1986, twenty-four of twenty-seven migrants about whom I collected information concerning kinship relations and residence abroad reported living in the same town and in close proximity (often rooming together) with either kinsmen, co-villagers, or co-nationals. It is important to remember this fact when appraising the impact (or lack thereof) of the migrant's experience in Arabia on his culture and social structure upon his return to Jordan.

For the migrants recorded in 1986 additional information was gathered on some regarding education, frequency of home visits, time spent on such visits, and how earnings were spent. Thirty-eight of forty-two or 90 percent of those from whom information was gathered had graduated from high school or had passed high school equivalency exams (see Table 2.10). Seventeen of forty-two or 40 percent had at least two years of higher education and another six or 14 percent had done postgraduate work or had professional education after initial college degrees. The education of this group of migrants was as surprisingly high as their intimate kinship connections in the diaspora.

Eight of the fifteen men on whom information was gathered visited their home village once a year, two twice a year, and two three times a year, only one visiting more than four times a year (see Table 2.11). Two visited once every two years, none visiting less than that. Some men telephoned the village. In 1986 there were more than thirty village households that had telephones and a long waiting list for phone installation. All twelve migrants from whom information was collected on the matter spent between one and three months on their visits, five, all teachers, spending three (summer) months.

Income earned in Arabia was frequently spent on building homes in the village, buying land there, the education of family members, cars and pickup trucks, and investments in small shops in the village or the adjoining district center. Some representative examples include a purchasing agent in the port of Jidda who became the business manager of a newspaper in the inland oasis of Tabuk making between $7,200 and 18,000 a year in the period 1978–86 who spent as follows: $6,250 a year on a rented apartment in Jidda and subsequently $2,750 a year on a rented apartment in Tabuk; $35,000 on a new house in Kufr al-Ma; and $8,750 on a piece of land in the nearby city of Irbid. In 1986 he was saving $750 a year and had $5,000 in the bank. His brother, an airport lighting technician who had been in Saudi Arabia since 1977, spent $32,000 on the building of a house in the village, $5,000 on his marriage, $5,000 on a failed investment for extracting salt from the Dead Sea and the Al-Azraq oasis, and $2,500 on a plot of land on the main highly-trafficked road near the village entrance. He also bought a pickup truck on installments for $3,200 and sold it when the above-mentioned company failed.

Examples of migrants with more modest incomes include the following: an automobile mechanic with an income of $6,000–12,000 a year who purchased a secondhand automobile in Saudi Arabia for $750 and tools for $250 and together with his wife, who is a cousin and a teacher in Arabia, was planning (1986) to build a cement house in the village for $5,000. They said that if they saved an additional $5,000 between them they would build a garage in the village for the same amount as the cost of the husband's workplace. In 1985–86 they had saved $5,000 but the previous year they had saved only $1,500. A driller on an oil rig from 1979–83 with an income of from $6,000 to 7,500 a year spent $12,500 on a village house and $9,250 on a village land plot, and invested $1,250 to capitalize a small village grocery shop. The surveyor who worked for a number of English companies doing road surveys in Riyadh from 1975 to 1984, beginning at $225 a month and ending at $2,500 a month plus travel and housing perquisites, but working only four months every year, invested $87,000 in a chicken farm near the village in 1984 including 6 acres and 10,000 chicks. While he was in Riyadh he saved an average of $1,500 a month and expended $500 a month on hospitality to fellow-villagers. An assistant personnel relations officer for a Saudi–Dutch cleaning and maintenance company who spent four years in Riyadh and had saved $15,000 was convinced by a fellow-villager to invest money in that villager's business enterprise. That villager paid off his own debts with half the money and drank up and gambled away the rest. In 1986 this returned migrant was engaged to be married with the remainder of his savings, $6,250. He had just gained employment as a clerk in a small bank in the adjoining district center when I left the village in June 1986.

The outstanding case of a big spender/generous man, depending on the construction placed on his behavior, is that of a butcher who worked for many years in Amman and left in 1976 for Jidda, where he gained employment as a foreman of a refrigerated meat warehouse, earning $500 a month. In addition he moonlighted as a cook in a restaurant featuring roasted chicken for $1,000 a month. Subsequently he went to Jordan and returned with an unrestricted visa that allowed him to work as an independent contractor, food merchant, and distributor of refrigerated chicken to companies, restaurants, and the Jidda airport, averaging $2,500–$3,750 a month. I asked him how he spent his money during the six years he was in Jidda. He said that he spent one half on drinking, women, and films and sent the other half back home as savings.

One of the earliest migrants to go as a teacher to Saudia Arabia in 1974 earned between $560 a month at the beginning and $1,600 a month in 1986 when I interviewed him. He built a large two-story house on a prize piece of land in the village, which cost $62,000 and $25,000 respectively. In 1986 he had $5,000 savings in the bank. He has spent $7,500 on the education of his brother, who is now finishing a local junior college. In highland Abha on the border of Yemen where he teaches he spends $2,500 a year in hospitality on the tribal Saudis with whom he associates. He said he was thinking of setting up a stonecutting workshop in the nearby city of Irbid on his return to Jordan in two years' time, but it required $25,000 in capital, which he did not have.

One of the most successful migrants in terms of earnings was a villager who went to work for Prince Saud as his receptionist/telephone switchboard operator in his company in Riyadh. He brought his wife and children to live with him after a few years when electricity was provided to his house through the good offices of the prince. He said that during his years in Saudi Arabia (1977–86) he saved about $225,000, or around $20,000 a year. He expended $52,000 on three successive loans to his brother in various enterprises including a bakery that failed, a pickup truck, and a brick-making workshop. He spent $62,000 on the higher education and marriage ($7,500) of his wife's son (from a previous marriage); $17,500 on land plots in the village; $75,000 on his village house and house plot; and $15,000 to open a hardware store specializing in aluminum frames for windows and doors in the adjoining district center. While he was in Riyadh he spent $6,250 a year on a rented apartment.

A final, much more modest migrant in terms of earnings and expenditures is a plasterer who went to Dhammam, Saudi Arabia in 1982, leaving his two wives and ten children back in the village. In 1986 he was saving $1,650 a month or $19,800 a year. He spent it all on his own household expenses and on payments to his estranged wife and her children.

The Migration Process, the Context, the Consequences

The discussion that follows draws on seven interviews with migrants to Saudi Arabia.[2] The migrants include two teachers, an educational administrator, an assistant public relations officer, a telephone operator turned translator and personnel supervisor, a foreman and warehouse specialist, and a plasterer. Among the matters described are daily work regimes, the process of recruitment including the guarantor (*kafil*) system, ethnic stratification, attitudes toward and appraisals of Saudis and other nationals working in Arabia, views of women's work outside the home, social and work relations with Saudis, perceived discrimination, and the various climes and locales in which work and home activities were pursued. Special attention will be given to the peculiar circumstances of encapsulation and isolation of co-villagers and co-Jordanians on the one hand and the development of intimate social relations with Saudis and other nationals on the other. In the analysis that follows I will discuss the relevance of the interviews for three processes of change: the shift from deferred to programmed decision-making, the development of neotraditional views, and the transvaluation of culture.[3] I will draw on the conversation-interviews, when pertinent, during the discussion. Finally, to place the Jordanian work diaspora to the Arabian peninsula in perspective and sharpen the focus on particular processes and institutions I will undertake a short comparative analysis of the similarities and differences of the diaspora of Turks to Germany, Tunisians to France, and Jordanians to Arabia.

Analysis

The circumstances that brought the migrants to Saudi Arabia differed widely from the teachers who applied in a formal and systematic fashion through the Jordanian government, first meeting several perquisites such as freedom from debt, obligation to the state, and teaching experience; to the warehouse foreman who went on a visitor's visa for three months, met fellow Jordanians employed in a company in Dammam (see map), and got them to act as intermediaries with company officials (who would act as guarantors) and to send a letter requesting his services; to the plasterer who met a Saudi socially in his village in Jordan who offered to act as a guarantor (a critical matter for nonprofessionals) and who sent him a work visa a month later.

The teacher turned educational administrator who went to Abha on the Yemen border (see map), on the other hand, answered an ad in an Amman newspaper, presumably from the Saudi Arabian Ministry of Education, and hired on for five years, but then, subsequently, after he became an educational administrator, contracted on a year-to-year basis with the Ministry. To go to Arabia, however, he had to forfeit future prospects of employment with the Jordanian government because of his previous broken contract due to his mother's illness while he was a trainee in Egypt. The telephone operator turned personnel supervisor also left for Arabia in a mood of pique after the municipality of Amman would not reward him and his colleagues for their creative work. These are not the only cases of men engaged in public employment who developed ambivalent attitudes towards the state in its bureaucratic aspect; in the case of the educational administrator, ambivalence towards both the Jordanian and the Saudi Arabian states.

Several migrants, particularly the teachers, stressed the sensitivity to and the importance of bureaucratic rank, promotion to rank, and its accompanying compensation rate and perquisites. Others, such as the personnel supervisor, the assistant public relations officer, and the oil field foreman became sensitive to company hierarchies including ethnic stratification: the American general manager of Santa Fe had his own separate domicile and dining facilities; the managers of Saudi Cemsto were Dutch; lower-echelon white-collar jobs were held by Jordanians and Lebanese; and Filipinos were the janitors. The only Saudi involved, the owner who lent his name to the company, was seldom if ever, seen by the great majority of workers. The existence of hierarchies and accompanying status differences was not confined to Saudi Arabia, however, as the example of the Jordanian "technician" in England who was forced to make separate housing arrangements by the Jordanian "engineers" on the same mission demonstrates.

The rewards for nonprofessionals who were "raiding Arabia" could be extremely high, as attested to by the assistant public relations officer who saved over $18,000 in three years or the surveyor referred to above who saved over $87,000 in nine years, which he invested in a chicken farm. A significant proportion of income was in the form of perquisites such as housing, travel, and food allowances. Those working in management positions received bonuses and substantial severance pay. These nonprofessionals were quick to jump from one employer to another in one location after another when the remuneration package differed significantly with different companies. Of course, these high rewards were also terminated summarily, as with the personnel supervisor and the foreman. These migrants also exemplify the variety of daily, weekly, and seasonal work rhythms pursued on the peninsula, from the teacher who commuted a fairly long distance on a daily or weekly basis between his home and his school, two completely different social milieus, and received a three-month summer vacation; to the workers on the oil fields, whether they were oil drillers or foremen in warehouses, who worked alternating one-month, day-night, twelve-hour shifts; to the plasterer who initially, in Dammam, worked six months and returned to Jordan for two months, but thereafter, from Qurayyat much nearer Jordan, returned to his village for rest and recuperation every two months for fifteen days.

What is remarkable about this occupationally diverse, and geographically and topographically scattered group of migrants is the peculiar and varied modes of social interaction and cultural exposure in which they participated. The assistant public relations officer traveled widely in Saudi Arabia, east, west, north, and south and in doing so gathered a great deal of knowledge about the country generally and its business culture in particular. But in Riyadh itself, where he worked and lived, he was encapsulated due to the timing and length of his work hours on the one hand and the presence of co-villagers and close relatives in the city with whom he spent nearly all his leisure hours on the other. In Riyadh he did not interact with Saudis or the Dutch who ran the company or the Filipinos who did much of its manual labor.

The schoolteacher who lived in humid coastal Layth (see map) but commuted to and taught in remote upland Atana forty miles away knew almost no one in Layth, but entered into close social relations with the pastoral people of Atana who constantly extended hospitality. "You don't feel you're a stranger, in Atana," he said, whereas in Layth he and his fellow-teachers invited no one, and no one invited them. The persons he got to know in a semiofficial capacity in Layth were two Egyptians and a Pakistani in the hospital. The foreman on the oil field near Dammam had no contact whatsoever with Saudis, but got to know the American general manager so well that the latter wished to adopt one of his children. The woman who went to teach in the remote hamlet of Al-Kur in northwestern Arabia got to know her fellow Egyptian and Sudanese teachers quite well but had no contact with Saudis, Europeans, or Asians. The educational administrator in Abha, on the other hand, got to know the Saudis of the district intimately, administered Saudi teachers in the course of his work for many years, and was able to discuss their strong points of character and foibles with sophistication. He had a markedly ambivalent attitude toward Saudis and Saudi Arabia. On the one hand he identified with them, was heavily involved in long-term reciprocal relations of hospitality, and spoke about how they reminded him of his own father who dressed like them. On the other hand he exuded the resentment of the migrant who was discriminated against in hospitals, in salary, and in promotion and tenure within the Saudi bureaucracy, and who constantly felt the need to work harder than the natives or run the risk of dismissal: "I've seen now that they've told the foreigners to go home," he said. "How long will they keep me?" The plasterer, on the other hand, interacted almost entirely with co-Jordanians (but not co-villagers) both at work and in his domicile. He took in stride and was even philosophical about his status as a foreigner and noncitizen worker in Arabia. "If I'm going to work for a Saudi," he said, "I only want his material possessions and not his friendship." When I asked him what he thought of Saudi Arabia he replied, "It is the best state among nations." Although he led this almost completely encapsulated existence (with co-Jordanians) in Saudi Arabia, paradoxically, he developed multiplex relations with the Saudi owner of the company[4] and accompanied him and his family on the pilgrimage to Mecca, a fact which entirely belies his statement negating the desire for friendship or his view that relations between foreigners and Saudis are or should be completely instrumental.

The migrants' explicit assessments of Saudi behavior and character as well as those of other nationalities were diverse and reflected not only the different circumstances in which they worked, the different social types they met, the length of time they stayed, and the frequency and intensity of their social interaction, but also their own ambitions and personalities. The migrants who tended to view Saudis as arrogant tended to have the least interaction with them, such as those who worked on the oil fields. This was not always so, however. The foreman of the refrigerated meat plant who became an independent food merchant in Jidda, referred to earlier, had considerable contact with Saudis in strictly business contexts. He thought that Jidda was beautiful, "a bit of Paris," as he said for its run of foreigners and the high life he enjoyed including drinking, women, and films. When I asked him what he thought of the Saudis, he said he viewed them as arrogant. They told him, "You (foreigners) are here as our servants."

On the other hand, the schoolteacher who regularly shared hospitality in the Bedouin encampment said about the Saudis, "If you are polite and courteous they will reciprocate." He liked the fact that among these semisedentarized folk there was no standing on ceremony. They were frank, open, and friendly with the implication that the inhabitants of Kufr al-Ma (a village that had become a municipality, having doubled in size, increased in wealth, and developed occupational differentiation and commuting patterns to cities) were no longer this way. As much as he liked them, he found the physical circumstances in which he lived very difficult.

The personnel supervisor who was in charge of Saudis was quite aware of the status incongruence of a foreigner ordering Saudi citizens around, and by implication aware of the tendency for Saudis to use their privileged status to loaf on the job. He got them to work by joking and dispensing overtime work to them. Whenever he was stopped by traffic policemen he apologized, and he never received a ticket. This polite and self-effacing attitude and demeanor apparently earned the affection of his Saudi employees who, he said, wept when he left Arabia. Though he was dealing with an entirely different social category of Saudis than the schoolteacher in Atana, he came to a similar conclusion: treatment of the migrant by Saudis depended on the migrant's treatment of Saudis. He noted, however, that Saudis in Riyadh treated their own Saudi neighbors more diffidently than Jordanians, inviting them for hospitality only on religious holidays.

When I asked the educational administrator in Abha what he thought of Saudi students he said that they had no brains. When I demurred he proceeded to explain that the Saudi welfare state assured the Saudi student, regardless of performance, of a job at a high salary. Even if the student flunked out he could get a well-paying job in the army. He then qualified his statement about the Saudis' laziness and lack of ambition by saying that those with whom he came into contact were of the "lowest class" and not the Saudi professionals who, presumably, worked hard and had ambition.

When he was a trainee in Cairo this administrator had liked the easygoing, fun-loving, cooperative attitude of Egyptians on the one hand but had deplored their weak family ties on the other, weak due to birth control, dispersion of the population through occupational mobility and the fall-off of visiting among close kinsmen, and a poverty that undermined a sharing ethic in the family. The teacher in Al-Kur found the Egyptians and Sudanese cordial but miserly; but the former were obsequious when faced with authority while the latter were rigid and would challenge directives from superiors without fear. None of the migrants mentioned above gave any indication of assimilating to Arabian culture or yearning to become Saudis.

The one migrant who nearly "assimilated" to another culture was the warehouse foreman.[5] Interestingly enough, this did not occur in Arabia but in Jordan while he was a hydrology supervisor in the desert over a number of years. He dressed like the Bedouin, wore his hair long, went along with them on their pastoral round, engaged in their entertainments, and even contemplated marrying a Bedouin woman.

This transformation was quite unlike the adaptation of the Abha administrator who dressed like the Saudis of the district and enjoyed long-term reciprocal hospitality with them, i.e., "acculturated" without ever thinking he could become one of them (though his son who was born there apparently has that option).[6] But even the Abha administrator's intercultural relations were more profound in their implications for change and adaptation than those of the two schoolteachers in northwest Arabia who, although they enjoyed the hospitality of a pastoral people, learned to understand their dialect of Arabic, and were treated as "kinsmen of the town," never engaged in long-term reciprocity or emulated their dress or demeanor. They underwent neither assimilation nor acculturation.

One aspect of the transvaluation of culture, i.e., the learning of new values and the development of new identities is the change in the mode of decision-making. Tutwiler, drawing on Ortiz (1973) has analyzed decision-making among Yemeni migrants to Arabia.[7] He distinguishes between "deferred" and "programmed" decision-making. The former process defers decisions till they have to be dealt with, maximizes subsistence security, and reduces risk and uncertainty by following tried-and-true methods and social arrangements, and by allocating resources on an ad hoc basis. Programmed decision-making calculates costs, risks, and probable benefits well in advance of initiatory actions and accepts greater risks. Michalak in analyzing Tunisian migration to France has added that programmed decision-making requires a (daily, monthly) budget and a timetable (for savings) together with an initial assessment of the amount needed to save/invest.[8] He observed that generally Tunisians moved from deferred ad hoc decision-making to programmed decision-making as they moved from the status of new unmarried migrants to veteran married migrants. My data neither supports nor negates this plausible conclusion. It does document an interesting and varied range of migrant experiences and attitudes. Certainly, many of the nonprofessional migrants, both blue collar and white collar, including both business managers and skilled tradesmen, those whom we have characterized as the "raiders in Arabia" were men on the move making sudden and ad hoc changes in employment and, often, occupations, as more lucrative employment opportunities opened up. One migrant not mentioned above switched from manager of transport and logistics for a Saudi company in Riyadh to accountant at the Canadian embassy in Jidda, although he had no previous training or experience in accountancy; his college degree had been in English literature! The purchasing agent in the port of Jidda who finally became a business manager of a newspaper in an inland oasis referred to below also held down jobs as a diver and a director of a camp for workers. The plasterer who met his Saudi guarantor quite by accident in a Jordanian village certainly had not planned to go to Arabia; neither did the technician returned from England who went to the peninsula in a fit of pique. The plasterer did little planning with respect to the disposal of his income, either, since it was all swallowed up in payments to his first estranged wife and in household expenses for his second wife and many children, expenses that his second wife managed.

As migrants began to earn substantial sums of money, they did begin planning how to dispose of it in the future. The Jordanian woman who taught in northern Arabia while her husband worked as a mechanic there was planning to build a house and, subsequently if savings allowed, a garage back in the village. The personnel manager who left in a fit of pique five years before, when I interviewed him in 1986 had calculated that he needed to work three more years on the peninsula, two years to finish construction of his village house and a third year to finish paying the installments on his car, which he had left in Arabia to avoid paying customs duties.

The foreman who had adopted a romantic attitude towards Bedouin life while he was a hydrology supervisor in the Jordanian desert, with respect to his earnings in the oil fields of the Arabian desert, spent some money on consumer items such as a TV, refrigerator, and wardrobes, but invested much the greater part of his income in various enterprises: chicken farm, olive trees, tractor, water tank with pump, storehouses. Most of these enterprises were unsuccessful, and his storehouses stood half-completed on the main road because his employment in Arabia was summarily terminated in 1983. But he obviously had been forced to engage in some planning and to take greater risks than he had ever done before.

The migrant who took the biggest risk without adequately calculating the costs and benefits was the assistant public relations officer who lost most of his savings, perhaps not so much because of the inherent unsoundness of the venture (other tile-making workshops in the area were operating successfully), but because he had not investigated or assessed the character of his co-entrepreneur adequately. It is interesting that both of these migrants afore-mentioned ended up getting lower-echelon office jobs, one in the government bureaucracy and the other in a bank, jobs they probably would have held had they never gone to Arabia.

As a result of their business failures, however, both had developed new attitudes on important matters: the public relations officer had developed a deep suspicion of his co-villagers, whom he now regarded as deceitful and untrustworthy (in Riyadh he had interacted with them intensively); and the former hydrologist who had interacted with the Bedouin had come into contact with an American manager with whom he had developed a significant social relationship.

Although most of the hydrologist's business ventures had failed, it would be false to consider him a failure as a migrant. He built a solid house, planted 300 olive trees that gave him a continuing if modest income as well as providing an important nutritive supplement to his household, and, not least significant, paid off his debts with his earnings in Arabia. Even the public relations officer, after his investment fiasco, still had saved enough to become betrothed and anticipate marriage.

Although most Jordanian migrants in Arabia were thrifty and some were niggardly, many made some investment in social relations, such as the schoolteacher who invited her Egyptian and Sudanese counterparts to her home. A few became deeply involved in expenditures on social relations, such as the educational administrator in Abha, though the bulk of his earnings were spent on building a house and buying land back in the village as well as providing for the education of his brothers.

Not all of the residents of Kufr al-Ma in the diaspora socialized together when they worked in the same city. A manager of transport and logistics in Riyadh (not mentioned above) said that he had invited his covillagers to share his hospitality there, but they were too busy "counting every single penny." He continued, "When I went to Riyadh I called the people from Kufr al-Ma on the telephone and invited them to come to the hotel (to socialize and receive hospitality). Do you know they didn't come because they didn't want to pay the taxi fare of ten riyals. There is a competition between cousins and close relatives; there is an intense competition." The co-villagers referred to were niggardly from his point of view, but with their more modest incomes, their thrift may have been part of programmed decision-making since taxi fare may have exceeded their daily budget.

There are two interesting points to be made here. One is that the strong "son-of-the-village" (*ibn al-balad*) ethos that dominated village life in the 1960s and required constant visiting and hospitality, among other things, apparently did not always or perhaps usually operate in the diaspora, although close relatives still got together frequently. The other, perhaps more significant point, is that the relatively affluent business manager still felt it necessary to invite his co-villagers and was offended when they demurred. This was so despite the fact that his education (he had a B.A. degree in English literature), his occupational status and income (he was a high-echelon business manager with a high salary), his sophisticated programmed decision-making (he ploughed back a significant proportion of his earnings into the company he helped manage), and his style-of-life (he dressed like a western businessman, traveled abroad, and enjoyed western entertainments) clearly set him apart from his fellow-villagers. Certainly, he had little in common with them, but he did not think so. When I asked this sophisticated business manager how he invested his money he replied that he gave much the larger portion of it to his father to do with as he chose. I replied, "But you're a businessman; don't you have ideas about how the money should be invested?" He replied, "The main thing (is) I just want my father to be happy." The manager had engaged in programmed decision-making with respect to part of his earnings, but in giving the bulk of his salary to his father he was investing in "social arrangements," clearly apart from any calculation of costs and benefits. Moreover, that he should continue to be concerned about his kinsmen and co-villagers in and out of the village, although he had emancipated himself from the village economically and in style-of-life and seldom visited it (though his wife lived in his parent's house in the village), indicates the complexity of the process of the transvaluation of culture and in this case its uneven, contradictory, and incomplete character.[9]

Each of the seven migrant interviews presents insights on whether attitudes change as a result of the migration experience, how they change, and to what degree. The technician-telephone operator turned personnel manager began his acculturation in England where he lived with an English family. This was an unusual experience. Few migrants—none in Arabia—lived with a family for any length of time. Those that did, including two in the U.S.A., one in Greece, and one in Turkey, developed special insights about the values that underlay various non-Arab cultures. The technician's acculturation continued on his return from England in Amman where he worked closely with an Englishman in the telecommunications center; and continued in several different milieus in Saudi Arabia where he lived with American managers in the same quarters on the Gulf and later in the foreign quarter of Riyadh. This succession of exposures to quite different cultures and subcultures was a quite frequent experience for Jordanian migrants to Pakistan, Greece, and the U.S.A. as well as Arabia. The technician's interpretation of his six-month living experience with the English family is interesting: he observed at first hand their close-knit kinship ties since he went with them on visits to relatives. But he continued to express the view that English families were, in general, weak. On the other hand, his fraternization with the American managers in Arabia convinced him that Americans had close and warm family ties as evidenced by their waiting day-by-day for letters from home and by the fact that one manager quit his lucrative job to return to the U.S.A. because his wife needed him. On the basis of extensive interviews in 1991 with four Jordanians in Texas who had been studying in the U.S.A. for from five to thirteen years (see Chapter 6 below), I can say that this technician knew more about American family values than many of them did.

This technician also came into regular contact with young Englishmen when he participated in the weight-lifting club. He very much enjoyed this introduction to this aspect of English youth culture, but he was shocked by their lack of modesty—by their nakedness in the shower room, as he was by the availability of contraceptives in public bathrooms. Despite his shock at the general freedom characterizing relations between the sexes in England, he explained this freedom in a rather sophisticated manner for a young man who had never been out of the country: "For us Muslims it is not good. For them (the English) it is normal. They have lived like that since childhood," i.e., in terms of cultural (but not ethical) relativism.

I frequently questioned migrants about their views of tribal law, which was a major and required mode of conflict resolution during my research in Jordan in the 1960s, the law stipulating certain procedures for cases involving violation of honor such as adultery, rape, burglary, slander, and other violations of modest behavior.[10] Generally speaking, when such a crime had been committed, responsibility on both the victim's and the perpetrator's side was collective and implicated relatives through the fifth degree of patrilineal descent. There was at that time no question whatsoever about the applicability of tribal law and collective responsibility to such cases even though civil law and Islamic law courts and codes existed to try them. By the 1980s the suitability of tribal law for fast-changing Jordan had become questioned, at least in the capital and in other towns. Both the schoolteacher at Layth and the educational administrator at Abha came out strongly against the principle of collective responsibility: "Revenge based on collective responsibility and punishment on one who has no blame is bad.... It should be the person (who committed the crime) himself (that) carries the burden of the penalty. Government law should operate," said the schoolteacher.

In reply to my question, "What are your views on tribal law?" the educational administrator replied, "Injustice or oppression of the person is not right. We are brothers; you err, I didn't. Religion says, 'Every person is held to account by himself.' Religion says, 'The killer (only) is killed.'" The concept of individual responsibility is strongly affirmed here, but the administrator's source for this principle was not state law (as was the teacher's) or secular principles, but Quranic verses. The administrator's statement is an instance of the reinterpretation of tradition and Islamization, not modernization or westernization.[11]

The one female teacher interviewed casts an interesting light on the attitude held about women's work outside the home. In 1959–60 when I first began conducting my research in Kufr al-Ma it was unthinkable to even discuss women's working outside the home and the village. This woman and others like her have not only left the village but also left the country. This pursuit of her profession abroad was possible and honorable because she had a *mahram,* a husband, a protector, literally, a person who made her sacrosanct. Her working in Arabia is not regarded as an instance of women's liberation either by herself or others, but as the normal exercise of an adult's right to pursue an occupational specialty for which they have been trained. A traditional role, male protector, has been extended into an entirely new situation—the diaspora—to serve novel purposes: both geographical and status mobility; or, if her behavior in leaving her village to work in a foreign country (and this was new and different) is to be interpreted as acculturation, it is certainly "controlled," i.e., the practice has been integrated into an existing value system and given a well-known label.[12]

Even when new skills reflecting new values have been developed, the construction put on them by the migrant is often otherwise. When I asked the former hydrologist how he got his initial job in Arabia, his reply clearly indicated programmed decision-making: he had gone to Amman to get a passport and visitor's visa for Saudi Arabia; then he went to the center of economic activity on the Gulf, Dammam, where he made contact with fellow-Jordanians; who in turn used their good offices to get a letter from the company sent back to Jordan requesting that he come to work. The former hydrologist, undoubtedly, knew about and planned for this sequence of events. But his definitive comment summing up his going to Arabia was, "I went by the way of chance; God smoothed the way for me and got me work." That is, a religious attitude determined his interpretation of events.

The educational administrator's reply to my question, "What are your views on women working outside the home?" also illustrates how change is interpreted not to be change. He replied, "I don't believe in it. She can work if she has no children. She can work in any arena: schools, ministries, as an engineer they are even working as aviators. The thing I oppose is a woman with five children (working)." I replied, "But in Kufr al-Ma several women with children teach." He said, "Here in Kufr al-Ma she has her mother or sister to help her. Where will she send her children? To her mother."

The administrator first makes an absolute statement of his position, and immediately hedges it with a set of conditional statements, taking into account marital status, wealth, and availability of kinswomen to help. When these statements themselves are questioned, he hedges them further, an eminently systematic approach in terms of increased contextualization and refinement. What is important here for the reinterpretation of tradition is that this modus operandi removes the position enunciated far from the original statement without, however, negating it.

Attitudes towards women's working outside the home, birth control, and the application of Islamic law focusing on the stipulated punishments (*ḥudud*) reflect not only a variety of opinions but also some patterned responses.[13] The unusual response on these matters was the technician turned telephone operator turned personnel manager's response. He said, "Religious people say it is against Islam, but it is good to have a small family. We will have one more (child). If I have ten, six will be mechanics in workshops." What is exceptional in his response is not his practice of birth control; other migrants practiced a form of birth control called "family planning" (i.e., the use of contraceptive methods, but those not involving a definitive cutoff of procreation by an operation) and viewed it as permitted by Islamic law and ethics. Rather, it was his championing of small families and his willingness to place himself in opposition to the religious establishment, as well as his charging his fellow-villagers with general ignorance about the matter. When I asked him how he felt about women working, however, he gave a qualified reply (without the initial absolute statement), and when I pressed him on one of the qualifications (how could nursing be approved when nurses worked among men) he replied, "But it is a revered job. There were so many nurses in Islam." The extension of women's work into a new sphere in the modern context was justified in terms of religious history.

The plasterer gave the stock answer on birth control, loosely quoting the Quran, "'It is forbidden,' God said. 'We will give you sustenance, you and your children.'" And when asked about women's work outside the home, he said, "No! God created her for the home only. If she leaves the home she departs from the religion of Islam and from the command of her husband."

But more migrants gave qualified replies such as those of the educational administrator or the teacher in Layth than absolute and stock answers such as the plasterer. In reply to my question, "What is your view of women working outside the home?" the teacher said, "Every country has its own views. If the work is honorable there is nothing to prevent it, but it is better if she works in her home. But if society needs her, it's okay. A school-teacher is okay." "What of a doctor?" I asked. "The doctor has to study and work outside the village. No. In the city it is possible that it (women's working outside the home) exists.... Teaching is okay with her safeguarding (*muḥafaTHa*)."

When I asked the woman teaching in Al-Kur about her view of women working outside the home, she replied, "I'd educate my daughter through university, if she qualified, and encourage her to be a teacher or a doctor." But when asked about engineering, she demurred: "Her (the engineer's) work is not in the office all the time; it is in the field with men." Nursing was also rejected as possible employment for women because, she said, there was "much mixing (of the sexes)" in that occupational situation too. The interesting point here is that this teacher's response, like that of the two male teachers/educators, is basically the same in form—an absolute statement followed by a series of hedges—and the same in one crucial point of content: the woman's honor must be safeguarded in her place of employment whether through reduction of interpersonal contact with the other sex or by close monitoring.

The series of hedges recorded in these interviews allows the tradition regarding women's work to be reinterpreted. The reinterpretation proceeds along certain lines taking into account marital status, availability of kinsmen, income, urban vs. rural residence, and, most important, the possibility of protecting the modesty and honor of women in the new social environment.[14] Note, the teacher in Layth begins his reply with a statement recognizing cultural relativity as a principle of evaluation, "Every country has its own views." Of concern to this teacher as to the educational administrator and capping their replies was an economic concern that the employment of women would adversely affect the employment of men.

Shortly after this teacher replied to my question, his father, a veteran cultivator, said, "Girls can work in typing, the land registry office, courts, educational offices; i.e., spread them around."

This is not the only instance of a discussion of interpersonal relations in which the reply of a father was more tolerant of new projects and arenas for women's activity than that of his son. This may reflect the increased influence among younger men of what some have termed "neofundamentalist" views that demand stricter adherence to certain aspects of Islamic law and ethics in order to affirm Muslim identity and authenticity against what they view as western neocolonialism, particularly its cultural penetration and undermining of Muslim family life and morals; as opposed to the views of certain fathers' more "neotraditional" orientation, more tolerant of non-Islamic customs (such as tribal law, community conflict-resolution, extended kinship ties, and folk medicine) as well as more tolerant of diverse Muslim views including Sufi and nonfundamentalist interpretations. This elder generation is also not as caught up in the necessity of responding politically and ideologically to the challenge of western economic and cultural domination.

It is difficult sometimes to interpret migrants' views about the kinds of social and socioreligious matters we have been discussing. The educational administrator told me, as we were discussing the general matter of his physical circumstances in Abha and the customs of the people there, that what was good about Saudi Arabia was that women sat absolutely by themselves; there was no mixing of men and women. He said that for Muslims it had to be this way (separate), and his houses in Abha and Jizan were divided in two with a section for men and one for women, each with its own bathroom. Is this statement a reflection of a "neofundamentalist" orientation: a new quest for authenticity and distinctiveness vis-à-vis non-Muslims by a closer adherence to what are perceived to be the correct Quranic norms? Or does this statement reflect a "neotraditional" orientation: one that values the customs of his own village as he knew them in his childhood and early manhood in the 1950s and 1960s when the segregation of sexes in public arenas was an accepted and generally observed custom? There is evidence for both interpretations since Saudi Arabia is, after all, heavily influenced by neofundamentalism at all levels of society and the educational administrator had lived in Saudi Arabia for twelve years. On the other hand, Kufr al-Ma definitely had and has a "modesty code" that antedates the so-called Islamic resurgence that began in the 1970s after the OPEC oil-pricing revolution.

Attitudes toward religion and society are also crystalized in views expressed about the character of Islamic rule in Saudi Arabia, particularly about the stipulated punishments (*ḥudud*). Only one migrant, the refrigerated meat plant supervisor turned food merchant in Jidda, stated outright that Saudi rule was no good: "They cut off heads there in the public square; (whereas) in Jordan they get fifteen years for murder; they whip you for drinking (in Saudi Arabia); yet drinking takes place; they (meaning certain restaurants) put liquor in bottles labeled 'health water'.... Some (Saudis) drank and then went and sat in the mosque," he said. Of course, the fact that he himself had consumed a lot of alcohol in Jidda could not be irrelevant for the formulation of his views. The technician turned personnel administrator was critical of Islamic rule in Saudi Arabia, saying "... there are some areas where they don't know Islam." He distinguished between Mecca and Medina, the holy cities, where people were pious, and Riyadh where many were not. He disapproved of the operation of the Islamic militia (*mutatawwa'in*) who indiscriminately chased people to the mosque at prayer times, even Buddhists!

On the other hand, when I asked him about the stipulated Islamic punishments, though he had never witnessed one, he said they were a good thing; they reduced the crime rate: "If one sees a head cut off, he will dream about it for a week; he will never do it (the crime)." The plasterer, who had witnessed the punishment of the cutting off of the right hand for theft on TV, said that he supported it 100 percent. There are many foreigners in Arabia; they leave the shops open, their automobiles open. (It is) to teach others a lesson. If I hear of the cutting off of the hand and I found a wallet in the street I'd leave it."

The teacher in Layth approved of the compulsory closing of shops fifteen minutes prior to the required five daily prayers. He had witnessed a beheading in Mecca and said, "The adulterer is killed [in fact, this is not so—the Quranic punishment for adultery is a flogging of 100 lashes of the whip]; the thief, his hand is cut off; and the drunkard is whipped.... The man who borrows 100,000 riyals is put in prison seven years till he has paid off the sum or brought witnesses that say he can't pay." He continued, "It is a good system, God's order," and he contrasted it with tribal law in Jordan which allows for acts of God and magnanimity (i.e., forgiveness by the victim or his family), both of which allow the perpetrator of the crime to go free. He praised the Islamic system of justice because on the one hand it took into account extenuating circumstances but on the other, criminals were not allowed to go free and the killer (only) was killed.

When I asked the woman schoolteacher about her view of the Islamic state in Arabia, she said, "They apply the Islamic system. They rule by the Quran. They limit the freedom of women. Yes!" This was a yes of affirmation, not resignation. Finally, the educational administrator when asked the question, said, "Islam is not the middle way. (They say in Saudi Arabia), '(Go to) the mosque! (It's time for) prayer, prayer! (It's time to) worship, worship!' The religious police say that. They ask the people to shut the shops at prayer time. He who doesn't pray is whipped." Regarding the punishment of beheading for murder he said, "How can I oppose God's judgement? The killer is killed...."

One can infer that the witnessing of the application of certain aspects of Islamic law in Saudi Arabia, particularly the stipulated punishments, reinforced the view of the overwhelming majority of migrants from Kufr al-Ma that the Islamic system was more just than others, including tribal law and the state laws of other Arab countries, and was a more effective deterrent. When I asked one migrant what thing he liked best about Saudi Arabia, he said, "Application of the religion of Islam."

Support for the application of Islamic social and legal norms in Saudi Arabia did not mean that migrants always approved of the way these norms were executed. One migrant, an airport lighting technician in the oasis of Jauf who had lived in Saudi Arabia for nine years, liked the Islamic system of social control because, he said, "Courts rule all the time by religion." He looked askance at tribal norms of reconciliation with all their complications and long, drawn-out negotiations. In the Islamic mode of justice they were dispensed with, and severe punishments were meted out quickly to the individuals responsible (only). He liked the Islamic mode of justice because it was quick, and because it did not allow for buying out the victim through compensation (as allowed and encouraged by tribal law). But he commented adversely on the operation of the religious militia in Jauf. They harassed him for sitting in the waiting room in the women's section of the hospital, accusing him of hanging around in order to ogle women when he was simply waiting for his wife to come out from a doctor's consultation. He said, ironically, that if he hadn't come to the hospital to wait for his wife, the religious police would have wanted to know why he had let his wife go to the hospital unescorted!

A Comparative Dimension: Turks in Germany and Jordanians in Arabia

The Turkish migration to Europe, beginning in the late 1950s after the formation of the European Economic Community (1957) and accelerating in the

1960s and 1970s, highlights certain aspects of the Jordanian migration to Arabia in the 1970s and 1980s. Keyder and Aksu-Koc have reviewed the literature on Turkish migration to Europe in a detailed and sophisticated manner in their (1988) book, and Abadan-Unat has characterized its phases in a (1986) article.[15] I shall draw on their description and analysis to bring out the similarities and differences of the two migration experiences. It should be noted that I will be generalizing extensively about the migration experience of Turks to Germany since the migration has been over a longer period than for Jordanians to Arabia, and it has passed through five separate phases. First let us consider the similarities.

The migrants to Germany as well as to Arabia were regarded as permanent foreigners. There was no provision for or expectation of their becoming citizens, and no attempt to integrate them educationally or politically into the receiving society. In Germany this permanent migrant-exile status is indicated in the term used to describe such migrants, "guest-workers." In 1978 the German government began to examine more integrative policies, but xenophobia towards Turkish workers in Germany reached a high pitch in 1983 when 120,000 workers returned to Turkey.[16] Although this kind of xenophobia did not arise in Saudi Arabia and Kuwait until the Gulf War in the winter-spring of 1991, directed mainly against Jordanians particularly of Palestinian extraction, and Yemenis, both of whom were summarily expelled; as a number of our migrant interviews indicated, Jordanians before that time were quite conscious of the limitations placed on their ability to integrate into Arabian society. This is the sense in which Abadan-Unat refers to the Turkish movement to Europe as a "shift of manpower" rather than "migration."

Both Jordanians and Turks stayed abroad more than four years with the Turks averaging much longer because the emigration began 10–15 years earlier. But the Jordanian migration to Arabia, particularly for those migrants working in northwestern Arabia, probably resembled more the Mexican migration to the southwestern United States than the Turkish migration to Germany in that it was not a once-and-for-all migration. Because of the adjacent borders (of Jordan and Saudi Arabia, and Mexico and the United States) for many migrants there was the option of short visits (for teachers long visits) or circular migration rather than a prolonged, rare or, no-return stay. German statistics for 1980 revealed that the mode number of years abroad of Turkish migrants was 10–15 years.[17] My statistics for Kufr al-Ma for 1986 indicate that the mode number was 7–9 years (see Table 2.7). The migrant experience abroad in both instances, then, was not a passing thing and allowed ample opportunity for such processes as acculturation, programmed decision-making, neotraditionalism, and the transvaluation of culture.

There is evidence in both cases that migrants returned to their home countries to engage in small-scale service or workshop enterprises in which competition was intense and financial success by no means guaranteed, rather than in industrial enterprises. This fact is perhaps related to the desires of the returnees in both cases to be self-employed. Turkish workers in Germany had been part of an industrial labor force, in a status and job they did not relish. Many Jordanian migrants, on the other hand, had been government employees in one way or another: as soldiers, teachers, clerks, and technicians. Many of these returned migrants, too, chose self-employment or employment in the private sector on their return.

In terms of economic success and cultural exposure, Keyder and Aksu-Koc characterize the majority of the Turkish returnees as either "returns of failure" (after a few years abroad without significant contacts with the host society and no substantial savings) or "returns of conservatism" (who come back without any change in their traditional norms, values, or life styles and only enough savings to invest in traditional enterprises like small shops or a small piece of land). They argue that in the future most Turkish migrants will be "returns of retirement" (the generally skilled and educated migrant who has successfully adapted to the host society and lived there with his family comes home with enough saved to retire in his old age). They argue that "returns of success or innovation" (who come back with new knowledge, skills, enough savings, and a desire to invest in new enterprises—to employ substantial numbers of workers) are few among Turks in Germany.[18] Furthermore, they argue that a substantial proportion of Turkish migrants' earnings are spent on consumer goods, much of it being "cosmetic consumption" and not signifying any change "in the traditional, rural life style."[19]

Our assessment of the impact of the migration of Jordanians to Arabia is not different in some respects. Most Jordanians return home to invest in petty enterprises that do not employ large numbers (e.g., a tile or cement block workshop in Kufr al-Ma employs four or five). On the other hand, to characterize investment in houses, land, marriages, and the higher education of children—and both the Jordanian and Turkish migrants had a special propensity to encourage and support education—as having little impact on society is taking an overly narrow view.

The strictly economic aspect aside, the whole question of the cultural impact of migration in the Jordanian–Arabian case is a complex matter in which generalization is difficult, as I suspect it is in the Turkish–German one. Television sets, I suppose could be considered "cosmetic consumption," though the authors don't specifically mention it, and yet TV broadcasts certainly have the potential to change attitudes, and not necessarily in the direction that most social scientists with an explicit/implicit evolutionary perspective would predict.

Keyder and Aksu-Koc certainly make a case for the view that Turkish workers in the European diaspora do not learn "modernity." The modernization school that they criticize argues that migration is a response to the decay of traditional ties and will accelerate the transition to industrial capitalism. Migrants in Europe, according to the theory, will learn the industrial ethos including work discipline and labor consciousness, return to their home countries, and "help their fellow workers at home adapt to more industrialization."[20] Keyder and Aksu-Koc argue, on the contrary, that Turkish workers in Germany were not well-integrated into German society and that they had developed "traditionalism" (rather than modernity) as a defense against alienation, i.e., they had developed conservative views emphasizing the integrity of family life, interpersonal morality, and religion. A similar argument can be made about some Jordanian migrants from Kufr al-Ma, as their attitudes towards and comments about family life, hospitality, relations of the sexes in public, the education of women, and the stipulated Islamic penalties above indicate. On the other hand, it can be argued more persuasively, as will be done in the succeeding chapters, that what is occurring is not a reaction to alienation, but a reinterpretation of tradition spurred by the startling new circumstances that Jordanian migrants encountered in the diaspora and at home, a reinterpretation that moves in a number of different directions by different individuals or even by the same individual at different times.

To return to the differences between the Turkish and Jordanian cases. By and large, Turkish migrants were drawn from the "bottom category of the rural upper stratum" and from "the middle stratum," although the Turkish government's initiatives through the Turkish Employment Service to form cooperatives that would encourage migration and investment of migrant earnings back in their villages in the late 1960s allowed some migrants from the lower rural stratum to qualify.[21] Michalak, referring to migrants from northwest Tunisia to France, also states that "it is not the poorest people who migrate. The poor have neither the minimal financial resources, nor networks with which to migrate, and they have no skills of even the most rudimentary kind...."[22]

The Jordanian migrants to Arabia did include children of the village's elite such as the doctor who early on settled in Medina (his father was a civil court clerk) and the logistics and personnel manager in Riyadh (whose father was a retired noncommissioned army officer), but they also included the plasterer (whose father had some village land and a very small shop) in a village where the contingent climate and the erosion of soils made dry cereal farming not even sufficient for subsistence, the teacher in Layth (whose father was a subsistence cultivator with a little land but supporting two wives and a very large family), the assistant public relations officer (whose father was also a subsistence cultivator with a little land), the airport lighting technician and the business manager of the newspaper (two brothers, whose father had been village mayor but poor and heavily in debt to village shopkeepers at his death), and the refrigerated meat plant foreman in Jidda (whose father was landless and impoverished).

Although the Turkish migration to Germany was dominated initially, in the early 1960s, by single urban males, by the late 1960s it had become dominated by married rural males. But these men, overwhelmingly, left their wives and children in Turkey. After 1974 and new German government policies aimed at family reunion, however, the number of Turkish wives and children accompanying men to the diaspora swelled. By 1980, 59 percent of the Turks in Germany were dependents, i.e., women and children.[23] Four-fifths of the villagers in Arabia on whom I have data were married in 1979 and almost all of them were married in 1986. In the earlier year very few brought their wives and children, but by 1986 almost half did so.

Jordanian migrants considered a variety of factors in determining whether to bring their wives and children to Arabia with them. One brought his wife after she secured a teaching position in Saudi Arabia; his brother, the airport lighting technician, brought his wife after she complained of living with his in-laws back in the village—she was a city girl; the telephone switchboard operator who worked for the Saudi prince brought his wife after his mentor provided electricity to his apartment; the teacher in Al-Kur came with her husband who was a necessary "protector"; the educational administrator in Abha brought his wife, mother, and children because he was going away for a long term and his hours were long (he worked nights as well) and he couldn't cook. Those who chose not to bring their wives to Arabia included the logistics and personnel manager in Riyadh who said that he was traveling all the time and his wife would not be able to cope alone, as well as a sales manager for Winston cigarettes who was also on the road most of the time; the surveyor whose work cycle put him in Arabia only four months out of every year; the plasterer whose relatively low income and large families made it necessary to save every piastre in Arabia; the refrigerated meat plant foreman who was up to high jinks in Jidda; the teacher in remote Layth who thought about bringing his wife the first year but changed his mind after he adapted to the customs of the Bedouinized population and better appreciated the difficulties of life for a family; and a bulldozer driver–independent contractor in Abha who arranged for a visit of his young wife and daughter for three months after he had worked in Abha for five years.

When I asked him why he didn't bring his family to stay, he said that he was engaged in private employment and "they" (meaning the government) didn't allow it—they allowed it only if one was engaged in public employment like teaching. The bulldozer driver-contractor's family's visit to Arabia was the only family visit to Arabia I recorded among all migrants from Kufr al-Ma. The telephone operator turned administrator in Khobar and Riyadh said that his cousin (the doctor who practiced in Medina) had his two wives with him, but he had a very large house. He continued, "But for me, I have no house; those (wives and children) there (will) see themselves as if in jail; the husband works from the morning until 2 p.m.: he has lunch and returns to work until 8 p.m." His company had allowed him to bring his wife, but he had refused, saying, "Why should we both be foreigners (here)?" Clearly, he viewed his stay in Saudi Arabia as a form of exile.

The migration to Arabia, overall then, was of married men without their dependents, though decreasingly so from the 1970s to the 1980s whereas more than fifteen years before, Turkish migrants' dependents outnumbered the male heads of households in the German diaspora.[24] It should be mentioned here that whereas migrants to Arabia were in overwhelming numbers married, student migrants from Kufr al-Ma to Pakistan, Greece, Russia, the United States, Saudi Arabia, and Egypt were overwhelmingly single. This fact has implications for a quite different migration experience than the one we have been describing and these implications will be pursued in the following chapters.

Although the Turkish migrant population is substantially more educated than the general Turkish population, with only 3.1 percent being illiterate and with a higher percentage of primary school graduates, occupationally the Turkish migration to Germany represented a brawn drain rather than a brain drain because a substantially lower percentage of migrants were high school graduates or had higher education than the general Turkish population.[25]

The Jordanian migrants to Arabia from Kufr al-Ma, on the other hand, were overwhelmingly high school graduates, with a substantial percentage having higher education, usually a two-year junior college diploma (see Table 2.10). The Jordanian migration to Arabia was a brain drain. In a 1985 survey of migration from a Jordanian village in the adjoining district to Kufr al-Ma, Seccombe also found that a considerable proportion of migrants were men who had substantial skills and experience, particularly teachers and soldiers serving in the military abroad; the latter generally had fifteen years or more of service in the Jordanian army.[26] Keely and Sacket found that migrants from Jordan were male (95 percent), age twenty to thirty-nine (80 percent), married (66 percent), white-collar (40 percent), and educated (33 percent had university degrees).[27] Abadan-Unat, on the other hand, suggests that the Turkish migrants in Germany are an underclass, doing the "dirty work—jobs that are dangerous, temporary, dead-end, undignified and menial."[28] This is certainly not the status of Jordanians in Arabia. Their education and skills place them in a superordinate position vis-à-vis many Saudis who, on the other hand, are citizens and wealthy. This makes the position of Jordanians in Arabia anomalous, but not underprivileged.

Jordanian migrants to Arabia, whether they were teachers in Abha or Layth or plasterers on the northern border or business managers in Riyadh or oil workers on the Gulf were going, overall, to a culturally and geographically similar country. This was not the case for Turks in Germany or Tunisians in France, both of whom had to grapple with the daunting facts of a different language, style-of-life, work ethic, housing, food, and for Germany and northern France, climate. This contrast can be overdone, however.

Migrants from the post-peasant village of Kufr al-Ma had by the 1970s many of the amenities of the towns including running piped water and electricity. To be posted in Al-Kur, Layth, the oil rigs of Abqaiq or, contrarily, the cosmopolitan city of Jidda or the puritanical capital of Riyadh required considerable adjustment. Moreover, the climate and housing differed radically from the cool highlands of Abha or Oman to the hot, steamy Red Sea littoral of Layth and Jizan to the restricted, dry inland oases of Jauf and Tabuk to the paradisiacal oasis of Al-Ayn. Nevertheless, there is no question that Jordanians in Arabia benefited from their speaking the same language and in certain parts of Arabia, though not all, coming from generally the same tribal background. Given this familiarity, it is striking that many Jordanians in Saudi Arabia had as little contact with Saudis as Turks had with Germans or Tunisians with French.

The single most important contrast between the Jordanian migration to Arabia and the Turkish migration to Germany is the fact that the residents of Kufr al-Ma did not sever their ties with the village community even after prolonged stays in Arabia. Those who could not make frequent visits home went for a long summer vacation; those who could not come home for the summer came home for the fast month of Ramadan; those who could not come home for the fast month, at least came home for a week to ten days to celebrate the festival of the breaking of the fast at the end of the fast month. Many migrants maintained telephonic communication with their families and sent remittances and letters at regular intervals. While abroad, as indicated above, many maintained contact with kinsmen and co-villagers in the diaspora. Returned migrants, in overwhelming numbers chose to continue living in the village, although most commuted to work outside of it. To my knowledge, no migrant from Kufr al-Ma married in Arabia, though several who went as single students to Greece, the United States, and Russia did. The future orientation of work migrants to Arabia back towards their own village was attested to by their investments in it: the purchase of land and the building and/or expansion and/or upgrading of houses there.

Of course, the community itself, to which they were clearly committed, was no longer in the 1980s a village. It had become electrified, had running, hot, and cold piped water, and had acquired paved roads and regular transport to the cities of Jordan. It had become a municipality and was able to borrow money to improve its roads, lighting, and trash collection, and was even making preliminary plans for a sewer system. Thus the attraction of the village was not simply that of family, kinship, and son-of-the-village social networks, and a style-of-life and public morality of which they approved, but also the amenities now available.

Much of what has just been described contrasts with the Turkish migration to Germany. On the one hand, as more men took their wives and children (and the latter constituted the majority of the Turkish population in Germany by the 1980s) to Germany, visits back to Turkey decreased in frequency, particularly after the German government implemented restrictions on the issue of work permits to foreign workers in 1974. Many Turks returned to Turkey after the recessions of the late 1960s, late 1970s, and late 1980s.[29] But the great majority remained, and as Keyder and Aksu-Koc state, by the late 1970s "a majority of the foreign workers in Europe have acquired the characterization of permanent migrants, and Turkish workers are no exception to this."[30]

On the other hand, one of the most commonly stated reasons for migrants' return to Turkey was "family fragmentation."[31] Elsewhere, Keyder and Aksu-Koc refer to the "disintegration of the household unit" as "the major impact of international labour migration on the composition of the (Turkish) family...."[32] There is no evidence to substantiate such an impact on Kufr al-Ma. The absence of one or more members of the family did not result in women being left in separate households alone or in role incompatibility due to the changing status of women.

The extended kinship network that supported the conjugal family and the ethos of co-villageship (though they were not what they were in 1959–60 when I first began my research), together with the frequent home visitation of migrants, communication through emissaries and kinsmen in the diaspora, and the tendency towards circulatory migration prevented disintegration of households and weakening of family ties.[33] The reinterpretation of tradition of the kind I have suggested above accommodated changing women's roles to the changing functions they took on, and the different circumstances and locales to which they were called on to adjust.

This is not to claim that the village and its component families were what they were in the 1960s before the onset of migration. Indeed, the village community has become less multiplex in its interpersonal relations and it is no longer an evenly-spun web of kinship in which every person can claim some kind of kin relationship (even if unverified) with every other (see chapter 7). Strains did arise between close kinsmen because of the absence of migrants, economic differentiation, status distinctions, and the weakening of the egalitarian ethos (guest house, hospitality, reciprocity of gifts and visits).

But there is very little evidence to indicate that as Jordanian migrants stayed in the diaspora for longer and longer periods, they developed a tendency to integrate (though not assimilate) into Arabian society as did Turkish workers in Germany. That is, there is no tendency for Jordanians in Arabia to become "permanent migrants" as Turks have become in Germany. The people of Kufr al-Ma did not lose their young as the Turks did in Germany.[34] It is this remarkable resiliency of social structure and ethos (discussed at length in chapter 7) along with the capacity to adapt to and reinterpret changing roles and situations that will be a continuing theme in the following chapters.

Notes

1. The pursuit for work outside the country had begun earlier, however, in 1955 when two migrants left for Beirut where they secured work as construction laborers, as longshoremen, and in cement and stonecutting workshops. Between 1955 and 1965, thirty-five migrants left for Lebanon where they usually spent between two and four months (the shortest stay was two weeks and the longest sixteen months) working as construction laborers, pipe fitters, fishermen, (electric wire and weaving) factory workers, smith's helpers, masons, and cement workshop laborers. Almost all worked in Beirut, although a few worked in Mount Lebanon, in the Beqa' Valley and outside Tripoli (as gardener, chicken farm attendant, mason, and factory clerk). The great majority of migrants were between the ages of twenty-one and thirty and on those for whom I have information, thirteen were married and seven single. Seven of the thirteen on whom I have information had less than a sixth grade education, two were illiterate, and only one had finished high school. Stays in Lebanon were limited by legal requirements and political conditions—most went on tourist visas that expired after two or three months and had to be renewed (and then only for short periods)—and by the entry of waves of cheap Syrian labor which drove down wages after economic recession in Syria. Twenty villagers went at one time in the summer of 1959 when it became possible for a short time for Jordanians to travel through Syria and into Lebanon on a Jordanian identity card (without passport or visa).

A number of villagers throughout this period pursued circulatory migration, returning to Jordan in summer months or during economic downturns or to rest or to get a new visa. Economic returns and savings were generally small. After ten years of circulatory migration the pioneer migrant saved 150 dinars, spending 100 to build a modest rough-hewn stone and adobe house in the village and 50 to buy eight goats. Most villagers returned to the village with only $75–100 saved after a few months' work. Two villagers were able to save enough to get married, and a third to pay off his wife's debts. This work migration was quite unlike that which followed in the 1970s in its brevity, low economic rewards, and social implications.

2. Six of the seven migrants are from Kufr al-Ma. The seventh, the foreman who worked for an Aramco affiliate near the oil fields, lived just outside the village limits in the adjoining district center of Deir Abu Said. None of the interviews was tape-recorded. I decided early in my field work that this mode of recording would inhibit and distort responses. I am not, therefore, able to produce a verbatim account of what was said. However, throughout my field work I did attempt to record responses as close as possible to what was said, making a point to reproduce key Arabic phrases when they seemed important for conveying shades of meaning perhaps untapped by English equivalents.

3. Deferred decision-making seeks to defer decisions till they have to be dealt with, maximizes subsistence security, and reduces risk and uncertainty by following tried-and-true methods and social arrangements and allocates resources on an ad hoc basis. Programmed decision-making calculates costs, risks, and probable benefits well in advance of initiatory actions and accepts a greater risk. For a discussion of the concepts in relation to Yemeni migrants to Saudi Arabia see Richard Tutwiler, Chapter Seven, pp. 352–55, "Tribe, Tribute and Trade: Social Class Formation in Highland Yemen," PhD dissertation, State University of New York at Binghamton, 1987. Neotraditionalism is an ideological orientation rooted in adherence to scripturalism (adherence to a holy scripture as a guide for modern life), appreciating the depth and complexity of the past Islamic tradition, but also recognizing the challenge of Western civilization and accepting the need for a selective acceptance of modern technology. See William E. Shepard, "Islam and Ideology: Towards a Typology," *International Journal of Middle East Studies,* Vol. 19, No. 3, August, 1987 for a discussion of neotraditionalism. See R. Antoun, *Understanding Fundamentalism: Christian, Islamic, and Jewish Movements,* AltaMira Press, 2001 for a discussion of the significance of scripturalism. The transvaluation of culture is the instilling of new attitudes reflecting new values and new identities such as cross-religious egalitarianism, humanism, materialism, skepticism, a positive stance toward innovation, an achievement ethic which channels rewards to high performers, and the sense of citizenship of a nation. For a discussion of the concept see Donald E. Smith, *Religion in Political Development,* 1970.

4. A multiplex relationship is one that serves many interests, e.g., economic, political, religious, recreational, and kinship, and in doing so affects and changes all in the direction of greater intimacy. Co-villagers in Kufr al-Ma, for instance, are likely to be not only neighbors and relatives but also worshipers in the same mosque, sharers of water, collaborators at harvest time, and mutually involved in local social control including gossip, compensation for injury, and mediation to reduce estrangement. See Max Gluckman, *The Judicial Process Among the Barotse of Northern Rhodesia,* p. 18 for a discussion of the concept.

5. Assimilation is the process of absorption of cultural traits along with their underlying values, thereby entailing a change of identity.

6. Acculturation is the process of borrowing cultural traits without a change in the basic values of the borrowing individual/group.

7. See Richard Tutwiler, Opis. cit.

8. See Laurence Michalak, "The Impact of Continuing and Return Migrants from Tunisia: Case Studies from the Tunisian Northwest," paper presented to the conference on "International Migration of Middle Easterners and North Africans: Comparing Diasporas" UCLA, May 1988.

9. For more information on this transport and logistics manager including an analysis of his migration experience in Pakistan and Arabia see chapter five below.

10. See Antoun, *Arab Village,* 1972, for details of such cases. See also a detailed description and analysis of a case of honor involving marriage and divorce in Kufr al-Ma in the 1960s entitled, "Institutionalized Deconfrontation: A Study of Conflict Resolution among Tribal Peasants in Jordan," in Paul Salem, editor, *Conflict Resolution in the Arab World,* American University of Beirut and Syracuse University Presses, 1997.

11. For a discussion of Islamization and its implications see Antoun, *Muslim Preacher in the Modern World,* 1989, Chapter Nine.

12. See Raymond Teske and Bardin Nelson, "Acculturation and Assimilation: A Clarification," for a discussion of various modes of controlled acculturation.

13. The *hudud* are the stipulated punishments in Islamic law, gross violations of Muslim mores that must be punished in this world (rather than the next). Those mentioned in the Quran include the punishments for adultery, theft, banditry, the drinking of intoxicating liquors, and falsely charging adultery. A specified punishment for apostasy was added by Muslim legal scholars (*fuqaha'*).

14. See Richard T. Antoun, "On the Modesty of Women in Arab Muslim Villages: A Study in the Accommodation of Traditions," *American Anthropologist,* Vol. 70, No. 4, August 1968 for an extensive description and analysis of the "modesty code" as it existed in Kufr al-Ma and other Muslim villages in the Middle East in the 1960s.

15. See Caglar Keyder and Ayhan Oksu-Koc, *External Labour Migration from Turkey and its Impact: An Evaluation of the Literature,* International Development Research Center, Canada, 1988, and Nermin Abadan-Unat, "Turkish Migration to Europe and the Middle East: Its Impact on Social Structure and Social Legislation," in Laurence Michalak and Jeswald Salacuse, editors, *Social Legislation in the Contemporary Middle East,* Institute of International Studies, University of California, 1986.

16. See Abadan-Unat, pp. 343–44.

17. See Keyder and Aksu-Koc, p. 47.

18. Keyder and Aksu-Koc are summarizing and applying an analysis by F.P. Cerase, "Migration and Social Change: Expectations and Delusions, Reflections upon the Return Flow from the United States to Italy," *International Migration Review,* Vol. 8, No. 2, 1974, to Turks returning to Germany.

19. See Keyder and Aksu-Koc, p. 127.

20. Keyder and Aksu-Koc, p. 88.

21. See Keyder and Aksu-Koc, p. 81 and Abadan-Unat, p. 331.

22. Michalak, p. 20.

23. See Keyder and Aksu-Koc, pp. 24–25.

24. Michalak, 1988, reports that the great majority of Tunisian men from the northwest also left their wives and families in Tunisia.

25. Keyder's and Aksu-Koc's conclusion is based on the Turkish census data of 1974 and 1975; see pp. 24–25.

26. See Ian Seccombe, "Labour Migration and the Transformation of a Village Economy: A Case Study from North-West Jordan," in Richard Lawless, editor, *The Middle East Village: Changing Economic and Social Relations,* Croom-Helm, 1987.

27. See Charles B. Keely and Basem Saket, "Jordanian Migrant Workers in the Arab Region: A Case Study of Consequences for Labor," *The Middle East Journal,* Vol. 38, No. 4, Autumn 1984, p. 689.

28. Abadan-Unat, p. 360.

29. See Keyder and Aksu-Koc, Chapter Three and Abadan-Unat, pp. 334–35 for details.

30. Keyder and Aksu-Koc, p. 48.

31. Keyder and Aksu-Koc, p. 50.

32. Keyder and Aksu-Koc, p. 119.

33. Ethos is the emotional tone, character, and quality of a people's life; its moral and aesthetic style and mood.

34. See Keyder and Aksu-Koc, p. 128.

APPENDIX

TABLE 2.1 • *Years of Initial Departure to Arabia*

Year	No. of Workers		Year	No. of Workers
1959	1		1973	1
1960	1		1974	7
1961	2		1975	11
1962	0		1976	12
1963	1		1977	19
1964	3		1978	9
1965	1		1979	3
1966	0		1980	5
1967	0		1981	8
1968	0		1982	2
1969	0		1983	11
1970	1		1984	2
1971	1		1985	0
1972	2			

TABLE 2.2 • *Occupations in Arabia*

Occupation	Year 1979	Year 1986	Occupation	Year 1979	Year 1986
Teacher	7	12	Typist	2	
University Registrar		1	Photographer	1	
Educational Administrator		1	Airport Lighting Specialist	1	1
Principal, Junior High School	1	1	Foreman	2	
Clerks[1]	7	1	Electrician	1	
Soldiers[2]	1	8	Surveyor	3	3
Managers[3]	1	8	Haberdasher		1
Accountants	1	4	Restaurant Owner		1
Pathologist, Health Department		1	Wholesale Food Merchant		1
			Mason	5	
Nurse	2	1	Auto Mechanic	3	2
Anesthesiologist, Health Department		1	Plasterer[4]	2	2
			Carpenter	1	
Doctor	1	1	Waiter (Restaurant)	1	1
Engineer, Civil	1	1	Worker (Construction Co.)	1	2
Translator	1	4	Driver	2 (truck)	2
Assistant Public Relations Officer		1	Bull-Dozer Driver[4]		1
Telephone Operator	3	2	Oil-Rig Driller	1	1

1. Clerks include one employed in the University of Riyadh, one employed in the Ministry of Justice, and one working for a prince in Abu Dhabi. Note too, the proliferation of white collar specializations in 1986 compared to 1979, e.g., the additions of a health department pathologist, an anesthesiologist, an assistant public relations officer, a wholesale food merchant and a personal supervisor.
2. The label "soldier" obscures the variety of specializations, including an anesthesiologist, an intelligence officer and a signal corps specialist.
3. The managers include the sales manager of Winston Cigarettes, the newspaper circulation manager in Jidda, two newspaper distribution managers, one in the Gulf and one in Tabuk, the manager of a construction company and the commercial affairs manager of a conglomerate controlling travel and duty-free shops in Riyadh and Jidda.
4. Both the plasterer and the bull-dozer driver are independent contractors.

TABLE 2.3 • *Locations of Places Migrants Have Worked in Arabia**

	Year	
Locations	1979	1986
NORTHERN BORDER TOTALS:	1	9**
Hafar al-Batin		2
'Ar'ar	1	2
Qaryat al-Ulya		1
Tabuk		4
INLAND OASIS TOTALS:	14	17
Al-Jauf	3	1
Ha'il		1
Al-Medina	1	4
Al-Ayn	10	11
RED SEA TOTALS:	4	6
Al-Kur (Wajh)		1
Lith		1
Jidda	4	4
GULF TOTALS:	14	15
UPPER GULF: Kuwait City	2	1
MIDDLE GULF:	9	7
Dammam	5	2
Dhahran	4	
Abqaiq		1
Bahrain		3
Khobar		1
LOWER GULF:	3	10**
Abu Dhabi (City)	1	2
Dubai		1
Sharjah		4
Al-Fujayrah		1
Sohar		1
Oman	2	
Ras al-Khaimah		1
YEMEN BORDER TOTALS:	3	8**
Abha	2	5
Jizan		2
San'a	1	
Khamis Mushait		1
CAPITAL: Riyadh	12	14

* Since some migrants worked in more than one place, the totals exceed the number of migrants.
** Significant increases from 1979 to 1986.

TABLE 2.4 • *Countries in Which Arabian Migrants Worked*

	Number of Migrants Year	
Country	1979	1986
Saudi Arabia	36	38
Abu Dhabi	11	15
Kuwait	2	1
Oman	2	1
Yemen	1	
Shariqa		4
Bahrain		3
Dubai		1
Ra's al-Khayma		1

TABLE 2.5 • *Age of Migrants in Arabia*

	Year	
Age Range	1979	1986
15–20	0	0
21–25	8	1
26–30	17	14
31–35	13	22
36–40	3	11
41–45	6	7
46–50	2	6
51+	2	5

TABLE 2.6 • *Sex of Migrants, Marital Status, Location of Spouses**

	Year	
Category	1979	1986
SEX:		
Male	51	58
Female	2	5
MARITAL STATUS:		
Married	42	61
Single	11	1
Betrothed	0	1
LOCATION OF SPOUSES:		
Spouses in Diaspora	10	29
Spouses in Jordan	33	34

* My information on location of spouses is incomplete.

TABLE 2.7 • *Number of Years Lived/Worked in Arabia*

Number of Years	Year	
Lived/Worked	1979	1986
Less than 1 year	0	0
1–3 years	28	14
4–6 years	20	16
7–9 years	3	23
10–12 years	1	8
13–15 years	0	4
16–18 years	0	2
19+ years	1	2

TABLE 2.8 • *Range of Incomes Earned in Arabia**

	Year	
Range of Incomes	1979	1986**
$600 or less monthly/$7,200 or less annually		6
$600–$900 monthly/$7,200–$10,800 annually	17	14
$900–$1,200 monthly/$10,800–$14,400 annually	10	10
$1,200–$1,500 monthly/$14,400–$18,400 annually	13	18
$1,500–$1,800 monthly/$18,400–$21,600 annually	4	5
$1,800+ monthly/$21,600+ annually	1	6

  * Information on income of migrants is incomplete.
** In 1986 for those for whom I had information.

    81% (42) made between $7,200–$10,000 per year
    63% (33) made between $10,000–$21,000 per year
    35% (18) made between $14,000–$18,000 per year

TABLE 2.9 • *Interpersonal Relational Patterns in Arabia**

	Year	
Pattern of Relations	1979	1986
Close relations with brothers	7	4
Close relations with 1st cousins	0	5
Close relations with 2nd–5th cousins	0	0
Close relations with co-clansmen	4	2
Close relations with co-villagers	1	1
Close relations with co-Jordanians	0	7
Living with co-Arabs	1	1
Living with Europeans/Americans	1	1
Living without contact with any of above	0	2

* Obviously my data here is incomplete for both years. My Participant
  observation in Kufr al-ma over 30 years leads me to infer that relationships
  with co-villagers and co-kinsmen, especially close kinsmen, is stronger than
  indicated in this table.

TABLE 2.10 • *Education of Migrants: 1986**

Number of Years Formal Schooling**	No. of Migrants
1–6 years	2
6–9 years	2
9–12 years	9
13–14 ears	17
15–16 years	6
17+ years	6

* Information on schooling of 1986 migrants is incomplete.

** To the best of my knowledge, no migrants from Kufr al-Ma are illiterate. My surmise, judging from the age of migrants, is that all migrants received some formal primary school education, which was compulsory in Jordan from the 1950s. Compulsory education was being enforced in the villages of Al-Kura sub-district by the middle 1950s.

TABLE 2.11 • *Frequency of Home Visits and Time: 1986**

Home-Visit Frequency	No. of Migrants
Once every two years	2
Once per year	8
Twice per year	2
Three times per year	2
Four times per year	0
More than four times per year	1

Time Spent on Visits	No. of Migrants
Less than one week	0
One week	1
One month	7
Two months	1
Three months	5
More than three months	0

* Information for most informants in the 1986 survey is lacking, but I have no reason for believing that the results of this convenience sample are misleading.

3

TWO SOJOURNERS ABROAD
MIGRATION FOR
HIGHER EDUCATION TO
ENGLAND AND GERMANY[1]

❧❧❧

One day in the winter of 1986 I was sitting in the men's guest room (*maḍafa*) of a large extended family, along with their relatives and neighbors, when a middle-aged man engaged me in conversation, indicating that he had just returned to Kufr al-Ma from Saudi Arabia where he was a traveling sales supervisor for Winston cigarettes!

My previous visit to the village in 1979 had alerted me to the growing importance of occupational mobility and transnational migration, and so I asked each of the seventeen men sitting around the guest room for their current occupation and place of work. Six were serving in the Jordanian army, two were teachers, two students, one a postal clerk, one a designer and interior decorator, and one a retired cultivator. Of the seventeen men only one, the postal clerk, worked in the village. The two teachers taught at junior colleges elsewhere in Jordan. One of the men serving his compulsory military service had just finished a BSc degree in agronomy from Peshawar University in Pakistan. The designer had a BA degree in fine arts from Cairo University. This was certainly a post-peasant society with a vengeance: not a single man worked the land and only one man ever had!

In the remainder of this chapter many of the interesting implications of transnational migration for rural communities in the Muslim world suggested above will be neglected. Rather, the description and analysis will concentrate on the implications of one type of migration, that for higher education, focusing particularly on those who have left the Arab world for education in northwestern Europe. This is perhaps the most radical type of migration in its implication for cultural change and the creation of a global society.

117

Unfortunately, the vast literature on international migration has been focused on labor migration and on the economic, demographic, and social implications of that migration on the economies and polities of sending and receiving countries.[2] Little attention has been paid to the interpersonal aspects of migration and the reactions of migrants to prolonged exposure to alien cultures and political systems and to radically different living circumstances. Even less attention has been paid to international migration for education. Eickelman and Piscatori's (1990) *Muslim Travelers: Pilgrimage, Migration, and the Religious Imagination* discusses migration mainly in terms of the quest for and the realization of religious identity. It points out that the institutions of *hajj* (annual pilgrimage to Mecca) and *hijrah* (the religious obligation of Muslims to migrate and simultaneously break ties, distance oneself from evil, and form new bonds of religious brotherhood) have institutionalized migration. In addition, the Quran and the Traditions of the Prophet have urged the quest for knowledge abroad, and Muslim scholars widely pursued knowledge peripatetically in the medieval world.[3]

However, in the modern Middle East the 1973 oil-pricing revolution triggered a quantum leap in transnational migration in which the pursuit of higher education played an important role, albeit in a completely different context: the pursuit of secular education to gain professional skills in a postmodern world in which national borders were being breached and multicultural societies established, willy-nilly, within national borders.[4]

The two case studies of Jordanian migrants described below begin to fill this gap in the literature, first and foremost, by focusing on the experiences of migrants and the humanistic implications of their quest for higher education abroad; and second, by exploring the degree to which, counterintuitively, the quest for secular education to gain professional skills continues to have religious dimensions. In addition, the chapter calls attention to the specific multicultural contexts in which migrants abroad seek to, alternatively or simultaneously, engage in important processes of accommodation, acculturation, assimilation, and reinterpretation or rejection of the particular traditions of the host societies and cultures into which they are plunged. Finally, it briefly evaluates the usefulness of concepts such as acculturation by refining them, and suggests the usefulness of others such as compartmentalization, preadaptation, encapsulation, the vicarious quest for identity, "living on the border," and "the constantly shifting center."

Two Students, Two Countries, Two Accommodations of Traditions[5]

Two students, one to Germany to study medicine, and one to Egypt to study Islamic law and subsequently to England to study linguistics, illustrate the possibilities of "acculturation, "assimilation," and "living on the border," three processes of sociocultural transformation to be explored below.[6] The young men, hence referred to as Ali and Yusuf, spent considerable periods abroad: Ali, fifteen years in Germany, and Yusuf, five years in Egypt and nine years in England.[7] They will be discussed in the order in which they left Jordan, Ali in 1963 and Yusuf in 1967.[8]

Assimilation and the Preservation of Religious Identity in Germany

Ali arrived at the University of Erlangen in West Germany in 1963. He spent his first year studying German and his second taking a premedical curriculum. He passed his medical exams in 1971, and thereafter specialized in surgery. From 1972 to 1980 he practised medicine in West Germany while pursuing his specialized studies.

In 1970, at the urging of a Lebanese fellow-student who had just married a Lebanese girl from Beirut, he went to Lebanon to visit the latter's family—she had an eligible unmarried sister. He went from Beirut to Jordan and returned with his father, who went with him to make the formal request of marriage. In 1970 he returned to Germany with his wife. Four of his five children were born there.

In 1980 he received a certificate of advanced medical learning from the head of hospital (*chef arzt*) and returned to Jordan, opening a medical practice in the regional capital of Irbid. The German head of hospital where he had practised medicine invited him to stay on permanently, telling him that he would deal with any bureaucracy involved: "You can do it all [practise all aspects of medicine] whether you're Arab or not." Ali turned down the offer.

He said in an interview that he had never contemplated marrying a German woman: "If I marry a German woman, I must stay (in Germany); if I brought her to Jordan it would be difficult for her." To understand his decisions to marry an Arab Muslim and to return to Jordan to practise his profession, it is necessary to note the circumstances of his early student life abroad and the views he developed of Germans and German culture. For seven years before his marriage he lived with German families as a lodger in their homes. When I asked him to describe his social relations in this period, he replied that he developed close relations with these families. They brought him out of his room every day to watch television; they brought cakes and coffee to his room during his late evening study hours; they washed his clothes; on weekends they took him with them on visits. He noted that Germans were energetic: they always went on hikes and for rides in the car; they always took an annual vacation outside Germany. All of this he viewed in a positive way.

He viewed university life and his professional work in German hospitals in an even more favorable light. He said that in these hospitals the patient was cared for to an extraordinary degree; medical care was extremely efficient—time was dear for Germans and they put it to good use—all lab tests were returned within three days; the patient was always matched with the appropriate care by a qualified specialist. He was impressed by the human concern demonstrated by the medical system: all persons were treated regardless of expense; no favoritism was shown to Germans; the chief physician treated each patient like a member of his family. None of the pejorative terms commonly used in the United States to describe a system of "socialized medicine" or a "welfare state" were found in his vocabulary.

But he also described what he viewed as the negative aspect of German family and social life. "After eighteen the child is independent and can marry whom she wishes [without receiving a parent's consent]. Both the husband and wife work, and this leads to problems," he said. Both men and women drank too much. I asked him, "Did you drink?" He replied, "You know what kind of family I have," referring to the piety of his father. He observed that the German father returned home after work and sat down in front of the television and watched whatever he preferred without considering the wishes of the other members of the family, behavior he considered egotistical. He noted that if two people quarreled in the street no one interfered; if they acted at all, they called the police. For him these behaviors clearly indicated a lack of human concern.

Ali's comments about German family life were not simply that. They had significance for a general worldview and way of life that was considered to be religiously appropriate, as became clear when I asked him at the end of the interview, "What is the importance of religion in Germany?" He replied that it was of little importance there. He elaborated, "In Germany they say, 'Religion is for the church not the office.'" He said that a German came to Jordan and went back to Germany and gave a lecture and said, "If you want to see a social (collective) life go to Jordan; if you want to see religion, go to the Middle East."

Ali was clearly a person with a drive to succeed who practised deferred gratification over a long period. He said he did not interact with Arab students in Germany (who proliferated in the 1970s) or enter into any of their organizations because it took up too much time. He said that for every grade of "excellent" in a subject, he paid reduced fees at the university.

I asked Ali whether, while abroad, he ever visited another student from Kufr al-Ma who had also gone to West Germany to study medicine or vice-versa. He replied that he had never visited him. "He has another mentality," he said. "He wants to drink and have his girlfriends. We have nothing in common. Every day he was with another girl. One day he came and visited me; he was with his secretary (i.e., his girlfriend)." To understand Ali's evaluation of German life and other aspects of his worldview it is necessary to understand his relationship with his father.[9]

Ali's father had finished primary school in the adjoining subdistrict center (which then was only a village) and junior high school in the market town of Irbid before World War II, an accomplishment that was unusual for a village boy at the time. After graduation he worked for three years as an Arabic-English translator on the oil pipeline that linked Kirkuk in Iraq with Haifa in Palestine, before serving as a customs officer in Amman for two years. He then married, opened a village shop, and engaged in small-time grain trading between Palestine and Transjordan for ten years prior to joining the Islamic court as clerk-usher in the nearby village and subdistrict center of Deir Abu Said between 1954 and 1963. From 1963, the year his son left for Germany, until 1970, the year of his death, he managed his own orchard—which he had planted—in the Jordan Valley on land he had purchased with a bank loan. He also engaged in various entrepreneurial activities including buying a tractor and a stonecutter, and, with his second son sometimes driving, renting them out to the area's cultivators. He used the profits to finance his son's medical education and to modernize his home, replacing its stone and adobe walls with cement and adding a colorful painted grille around each window.

Two things stand out about Ali's father and his family background. One is the aura of religious piety in which he grew up. The name of the family, itself, *al-shari'a*, literally, "the way," meaning the Muslim way and, more specifically, the whole code of Islamic law and ethics, was attached to the family as a result of their reputation for piety and religious learning. The other thing is Ali's father's early contact with foreigners through his position as translator and customs officer and his commitment to material modernization and pioneering entrepreneurship (that was only moderately successful)—no one else in the subdistrict had introduced tractors or stonecutters at the time. Notable is the fact that in 1965 Ali's father borrowed money from the bank at interest to finance his investments. Five years before, securing bank loans with interest (referred to as *riba'* or usury by some Muslim scholars) had been a subject of debate in the village, and the consensus, particularly among the pious village elders, was against it.

In a certain sense Ali's student life and professional training were a vicarious realization of his father's goals and feelings. His father had not been able to continue his schooling because his own father had died and his uncles could not afford to continue his education in town. Ali's father had loved his mother, who suffered for many years because doctors were not able to diagnose or treat the illness which led to her early demise. In Ali's words, "My father always had it in his mind—it was his dream—that I should be a doctor; he planted the idea in my mind."

I asked Ali, "What is your view of your childhood in the village?" He replied, "What my children have I didn't have. It was a good memory because my father was good to me." In another interview I asked him the same question and he replied, "I didn't have everything I wanted, but I had everything I needed. My father monitored my activities, even when I became adult." He said that his younger brothers got away with a lot more. Ali continued, "There was mutual love between us," and he proceeded to give a trivial but nevertheless important example: "I hated smoking; my father was a constant smoker; if I came in and sat down my father would throw away his cigarette." I asked Ali, "Did your father send letters to you in Germany?" He replied, "Yes, the most important advice he gave me was, 'I enjoin you to fear God (be pious, *ittaqa allah*).'" Ali said that his father meant by that that he should abstain from alcohol and running around with women. He said that the result (of his father's advice) was that he finished his medical studies in a relatively short period of time. I asked Ali, as I did all migrants, what he thought of tribal law in Jordan, what he thought of Jordanian television, and what he thought of the unemployment problem in Jordan. His answers reveal his orientation towards modernization and modernity and the relationship of that orientation to Islam, government, and the socioeconomic order.[10]

He said that tribal law had both positive and negative sides. The positive side was that it helped solve problems. But it was "backwards, a thing of the last century. The king wants it," he said. I replied, "The people came and asked the king for it," (i.e., to restore tribal law after it had been abolished by government edict). He replied, "The people, the Pasha—if the (civil) law is not here, they have no value. It is difficult now; if two pupils twelve years old, kick one another and one gets a fracture, they [the perpetrator's patrilineal relatives] must go to his family and pay. I'm not completely against tribal law, but if they have a problem they take not what we have now [i.e., civil law]. Life [today] is not the same as forty years ago."[11]

In answer to my question, "What is the impact of television in Jordan?" he replied:

> Television in Jordan has a broad effect: [first] in science, everybody can see the civilized countries. They [Jordanians] try to say we have and others haven't. They know now how strong they [western countries] are. Second, they now see that they themselves have nothing and other countries have so much. Third, when you see how beautiful other countries are, and they [Jordanians] don't have [that beauty]. Fourth, in medicine we know now that we have not: we have no hospitals [in the district] like *madinat ḥusayn* [the so-called king's hospital in Amman]. Not everyone can go there—only people in the army [and their families]. People became jealous of the West as a result of television. Television [also] brings out the negative side of western civilization: how to be a drunkard; for girls, sometimes we see in film what girls do with their [boy] friends; it [sexual immorality] is against our religion. Films in Germany are native [to Germany], but our films are from abroad. Too many people see what is on the television screen as real. They see the same forty people every week [on the television screen].

Finally, in answer to my question, "What is the solution to the unemployment problem in Jordan?" he replied:

> "Providing jobs for all the graduates of institutes and universities." He said that the Germans distinguished many different occupational statuses: *hilfsarbeiter* (assistant worker), *arbeiter* (worker), specialist, master, and engineer. "Jordan," he said, "only had the worker on the one hand and the engineer on the other and nothing in between." He continued, "In Germany everything is according to certificates; the shoemaker and the barber have to have certificates." He said that the educational institutions in Jordan only gave academic degrees. He said that there was only one trade school in Jordan.

"What is the solution to the problem of unemployment?" I asked again. "The solution," he replied "was the founding of trade schools in all specialties," i.e., the country needed technical experts. I said, "But aren't there lots of people who can fix televisions?" He replied, "They don't really know how to fix televisions; they just fool around with them."

Ali is perhaps the most "modern" of the two migrants measured in terms of his commitment to science and its application to societal improvement and individual welfare, particularly in the field of medicine where he observed and clearly vouched for the superior German hospitals, personal medical care, and match of specializations with individual needs. In his evaluation of the impact of television, Ali seemed to equate progress with science and applied science, and in his earlier remarks on the German health system, with the effective use of time.

He also stipulated what he believed to be a superior German socioeconomic system in his view that the unemployment problem in Jordan would be solved by the differentiation of roles and the hierarchicalization of society: differential training and distribution of knowledge and skills and formalization of hierarchy by the issuing of certificates at all levels. This commitment to the development of a necessarily differentiated and hierarchical society is interesting because in his earlier remark on German religious attitudes he repudiated the notion that religion should be separated out from office (i.e., government and business).

In some respects Ali's views of how television represented the civilized West as opposed, by direct implication, to uncivilized Jordan, as well as his earlier story of how the German traveler found religion and collective life in the Middle East (and not in Germany) is a caricature of Western "orientalist" discourse. In this respect Ali not only acculturated to German ways but assimilated them in the sense of identifying with their underlying values: effective use of time, material modernization, hierarchicalization, human concern for the individual, and a universalistic system of rewards that did not recognize ethnic differences—though his remarks about the German hospital director's offer indicated that his ethnic identity had not in fact been cancelled. His qualified response regarding his view of tribal law clearly relegated it low on the ladder of progress, a vestigial institution—now that civil law and state order had emerged. All this seems to indicate that Ali went to Europe and returned as a cognitive retread.

But his remarks about television and civilization end with a return to a persistent theme in the interview: western civilization is deeply flawed by its immorality—familial, sexual, and alcoholic. This theme emerged as an explanation of his refusal to visit the other son of the village in Germany, it colored his description of German family life, and it was dramatized in his father's admonition in his letter.

More significant than either the strictly sexual or the alcoholic dimension is the broader immorality of German familial/societal life: When both husband and wife work, and the daughter is free at age eighteen (as opposed to monitored, as Ali was by his father into adulthood) to make her own decisions, then, truly, the world has been turned topsy-turvy, and an ordered and religious way of life cannot be lived. Thus Ali married within his own religion and ethnic tradition and decided to return to Jordan to practise medicine, even after he had an opportunity to do otherwise in a society that he admired for its educational system, quest for knowledge, application of science, efficiency, and fairness. How could a Muslim lead a meaningful life in a society where religion was barred from office?

The theme of the survival of the religious person in the secular society emerges again, but with a very different twist and involving a different father-son relationship with Yusuf, the migrant to England.

Preadaptation and Controlled Acculturation in Cairo, London, and Leeds

Yusuf's early peripatetic schooling was a forerunner and perhaps preadapter to his later peripatetic higher education. He attended primary school in three different locations in Jordan, only the first two years being in Kufr al-Ma; for the remainder of his early schooling he attended junior high school in the northern border town of Ramtha where his father was a customs officer; his first two years of high school were spent in Deir Abu Said, the subdistrict center adjoining Kufr al-Ma because his father was now posted there as a clerk of civil court; while his final year of high school was spent on the West Bank in Nablus at a special school oriented toward preparing students for the religious university of Al-Azhar in Cairo, which he entered in 1967.

I asked Yusuf about his relationship with students of other nationalities in Cairo and with Egyptians. He said that for the first three months he had lived in university dormitories together with Africans, Malaysians, and Indonesians, but had moved out thereafter and lived in a series of flats by himself. He found the quarters at the university very crowded with ten to fifteen students in one block, and the food was unsavory. I asked whether he maintained contact with students whom he had met there. He replied that he still has contact with one Bahraini who is the director of an Islamic college and with a Tanzanian who is a teacher in Ajman. He also has a few Egyptian friends who teach at Cairo University and with whom he stayed on a return visit in 1985. His closest ties from his student days were with the four Jordanians who went with him to Al-Azhar from the religious high school in Nablus; he still corresponds with all of them.

I asked Yusuf whether he got to know many Egyptians. He replied, "The nature of the Egyptian is open. If any stranger comes, they say, 'Hello, where are you from?' You get to know them." They would go out together and engage in reciprocal hospitality. I asked Yusuf what he thought of Egyptian character. He replied, "Very open. They are excellent; they laugh; they are helpful; greedy; some take you for a friend in their own interest; they like money very much; they will introduce you to the whole family; they don't feel shame (as Jordanians do) about introducing you to their women." "What did you feel about this contact with women?" I asked. He replied, "I liked it. It was very nice. That was my impression when I was there."

Yusuf's view of Egyptian (specifically Cairene) character changed somewhat in 1985 when he returned for a visit:

> They are still open. Greedy. They like you for your money. [But] morals are [now] degraded. A man gives you his word, but it isn't worth anything. If you ask him to do anything he won't do it unless for money. For instance, filling out papers—he won't do it unless it's for money.... When I was there in 1967 you'd go to any shop, they'd give you the right answer [if you asked directions]; now he'll tell you, "I don't know."

I asked Yusuf, "Are Jordanians discriminated against in Egypt?" He replied, "Jordanians are all considered Arabs along with Syrians, Palestinians, Iraqis. The Egyptians don't distinguish between them unless there are political problems (i.e., government-to-government problems). There were none at the time."

I asked Yusuf what he thought of Egyptian women. He said that they were very poor, and "When a foreign man came they said, 'Hi' and treated him as if he were the prime minister of his country."

I asked Yusuf how he evaluated his education at Al-Azhar. He replied, "The only weakness is that they didn't have foreign languages—no French or English; the other aspects were excellent." While at Al-Azhar he focused his studies on the Quran, the Traditions of the Prophet, Islamic law (*fiqh*), principles of Islamic law (*uṣul al-fiqh*), *qanun* which, he said, included study of both Islamic and civil law and their interrelationship including the operation of the mixed courts, Arabic language and literature, oratory, and Islamic history. He specialized in the Shafa'i school of law because, he said, most Jordanians follow that school. I asked him whether memorization was an important part of his studies. He replied that he had memorized one-third of the Quran, a few Traditions of the Prophet on each subject, and verses of both pre- and post-Islamic poetry. I asked him how he evaluated his teachers at Al-Azhar. He said that the lecturers were advanced in years, and so they were good, i.e., advanced in knowledge; they were all Egyptians. He said that you could go to the professor's house, and he would help you if you had any difficulties; he did not go because he had none, but others went.

He received a BA degree in religious law and state law (*al-shari'a wa al-qanun*) from Al-Azhar in 1971. His father wanted him to return home, obtain a position in the bureaucracy (nearly all teaching positions in Jordan are government positions), start earning money—since he had two younger brothers who needed educating—and settle down. Yusuf insisted on continuing his education. His father acquiesced to another year at Al-Azhar studying educational psychology (and thereby enhancing his teaching credentials); he received his diploma (MA degree) in 1972 and began exploring the opportunities of continuing his studies abroad. One Egyptian professor suggested studying in England. So even though his father adamantly opposed such a move, and without his knowledge or consent, Yusuf, as he said:

I packed my suitcase. I had a thousand dollars in my pocket. At that time I thought I'd stay one or two years working and learning the language [before continuing Islamic studies in England]. When I went in 1972 I didn't know anybody in England, not a single person.

After his departure for England, Yusuf's father cut off communication and correspondence with him for over two years.

Yusuf's Islamic education at Al-Azhar had a direct impact on the pattern of relationships he formed both with other Muslims in England and with the English both in London and Leeds. When he arrived in Leeds in 1976 he found a very active Muslim religious movement dominated by Pakistanis called, *al-da'wa,* "The Mission (of spreading Islam)." There Muslims centered their activities around a mosque in Leeds and engaged in periodic missionary campaigns of religious intensification. As Yusuf described it:

They continually urged me to go on their campaigns which involved sleeping in the mosque and then going and preaching in various people's houses, saying, "Peace be upon you. Are you a Muslim? Do you pray? Why not? Do you fast? Why not?" Then they called the person, or (if he resisted) dragged him to the mosque for prayer.

Because Yusuf did not drink and because he did not date girls, they regarded him as one of them. More important, Yusuf quickly became well-known in the local Muslim, mainly Pakistani, community in Leeds when it was discovered that he was a graduate of Al-Azhar and that he recited the Quran better than they did. They made him the prayer-leader (*imam*) of the mosque, and so he assumed a position of leadership in the diaspora as the *shaykh* of the local mosque, which involved not only leading congregational worship on Friday but also giving children lessons in the Quran.

In Leeds he interacted mainly with Pakistanis since, he said, "The English are very conservative and difficult to get to know." He stopped participating actively in the *da'wa* movement, however, because he had to pursue his studies and also, by implication, because he did not particularly care for their overly aggressive missionary style. During this time he became acquainted with the works of the leading Pakistani fundamentalist scholar, Abu A'la al-Ma'dudi, and he mentioned that one of the Pakistani students at Leeds and a friend of his, who was one of Ma'dudi's students, later became Minister of Education in Pakistan.

Yusuf's other arena of activity and social network at Leeds was the university. Whereas he characterized his four years in London, 1972–76, as "mixing with people from society," he characterized his life in Leeds as "weekdays at the university and weekends at the mosque." He said that he mixed with students at the university, and they exchanged hospitality. He elaborated, "Student life was very good, but it was entirely different outside [the university gates]. The [English] students themselves criticized society. The man in the street, you can't get to know; only the university students; they are middle class; one was the son of a knight."

I asked him if he got to know English girls at the university. He said that there was a common room where all the students met, but he never got to know any of the girls. When I pressed him further about his impression of English women he replied:

> You have to get to know the English girl. Arab students are influenced by films. Most of my extra time—because I was a *shaykh* (religious scholar)—I spent in the mosque or at religio-social get-togethers. I spent my extra time in the library—I had a special room at the library.

Then he returned to the previous subject of English women, commenting, "It is not difficult to grab a girl [i.e., to get a date]. [But] she has no intention of going with you to your house—just because she went [with you] for tea or coffee."

He established an important and satisfying relationship with his mentor at the university, the head of the Semitics department who was a Yemeni Jew with whom he still corresponds. It was he, in fact, who convinced him to switch from general Islamic and Middle Eastern studies to research in linguistics: Yusuf's PhD dissertation in descriptive linguistics was on the Arabic dialects of the Jordan Valley. It was this professor who wanted him to stay as a permanent member of the linguistics department at Leeds when he graduated. He said that he still corresponded with him.

When I asked Yusuf if he had ever thought of settling in England, he mentioned the fact that the head of the department had asked him to stay and elaborated, "No, they [the English] look on you as second class. I hated it. I had the opportunity of staying—working there as a teacher. The head of the department even now wants me to come and teach as Lecturer." He said that he would consider going to England as a Visiting Professor [only]. His final statement on the subject was telling:

> You're not inside the academic community all the time. You have to go home and have neighbors, and if you don't have good neighbours you won't be happy.

Yusuf had nothing but praise for the English university system. He much preferred the concentration on one course the whole year with an end-of-the-year exam to the American semester and credit system, proliferating shorter courses and electives (which was the system prevailing at the university in Jordan where he taught). But in Leeds if his weekly round oscillated between the space of the university and the space of the mosque, there was a third and encompassing space—the world—which compromised both of these confined and limited spaces and made assimilation impossible.

To understand the relationships he had with the English and the attitudes he developed towards them we must return to the circumstances of his arrival in London and his four-year experience there. On his first Friday in London he asked someone at the hotel at which he was staying where the nearest mosque was, and he was directed to the Islamic Cultural Center, where he met a graduate of Al-Azhar who worked as the *imam* of the mosque. Initially, he worked at this Center as a clerk and spent four months studying English. For the following three years he taught Arabic in various English grammar schools and also gave private lessons, all of these positions having been arranged through the Islamic Cultural Center. During these four years in London he lived happily. He saved money for his future education (the forty pounds a week he earned was more than enough to cover his frugal living expenses) and he bought a car.

I asked him, "How did you spend your leisure time in London?" He said that he traveled. I asked, "Where did you go?" He replied, "Anywhere. I would get in my car and go. I know England more than Jordan. I went everywhere. I stayed overnight in only a few places. I went by myself. I liked to go by myself." When I asked him why he didn't go with others, he replied, "Why would I want to do that?" He said it was a bother to take other people because then you had to take care of them if something happened to them. He clearly enjoyed the freedom of his new life. I asked him whether he attended films or plays in London. He replied that he had no time to attend films or plays: he went to work at eight in the morning and did not return to his flat till eight in the evening. It must be noted again that he was saving money in order to apply to a graduate program at an English university (he applied to six and Leeds was the first to admit him). During this entire period in London he lived in single-room flats where he cooked his own meals; otherwise he ate at the Islamic Center. He said that he never got to know any of the people living in the adjoining flats. Whereas in Leeds he developed a largely Pakistani social network outside the university, in London he said, "I mixed with people from society"; by this he meant Pakistanis and Indians as well as English Muslims at the Islamic Cultural Center.

Just as they were to be later in Leeds, his social relations in London were highly structured and limited in part as a result of his Muslim higher education and his work, in part as a result of his economic circumstances as an aspiring and later struggling student, and in part as a result of his own staunchly independent (some would consider him a loner), goal-oriented, and highly curious (with respect to foreigners and other cultures) character. What is unusual about his relationships with the English he met in London in the course of his work is that although as a foreigner from a part of the world formerly dominated by them and presumably, therefore, inferior in status, as a teacher he was always in a superordinate position. Over a four-year period he did not get to know any of the students he taught in London or their families outside of class, although a few of the adults he tutored invited him for tea or dinner. His egalitarian relationships with English persons in Leeds and his superordinate relationships with them in London almost always took place within restricted and formal milieus: the university in Leeds and the grammar school classroom in London. The one important egalitarian relationship he had with English people "in the world" was in a religious (also specific) context. Regularly, once a year, he attended a three-day "Conference of Concordance" between Muslims and Christians. He much enjoyed interacting with others at these ecumenical meetings, and through them he developed a friendship with a certain vicar with whom he exchanged hospitality.

Otherwise, in the world, and his own perception must have been strengthened by his interactions with South Asians in London (whom he resembled to some degree, being short and rather dark in complexion), he viewed the English as "conservative." Yusuf elaborated, "They didn't mix with foreigners, and especially blacks; they avoided anyone not from Europe. They showed jealousy to Arabs because [they believed] they were all rich."

When I asked Yusuf what he liked best about the English, he replied that he liked the system of government and social order:

> Everyone had the right to do what he likes. Oppose what he likes. The government, talking without any opposition. I like it. The way they [the English] behave—from the social side the way they treat people. From the religious side, if anybody argues about religion, they say "Okay, do what you like." They forced everybody riding motor bikes to have a motor helmet. The Sikhs said they couldn't take their turbans off, so the government allowed it [i.e., to keep them on].

He liked the English countryside and the fact that "any kind of food in the world is available, eastern and western." He even said he liked the conservatism of the English, but then added: "But not the way they closed themselves for themselves. If they had a bit of openness it would be better."

When I asked Yusuf what he didn't like about the English he said:

> Some of them are arrogant. Everyone from the Middle East is [considered] riff-raff. [They think to themselves], "We colonized them." From the inside you can't open up people's hearts [but] they dislike the Arabs: for one thing they are Muslims; the second thing, they are rich. But if he [the Englishman] has an interest involved [e.g., a company doing business in the Middle East] they make propaganda for the Arabs.

At the end of the interview Yusuf looked at me directly and asked, "Why do they [Westerners] dislike Muslims?"

His life in London, then, gave him strong and favorable views of English democracy and religious pluralism, although that democracy and pluralism were flawed by racial bigotry, ethnic arrogance, and a certain insularity of mind and social relations. But the life he led in London, like the life he led in Leeds, was encapsulated, encapsulated even at an imaginative level since he never frequented films or plays.

His relations with and attitudes toward English women and his views of relations between the sexes provide further insight into the mode of acculturation he pursued in England. His exposure to Egyptian women, in a way, preadapted him to social life in England: For the first time (unlike the rural tribal society of Jordan from which he came) in Egypt he was able to interact with unrelated women in a free and open manner within the contexts of visits to the families of his friends and classmates. He enjoyed that contact. I asked him during the interview, "What do you think of relationships between the sexes in England?" He said that they did not strike him as extraordinary. He had gone to Germany for two months during the summer of 1970 to work—he secured a job with a shipping company numbering cartons and putting them on a truck. When I asked him whether he made much money, he replied that he had gone to Germany "just to see the life," not to make money, so that when he came to England the (public) kissing and hugging (among couples) did not strike him as unusual. One chap below his (German) flat was always drunk, he said, and often invited him in. While in Germany he worked alongside other Arabs at the company, roomed with two Jordanians, and later toured Europe by car with them. Thus, by the time he arrived in England Yusuf already had two preadaptive experiences in Egypt and Germany.

I asked Yusuf whether he ever thought of marrying an English girl. His father had told me earlier that Yusuf had written a letter to him toward the end of his stay suggesting the possibility of marriage.[12] He replied to my question:

> I wrote to my father just proposing the idea of marrying an [English] girl. I had no one in particular in mind. I just proposed the idea. First, I never considered it seriously because I wouldn't be able to find a virgin girl, or I would have to go deep into the countryside there. A vicar told me once that [in one country district] once you get engaged to a girl you have to marry her; you couldn't go out with her privately; you could only sit around with her family.

I interjected, "You must have been entertaining the notion of marriage or you wouldn't have written the letter." He replied that he wrote the letter because of the possibility of his staying in England, saying, "You know how it is when you're abroad—many ideas go through your mind."

Yusuf's actual relations with English men and women were an interesting mixture of freedom and self-control. He greeted girls on the university campus and spoke with them in the common room (something of which the members of the *da'wa* movement disapproved), but he never dated them. He attended mixed gatherings and even parties hosted by the ecumenical conference, but he never drank, and if drinking became blatant, he left. The vicar, knowing this, never offered alcohol to guests when Yusuf was present. He was not disturbed by husbands and wives kissing in public, regarding it as a "custom." However, he strictly observed the Muslim food taboos on pork and alcohol. Yusuf's behavior was an interesting example of "controlled acculturation": picking and choosing what to borrow and avoiding those acts/beliefs that undermined one's basic values.[13] Yusuf's ability to control acculturation in this fashion was facilitated by his superordinate status (as teacher and *imam*) among both Muslims and non-Muslims in specific spaces of work and study; by the varied preadaptive experiences he had; as well as by the considerable travel he undertook within England.

The latter two experiences inside and outside the country allowed him to develop some empathy, tolerance, and a certain sense of cultural relativity toward many of the alien customs he witnessed, whether in Egypt, Germany, or Great Britain.

Be this as it may, in the end his evaluation of English life and his own worldview was religious. Indeed, it was in England that his Muslim identity was shaped and sharpened. I have no evidence that he was particularly pious as a youth. He was sent to a religious high school in Nablus in part because the high school he attended in Transjordan had no science program, and he could not qualify for other professions such as medicine or engineering. But he returned to Jordan in 1980 with a clipped beard, an indicator of his religious identity and commitment.

His condemnatory religious evaluation of English life emerged at the end of a conversation we had about his reaction to English ways, including public kissing and the consumption of alcohol. He said, referring to English life in general:

> They are all working for themselves [i.e., without God's plan]. Women work because they [the family] can't afford [to buy] a telephone [otherwise]. Women would like to stay home; over 60% don't want to work. After 18 they leave the house. A girl, a secretary, living at home, gives 10 pounds a week as rent to her father! She saw the check I received from my father for 1,000 pounds. [After Yusuf entered the university his father relented and began sending him money as did his elder brother who was a doctor in Saudi Arabia.] She was astonished [by that]. Sometimes the parents even rent the house to the son!

Despite his observation of free, public cross-sex relationships over a long period of time including women's active participation in the workforce, Yusuf regarded English women as essentially conservative. They had been profaned and family life undermined by a topsy-turvy secular world where women had to work, children paid rent to their parents, and God's plan for the family and society had been abandoned.

In Jordan I observed that Yusuf's interpersonal relationships reflected the same kind of controlled acculturation that had organized his life abroad. At the time of interview he was a professor at the university. He invited me to his house in town for dinner along with a mutual friend from the village who was also his patrilineal kinsman and a small shopkeeper in the same town. Earlier I had met his Jordanian wife and his wife's sister in his university office, and he introduced them to me effusively, and we had a very pleasant conversation. Weeks later, I spent several hours at his home, and I never saw his wife, who prepared the meal in the kitchen and did not join us either during or after dinner. Both Yusuf and his patrilineal kinsman excused themselves after the meal to perform their evening prayers.

Yusuf's pattern of interpersonal and gender relationships in Jordan, then, reflected exactly the same kind of compartmentalization as in England: the university was a space of relatively free interaction between the sexes; the world and the home were not.[14]

Yusuf's view of the role of religion and, in particular, of an Islamic society and how best it could be achieved, and the state, and the proper relationship of Muslims to it emerged in our conversation that evening. We discussed the question of whether various Muslim groups favored setting up an Islamic state, and, if so, whether it should be done now or in the future. I said that the Egyptian Islamic movement, *takfir wa al-hijra* (expiation for sins and emigration) wanted to postpone setting up an Islamic society until after an Islamic state was established. Yusuf immediately quoted a Tradition of the Prophet: *inna allaha yaz'aju bi sultanan ma la yaz'aju bil qur'anan,* literally, "God can arouse through the ruler what cannot be stirred up through the Quran." He said that God gave the sultan more (coercive) power than the Quran (to move people). If the king wanted an Islamic state, he would bring it into being whether the people liked it or not. He continued:

> The Quran is with everybody, but they don't practice it. People want to marry, educate their sons or make money for themselves, and they will pray. But when you tell them to practice the Quran they will find it difficult. They won't take their money out of the bank (as some Muslim interpretations of the Quran require since banks take interest, i.e., usury) because they are receiving interest (i.e., monetary benefit).

Regarding the movement, *takfir wal al-hijra,* Yusuf viewed it as against civilization, against everything western, e.g., radios, televisions, and telephones. Yusuf continued, "Today (in Jordan) everyone who opposes the government is popular. Preachers who preach against the government get a following, and then the government tries to co-opt them by giving them a position in the government. People then turn away from them (and the government knows this) unless they refuse government appointment (he knew of only one man who did so) in which case they become even more popular." He continued, "There are two ways of getting Islamic society: by government edict (or) gradually by means of education. The rector of the university could say, 'Everyone shall wear modest dress or not be allowed inside university gates.' (Similarly) there are two faces of the Muslim Brotherhood: Let the government do what it wants or appear to hold their view; privately work against particular individuals who are not considered Muslim, through private meetings, scouts, karati. The *da'wa* (movement) move around (like this) as missionaries."

Yusuf's view of the Islamic society and how to work for it, of the state, and of the Islamic movements was complex. On the one hand he was strongly attached to establishing religion by authoritarian mechanisms; on the other hand he realized the advantages of gradualism and religious intensification through piecemeal missionary activity. On the one hand he understood the need for dissimulation and accommodation with the non-Muslim state and criticized blatant attempts by fundamentalists to curry favor with the populace by attacking it. On the other hand, he clearly admired the one preacher who defied the state and refused government appointment. He understood that the basic problem for Islamic movements was the human inclination to pursue the instrumental and status-enhancing goals accepted by society—marriage, money, office—rather than practice the norms laid down by the inimitable Quran.

How these views can be, are or will be accommodated to the views he evolved in England is entirely unclear. In Leeds, although he generally approved of the *da'wa* movement and played a key role in their mosque activities, he looked askance at their aggressive methods, and I have no evidence that he ever participated in their missionary campaigns in Jordan. He rejected out of hand the idea that technological modernization should be rejected as corrupt and un-Muslim. But he accepted the fundamentalist view of the corruption of the body social in the West and the necessity of preserving a moral as well as a gender division of labor in accord with Islamic norms. How he has, is, or will reconcile his admiration for English democracy and religious pluralism with his admiration for an authoritarian solution by God's action through rulers is entirely unclear. With such an accommodation or lack of it, the course of Jordanian society and other Muslim societies in Asia, Africa, and not least, Europe will depend.

Notes

1. This chapter is a different version of an essay first published in Akbar Ahmed and Hastings Donnan, editors, *Islam, Globalization and Modernity,* Routledge, London, 1994.
2. See Eades (1987) and Kearny (1986) for reviews of the anthropological and social scientific literature on migration.
3. See the articles by Masud and Gellens in Eickelman and Piscatori on these points.
4. In this book I am not using the term, "multicultural" in the context of the social, educational, and political movement in the United States in the late twentieth century: the movement that rejects assimilation of ethnic minorities as a model, rejects oppression of minority cultures through discrimination and prejudice, and seeks the economic and political integration of minorities without the reduction of their cultures to uniformity (see Nathan Glazer, *We Are All Multiculturalists,* 1997 for details). Rather, I am using it in a broader general sense to indicate the fact that cultural and ethnic difference has become a global fact and the local context with which the overwhelming majority of transnational migrants, wherever they settle, must contend.
5. For a detailed definition, description, and analysis of the accommodation of traditions see Antoun, "On the Modesty of Women in Arab Muslim Villages" 1968.
6. Acculturation is the process of borrowing cultural traits without a change in the basic values of the borrowing individual. Assimilation is the process of absorption of cultural traits along with their underlying values, thereby entailing a change of individual identity. 'Living on the border' is the psychological state and sociocultural process of linking seemingly separate sociocultural worlds in a conjoint and viable mode of livelihood and style of life. It often (but not necessarily) involves sporadic geographical mobility. The works on which I draw for the development of these concepts are Teske and Nelson 1974 and Rouse 1991. I have also found Fischer's and Abedi's discussion of 'the crazy space between exile and migration' useful and provocative (1990: particularly, ch. 5).
7. The two students, then returned, were interviewed in Jordan in 1986.

8. A third young man, Zayd, illustrates the same processes of accommodation, acculturation, assimilation, and the reinterpretation of traditions as well as the concepts of encapsulation, compartmentalization, and particularly, "living on the border, but in a very different milieu, the United States. See chapter 6 below for details.

9. For a capsule portrait of Ali's father see Antoun, *Low-Key Politics: Local-Level Leadership and Change in the Middle East,* 1979: 220–21; and for his leadership attributes see table 7, 214–15.

10. I am using the terms modernity and modernization in Nash's sense: "Modernity is the social, cultural and psychological framework which facilitates the application of tested knowledge to all phases and branches of production. Modernization is the process of transformation toward the establishment and institutionalization of the framework of modernity." See Nash 1977.

11. In the 1980s a movement occurred, mainly inspired by urban intellectuals, to abolish tribal law in Jordan. Tribal law stipulated collective responsibility both on the perpetrator's and the victim's side for individual crimes of honor (like murder, automobile homicide, rape, burglary, elopement, and other violations of the modesty code), the appointment of tribal arbitrators (from among the elders of the region), and the imposition of truce periods, banishment, and eventual reconciliation (*sulha*). In Jordan the process of tribal law moved in tandem with the prosecution of crimes of honor by civil and criminal courts, and the outcomes of the two processes were intertwined. The system of tribal law was officially abolished by edict in the 1980s, but soon thereafter reinstated by the king after petitions for reinstatement were brought by tribal representatives, particularly from southern Jordan.

12. For a portrait of Yusuf's father see Antoun 1979: 221–23 and table 7, 214–15.

13. See Teske and Nelson 1974 for a discussion of the concept of antagonistic acculturation.

14. In Jordan Yusuf also sharply compartmentalized his urban and his village relations. He rarely visited the village; and when he did so, he visited only his parents and in-laws whom he considered enlightened. Villagers had taken umbrage when he did not invite them to his wedding in town.

4
MIGRANTS TO GREECE LIVING IN THE WORLD, INTEGRATION, AND MAINTAINING ETHNIC IDENTITY

The overwhelming majority of international migrants for higher education (to fourteen different countries) have returned to Jordan to live and work after finishing their degrees. The two exceptions to this pattern are those who went to study in Greece and the United States. It is the former group of nine young men who left Jordan for Greece between 1968 and 1983 that is the subject of this chapter. Greece and the United States are also the only countries where a substantial number of Jordanians married foreign women. This chapter will focus on the key mechanisms, cultural, social, economic, and political, that have allowed Jordanian integration into Greek society: the Greek consanguine family,[1] the dowry custom, the custom of courtship, the Greek ethos (toward the stranger and living in the world),[2] the status match of rural Greeks and tribal Jordanians, Greek government policy toward immigrants, and the concentration of migrants around Aristoteles University and the city of Salonika in northern Greece. This chapter will also focus on the mechanisms that have allowed and facilitated the maintenance of ethnic identity by Jordanians, e.g., impression management, dissimulation (*taqiyya*), "passing," symbolic ethnicity, the Muslim structure of marriage, and the "reidentification by alters."

In some respects the Greek case represents the opposite end of the continuum illustrated by the Jordanian migrants reaching abroad through the army discussed in chapter one. These latter migrants were, for the most part, encapsulated within army base, classroom, barracks, and army club; when they ventured off base it was for very brief periods, meeting members of host societies in confined settings such as bars, sporting events, cinemas, and hospitals. None of the army migrants indicated a desire to return to the U.S.A. as permanent immigrants, though one indicated a desire to return to work.

The students in Greece, on the other hand, were all young single men who spent long periods, between four and fourteen years, attaining a degree, in a relatively open society where they studied with Greeks, worked with them, dated and courted Greek women, married and raised children, and in a number of cases were absorbed into the consanguine families of their wives.

The Jordanian migrant's experience in Greece shares certain attributes with migrants for education to the United States (particularly illustrated by Zayd, the Jordanian migrant to Houston discussed in chapter six), e.g., long-term studying, working, dating, courtship, and marriage. But the United States did not prove to be as open and receptive a society for Jordanian students as did Greece. Zayd and other Jordanians in Texas did not have many—in the former's case any—American male friends, though they had many "girlfriends"; they did not interact much with Americans outside of work/study contexts; they were rarely invited to American homes; dating and courtship were conducted, for the most part, in isolation from the families of the concerned women, the families being in any case conjugal rather than consanguine; two of the five marriages to Americans ended in divorce; and three of the five men definitely indicated a desire to return to Jordan after working for a period in the United States.[3]

The migrant experience in Greece also shares similarities with the Jordanian migrant experience, also for education, in Pakistan. A pioneering student went to Pakistan in 1972 and started a chain migration process, similar to that in Greece, that drew over twenty students from Kufr al-Ma. Initially, the migration, like that to Greece, was long-term (at least five years) and regionally focused around a single university, Fazelabad, in the city of Lyallpur in the Punjab. A significant factor in directing migration to both Greece and Pakistan was its relative cheapness (though education in Pakistan was cheaper than in Greece, a fact that might have accounted for more than twice the number of students going to Pakistan as Greece). Pakistan was favored by Jordanians for two other reasons: it was Muslim and the language of instruction was English, the foreign language commonly taught in Jordanian secondary schools. Greece, on the other hand, had a completely different language which had to be mastered before substantive study could proceed; a six-month to one-year study of Greek was initially required. And Greece had a completely different religious tradition, Greek Orthodoxy, with a long history of animosity toward two Muslim polities: Ottoman Turkey, which ruled Greece for almost four hundred years, and modern Turkey, which had overrun much of the Greek population of Cyprus (in 1974) while most of the Jordanian migrants were studying in Greece. And yet six of the nine students who went to Greece married Greek women and four of the nine have settled permanently in Greece. Only one of twenty-seven students married a Pakistani, and none have stayed in Pakistan.

The counterintuitive conclusion that Jordanian Arab Muslims of tribal back-ground would find most congenial a society and a culture with which they shared neither language nor religion (Greece) rather than one with which they shared religion (Pakistan) or others that had a substantially higher standard of living and a reputation for being the open democratic societies, par excellence (the United States and Great Britain), is one that will be explained below.

Students in Greece

The nine students who went to Greece to pursue higher education are repre-sented in Table 4.1 following, together with their pertinent social structural and migration attributes. They are listed in the order in which they went to Greece.

Migrant One was quickly followed by Two and Three, and they were followed two years later by Four, Five, and Six, and by Seven a year later. The Greek case is clearly one of chain migration in which students often returned to Jordan dur-ing the summer vacation, spread the word, and urged their peers among their rel-atives and friends to join them. Two and Five are brothers as are Three and Nine. Seven is Three's uncle, and they roomed together for three years. One and Seven are related by marriage. The last column in Table 4.1 demonstrates that all mi-grants except the first in his initial year (who lived alone, i.e., without ethnic com-rades), lived in the diaspora in the presence of other kinsmen from the village, most with members of the same clan, and many in the presence of close cousins, first cousins, or brothers. As chapter two on migration to Arabia indicated, the presence of sons of the village in the same city is not a necessary indication of fre-quent interaction. In Greece, however, the occupational designation of "stu-dent," studying the same subject (medicine or engineering), and at the same institution, Aristoteles University, produced a great deal of interaction and mu-tual support, particularly in early years, among sons of the village. Most of the migration group, then, clustered in time, space, educational institution, and in kinship connection. Only Eight[4] and Five spent any part of their student career outside of Salonika, the former a year and the latter six months in Athens.

Several of these migrants were exposed to other countries and cultures before they came to Greece or after they left it, or both. One took his Greek wife to the Emirate of Sharja on the Persian Gulf after he obtained a job there as an engi-neer. Two had spent a year at the Arab University in Beirut studying Arabic be-fore he came to Greece. Seven had spent a year at Baghdad University in Iraq studying geography before entering Aristoteles University in Salonika. Eight had spent two months in Ankara, Turkey intending to study medicine when the de-teriorating political situation resulted in student demonstrations, urban violence, and the sporadic closing of the universities, at which point he returned to Jordan and secured the army scholarship to study medicine in Greece. Six departed for

TABLE 4.1 • Migrants to Greece*

Migrant Number	Age*	Marital Status	Children	Spouse's Nationality	Place Studied	Time Spent There	Year Began	Specialization	Yrs Studied Beyond HS	Date Finished	Highest Degree	Scholarship	Current Occupation Place	Income	Work Location	Army Service	Frequency of Visits to Jordan	Kinship Patterns
1	43 (1993)	M	Yes	Greek	Salonika Aristoteles University	14 yrs	1968	Engineering	14	1982	BE	No	Restauranter		Salonika	No		1st yr Alone; 2nd yr co-Villagers; 4th yr, Affines
2	42 (1993)	M	Yes 2	Greek	Salonkia Aristoteles	7 yrs	1969	Medicine General Practitioner	7	1976	MD	No	Doctor	$90,000	Salonika	No	1 yr (6 yrs)	Clansmen
3	40	M		Greek	Salonika Aristoteles	7 yrs	1969	Medicine General Practitioner	7	1976	MD	No	Doctor		Salonika	No		1st yr Villagers; 3rd yr Cousins
4	33	M	Yes 2	Greek	Salonika Aristoteles	7 yrs	1978	Medicine Gynecology & Obstetrics	7	1971	MD	No	Doctor	$10,056	Irbid Jordan	No		Clansmen
5	38 (1991)	M	Yes 1	American	Salonika, Athens Merchant Marine Academy	4 yrs	1971	Radio Navigation	4	1975	Captain's Certificate	No	Captain, Geodetic Ship	$37,000+	Gulf of Mexico	No	Once (every 2½ yrs)	Brothers
6	39	M	Yes	Jordanian KM	Salonika	2 mo	1971	Veterinary Medicine Pakistan	6	1976	VMD	No	Veterinarian, Dept of Agric	285 DM	Deir Abu Said Jordan	No		
7	37	M	No	Greek	Salonika Aristoteles	12 yrs	1972	Veterinary Medicine	11	1983	VMD	No	UE		Jordan	No		1st Cousin
8	27	M	Yes	Greek	Athens Univ 1 yr / Salonika Aristoteles 6 yr	7 yrs	1978	Medicine General Practitioner	7	1985	MD	Yes (8 yrs)	Doctor (Army Hospital)	$5,400	Jordan	Yes (20 yrs) commitment		Co-Villagers
9	33 (1998)	S	No	—	Salonika Aristoteles	10 yrs	1983	Engineering (Computer)	10	1989	BE	No	Engineer Al-Bait Univ. Jordan (1998)		Salonika	No		Brothers

*Unless otherwise specified, data collected including ages refers to 1986.

Pakistan after only two months in Greece because he found learning Greek a daunting task; in Pakistan the instruction was in English. Much later, after graduating from Fazelabad University in Pakistan, he studied at London University's Royal Veterinary College for a year. And Five, after joining the Greek merchant marine and sailing the three continents, went to the United States, where he married an American. He presently works as a captain on a geodetic ship in the Gulf of Mexico. Multinational and multicultural exposure is a general characteristic of migrant life whether through work, education, or the army, as the last three chapters have demonstrated. A frequent attribute of migrants to one country is that they have gone or will go to others, as is fitting in a postmodern global society in which national boundaries are frequently crisscrossed, local rootedness challenged, and national and ethnic identities complicated.

Occupationally, the migrants to Greece concentrated on the standard professions, medicine and engineering, whereas, for instance, those to Pakistan concentrated on English (5), food technology and nutrition (4), and animal husbandry (3) and those to the United States on business management. By the time Jordanian migrants began going in numbers to Pakistan and the United States, approximately ten years after the pioneer student went to Greece, the number of doctors and engineers in Jordan had increased to the extent that there was white-collar unemployment in those professions. Indeed, when interviewed in 1986, Seven, the veterinarian, after serving a two-year internship in the nutrition department in Jordan, was unemployed.

Significantly, only one student to Greece, Eight, served in the Jordanian army; he had received the army scholarship that required twenty years of medical service as an army officer on completion of studies; in 1986 he was working as a doctor in a Jordanian army hospital. The student track and the army track, then, tended to be mutually exclusive. This was not the case by the late 1970s and 1980s, when army regulations tightened and a number of graduates from Pakistani universities were required to serve a two-year enlistment on their return to Jordan.

Eight of the nine migrants are married. Six of them married Greek women with the first three to arrive remaining in Greece as permanent residents along with the last. Four, Seven, and Eight brought their Greek wives to Jordan after finishing their academic degrees, and two of the wives were living in Kufr al-Ma at the time interviews were conducted in 1986. All three were housewives at the time. In Greece, however, one had worked as a seamstress and another as an assistant surveyor while studying architecture at the university. Of the wives who remained in Greece, to my knowledge, only the wife of Two was working outside the home; she worked as a bookkeeper for a textile factory. Three of the men interviewed, Four, Seven, and Eight, stated that their wives had received a substantial dowry on marriage: land and a furnished apartment; a house; and 6,000 dinars (ci. $15,000). The significance of dowry for the integration of Jordanian men will be discussed below.

Finally, only one student, Six, was unable to adjust to Greek life, leaving after a two-month stay because of language difficulties. And only one, Seven, criticized Greek culture and society in the course of our conversations.

Analysis

We begin with a paradox. It is precisely in the country with substantial differences of religion and language, Greece, that the largest percentage of Jordanians chose to marry out of their ethnic group (6/8) and, subsequently, chose not to return to Jordan to live and work (4/8).[5] And it is precisely in the countries with the largest shared cultural content (of language, religion, and tribal custom), Saudi Arabia and the Arabian Gulf, that regular contact with the native population was most restricted. As chapter two indicated, Jordanians in Arabia lived in a segmented class and ethnic society where, with a few exceptions, regular contact with Saudis and other natives was lacking, whether in work, residence, or leisure. There were no marriages of Jordanians with either Saudis or residents of the Arabian Gulf. The only general exception to this encapsulation may be the case of the seven Jordanian students who went to study at Arabian universities.[6]

Again, counterintuitively, as documented in chapter two, Jordanians in Arabia were not exposed to a homogeneous physical, social, or cultural environment. On the contrary, some lived in highlands, some in the desert, some in oases; some in the oil fields, some in cosmopolitan Jidda, and some in puritanical Riyadh. They engaged in thirty-four different occupations, and had different community rhythms, different work/vacation rhythms, varied modes of finding jobs and contracting work, varied patterns of social interaction and cultural exposure (with Asians, Arabs—but not Arabians—Europeans, and North Americans), and varied attitudes toward the native Arabians, from ambivalent to critical to pragmatic.

Although language was a problem for migrant Six (who left Greece for Pakistan on account of it) and for migrant Four (who said he would choose to study elsewhere because of the difficulty of learning Greek, if he had to do it all over again); and religion was a problem for migrant Five, who broke off a serious relationship with a Greek woman on account of her father's religiosity, the remarkable fact is that Jordanians found Greece to be an open society where they studied, worked, and spent their leisure time with Greeks, courted and married their women, and acculturated to their society in a very successful manner.

Indeed, the Greek experience represents the opposite end of the interaction and acculturation continuum represented by migrants reaching abroad through the Jordanian army: the latter's short-term encapsulated stays in the western world in barracks, classrooms, and base clubs, or off base in discos, hospitals, and embassies, produced shock at the immodesty of western ways despite their admiration of that world's order, cleanliness, and honesty. Only one Jordanian soldier indicated a desire to return to the diaspora for the long term, but that was to obtain a green card (to work) and not to settle.

Many factors entered into this remarkable adaptation of Jordanians to Greek society. A demographic and geographic factor ought to be stressed at the outset. Unlike the workers who scattered all over the Arabian peninsula into diverse ecological and occupational niches and who ranged in age from twenty-six to fifty, the Jordanians who went to Greece were all young (in their twenties), all students, all single, and all located in the city of Salonika in northern Greece at the same university, studying, with one exception, the same or related subjects. This demographic, occupational, spatial, and institutional concentration provided mutual support in the first most difficult part of a long (usually seven years) process of study, work, and exposure to a foreign culture.

The conversations with the migrants mentioned above record a substantial positive reaction to Greek society and culture in its diverse aspects, a reaction that contrasts significantly with the frequently ambivalent reaction of Jordanian migrants to Arabia. In evaluating Greeks and their way of life, migrant Four said, "The Greek greets you and talks with you and offers cigarettes, and you can ask him questions." He continued, "The Greeks favor the Arabs. If you don't bring up their religion, they respect you." He had no difficulties with discrimination from students, bureaucrats, or professors. Five, who found religion a stumbling block to his integration into Greek society, nevertheless stated, "The Greeks, if you know them very well, they accept you, and they are a fun people." He continued, "I was treated like a Greek—not an Arab." He was referring here to his treatment by Greek sailors during his four years as an officer on Greek merchant ships. He enjoyed the company of Greek sailors, whom he found to be friendly, filled with a joy for life, similarly interested in exploring the world, and accepting of him—they gave him a Greek nickname, "Jordanus." This was by contrast to his later experience with American sailors, whom he found to be provincial, lacking in emotional depth, given to unpredictable mood swings, and prone to "carry their troubles with them on to the ship." Comparing Greeks to Americans after living eleven years in the U.S.A., he found Americans less friendly and reliable than Greeks, and after political crises such as the Gulf War, he feared discrimination from the former.

On being asked his opinion of Greeks, Eight said, "They were very good," and he continued, "The Greek favors the Greek, but if you are gentle, they treat you like one of them." On being asked what the difference was between Greece and Jordan, Two said, "All the circumstances (of life) differed. Life here (in Greece) is all freedom—more than Jordan, more than any Arab country." On his initial arrival, Greeks—ordinary people outside the university—helped him a lot: they lent him money and helped him find a house. This is not to say that Jordanians did not criticize aspects of Greek society and culture. Seven gave a negative view, citing the politicization of Greek universities, the absence of achievement motiva-

141

tion among the students, the decline of respect for elders (the son didn't respect the father), and the decline of religiosity. He regarded Greek life as being guided by the quest for pleasure—"a people that likes to enjoy themselves"—which, unlike his Jordanian peers, he interpreted negatively. But even Seven regarded certain aspects of Greek life positively: Greek food, the organization of the Greek home, the higher standard of living, the existence of the honor code in the Greek country-side (from where he selected his wife), the more positive role of Greek govern-ment in securing employment for its people, and the fact that the Greeks were "an eastern people," favoring boys over girls.

These dominantly positive views of Greek society reflected the Jordanian stu-dents' acculturation to and integration into Greek society. This acculturation and integration resulted in part from the openness of Greek society to foreign stu-dents, the mode and duration of student life, and the policies of the Greek gov-ernment and Greek universities. Students pursuing medical and engineering degrees engaged in a long-term quest that could not be concluded without con-siderable engagement with Greek society and culture. The Greek universities re-quired all foreign students to spend at the optimum, the first year, and at the minimum, the first six months learning Greek before they undertook their sub-stantive studies. Most students from Kufr al-Ma were forced to work to provide their own income to continue their studies. This engagement in work both lengthened the duration of their stay in Greece and brought them into contact with other Greeks in a situation where they had to understand the culture—they could not just be students within university gates. All students lived in the city of Salonika (and not in dormitories): coresidence with Greeks in the same rooming houses also accelerated acculturation: some Jordanian students met Greek women there, dated them, and in some instances married them. Other students roomed with Greeks, e.g., Four who roomed with a divorced Greek and his young child for five years. This continuous social intercourse with Greeks (though one must not overstress this point since many of the migrants from Kufr al-Ma roomed together the first few years) was facilitated by a particular aspect of the Greek ethos encouraged by the Mediterranean climate, the penchant for spending long evening leisure hours in public space: promenades in the streets and squares and dinner in restaurants and tavernas. The constant contact of young single men with Greeks within the neighborhood and in public spaces over a long period and in a society that lacked the ethnic stratification of the kind found in Arabia could not but result in acculturation to and positive attitudes to-ward Greek society and culture.

For certain Greek women there was an important consideration of status and subculture in their attraction to Jordanian men from Kufr al-Ma. Relatively poor working-class women of rural origins who aspired to middle-class status—exactly the kind of women to be found in rooming houses and in factories in Salonika—found aspiring professionals (doctors and engineers) a good marriage prospect. The tribal background of the Jordanian men and the rural background of Greek women, both of which engendered social conservatism, provided a basis for enduring courtship and marriage despite linguistic and religious differences. The Greek government's policy toward migrants—again contrasting specifically with Saudi Arabia and the Gulf—also facilitated such bonding since foreign students were allowed to work in Greece, to contract civil marriages, and to receive citizenship.

All of the factors mentioned above resulted in the fact that Jordanian students pursuing higher education in Greece, despite the substantial difference in language and religion, did not suffer from the status incongruence to which migrants to Arabia were subjected. That is, they were not ranked down on some attributes and up on others relative to the native population. Whereas Jordanian migrants in Arabia were mainly white-collar workers with professional and semiprofessional skills (e.g., translators, clerks, teachers, business managers, health specialists, noncommissioned officers) and, thereby, higher in status than most Saudis and Abu Dhabians, they were much lower in income than the natives who in addition to their salaries received all the social welfare benefits of the oil state. In addition, Jordanians were barred from marriage with native women, *de facto,* and barred from citizenship, *de jure.* Jordanian students in Greece, on the other hand, had, as aspiring professionals, a high status that was not negated by their ethnic origin or, for most, by their religion.

Jordanian men did not simply acculturate to Greek life, however. They assimilated to it, if by assimilation is meant acceptance of the values that underlay the culture. Yet none of the migrants, to my knowledge, lost their ethnic identity.[7] They remained consciously Arab, Jordanian, and Muslim. This fact poses a problem and raises a question. How could Jordanians assimilate and yet maintain their ethnic identity? That is, how can one accept many of the most important values of another culture and yet reject its society as a reference group?

As pointed out in chapter three, acculturation in northwest Europe was usually controlled and selective. Likewise, assimilation in Greece was also incomplete and selective. Ali, the migrant to Germany, assimilated the German values of effective use of time (efficiency), material modernization, hierarchicalization of the workforce, concern for the individual, a universalistic system of rewards, and the application of science. Yet he rejected the sexual, alcoholic, and familial immorality of German society: it was wrong for young men and women to date, for both husbands and wives to work outside the home, and for daughters to leave home at eighteen. Ali segregated his home life (he had married a Muslim woman of Arab origin) from his work life (one guided by German values). Migrant Two also assimilated large areas of Greek culture, but they were different from those assimilated by Ali. He came to appreciate certain aspects of the sexual freedom of Greek society, including the zest for courtship, the fun-loving style-of-life, the television portrayals of love and family life, and the integrity of the conjugal family. When I asked him about how his prospective wife's parents reacted when they learned that their daughter was to be married by a Muslim shaykh, he replied, "This was an agreement between me and my wife." And when I asked him if he was happy with his life in Greece, he replied, "I like to live at home (with my wife and children). I'm happy there." That was where he spent his leisure time. Indeed, Two had made the two-worker conjugal family the basis of his marriage. Unlike Ali, he had assimilated Greek values relating to the mode of family life as well as work life. But he too had maintained his ethnic identity intact: he had insisted on a Muslim marriage contract, required his wife and daughter to observe a modesty code in their dress, and, referring to his wife, said, "I tried to change her mind from Greek to Arab," while saying about himself, "My thinking is Arab right up to the present." His wife agreed with this assessment, saying, "He is a true Arab."

Forging a New Identity in the Diaspora

Describing the process as one of partial assimilation and maintenance of ethnic identity does not, however, reveal its true character. What migrant Two as well as Ali in Germany, Yusuf in England, and Zayd in the U.S.A. were doing was forging a new identity in the diaspora. Yusuf did this particularly with respect to the religious component of his identity as he took on the roles of Azharite, *imam,* follower of Ma'dudi, rejecter of the Da'wa (organization's *modus operandi*), and participant in ecumenical dialogues with Christians in England. And Zayd did it with respect to his wider understanding of the Arab and Jordanian component of his identity as he interacted with non-Arab women and Arab (but non-Jordanian, i.e., Lebanese, Syrian, and Arabian) men in and out of school during his first five years in Houston; and with other Jordanians and Palestinians in leisure activities in his later years there.

It is this process of forging a new identity in the diaspora in Greece that I now wish to examine in greater detail. We must first distinguish between the various specific processes/mechanisms utilized in forging that identity, some of which, such as preadaptation, controlled acculturation, and becoming modern, have already been discussed above; and others that will now become the subject of discussion: symbolic ethnicity, impression management, the affirmation of a core identity, the reinterpretation of tradition, and the absorption into the Greek consanguine family.

Naming is one symbolic process that assumed great importance. How this worked is illustrated by migrants Two and Five. Although Two's children were registered under their official Muslim name, i.e., a peculiar version of their father's patrilineal pedigree, they were known in school by their mother's father's name, i.e., by a Greek name.[8] Migrant Two and his wife had discussed the matter of naming and had decided to facilitate the acceptance of their children in Greek rural society by giving them Greek first names. Two had addressed his daughter when she was small by an Arabic name, *nur,* but he eventually dropped the usage. The utilization of names to "pass" in Greek society is an example of what an anthropologist, Berreman, has referred to as impression management and a sociologist, Goffmann, as "the presentation of self in everyday life."[9] Both Berreman and Goffmann assume that life is a performance and that men and women are the actors in it. Here, naming is also an aspect of symbolic ethnicity used to facilitate integration and assimilation. In the Middle East a special term, *taqiyya* ("dissimulation") is used to indicate the use of names, dress, ritual, and etiquette on the part of a religious minority to emulate the identity of the majority group and, thereby, gain acceptance and pass (unnoticed). Dissimulation and impression management also allow the individual to maintain their ethnic identity, and in the Middle East, even to practice the rituals that affirm it in secret.[10]

Another peculiar aspect of symbolic ethnicity involving naming was described by Five when he discussed his relations with Greek sailors. He said, "I was the only officer on the ship who was a foreigner. They never called me 'Muhammad'; they called me, 'Jordanus' (from the Greek name for the Jordan River)." By this mechanism, which I term, "reidentification by alter," the host group, here Greek sailors, create a fictive name that allows the group to treat ego as a friend, one of them, i.e., a Christian, rather than as a Muslim (for most Greeks, a Turk), i.e., a potential enemy. Two, the doctor, was also reidentified by his patients in a variant version of this process. When I asked him, "Do people at your clinic realize that you are a foreigner?" he replied that they didn't ask unless they heard his name. They would realize from his accent that he wasn't from mainland Greece; they inferred that he was a *bandi*, i.e., one of the Greeks who had come over from Turkey in the mass exchange of populations in the first quarter of the century, one who had maintained the peculiar accent of Greeks from Turkey. Here, again, supplied with culturally dissonant information, his accent, the audience reidentifies the subject to explain (away) the incongruity. In the United States, on the other hand, Five said that he wanted his children to have Arab and Muslim names, to which his wife was amenable, as long as they could have a Christmas tree and an Easter basket. Migrants Four and Seven, living in Jordan with Greek wives, reflected a third pattern: they gave their sons an Arab name and their daughters a Greek name. This choice squares with the patrilineal rule of descent in Jordan by which the father gives his name/identity to his children whereas the mother does not. Assuming the daughter marries a Jordanian Muslim in Jordan, her children would also be Jordanians and Muslims.

Symbolic ethnicity, as documented by Alba for second and third generation American immigrant populations, assumes importance only after substantial erosion of ethnic cultural content has taken place.[11] This certainly seems to be the case of Two, who does not pray or fast, who has not taught his children Arabic, and who occasionally drinks retsina and eats pork. On entering his house in a town in northern Greece, I was struck by the scene of the Ka'aba in Mecca, framed and prominently displayed on the wall between the salon and the main staircase leading to the second floor. As the interview/conversation with him recorded above, demonstrated, he was insistent on his wife and daughter observing what he considered a modest dress code. Both the modest dress code and the Ka'aba scene were indicators of symbolic ethnicity.

But the focus on dress and a modesty code for men and women, particularly for women, is more than an aspect of symbolic ethnicity. In rural Jordan and many other Arab Muslim peasant societies the modesty of women has been and remains a cultural focus.[12] The modesty of women is a core component of rural Jordanian ethnic identity, and not simply a vestigial symbolic element. Two insists on proper clothing for his daughter and wife; as he said, "They should not be naked." He restricted the hours when his daughter could be out of the house, and when she left, she had to leave a note stating where she was and when she would be back. He did not allow his wife to date other men while he was courting her, and he never dated other women in Greece before or after marriage, and he never thought of doing so. When I asked him whether he ever considered marrying a girl who was in the university, he said that he didn't because he had the idea that they dated other men before, i.e., they were impure. And when I asked him what the differences between rural and urban life were, he said that both rural and urban Jordanians had the same values, mentioning four; two of the four related to the importance of children and their care. Two's core identity clearly focused on the life and proper behavior of the conjugal family, the observance of the modesty code between the sexes, and his legal Muslim marriage.

Four has two married sisters with children who were both working outside the home as teachers, and a third sister in junior college studying accounting, and he has two nieces, one of whom is a nurse and the other a midwife. Both he and his father had encouraged them to pursue higher education. But his concluding comment with regard to married women was, "They all have problems; it is preferable if they stay in the house: (the husband would) find the food hot, the clothes clean, and the children looked after." Two had previously stated that part of his initial problem of adjustment in Greece, particularly with respect to his courtship, was that "in Jordan I was used to a system in which women stayed in the house." Four, like Ali in Germany, credited his father with instilling in him certain behavioral dispositions that stuck: he brought him up not to smoke or gamble, and he kept him in the house at night rather than permitting him to participate in frivolous activities like attending wedding celebrations; on the other hand, he placed responsibility on him when he was young.

If Two's core identity focused on his commitment to/happiness with his conjugal family, and his adherence to a modesty code, and Four's core identity on a sexual division of labor between spouses that defined the wife's place as in the home, a view endorsed by both Seven and Eight, and on norms inculcated by his father in childhood; Seven's identity focused on a particular view of his childhood past, in a Jordanian village when "the hearts of the people were good" and "there was no deception or duplicity"; "when the whole patrilineage used to meet

146

in the house of the elder," mutual visiting was frequent, and people were not too tired (from work and commuting) to pay attention to one another.[13] For Seven, the present represented the breakdown of kinship ties, both extended and close, the deterioration of morals, the proliferation of problems, the decline of sociability (sitting at home in front of TV rather than in the clan guest house) and the loss of the simple life.[14] It is against this rather (but not completely) idyllic view of a Jordanian "folk" society that one must interpret his comments about contemporary Greek society. Seven's account of life in Greece today as opposed to life in the Jordanian village of his birth and rearing might have come out of Robert Redfield's (1930s) dichotomous description of the folk-urban continuum in Yucatan contrasting harmonious collective life and religious piety with "disorganization," "secularization," and individualization.[15] Seven speaks of the politicization of the young, their absorption in pleasure, the lack of respect for the aged, the decline of religious piety, and the preponderance of sexual mingling, i.e., all the problems associated with freedom.

Although both migrants Two and Five were modernizers in many respects as observed below, and both had married foreign women, neither had "dated" in the commonly understood sense of the term. Two had never dated women; he had courted his wife. Five had also courted his wife over three continents, and he had gone out regularly with one Greek woman during his stay in Greece, to the point where they had considered marriage. But he always went out with her as part of a larger group of friends. It was an "eastern" and not a "western" mode of sociability. Moreover, he never consumed alcohol in Greece. He would go into bars with his fellow sailors in various ports, sit a few minutes and leave. This behavior could be construed as impression management, on the one hand, and symbolic ethnicity on the other, but it was more than that. Five's refusal to drink, like Four's refusal to gamble and smoke (particularly significant in view of the latter's indulging in alcohol), were indicators of his core Muslim identity, as was his special trip to Jordan to have the village shaykh draw up a Muslim contract of marriage shortly after he had a civil marriage in the United States.

The development of a core identity in the diaspora in all cases involved components of modernity. I have already defined modernity as the social, cultural, and psychological framework that facilitates the application of tested knowledge to all phases of production. Since all the migrants to Greece were students of higher education seeking professional training and expertise, there can be no doubt that within their disciplinary fields they supported the search for knowledge and a positive stance toward innovation. Their career goals explicitly assumed and anticipated the fostering of social mobility, and an achievement ethic that channeled rewards to high performers as well as universalistic standards of expertise, recruitment, and promotion, and programmed decision-making, implying planning and discipline. Modernity also involved the constant seeking of technological and educational self-improvement. Underlying many of these values is the assumption of individual freedom and responsibility.

Since his graduation from the merchant marine academy in Greece, Five had been engaged in a constant upgrading of his professional skills that allowed him to gain promotion from first mate to captain, and thence to captain of ships of increasingly larger tonnage. He gave as one reason that he could not return to Jordan to live and work the fact that he would not be covered by medical insurance there, indicating a commitment to programmed decision-making. Four is thinking of returning to Greece to finish his subspecialty training in medicine, and he is planning to participate in a family planning training course in Tunis. When I asked Four how the unemployment problem could be solved in Jordan, he replied that he had persuaded one brother to study computers, another to study English, and a sister to develop secretarial and administrative skills, i.e., the solution was acquiring semiprofessional and practical skills through education. And he emphasized as a positive fact that he had been brought up in a mobile in-the-world urban environment that valued education as a result of his father's occupational mobility and his mother's (cosmopolitan) Palestinian background.

Seven decried the absence of achievement motivation in Greek students as well as the lack of freedom in his childhood for the young man to express his views in front of the elders, though he was clearly of two minds about the implications of freedom as his remarks about social mixing indicate. His critical view of the Jordanian army emphasized the waste of manpower that impacted negatively on useful employment and production, and the inegalitarian character of army rewards vis-à-vis the rest of society. Eight affirmed the superiority of town and city life over village life by declaring that the town had more educational opportunities.

The most consistent evidence of the commitment to aspects of modernity was in the attitudes toward birth control and tribal law. All migrants endorsed family planning (though not birth control, which they construed as the definitive cutting off of procreation by an operation on the male or female, except Four, who endorsed tubal ligation). Family planning was necessary "to fulfill (one's) obligation to children" (Eight); "how will my brother with fourteen children get along on a salary of 100 dinars a month" (migrant Seven); "if they practice family planning they can live better; if I have two or three children I can do everything for them" (Two). Not only was planning accentuated here, but also concern for the conjugal (and not the consanguine) family, the basis of a modern mobile society.

The attitudes toward tribal law in Jordan were complex and sometimes ambivalent. But the answers of all migrants reflected aspects of modernity: Two asked, "Why should the head of the clan, a simple man, why should he have the law in his own hands?" This statement dismissed those without a formal education from potential leadership in a modern society. Four stated, "It (tribal law) is not good.... It is based on traditions (*taqalid*). A hundred years ago they rode in camels, today in planes." His evolutionary view equates tribal law with obsolescent vestigial institutions. Seven stated, "If there was civil law, the Rihaba (a neighboring village) case (of honor) would have ended with one dead not three." He went on to say that only Jordan (among Arab countries) had tribal law. Here tribal law is associated with revenge and excessive violence as opposed to civil law, associated with order and the state. Five said about tribal law, "The older people get together and make a decision, but not in the right way. The killers get away." His view accentuates the cancellation of individual responsibility and the dominance of a gerontocracy, both negations of important aspects of modernity. Migrant Eight made this commitment to individual responsibility and the repudiation of collective responsibility even more explicit when he said, "Why should I have to flee to another area on account of some ass (i.e., a kinsman who has perpetrated a crime on a member of another group)?"

However, the process of forging a new identity is not a matter of choosing between certain core values and behaviors associated with one's early upbringing on the one hand and the values and behaviors associated with modernity in the diaspora on the other. The process of forging a new identity is part of a constant process of reinterpretation of tradition. Handler and Linnekin (1984) have pointed out that there is no such thing as "tradition," if what is meant is an unchanging body of custom passed on from one generation to the next. New meaning is constantly being given to custom by the addition or subtraction or rearrangement of cultural content, e.g., changes in dress or the design or redesign of a national flag over time. But even when the custom/cultural content is exactly the same form from one generation to the next, its meaning cannot be the same because the context is very different. The American flag raised on the Pacific island of Iwo Jima by the marines during World War II has a much different meaning for many Americans than the American flags burned by war protesters during the Vietnam War or the flag that was the subject of the Supreme Court decision on flag-burning just prior to the Gulf War.

Attempts are always made to reinterpret tradition/custom in light of the new circumstances, and usually, to claim the legitimacy of an unchanging tradition at the same time. Thus, when asked about family planning, migrant Seven said, "Religion ordains the ordering of progeny (*tansik al-nasl*). One should plan for three or four children only." This view was not propounded in the village twenty-five years before, when I began doing my field work, a time when neither overpopulation nor unemployment were major problems. Reinterpretation of tradition on this issue has proceeded along the lines of distinguishing between birth control (*tahdid al-nasl*), which is almost universally decried (i.e., an operation that definitively cuts off future procreation) as being against God's law, and family planning (i.e., the use of various, but not all, contraceptive methods), which is construed as being part of a rational person's behavior in the modern world. When I asked Two about how he reconciled the considerable difference in religious traditions between him and his wife, part of his answer was that neither he nor his wife were regular practicing devotees of their religions. But then he added, "God is one, whether in Jordan or in Greece." This statement constituted a universalistic reinterpretation of religious theology. But it in no way diminished Two's strong identity as a Muslim.

The modesty code involving the code of honor and dress, among other things, is a fundamental aspect of the mores of rural Jordan and a continuing cultural focus. In 1960 for both sexes it required covering the head as well as the limbs, legs to the ankles, arms to the wrist. By 1986 the requirement of headcovering was modified for men (though most men above the age of forty continued to wear headdress in public) but not for women. For both sexes covering the limbs was still required. Village women who were now schoolteachers in district schools now wore long dresses secured to the neck and reaching below the knee with limbs still covered. I have referred above to migrant Two's concern for the modesty of his wife and daughter in the diaspora. In my conversations with him, he said, regarding his wife during their courtship, "I tried to change her mind from Greek to Arab," and he gave as an example, dress: "Shorts were okay (for his wife and daughter) but not short shorts (i.e., only slacks or shorts to the knee)." Slacks are absolutely forbidden in Kufr al-Ma (those who wear them in the city are suspected of being prostitutes), and the idea of wearing shorts there is unimaginable. Two's reinterpretation of the Jordanian modesty code was quite substantial, to say the least, but, for him, it was the preservation of a tradition.

When I asked Four about appropriate occupations for unmarried women, he began by observing that in Greece women drove buses; then he listed the names of suitable occupations for women: teaching, working in a company, in a bank, seamstress, hairdressing. He concluded by exclaiming, "(But) in Jordan driving a bus, after two hundred years!" The key difference between allowed and disallowed occupations seems to reflect three principles. The allowed occupations are, first, those in which sex segregation is practiced, e.g., teaching, hairdressing. Second, those in which monitoring of women's activities by a responsible authority can take place, e.g., in a bank or company. Third, all the allowed occupations are either respectable white-collar occupations, e.g., bank clerk or company secretary, or occupations that can be carried on in the home, e.g., seamstress. The bus driving job was disqualified on all counts: continual sexual mixing rather than segregation prevailed; the bus driver could not be monitored since the bus was moving from place to place; and bus driving was not a responsible, safe, white-collar occupation. On the contrary, it exposed women in a continuous way to a constantly changing mix of strangers.

The reinterpretation of tradition with regard to women's work/study outside the community, an unimaginable possibility for village women when I began my research in Kufr al-Ma in 1959, has now moved to allow it in a variety of occupations provided the woman's honor is safeguarded at work/school either by sex segregation or restriction of cross-sex interaction or by close monitoring of her activity by responsible parties. As pointed out in the preceding chapters, sometimes the generation of fathers is more flexible in its reinterpretation of the honor/modesty code than the generation of sons. That is, not all reinterpretations of traditions are the same. Indeed, given the variety of circumstances in which migrants find themselves at different times in different places it would be surprising if they were.

Mechanisms of Integration

Several mechanisms have allowed migrants to integrate into the societies of the diaspora, to acculturate successfully, and at the same time to maintain ethnic identity. Many of these mechanisms were mentioned in chapter three, e.g., the vicarious (son for father) pursuit of professional identity for Ali in Germany, the preadaptive experiences of Yusuf in Egypt and Germany and his resort to controlled acculturation in England, and the basketball group for Zayd in the U.S.A. In Greece, besides impression management and symbolic ethnicity, the key survival mechanism seems to be absorption of the migrant into the consanguine family of his Greek fiance/bride/wife. When I asked migrant Eight about the kind of social contacts he had in Greece, he said that he leaned to the relatives of his wife, continuing, "I wasn't a stranger there." Seven, describing the circumstances of his marriage, stated that he met his Greek wife through her sister, who was a student at the university. Even before they were married his fiance used to lend him money, and her parents supported the marriage. She was given a handsome dowry (a house) by her family, as was the wife of Eight (6,000 dinars).

However, it is migrant Two's relationship to his wife's consanguine family, perhaps atypical perhaps not, that elucidates the full potential and significance of the consanguine family as a survival mechanism in the diaspora. I have emphasized Two's devotion to his conjugal family, his pursuit of his leisure time at home, and his ideological commitment to that family, as attested to by the early agreement between him and his wife that both should work for its well-being, as well as by his unwillingness to move to Jordan to live and work because it would adversely affect his children. His comment that service in the Jordanian army allowed the son to emancipate himself economically from reliance on his father, in contrast to the Greek army, was another indication of his acceptance of the conjugal family model.

But migrant Two's acceptance by and absorption into his wife's consanguine family was critical for his integration into Greek society and his acculturation to it. This absorption has many facets. Two lived in a row house on the outskirts of town next to one sister-in-law. The children of the sisters were constantly playing together. In 1993, at the time I interviewed him, he had no phone, and this had been the case for many years. All phone calls to him or his wife came to his sister-in-law's house and were relayed to him. Two and his wife ate out two nights a week at the taverna of his other sister-in-law and her husband—those evening gatherings went on for many hours. Every Friday evening the families of the three sisters and their parents gathered at the home of one sister. Two's mother-in-law took his children into her house in a village seven kilometers out of town for between four and eight years, a house to which he and his wife came and stayed over on weekends. This arrangement allowed both Two and his wife to work. Two's father-in-law, a farmer who raised tobacco and wheat, sharecropped Two's tobacco plot along with his own. And Two's brother-in-law was fond of him, and had been very supportive of his sister's marriage, helping to talk his parents into approving it. The support that his wife's consanguine family gave to Two, then, was wide-ranging and intense, comprising economic cooperation in a number of ways, commensal unity, communication funnel, constant sociability, and not least, psychological support.

Five, Two's brother, on the other hand, had left Greece, in part, because he realized that absorption into his prospective Greek wife's consanguine family was impossible. It is significant that an important aspect of his adaptation to the United States in his early years there was the critical support his prospective and later actual brother-in-law gave him to secure immigration papers, housing, and employment, and even to support and arrange marriage itself.[16]

The absorption of the Jordanian husband into the Greek wife's consanguine family is, however, only one, if perhaps the most important, factor leading to his integration into Greek society. Other factors include: an open Greek society emphasizing hospitality, interfamily visiting, collective dating, and enjoyment of food, drink, dance, and song in public arenas; the concentration of students in Salonika and around Aristoteles University; the necessity of Jordanian students to live and work outside the university; the necessity to learn Greek before anything else; the favorable government policy toward foreign students; and the status (upward-mobile) and cultural (conservative) match between rural Greeks and tribal Jordanians.

Notes

1. Following Linton, 1936, the "consanguine family" is defined as that in which the parent-child tie and the sibling tie are given more weight than the husband-wife tie. The latter family type is defined by Linton as the "conjugal family." In the consanguine family, the in-marrying spouse (in the Greek case the Jordanian husband) is absorbed into the family of the in-place spouse. For details see Linton, *The Study of Man,* chapter four. I have found Linton's early terminology much more useful than those proposed later by other anthropologists such as Levi-Strauss, Murdock, Radcliffe-Brown, and Fortes, e.g., "nuclear," "elementary," "extended," "joint," because it focuses attention on the critical nature of *different* family dyads in *different* cultures.
2. "Living in the world" in the Greek context refers to the *joie de vivre* expressed in Greek culture through hospitality, an emphasis on family life and regular interfamily visiting, and an enjoyment of food, drink, dance, song, and public entertainment in public arenas such as the taverna and the theatre.
3. See chapter six below for the details of Jordanian migrant life in the United States.
4. To avoid ambiguity, capitalized numbers refer to migrants on table one; noncapitalized numbers designate ordinary numbers. I have discussed Eight's migrant experiences in the chapter

on migrants to Greece rather than in the chapter on migration through the army because his experiences as a student paralleled those of other students in most respects and outweighed the impact of his formal army status while in Greece.

5. I have excepted Six from the descriptive statistics here because he only stayed in Greece two months and subsequently pursued his higher education and professional training in Pakistan where he stayed five years.

6. A few other Jordanians did have regular contact with Saudis, e.g., the educator on the rural Yemen border, the business manager in Jidda and Riyadh, and the traveling sales manager of Winston cigarettes.

7. Migrant One spent the longest period in Greece, fourteen years, and married a Greek woman in a Christian marriage ceremony. He seems, by far, the best candidate for complete assimilation and identity change. And yet he returned to Jordan with his wife and family, seeking work there after he received his engineering degree. Failing that, he secured a job in an Arab Muslim country on the Gulf, taking his family with him. My inference is that this was not a man who had lost his ethnic identity.

8. In Jordan a person's name is his/her patrilineal pedigree, i.e., the given name, the father's name, the paternal grandfather's name, etc. up the line of patrilineal ancestors. In Greece one was required to list one's father's name first, then the given name, then the family name. For a symbolic and functional analysis of the Jordanian naming system in rural areas see Antoun, "On the Significance of Names in an Arab Village," *Ethnology,* 1968.

9. Berreman discusses impression management by the anthropologist in the context of field work in "Behind Many Masks: Impression Management in a Himalayan Village," Society for Applied Anthropology, 1962. Goffmann in a much-read book which bears the same title as the process described, *The Presentation of Self in Everyday Life,* 1959, views all life as a performance with back-stage and front-stage behavior.

10. For a discussion of the implications of symbolic ethnicity see Richard Alba, *Ethnic Identity: The Transformation of White America,* 1990, chapter 3. For a discussion of *taqiyya* check that rubric in the *Encyclopaedia of Islam,* New Edition.

11. See Alba, chapters 1 and 8.

12. See Antoun, "On the Modesty of Women in Arab Muslim Villages: An Accommodation of Traditions," *American Anthropologist,* 1968 for a detailed analysis of the modesty code.

13. Zayd's core religious identity was also based on childhood memories of chanting the Quran and rising just after dawn with his father while the latter performed morning prayers.

14. See chapter seven below for a description and analysis of the decline of the *madafa* and of the village's "moral society."

15. See Robert Redfield, *The Folk Culture of Yucatan,* 1941, for details.

16. See chapter six below for the description and analysis of Jordanian migrants to the United States and Five's (Bahhar's) experience there.

5

THE QUEST FOR EDUCATION
IN PAKISTAN:
THE VARIETY OF EXPERIENCE
IN A GLOBAL SOCIETY

The largest number of students from Kufr al-Ma seeking higher education abroad by far (twenty-seven) went to Pakistan. In some ways they resembled the eight students who went to Greece: They were young (in their twenties), unmarried, and led by a pathfinder (migrant One in Table 5.1), who in turn recruited other close kinsmen and co-villagers (Two, Three, and Four in Table 5.1) in a process of chain migration that was still continuing (five students were still in Pakistan) when I conducted interviews with returned migrants in Kufr al-Ma in 1986. The pathfinder is the student who leads the way for other clan or village mates to follow. There was a pathfinder for Russia, one for Greece, one for the United States, and one for Pakistan.

All interviews were with students who had finished their studies and returned to Kufr al-Ma, not to work or even in many cases to live—most worked elsewhere in Jordan, e.g., Amman, Irbid, Aqaba (see Table 5.2). But in all cases, though they did not live there, their families (wives, children, parents) continued to do so, and therefore they returned to the village on every possible occasion including weekends, if feasible. The students in Pakistan, like those in Greece, stayed for long periods, usually six years with infrequent visits home (often only twice). In both Pakistan and Greece academic life was disrupted by strikes that extended the period of study, sometimes a year or more, and in both countries (with one exception in Greece) students were entirely dependent on their own resources and on financial support from home, none receiving scholarships. In both cases the main motivation for choosing Pakistan/Greece was the cheapness of university life and of subsistence in general, as well as the facilitation of the admission process,

TABLE 5.1 • *Migrants to Pakistan*[1]

Migrant Number	Age	Marital Status	Children	Spouse's Nationality	Spouse's Kinship Relation	Place Studied	Time Spent	Year Began	Year Finished	Specialization	Yrs Studied Beyond HS	Highest Degree	Scholarship	Current Occupation	Work Location	Monthly Income	Army Service	Frequency of Visits to Jordan	Kinship Partners
*1	32	M	3	Jordanian, KM	Same Lineage	Feisalabad Univ Feisalabad / London Univ Royal Vet Col / Aristoteles Univ Salonika, Greece	5 yrs / 13 mo / 2 mo	1972 / 1981 / 1971	1977 / 1982 / —	Veterinary Medicine	6+	M Vet Science	No	Veterinarian—Dept of Agricul	Deir Abu Said, Jordan	285D	No		Alone—Clansmen & Brothers
2	25 1974					Karachi Univ		1973		Medicine Bacteriology	7+		No						
3		M				Feisalabad Univ Feisalabad		1981		Veterinary Medicine		B Vet Medicine	No	Veterinarian	Dhilayl, Zerqa				
*4	31	M	Y	Pakistani		Sind Univ Hyderabad	5 yrs	1975	1980	English Literature	5	BA	No	Commercial Affairs Mgr Saudi Co,	Amman	600D + 10% com on sales	No		Jordanians & co-villagers
5						Feisalabad Univ Feisalabad		1977		Geology			No						
*6	28	S				Karachi Univ	5 yrs	1977	1982	Psychology	5	BA Honors Psychology	No	—			Yes 83-85	Once per 2 yr (2M) summ/winter	Jordanians
*7	26	S				Feisalabad Univ Feisalabad	5 yrs	1978	1983	Animal Husbandry	5		No	Laboratory Supervisor Univ Zoology Dept	Jordan	160D	Yes 83-85		

No.	Age				University	Dur.	Years	Field	Yrs	Degree	Emp.	Job	Location	Car	Return	Freq.	Relation
*8	30	M	Jordanian, KM	Same Lineage	Feisalabad Univ Feisalabad	5 yrs	1978 1983	Food Technology	5	B.Sc Agric	No	Laboratory Spec	Ministry of Supply, Aqaba	230D	No	Once (2M) in 5 yrs (summ)	Clansmen
*9	27	S			Peshawar Univ	6 yrs	1978 1984	Agriculture	4+	B.Sc Agric	No				Yes 84–86		Alone Jordanians
*10	30	M	Jordanian, KM		Feisalabad Univ Feisalabad	4 yrs	1978 1982	Food Technology	4	B.Sc Agric	No	Asst Laboratory Dir	Ministry of Supply, Amman	180D		Once (2M) in 5 yrs (summ)	Cousins
*11	26	M	Jordanian, KM	Same Clan	Feisalabad Univ Feisalabad Peshawar Univ	4 yrs	1979 1983	Animal Husbandry, Entomology	4	B.Sc Animal Husbandry	No	Unemployed			Yes 83–85		
12	32	M 1			Sind Univ Hyderabad; Univ of Colorado Boulder	3 yrs	1979 1983	English Lit; Science & Technology	4+	BA English; MA Sci & Technol		Translator	Saudi Consulate Kansas City				Alone
13	24	S			Karachi Univ Sind Univ, Hyderabad	6 yrs	1980 1984	English; English	6+	BA English	No	Studying for MA	Hyderabad		Yes		First Cousins
14	25	S			Karachi Univ		1980	Political Science									First Cousins
15	24	S			Karachi Univ	4 yrs	1981 1985	Political Science	4	BA	No	Studying for MA	Karachi				First Cousins
16	26				Karachi Univ	5 yrs	1981 1985	Journalism	4+	BA Studying for MA	No		Ministry of Development, Amman		Yes		
17	25 1991	S			Avionics Inst Karachi	3 yrs	1986 1989	Aviation Maintenance Tech				Asst Aeronautical Engineer	Alia, Amman		Yes		First Cousins
18	24	S			Feisalabad Univ Feisalabad		1982	Food Technology			No	Student	Feisalabad				Brothers

(continued)

157

TABLE 5.1 • *Migrants to Pakistan¹ (continued)*

Migrant Number	Age	Marital Status	Children	Spouse's Nationality	Spouse's Kinship Relation	Place Studied	Time Spent	Year Began	Year Finished	Specialization	Yrs Studied Beyond HS	Highest Degree	Scholarship	Current Occupation	Work Location	Monthly Income	Army Service	Frequency of Visits to Jordan	Kinship Partners
19	27 1991	S				Avionics Inst Karachi	7 yrs	1982	1990	Aviation Maintenance Tech	3		No	Pilot, Jordan Nat Airlines	Amman		No		Clansmen
20	23	Eng		Jordanian	Same Clan	Sind Univ, Hyderabad		1982		English		BA English	No	Studying for MA	Pakistan				
21	24	S				Karachi Univ		1982		English			No	Student	Karachi				co-villagers
22	23	S				Feisalabad Univ	1 yr	1982		Veterinary Med	4		No	Student	Lahore				
						Punjab Univ Lahore	3 yr	1983		Dentistry									
23	25	S				Feisalabad Univ Feisalabad		1983		Agriculture				Student	Feisalabad				Cousins
24	24					Yarmouk Univ		1980		Economics & Politics		BA							
								1984		Islamic Lit			No	Student	Pakistan				
25						Karachi Univ				Journalism									
26						Feisalabad Univ Feisalabad				Food Technology				Canning Co.	Irbid				
27		S				Feisalabad Univ Feisalabad				Animal Husbandry			No						Clansmen

¹All data on migrants including ages pertains to the year 1986 (when data was collected) except migrants 2, 17, and 19 for whom information including ages pertains to the years 1974, 1991, and 1991 respectively.
*Indicates students interviewed.

158

TABLE 5.2 • *Migration to Pakistan: Incidence and Totals[1]*

Age	No. Students	Marital Status	No. Students	Place Studied	No. Students
21–25	11**	Married	6	Feisalabad	11**
26–30	7	Single	13**	Karachi	10*
31–35	4	Engaged	1	Hyderabad	4
No Info	5	No Info	7	Peshawar	2
				Lahore	1
				No Info	1

Specialization	No. Students	Education	Year Began	Year Ended
English/Literature	5**	1972	1	
Food Technology	4*	1973	1	
Animal Husbandry	3	1974	0	
Veterinary Medicine	2	1975	1	
Agriculture	2	1976	0	
Journalism	2	1977	2	1
Avionics	2	1978	4**	0
Political Science	2	1979	2	0
Bacteriology	1	1980	2	1
Psychology	1	1981	4**	1
Islamic Literature	1	1982	3*	2
Dentistry	1	1983	2	4**
Unknown	1	1984	1	3*
		1985	0	2
		1986	0	
		1987		
		1988		
		1989		
		1990		1

Educational Status	No. Students	Time Spent in Pakistan	No. Students
Finished	18**	1 year	0
Studying	8	2 years	0
No Info	1	3 years	3*
		4 years	3*
		5 years	6**
		6 years	2
		7 years	1

**Signifies Highest Number
*Signifies Next Highest Number
[1]Total Number of Students on whom data was gathered, 27.

(continued)

TABLE 5.2 • *Migration to Pakistan: Incidence and Totals[1] (continued)*

Highest Degree	No. Students	Current Occupation	No. Students	Work Location	No. Students
BA (studying)	1	Lab Supervisor/Specialist	3*	Amman	6**
BA (finished)	5*	Student (3 for MA)	8**	Irbid	1
BS (finished)	6**	Veterinarian	2	Zerqa	1
MA (studying)	3	Business Manager	1	Deir Abu Said	1
MS (studying)	1	Aeronautical Engineer	1	Aqaba	1
MA (finished)	1	Pilot	1	Pakistan (student)	8**
No Info	13	Canning Company	1	Kansas City	1
		Specialist	1	Kerak	1
		Translator	1		
		Unemployed	1		
		No Info	8		

Kinship Pattern	No. Students		Total	Army Service	No. Students
Brothers	s/d	2	2	Yes	5**
1st Cousins	s/s	2	4**	No	5**
2nd–5th Cousins	s/d	2	2	No Info	17
Clansmen	s/s	3	4**		
	s/d	1			
Villagers	s/s	1	2		
	s/d	1			
Jordanians	s/s	1	2		
	s/d	1			
Alone			3*		
No Info			11		

s/d = Studied a Different Specialization in the Same Place
s/s = Studied the Same Specialization in the Same Place

compared with Arab countries (e.g., Iraq and Egypt, where difficult inter-Arab political relations often raised barriers for students from other Arab countries). Finally, the period of migration for education was generally the same, ranging from 1968 to 1986.

On the other hand, the Jordanian student experience in Pakistan was distinctive and, in some ways, radically different from that in Greece. Language was a considerable barrier to Jordanians in Greece, and all students were required as a matter of university (government) policy to concentrate on Greek in the first year of studies. In Pakistan all university lectures were in English, which was the second language of Jordan, and so Jordanians actually had a linguistic advantage over many Pakistanis, who went up to the professor after class and asked him/her to repeat the main points of the lecture in Urdu. There was no formal attempt made by Pakistani universities to teach either English or Urdu to foreign students.

Greece is a staunchly Christian Orthodox country that commemorates many religious holidays and saint days, and has a history of confrontation with Ottoman and Republican Turkey, both associated with Islam in the popular consciousness whereas Pakistan is a staunchly Muslim country. Indeed, the rationale of its separation from India and establishment as an independent nation in 1947 was its Muslim identity.[1] This difference in religious identity and culture had an impact on Jordanian student experiences in Greece and Pakistan, particularly outside the university, both generally and specifically, as a number of the student interviews reveal.

The concentration of migrants in academic and urban centers was quite different in the two countries. In Greece all students studied at Aristoteles University and lived in or around the city of Salonika in northern Greece for almost the entire period of their stay. Those who have remained in Greece after their student days are still living in that region. The students who went to Pakistan were dispersed, for the most part, in four universities and four cities (Karachi, Hyderabad, Lyallpur, and Peshawar; see Table 5.2 for numbers) in three strikingly different regions, geographically, topographically, ethnically, and culturally: Sind, Punjab, and the Northwest Frontier. The Pakistani government-university system assigned students places in different universities depending on their disciplinary focus and their academic proficiency.

In Greece almost all students studied some form of medicine or engineering. In Pakistan there was a concentration on English/English literature, food technology, and animal husbandry. But students also studied a wide variety of other subjects including journalism, political science, veterinary medicine, aeronautical engineering, agriculture, and psychology (see Tables 5.1 and 5.2).

In Greece almost all students worked intermittently or constantly during their period of study in order to supplement their income. In Pakistan, to my knowledge, no students worked, though one, migrant Four, worked without pay for Arabian businessmen in Karachi. In Greece all students lived off campus in rooming houses or in single rooms with families in the city of Salonika. In Pakistan the overwhelming majority lived on campus, in part because of the cheapness of room and board there and in part because of transport problems in congested cities for those who did not have an automobile.[2]

In Greece Jordanian students seem to have been accepted as equals inside the universities. Outside academia they may have been looked down upon by Greeks of high economic and social status; but for the working class and lower middle class Greeks with whom they came into contact in rooming houses, they seem to have been regarded as equals and upward-mobile aspirants to professional status. In Pakistan, on the other hand, Jordanians were often fawned upon by the generality of the population they met in public spaces such as urban markets and rural villages, since they were regarded as carrying religious blessing, coming from "the holy land." Inside the university and in relations with educated Pakistanis outside it, the students were regarded as equals (by professors) and superiors (by students) in economic status as judged by their style-of-life, which included patronizing restaurants and cinemas and dating Pakistani undergraduates.[3] Their economic status was clearly superior to that of the great majority of Pakistani students and even some professors, a fact which led to envy, resentment, and some antagonism on the part of the latter, who were particularly sensitive to matters of honor, i.e., the preservation of the honor of Pakistani women from foreign men whom they believed to have illicit designs.

In any case, in accord with the factors noted above, Jordanians in Greece learned Greek, worked alongside Greeks, lived with them, courted Greek women, and (six of eight) married them. As a result of these experiences they acculturated rapidly, and assimilated to Greek society and culture. On the other hand, most of the Jordanian students in Pakistan led a much more encapsulated life; never assimilated or even acculturated (in the interviews some said they could not tolerate Pakistani food) to Pakistani culture in its various distinctive versions; and though some dated Pakistani women, and a few courted them, only one (Migrant Four) married a Pakistani.[4]

Even in those respects in which the transnational migrations for education to Greece and Pakistan were broadly similar, significant differences existed. Although the time period for the migration was broadly the same, the migration to Greece began and ended earlier; the first student left Jordan in 1968 and the last in 1983 (for a comparison with Pakistan see Table 5.2). In 1986 at the time of most interviews, only one active student remained in Greece whereas five remained in Pakistan. In 1986 those returning from Greece or remaining and working there were, without exception, in their thirties whereas those returning from Pakistan were in their twenties and early thirties.

Although the mode number of years spent in Pakistan and Greece was six and seven, respectively, no Jordanian from Kufr al-Ma studied in Pakistan more than six years whereas three students studied in Greece for considerably longer periods, ten to fourteen years (see Tables 5.1 and 5.2). Although in both countries intermittent strikes prolonged the period of study, in Pakistan the strikes were more frequent, were longer in duration, and had more diverse and surprising consequences for student life, as will be described below.

Although the process of transnational migration is described as the chain migration of close kinsmen and co-villagers in both cases, the implications of these migrations are socially quite different for the village of Kufr al-Ma. Most of the migrants to Greece were related—two pairs of brothers, a student and his affine, and a student and his nephew. But this migration network did not have significant effects on the community of Kufr al-Ma in terms of social patterning. In Pakistan, on the other hand, four sets of siblings and cousins (1, 7, and 18; 4 and 20; 3, 5, 11, and 27; and 12, 14, and 15—see Table 5.1) were themselves becoming linked by marriage and, thereby, in the process of constructing a competing village elite and informal political clique based on migration, investment in higher education and land, and in the case of the fathers of the first two sets, longtime experience as officers in the Jordanian Army, now in retirement (see chapter 1 for details). Thus, although the migration recruitment process for the two countries was nearly identical, in only one (Pakistan) was the migration network parlayed into status/power claims at the local level.

Finally, although all students pursued higher education abroad for the purpose of attaining professional or semiprofessional goals, all Jordanian students in Pakistan returned to Jordan to pursue these goals whereas half the students who went to Greece remained there to pursue their professions after graduation. No doubt the difference in standard of living, salary, and employment opportunities between the two countries, in addition to the social and cultural factors discussed above, accounted for the difference.

Analysis

The last chapter posed the question, How was it that Jordanian students in Greece acculturated, assimilated, and yet maintained their ethnic identity as Jordanians, Arabs, and Muslims? And it proceeded to discuss a variety of mechanisms that allowed societal integration while at the same time reinterpreting tradition to give new cultural content to that ethnic identity.

In Pakistan many factors prevented acculturation, assimilation, and the reformulation of identity: the Jordanian students' economic status and style-of-life, special religious origin, spatial dispersion in various cities and universities, tribal ethos, and societal encapsulation with respect to residence, work, marriage, and linguistic attainment. Rather, Jordanians in Pakistan were sojourners who, by and large, fostered their educational and career goals in a favorable environment. What is striking in the Pakistani case is the astonishing variety of student experiences and the unusual mix of people, ideas, and attitudes in a complex, mobile, global society. In this section the role of students as encapsulated sojourners will be analyzed, and in the next, the varied character of their local interaction in a global society will be delineated, along with their attitudes toward leading social issues.

The social relations of Jordanian students in Pakistan fall somewhere between the pattern of Jordanian workers in Arabia and Jordanian students in Greece. Whereas the latter became integrated in a relatively open society by study, work, residence, and social mixing, the workers in Arabia were, in various degrees, encapsulated in a society segmented by nationality, ethnicity, and class. It was a society in which citizenship, marriage, and regular neighborly interaction were not possible. Indeed, one of the conclusions of chapter two was that work relations were segmented as well, with Jordanians in Arabia interacting more with Europeans, North Americans, and Asians than with Saudis or Gulf Arabs.

A number of Jordanian students in Pakistan (e.g., Seven, Nine) also indicated that they had extensive relations with foreign students and rather restricted relations with Pakistanis as a result of their residential encapsulation (rooming on campus with other students from Kufr al-Ma or Jordanians), higher economic status, lack of work relations, ignorance of Urdu, dislike of Pakistani food, and revulsion at certain aspects of urban and rural poverty, e.g., dirt and extremes of opulence and deprivation.[5]

The relations of Jordanian students with Pakistani co-eds is particularly revealing in this regard. Most of those interviewed had opinions about Pakistani women, several admitted to dating them, and four (Four, Eight, Nine, and Ten) considered marriage. Only one, Four, did so. Most of those who dated Pakistani women complained about the restriction placed on such activity: the only places opposite sexes could meet on the campus were in the classroom and library; cafeterias on campus were segregated by sex; one could take a date to a restaurant, to the cinema (though one migrant denied this), or to a park outside the university, but generally, students complained about the lack of appropriate arenas for socializing outside the university as well. In addition, students complained about the resentful reaction of Pakistani students and particularly professors to their dating Pakistani women: Migrant Four referred to Pakistanis as "narrow-minded" and said that "even in the university it was very hard to deal with people." He said that many on the campus who saw a Jordanian walking with a Pakistani girl regarded it as "betrayal," presumably of her as well as the society's honor. Ten stated that dating a Pakistani girl could get a student blackballed by a professor, and Nine accused Pakistanis of "fanaticism" (*ta'assub*), saying that one of his professors objected to his fraternizing with a female professor by walking with her openly on the campus; he would have failed him on his viver (final oral exam) but for a lucky coincidence.

Many Jordanian students, then, had considerable contact with Pakistani women in a way unimaginable in Arabia, but they felt the constraints of the surrounding society, sometimes acutely. Just as important, all but one were dissuaded by parents or elder brothers from marriage on either ethnic ["No [outmarriage], Arabs like to marry Arabs" (Eight); "they (Pakistanis) have their distinctive customs" (Ten)]; or economic ["Praise be to God. I did not marry; circumstances were difficult—there were many expenses" (Nine)] grounds. Even Four, who married a Pakistani, never went to her parents' house, although he interacted regularly with her father on the campus (he was a professor) and with her in the library and, occasionally, the cinema, until his parents came from Jordan many years later to ask her family for her hand in marriage for their son.

The most extreme statement of ethnic difference was expressed by migrant Six when I asked him whether he ever contemplated marrying a Pakistani. He replied, "They are totally different: their customs; in beauty; Arab women are more beautiful and preferable." On the other hand, he criticized Pakistani women for trying to imitate the West and doing so only superficially, and for lording it over their husbands in control and ownership of property and (excessive) freedom of social life, both antithetical to Jordanian custom "where the man is prince ... and the woman is in the house."

It is interesting that the one Jordanian who married a Pakistani gave a completely different appraisal, when I asked him, "How do you compare Pakistani women with Jordanian women?" He replied, "As a wife I prefer the Pakistanis: they are faithful and simple and accept any way of life." Indeed, this characterization seems to have been borne out in her case since Four took his wife straight to Kufr al-Ma to his parents' house, where she remained—and still lives—while he worked for years in Saudi Arabia and later Amman.

While, therefore, Jordanian student social life was much more open in Pakistan than worker or student life in Arabia, it was extremely constrained when compared with Jordanian student life in Greece. There the combination of aspirant professional status and a tribal ethos proved a good match for the culture and upward mobile aspirations of rural Greek women, providing a similar base of social conservatism that led to courtship and marriage of a significant majority (six of eight) of Jordanian men in Greece.

On the other hand, most students said they were treated well in Pakistan, whether because they were of the same religion, because they were from "the holy land" and therefore superior Muslims (people in rural areas tried to touch them to gain blessing), because of their high economic status, because of the special relations between Pakistan and Jordan cultivated by Crown Prince Hasan (who married a Pakistani) and the ruler, General Zia al-Haq (who served on a military mission to Jordan for some time), or because Pakistanis were "a simple people" who were friendly and helpful.

The two most critical appraisals of Pakistan/Pakistanis (by Four and Nine) were still unstinting in their praise for the Pakistani educational system, commenting on the regularity of the exams, the quality of the professors, and their readiness to help.[6] Their critical remarks were mainly in the context of cross-sex relations, which Pakistanis related to honor and cultural pride: foreign Jordanian men pursuing Pakistani women. A few mentioned favoritism toward Pakistanis on the part of Pakistani professors, but others denied its existence, and some stated, contrarily, that the foreigners were the ones favored. Even Nine, when asked if he would go again to Pakistan for an education replied, "Yes, Pakistan still has grace (*fadl*); it was she that taught me." Only one person, the same Nine, placed a negative construction on the readiness of Pakistanis, whether students, professors, police, bureaucrats, or taxi drivers, to please foreigners. He said, "(They are) a people impressed by (British) colonialism; it got them to be passive and implanted fear in them."

The Jordanian tribal ethos, stressing familistic and egalitarian values and a histrionic, forthright, gregarious, and confrontational style played out differently in Pakistan than it did in Greece. Whereas in the latter country it paved the way for courtship and marriage and fraternization with Greeks, in the former it clashed with the ethos of the Pakistani middle class and bureaucracy, which stressed civility, diffidence, and punctuality, as well as the Pakistani social system, which stressed respect for differences of status and ethnicity;[7] it led in some cases to abrasive relations between Jordanian students intent on enjoying their new social freedom and Pakistani professors and bureaucrats intent on preserving the honor of their women and the rules that governed social relations within the university and outside it.

Language perhaps even more than religion, economic status, residential segregation, or cultural pride, played a key role in fostering the encapsulation of the great majority of Jordanian students in Pakistan. English was the lingua franca of Pakistani society, particularly in all formal contexts such as government offices, municipal offices, the university, and large business concerns. English was the second language of Jordan. That did not mean that all educated Jordanians spoke it well or even at all. Many did not have a good reading proficiency because secondary school instruction in Jordan was in Arabic; the only opportunity for learning English outside of school for rural Jordanians was the passive experience of watching television programs (which were alternated on successive nights with programming in Arabic) in English on Jordanian television. If Jordanians had an initial, if not comfortable, understanding of English, they had no understanding of Urdu, the national language of Pakistan. There was no attempt by Pakistani universities (or the government) to teach the official national language to foreign students.[8] Most students from Kufr al-Ma said that learning Urdu was unnecessary, although some did pick up some knowledge while dealing in the bazaar. Only one student (Seven) talked at all about Urdu and its components.

The language situation in Pakistan is much more complex than suggested above, however. Urdu is the national language, but Pakistan is divided into very distinct geographical regions (Sind, Punjab, Baluchistan, and the Northwest Frontier), and these regions are occupied by quite distinctive ethnic groups speaking different languages, e.g., Sindi, Punjabi, Baluchi, and Pushtu. Many Pakistanis in these regions spoke neither English nor Urdu. In addition, in the large cities other languages (as well as Urdu) were spoken by the *muhajirs,* the people who came from India as refugees at the time of the partition of Pakistan from India in the late 1940s.[9] More recently (1980s), other refugees from Afghanistan have come to Pakistan speaking still other languages as a result of the Soviet-Afghan War.[10] For any Jordanian to have acculturated or assimilated, it would have been necessary to learn more than one language—besides English—and that language would have differed, depending on what part of Pakistan he lived in, and, indeed, what part of a particular city he resided in.

The mosaic (of language and culture) in Pakistan differed quite dramatically from the ethnic situation in Greece which, regardless of its regional differences and the distinction between classical high Greek (*katharaevousa*) and popular modern Greek (*dimotiki*), was a relatively homogeneous country with a single language to learn. Moreover, unlike Pakistan, the language of instruction in the university was still the language of the country, though lectures in Greek universities were often in the classical language. Thus in Greece a mastery of the academic discourse complemented the learning of the popular discourse. Even if Urdu had been the language of instruction at Pakistani universities (and there is a drive by the government in that direction), its mastery would not necessarily have constituted an entree into the language of the region or the city of residence. In many areas it most certainly did not.

There is a social psychological dimension to the process of learning a foreign language that is important here. Learning a strange language involves a great investment of time, energy, and extraordinary effort—indeed, it is painful for many. Migrant One left Greece for Pakistan on account of his difficulty with Greek; and Migrant Four, who thoroughly enjoyed Greece, said the Greeks liked the Arabs, and took a Greek as wife, when I asked him whether he would go to Greece for an education were he to do it all over again, replied in the negative, citing the difficulty in learning the language. But there is another side to the process of language learning. Though it may be painful, once achieved, it leads to an exploration of a new universe of discourse, to an appreciation of new experiences, and in Greece, to an enjoyment of new and exciting cross-sex social relations; and in the process to an appreciation of, and finally, acceptance of many aspects of another way of life and worldview. The language situation in Pakistan foreclosed this possibility for Jordanian students. Both the pain and the pleasures of acculturation, assimilation, and forging a new identity were avoided there and their implications totally absent.

Astonishing Mixture, Mobility, and Diversity on a Global Stage

In assessing the significance of the new industrialization in the late twentieth century, Frances Rothstein has stated:

> Wherever we are in the "developed" world, we are increasingly likely to encounter people from the countries that anthropologists have traditionally studied [i.e., the third world]. Moreover, when we are in the field in the "developing" world, there are constant reminders of the First World. The overlap in people, things, behavior and ideas between the First and Third, core and periphery, or developing and developed, worlds and the variations within these categories are so great that the categories are useful only if we see them as points on a continuum....[11]

She continues, "The global factory is comprised of local actors and events, but the stage on which they play is the world."[12] Rothstein's insightful observations and trenchant metaphors are not just relevant to new industrialization, but also to transnational migration for higher education at the end of the century. And they do not simply characterize relations between first and third worlds, but also relations between second and third worlds and, as in the case discussed here, between third and third: the Jordanian students who went to Pakistan met not only Pakistanis, but also Yemenis, Iraqis, Sudanis, Egyptians, Saudis, Mauritians, Iranians, Turks, Thais, and Malays. One of the peculiar ramifications of the repeated and extended strikes and demonstrations that took place in Pakistan in the 1970s and 1980s is that they drove Jordanian students out of their dormitories and out of their universities to explore—with other foreign students—many other parts of Pakistan that they might otherwise not have seen. Out of this interaction developed friendship and later correspondence.

Migrant Nine, on the other hand, filled in a hiatus in study by walking across the border to Afghanistan in the middle of the Afghan-Russian War, at the behest of a British journalist, to take photographs of the *mujahidin,* the Afghan resistance fighters. The journalist lacked photographs for his journalistic piece. When I asked Nine in a tone of astonishment, if he had been well recompensed for his efforts, he replied, "Not at all, I did it for the (Muslim) cause." Nine's experience in rough-tough Peshawar, where he was held up by a thug on campus and where he and his roommate hired a servant to do the cooking after moving off the campus, was totally different than the experience of migrant Four who, in the period of disruption caused by strikes, left Hyderabad with a friend for Karachi where he acted as interpreter, *gratis,* for Saudi businessmen come to Pakistan to recruit Pakistani labor for their construction enterprises in Arabia. For Four these contacts were instrumental in landing a managerial job in Saudi Arabia when he went there a year later. The student of English literature became a successful businessman in Arabia, and the critical experience and social network that led to that result was forged in Karachi!

This unpredictable mix of experiences was matched by improbable turnings (of events and attitudes). Four, whose dislike of Pakistan was so great he said he ran away from the country as soon as his last year of study was finished—although he loved Pakistani food, had many Pakistani girlfriends, and praised Pakistani education—was the one Jordanian who married a Pakistani! And Nine who, though he complained of Pakistani fanaticism (while at the same time admiring Pakistanis' "holding fast to their religion"), felt constrained by a Pakistani professor, lacked any Pakistani friends, and was rejected in his marriage proposal by a Pakistani co-ed, would do it all over again (return to Pakistan for education) if given another chance.

Migrant Ten, on the other hand, was invited by Pakistani students to their homes and traveled up and down the length of Pakistan to cities eight hundred miles apart in addition to visiting and sleeping in a Pakistani village. He enjoyed socializing actively with Pakistanis and followed and engaged in political party debates with them on campus (as opposed to Four, who was active in the "Jordanian" Union on campus), he went on collective dates (the only student to mention such activity), and he studied together with Pakistani students (again the only one to mention it); these students, in turn, bailed him out of difficult situations with local authorities. In addition, he was the only student to compete successfully in intercollegiate athletics. But with all that, he followed his brother's advice and rejected the option of marriage to a Pakistani.

In contrast to those who made many friends and tramped all around Pakistan were students like Six and Eleven who, it seems, on the occasion of strikes went back to their rooms on campus or to the library, and socialized with their relatives, co-villagers, and other Jordanians with whom they shared a common "Arab mess," again, on campus. When they left the campus to recreate, they went together. This category of students tended to dichotomize and evaluate their experience in Pakistan as between inside and good (the university) and outside and bad (the population at large): Migrant Eleven said that the people were not good; they were composed of the few rich and the many poor whereas "the professors are patient and help the students; one can ask any professor for help, and he will help him (the student), even if it isn't his professor." And Migrant Six said about the inside (university) that the labs, books, and exam system were "American-(style)," i.e., of good quality. He said that the professors were all good and well-educated, rather than the reverse, and that in fact they favored the Arabs over native Pakistanis rather than the reverse. On the other hand, of the outside he said: "Pakistan didn't please me at all … there was a lack of places for distraction and recreation … there was one park … no coffee houses." And regarding Pakistani women, the (middle-class) women of Karachi, he said, didn't care about virginity, imitated the West, left child-rearing to servants, and exercised control over property and over their husbands (all negatives). This segregation of different arenas of experience and dichotomized evaluation of them is reminiscent of Yusuf's trichotomized world in Leeds, England (chapter three)—as between university (on weekdays), mosque (on weekends), and the outside (world)—which rejected him. Only, here in Pakistan, it was the students—well accepted at the university and even fawned upon by poor pious Muslims outside it—who rejected the (outside) world.

How did these remarkably diverse student experiences affect the views of Jordanians regarding leading social questions in Jordan such as women's work outside the home, birth control, unemployment, and regarding their own identity and upbringing in a tribal, peasant village? It would be difficult, if not impossible to establish causal links between a particular migration experience and particular views on social questions in the home country. What can be established, however, is the existence of a diversity of viewpoints by migrants on particular social questions, reflecting different value orientations as opposed to a uniform viewpoint reflecting a single value orientation. It is the very fact of diversity of viewpoints that is the significant factor.

I gathered no data suggesting a diversity of viewpoints on matters such as tribal law, women's work outside the home, or birth control during a year of participant observation in Kufr al-Ma in 1959–60 and three shorter periods of field work between 1966 and 1967.[13] In general, tribal law as applied in the guest houses of the village was not only accepted, but also favored over resort to the civil court as attested to by the existence of fifteen guest houses in the village and their nightly activity.[14] In the 1960s no one ever suggested that a girl from the village would ever be permitted to work outside it. In the 1960s there was a village girls' school through the third grade! And no one dared to pose the question, never mind discuss, whether birth control was appropriate.

In 1986 when I asked migrants to Pakistan what their views of tribal law were, I received a variety of opinions: Migrant Six said that it had only bad points, that state law was supplanting it, that it resulted in favoritism by the government to some tribes and not others, that it produced social dissension, and that it was favored by the older generation, not the younger. Migrant Nine, on the other hand, said that tribal law "has its evils and its good points," the good being the resolution of disputes at the local level, avoiding state involvement (what Eleven saw as a strength, Nine saw as a weakness), and the strengthening of extended family ties; and the bad being that individual responsibility and retaliation is effaced and replaced by collective responsibility and collective retaliation.[15] Migrant Ten, however, endorsed tribal law without reservations: It is efficient, time-saving, face-to-face (and thereby satisfying), provides effective arbitration, and affirms the values of honor, forgiveness, and magnanimity. Migrant Eight, however, rather than elaborate a series of reasons/rationales, summed up his position in only one sentence: "When a person makes a mistake, should we rope in all of the people in the mistake?"

Migrant Eight gave me a similar succinct answer to the question, "What is your view of birth control?" saying he didn't agree with it: "When God creates them, he will take care of them." Migrant Seven made similar pithy remarks indicating the religious source of opposition to birth control: "What comes from God will be better," and "What God brings (i.e., progeny) is good." Migrant Four, on the contrary was a champion of birth control, saying that it should be followed by all the people, that there ought to be teams to give instructions to villagers, and information centers. When confronted with the religious argument against it, he countered, "Shouldn't you give your sons and daughters a good life?" When I asked migrant Ten whether he favored birth control (*tahdid al-nasl*), he replied quickly, "It is not acceptable in our religion," but then added, "Increasing population, we have to plan for that" ... and "family planning (*tanTHim al-nasl*) is acceptable." Migrant Six made the same distinction between birth control (prohibited) and family planning (approved), but then made a further distinction that no other made between what was approved for the individual as opposed to the state: "Each person is free (to plan births) but for the government such as China to limit birth, no." Migrant Nine, on the other hand, not only supported family planning, but was also collecting information in newspapers about new, more efficient methods.

Views on women's working outside the house were similarly diverse, running a gamut of permissions and prohibitions of particular occupations. Migrant Four gave the most permissive views, saying, "Life is expensive and women can compete with men in doing any work," and he specifically endorsed women as engineers, nurses, and secretaries. When I asked him how far he would allow his daughter to be educated, he replied, "As much as she likes." Migrant Seven regarded practically every occupation as open to women's work, including airline pilots, ruling out only those jobs that involved excessive physical labor, and ending his views on the matter by saying, "I'm looking for an educated girl (wife) who can help me in my life."

Migrant Nine, on the other hand, gave a more cautious and hedged view of women's working outside the home: "Within a limited scope (yes)—in education and not civil engineering, as a doctor, but one specializing in women's diseases," (i.e., only in occupations with a clientele of women or children). Work as secretary was all right, but only up to 1 p.m. (so she could return home and fulfill her duties there), and not after she was married.

Migrant Eight restricted women's occupations much more sharply, ruling out medicine, law, and engineering on the basis of religion and allowing women to work only as teachers, and only in a girls' school. Migrant Ten gave the most substantial view of the restriction of women's occupations and the rationale for doing so: Her principal role in society was as daughter and wife, i.e., as helper in the home. Work outside the home ruined her reputation and her marriage prospects because she is thrown into contact with unrelated males (like male nurses, bank clerks, and engineers) who, it is assumed, will take advantage of her. Ten would promote her education beyond high school (which is segregated by sex) only if she attended a women's junior college. Note, these conservative views are held by the Jordanian migrant who was most outgoing in Pakistan, and most involved in campus affairs, athletics, collective dating, and travel.

To what degree is this diversity of opinion a product of the migration experience? It is impossible to say. But it would be implausible to argue that the transnational migration for education of young men thrown into contact with a variety of "cultural others" under unusual circumstances over a long period of time, did not help bring about the pluralization of private belief that is so evident in the statements of the men recorded above. Indeed, this pluralization of private belief became a marker of modernity in Europe and North America after the Enlightenment and was usually accompanied by the relativization of public values.[16] It is possible that transnational migration in the third world is the functional analogue of the Enlightenment and the French Revolution in Europe in pluralizing beliefs. Whether it will have the effect of relativizing public values is still to be seen.

Although the pluralization of beliefs is certainly in evidence in the statements of the returned migrants in Kufr al-Ma, what may be the dominant concomitant process is the reinterpretation of tradition rather than the relativization of public values. That is, new cultural content is being accommodated to distinctly new demographic, technological, and social structural circumstances in a logically articulated cultural discourse. Thus, although migrants take a variety of positions on birth control, they seem consistently to distinguish between "the limiting of progeny" (*taḥdid al-nasl*), i.e., birth control, i.e., an operation on husband or wife to definitively cut off future procreation; and "the organization of progeny (*tanTHim al-nasl*), i.e., family planning, i.e., the spacing out of births. Similarly, although the wide-ranging discussion of the possibilities of women working outside the home and outside the community is a startling development in Kufr al-Ma considering the possibilities of such work in 1960—there was none—a reasoned and coherent discourse has developed to reinterpret the modesty code that prevailed in 1960; this code ruled out not only women's work outside the community, but also all cross-sex communication with unrelated males in public arenas within or without the village.[17]

The new discourse allows women's education and work outside the community provided certain principles are adhered to—those that protect and preserve the honor of the woman in public arenas and maintain the integrity of the family and the welfare of children: sex segregation, avoidance, accessible monitoring, close proximity to the home, restricted work hours, safe transportation, and respectable white-collar employment.

One question that I posed to return migrants, not only from Pakistan, but also from Greece, the United States, Russia, and Western Europe was answered in a variety of ways, but with a remarkable unity of evaluation with a very few exceptions. That was the question, "What is/are your view/reflections of your childhood upbringing in Kufr al-Ma?" The replies were in the overwhelming majority positive. Nine made the most negative statement, saying, "They used to socialize by striking (the child).... There was poverty in those days." But then he said about the father who struck him, "The village used to respect my father (who was the mayor). Why shouldn't I be respected too? (I thought) if I study people will respect me. If I'm an agricultural engineer I can give any person what he wants." He said the corporal punishment had no effect on him. Despite its administration by his father, the latter provided a successful career role model for him.

Migrant Eight also began by discounting the past when he said that life after migration was better. But then he said, "The upbringing was good; formerly there were closer social relations."

The more usual evaluations were strongly positive. For instance, Seven said, "I remember my childhood, all of it. It was a happy one. There was no restriction.... There was nothing bad about my childhood that I remember, especially elementary school." After stating that he preferred to live in the city on account of its superior educational facilities, migrant Six said, "I yearn to return to my childhood."

But it was Migrant Ten who expressed most clearly the near-unanimous view that the migrants' early life in a tribal peasant village reflected all the positive values of an organic society:

Some traditions are good: respect for others, good relations, not making problems with others, treatment as equals, (the community as) one body (as opposed to) feeling jealousy. Today if you're rich everyone feels jealousy. (Nowadays) the social bond involves taking your rights and giving good treatment. Most customs are good; (to) feel like one family and visit one another.

When I asked Ten whether there were bad traditions, he said, "People still are good. Relations between villages are better than cities. To let your neighbor die from hunger is not good; to let neighbors face difficulties is not good." And when I asked him about whether he received physical punishment as a child, he replied, "From parents it is not punishment. If they (the children) make a mistake (punishment) is good."

Despite the pluralization of private belief, the migrants to Pakistan retained a strong sense of identification with the values of an organic society and a multiplex community in which human/social values were given priority. They realized nostalgically that this organic world and this multiplex community had substantially disappeared, but they were still attached to its values, and that attachment affirmed their strong sense of identity as family members, sons of tribesmen, Arabs and Muslims. It allowed them to take their varied, sometimes exhilarating, sometimes repulsive, and sometimes seductive experiences abroad in stride. When in doubt about the choices they should make in the Pakistani diaspora, they returned to their villages or through correspondence, consulted their family members, and accepted their advice, though they did not always agree with its rationale or the specific beliefs that accompanied it.

Notes

1. See the essays devoted to Pakistan by Binder, Cohen, Esposito, and Harrison in Ali Banuazizi and Marvin Weiner, editors, *The State, Religion, and Ethnic Politics: Afghanistan, Iran, and Pakistan,* Syracuse University Press, 1986, for a discussion of the importance of religion and language in the development of modern Pakistan.
2. The only two students who lived off the campus about whom I have information were Six and Nine. Nine was forced off the campus in Peshawar when the university closed following a prolonged strike. Six roomed off the campus with a Palestinian for a year, and then returned to the campus for his final two years.
3. The accounts by migrant students of dating Pakistani undergraduates must be viewed skeptically. Undergraduate women usually went to separate women's colleges. At Faisalabad and Peshawar universities there were very few female students. Personal communication, Iftikhar Ahmed.
4. Many never acclimatized, complaining of the intense heat, though at the same time they loved the rivers, the valleys, and the verdant fields. Some complained of being sick, and one, at least, had malaria.
5. There are exceptions to most of these generalizations, e.g., Four said he loved Pakistani food and Ten mixed with Pakistani students, studied with them, and in his appraisal called them "lovely boys."

6. The examination system in Pakistan varies from university to university. Some universities still follow the semester system whereas others have changed to annual examinations (the British system). The semester system was introduced in universities during the early '70s, but it didn't work in many universities for a variety of reasons: inadequate experience with the system; deficiency in human and financial resources; and lack of commitment to the system. Therefore many universities returned to the annual exam system after a few years of experimenting with the semester system.

7. Not only status but caste differences. Pakistan has castes in many parts of the country in the sense of rigidly separate, hierarchically ordered sets of localized social groups. Occupations are ranked and groups often interact according to a nonmonetary set of reciprocal social services that reflect that ranking. But the castes of Pakistan are not like Indian castes in that they lack the ritual and symbolic system based on the concept of purity that orders and compares the ranked groups in a homologous fashion. In the Punjab the emphasis is more on the clan or *biraderi* system, the latter being the smallest endogamous group representing the meaningful unit for marriage ties and dispute settlement.

8. This laissez-faire policy is similar to that of universities in the United States which make no effort to teach incoming foreign students English, although they do provide remedial instruction.

9. Urdu is understood and spoken in all Pakistani cities and towns and is the native language of many of the *muhajirs* who lived in India before the partition of Indian and Pakistan in 1947. But it is not spoken or understood in many rural areas of the country.

10. See the essays by Leonard Binder and Selig Harrison in Ali Banuazizi and Myron Weiner, editors, *The State, Religion, and Ethnic Politics* for a description of the linguistic situation in Pakistan. See also Soofia Mumtaz, "The Dynamics of Changing Ethnic Boundaries: A Case Study of Karachi," *The Pakistani Development Review,* Vol. 29, No. 3 and 4, 1990, for a description of the linguistic situation in that city.

11. Frances Rothstein, "Conclusion: New Waves and Old—Industrialization, Labor, and the Struggle for a New World Order," in F. Rothstein and M. Blim, *Anthropology and the Global Factory: Studies of the New Industrialization in the Late Twentieth Century,* p. 239.

12. Ibid.

13. During these field trips I was not focused on these topics and did not administer a questionnaire or conduct specific interviews on them. However, I am sure that my participant observation in a community with which I was very familiar would have uncovered such diverse viewpoints.

14. See Richard Antoun, *Arab Village,* for a description of the guest house in Kufr al-Ma. See also Antoun, *Muslim Preacher in the Modern World,* chapter 4, table 4 for a comparison of the guest house with other arenas of village activity, the mosque and the bureaucrat's office. For an extended description and analysis of the mediation of a dispute in the guest house in 1960 see Antoun, "Institutionalized Deconfrontation: A Case Study of Conflict Resolution among Tribal Peasants in Jordan," in Paul Salem, editor, *Conflict Resolution in the Arab World,* American University of Beirut Press, 1997 and Syracuse University Press, 1998.

15. By individual responsibility and retaliation is meant that only the culprit is responsible for his acts and not his kinsmen, and only the culprit is punished (by the state); collective responsibility, on the other hand, means that the patrilineal kinsmen of the culprit are responsible for his acts and that any of them are legitimate targets of retaliation by the members of the victim's patrilineal group.

16. See Bruce Lawrence, *Defenders of God,* particularly chapter four for a discussion of this process.

17. See Antoun, 1968 for a detailed description and analysis of the modesty code.

6

Longer Stay, Faster Change, Ruder Shock: Migrants to the United States, Coping with Mobility, Reinterpreting Tradition, and Evolving Identities

The focus of this book is the experience of transnational migration in its personal and humanistic aspects and in its various multicultural contexts. In the two previous chapters I recorded the reaction of migrants for higher education to prolonged exposure to two alien cultures (Greek and Pakistani), two different social systems, and radically different living circumstances. The students traveling the farthest, spending the longest periods of time abroad, and encountering the hardest cultural shocks were those to the United States. It was only in the United States that students were subject to continuous changes in numerous aspects of their lives: schools attended, professional goals, place of residence, place of work, women dated, and cars bought and sold.

Like the migrants to Greece, those to the United States learned the native language, worked and lived outside the university campus, and dated, courted, and married the women of the host culture. But unlike the Greek case, the integration of Jordanians into American culture and society was not relatively smooth; on the contrary, it was problematic. Like the migrants to Pakistan, the migrants to the United States knew the host country's language as the second language of their own country; encountered extreme economic and class differences; and were thrust into largely urban and highly multicultural environments. But the reactions of the two migrant groups to such circumstances were quite different. Those to Pakistan, with a few exceptions, engaged in limited interaction with the host population and withdrew behind university gates. Those to the United States engaged in intensive, if focused, social interaction and experimentation. Because both the problems and patterns of social structural integration and the rate and pervasiveness of change in the United States differed, the problems of identity in the United States and their modes of resolution also differed.

This chapter first records four migrant experiences as recorded in interview-conversations.[1] Then it analyzes and compares the modes of integration and encapsulation in the United States and the varying degrees of preadaptation and acculturation, and examines the question of how various migrants reinterpreted traditions and evolved social identities to deal with fragmented social spaces and to accommodate the several demands of a global society.

Migrants to the United States: Similarities

Although much of the interest of the present chapter lies in the great variety of circumstances, personal and social attributes, adjustments, and worldviews of the four migrants to the United States, there are also important similarities that should be pointed out at the outset. Table 6.1 presents the migrants in order of age and lists some of their important personal and migration attributes.

All the migrants received a green (working) card, and some attained subsequent citizenship through marriage with Americans. All live in small apartments, four of five in one-bedroom apartments.[2] All are hardworking, working overtime, from fifty to eight-four hours a week. Dan has two jobs and works fifty to eight-four hours a week, with his main job from 12 midnight to 9 a.m. Zayd has one job which involves working three to five days a week with quite irregular and late night hours. Bahhar's life at sea involves absence from family for one or two months, followed by shore leaves of a month or more. Until they finished their formal education all the students except one worked almost all their spare time while pursuing their studies. Three of four came to the United States for a higher education, and the fourth has studied on his own to upgrade his occupational status.

Those who went to school took a very long time to finish their degrees; the two who finished took seven and ten years respectively to finish a four-year degree; the third dropped out after 2½ years and has little intention of returning. The common experience has been that of running out of money, having to work to support themselves, cutting back on studies because of limited resources, and extending the period of study in the United States. This experience has led to an unusually prolonged period of acculturation in the U.S.A.

All migrants are nonpracticing Muslims, but all have a Muslim identity and wish to pass that identity, or at least pass their cultural identity, on to their children. But all see a good part of their working lives as being spent in the United States with their families. Three of the four intend to return permanently to Jor-

TABLE 6.1 • *Migrants to the United States*

Name	Age	Kinship Support in Disapora	Occupation	Marital Status	Yrs in USA	Acculturation	Ed Degree	Inner/Outer Directedness[5]
'Isam	23	Bros²/Close Cousin	Manager Red Lobster Restaurant	M	5	Thru American Mentor/Bros/Wife	——— [1]	I/D due to sibling rivalry
Zayd	30	Close Cousin	Chauffeur	D	11	Thru Girlfriends/ Wife	B Business Management [4]⁴ (11)	I/D to fulfill his father's trust
Bahhar	38	Bros²/___	Captain Merchant Marine	M	11	Thru Wife/B-I-L/ M-I-L	Radio/Naval Science [2] (2+)	O/D job I/D courtship/marriage
Dan	43	(Ohio)³ ___/(Texas), Co-villagers	Night Auditor, Dallas-Fort Worth Airport	D	13	Wife/American Mentor	Business Mangement [4] & Accounting (7)	I/D to prove himself after severance from army

[1] 'Isam dropped out of college after 2½ years.

[2] Bahhar left off rooming with his brother in Greece to advance his language learning; Isam left his Syrian roommate and brother in San Antonio to advance his English.

[3] Dan's main economic opportunity came through his American mentor; he cut off kinship ties with his village (no visit in 13 years); yet he used his (Arab) ethnicity to get jobs in Ohio and Texas.

[4] Numbers in brackets indicate the number of years it is supposed to take for (American) students to get the degree; numbers in parentheses indicate the number of years it took the migrant to get his degree.

[5] The terms are derived from David Reisman's *The Lonely Crowd*, 1955.

dan. As a result of their long exposure to American society and culture all the migrants have acculturated in dress, language idiom, and politeness formulas, and three of the four entered the dating game with the zest of young men coming from rural Arab societies in which cross-sex interpersonal relations outside the family were relatively closed.

Dan

NAME: (6/9/91 from my interview with Dan in Arlington Texas). His full name carried his patrilineal pedigree in Arabic. But everybody in the U.S.A. began calling him (the pejorative) "Abdul" so he went by the name of "Dan."

EDUCATION: High School, Irbid, Jordan (Science track), 1968. Royal Military College, Amman, Jordan, 1968–69. Pakistani Naval School (PNS Himalya), Karachi, Pakistan, 1969–70. The school was on an island. The aim was to establish a Jordanian Navy. He got an excellent education. They were really serious. "Here in the United States they give you freedom to study; one can change studies; one can drop (a course) if one is not doing well. There you have to take the curriculum, and you have to pass. It was a discipline. A foreign officer wanted to do well because he was competing with Pakistani officers."

I asked what life in Pakistan was like. "Miserable. It was too hot and humid. I hate to see somebody who is poor; that ruins your happiness." He was mad at the government for not taking care of the people. There were two layers (of society there)—the extremely rich and the extremely poor. He saw people who were completely naked. "The government has a responsibility. They should cut the bureaucrats' salaries by 5 rupees and clothe the people." They then decided that the Jordanian part of Aqaba was too narrow for a Navy, and he was transferred to the Army in 1973. He was transferred to the King's palace, and he took the Basic Tank Course for officers.

He was a tank officer till he retired. He never fought in any war. He registered at the University of Dayton to study electrical engineering in 1978. The tuition was $1,300 a semester. Because he had a job he had to transfer to Cincinnati Metropolitan College where he stayed from 1979 to 1982. He got an Associate's degree in Accounting and Finance in 1982. He stayed there for three quarters with a $1,000 tuition each quarter. He took twelve credit hours for three years (because he was working). Then he spent one year out of school, working, but also for rest and refreshment. By chance a professor came to the restaurant where he worked and gave him his card where he taught at Wilmington College. He registered at Wilmington College (a suburb of Cincinnati) in 1983 to continue working for his BA in Management. He had already taken accounting courses so he took mainly management courses for a double major. Among the courses he took were statistics, quantitative analysis, philosophy, international management—he hated philosophy. "What we read had no relationship to the lectures," he said. In 1984 he received his BA degree in Management, Accounting, and Finance.

I asked him how he evaluated his education in the United States. He said that he regrets that he did not continue at the University of Dayton; he would have been a much better student there. It was a private religious college where they paid attention to student needs; if they saw a weak point, they helped. The professors gave you their home number to call if you were in trouble. It was a small community. The college was possibly Catholic; he wasn't sure. They had their own activities, amusements; they had a nice library. Cincinnati Metropolitan College was very small and gave only an associate's degree. They wanted you out as soon as possible. It was designed to help adults get out fast and find a job. He had a difficult time competing (in school) while working. Wilmington College was between the other two. It was a Quaker college. Their specialty was agriculture. He took twenty credit hours there and got all As. In 1983 he got a government student loan of $2,500.

GIRLFRIENDS, ECONOMICS, AND MARRIAGE: In 1983 he got a student loan of $2,500, and his new girlfriend was working as a clothing manager in Cincinnati. She was helping him and they lived together for three years.

He said that he had married an American and was divorced. **I asked him how they met.** He had a friend who had married her sister. "She was 18 years old; she was after me. I treated her as a sister; she changed her mind (and became romantically inclined). I loved her but there was too much of an age difference. I was pure and innocent (then)." It was a different tradition and culture. They fought at breakfast. **"Over what?" I asked.** He didn't want to eat bacon; she talked about "that stupid religion that wouldn't permit a man to eat bacon." She said Muslims put veils on their wives. "She approached me one day, saying she wanted to become a Muslim. She was scared." She divorced him. She was a student at the University of Dayton; she had just finished high school. Her mother got the divorce because he couldn't afford it. They were married just six months. **I asked what he thought the basic problem was.** He said he was strongly Arab and was unable to accommodate to a new society. "When someone said, 'Hi' to her (when they were walking on the campus) I became suspicious," he said. She smiled at her former boyfriends. I told her, "You shouldn't say, 'Hi,' to anybody."

WORK HISTORY: He is a night auditor at the Dallas-Fort Worth Airport, earning $13,000 a year plus overtime for a total of $18,000. He said he took the job because he wanted to get the experience following his accounting degree. The airport had many concessions like restaurants and motels; he audited the receipts to see if sales equaled tender (money collected). There were twelve outlets in the airport. He entered the data into the computer. He balanced credit cards.

In Ohio he had been a restaurant manager at Gold Star Chili Inc. from 1979 to 1983. He worked eighteen hours a day for three years at $5 an hour and he worked at the commissary for eight hours (or fewer if he was efficient). He made $18,000 a year as base salary plus $4,000 at the commissary during the summer for a total of $22,000.

How could you possibly manage such a workload? He used to go home bursting with tension. He cooked the chili on the stove and he cleaned machines with lime and shined them and cooked and cut meat. Inside the machine it was 140 degrees. When I indicated my surprise with an interjection, he said, "I had no other choice." He never wrote to his father (or his family) for aid because they were mad at him, so he had to do it on his own. He had to make good and show people. He worked in the commissary every summer till 1982 to earn the tuition for college, and he was going to school full-time. He lived across the street from the commissary. At the restaurant where he worked they treated him like a member of the family. He was always at their home; he ate their food; they helped finance his car. He said, "My friend who encouraged me to come to the States was from Jordan, a family from Fuhays, 5 miles west of Amman." In 1984 (the year he got his degree) a professor encouraged him to open up a restaurant together, the Pasta Palace. They got a loan of $80,000 from the bank. They went in 50/50; he owned five hundred shares. But then the professor had a quadruple heart bypass operation. So in 1984 he became the co-owner and manager of the Pasta Palace. He created his own menu and recipes, all freshly prepared. The Olive Garden chain plagiarized him. He had had his own experience at the commissary; he just added spices. They paid interest of 12 percent on their loan. In 1985 after his bypass operation, the professor said he had to get out of the enterprise, but he said not to worry; his mother was a millionaire. The professor didn't want to wait to make it a going concern. "They brought in someone else to buy the business and be my partner; they wanted me to teach him everything I knew about management." He refused to give the new owner his recipes. His partner, the professor, told him if he wanted to get out of the business, he'd cover his debt.

EMPLOYMENT IN TEXAS: In July 1985 he left Ohio and came to Dallas to live with two friends, from the Ajlun district of Jordan, the same district as Kufr al-Ma. From January 1986 to 1989 he worked as a telemarketer for American Airlines in Fort Worth for $20,000 a year. He got this job also by reading a newspaper ad. They sold services on the phone and answered clients' calls, and helped them get the services they wanted. In 1986 he won the prize for the highest sales rep in American Airlines. They took them to New York City as a reward. He was paid $6 an hour for that job. At the same time he worked in an Italian restaurant in Fort Worth. He got this job also from reading a newspaper ad. He worked there one year in 1986. The owner was an Iranian and hired him on the spot. It was a five-star restaurant. Till now they are friends.

From 1987 to 1989 he was store manager of a 7-11 store. He got this job through Jordanian friends. He made $22,000 from his job as store manager and $6,000 from his telemarketer job with American Airlines. He got someone to sub for him for four hours, 6–10 p.m., at the restaurant in order to moonlight on the American Airlines job.

The American Airlines job improved his English language, gave him contact with the public, and got him used to different accents. I asked how he got the telemarketer job. He replied, through the newspaper. "I said I had never done it before. I was honest. There was a beautiful lady there who said, 'I'm sure you'll do well.'" But he was always looking for an accountant's job (since that was his degree). From 1989 to 1991 he worked as the night auditor at the Dallas–Fort Worth airport. In addition he's worked as a one-person clerk-manager at a grocery store four hours a day.

I asked him whether he felt adequately rewarded for his work. He said, "I learned a lot, but I never reached what I wanted. If I'd stayed (with my previous job as store manager) I'd be making $35,000. But my goal was to work as an accountant; to be off weekends. After I return from Jordan I will look for an accounting job."

WORK-CYCLE: Presently he works twelve to fourteen hours a day and gets only Sunday off. That's why he wants to return to the U.S. and get an accountant's job, so he can work a five-day week. He finishes work around 9 a.m. and comes back to his apartment to sleep; he gets up around 2 or 3 p.m. On the Sunday he entertained me that's what he did; perhaps got up a bit earlier.

RESIDENCE: **I asked where he lived and with whom.** He lived in apartments from day one, except in Dayton where he lived in a dormitory. He has had guests like his Ajlun friends who have lived with him.

ARMY SERVICE: He was an airport security officer with The Royal Jordanian Airlines and traveled widely for one year. Then he spent one year as an embassy military guard at the Jordanian Embassy in London. As a captain he drew a base salary of 120 dinars a month plus 200 dinars for guarding the embassy. In 1977 he became Chief of Guard of the Jordanian Embassy in London. "There was this guy, a Jordanian, who was in the United States, already going to the University of Dayton." He encouraged him to come and offered his help by sending application forms. **I asked him what he saved from his army salary.** He replied that he never saved anything. He said that if you didn't get retirement in the army, you got severance pay: for every year you served you got two months' salary plus your housing allotment was given back. He got $8,000 severance pay.

SPENDING: I asked him what he spent his money on (since he said that he never saved anything). He replied that he spent his money on women, food, cars, and an education. Later he told me that he is currently spending $200 a month on telephone calls to Jordan (he is going there in July) and $100 a week on dating and good food. He said he has never saved anything and still doesn't. Currently his apartment costs $360 a month. He found it by inquiring, not through Arab friends. He pays $180 a month on a Nissan FX200, a used luxury car; previously he had another used luxury car, a Ford Crown-Victoria LTD for which he paid $6,000.[3] He said you can usually buy a used luxury car for $2–3,000. He has had eight cars; he's cracked up two.[4]

TIES WITH ARABS: [Note that his coming to the U.S. was facilitated by one Jordanian; he first lived with another; and that another Jordanian family almost adopted him and gave him part-time employment.] In Arlington once or twice a week he gets together with other Arabs at Denny's for a cup of coffee. Movies and films are for young kids and he didn't go to them. After the Iran-Iraq war he got hooked on TV. Ninety-nine percent of his friends are Arab-American. [All the calls he got while I was interviewing him that Sunday, more than twelve, were in Arabic.] One percent are Americans. He said he liked them (Americans), but "you had to get out of yourself to match their personality. You have to feel at home with your own people." [He liked Americans but felt uncomfortable with them in nonwork situations.][5]

I asked Dan what he thought about the relationship between the sexes when he arrived in the United States. At Dayton he was shocked. He didn't see what was portrayed in the movies. He saw industrialization; real life. "It is not that great a deal," he said. He had thought that the U.S. was civilized, humanized. "Some of my village people are more civilized." How so, I asked? "It's not what car you own, but your way of thinking. An average person in Kufr al-Ma believes in God and cares about human beings."

Did you ever suffer from discrimination? A few showed discrimination. "Here you are an Arab or a Muslim." He almost had a fight at Denny's the other day because they were speaking Arabic. A guy was sitting with his girlfriend in the next booth and moved away, saying to the waitress that they should either speak English or get out. Dan got mad and told him off, saying, "You're neither civilized nor educated." As a village person he grew up in a very religious milieu. "I can't remember looking at a girl's face (when we passed in the village way); we used to look down at the ground (out of modesty). (Since then) I've had my share. It was shocking. I was too shy to ask a girl out at Dayton and Cincinnati. They came and took me out. I really liked it. I think it's neat. Now we're more Americanized. But marrying (an American)? I really had a bad experience. All they (American girls) care about is having fun and getting drunk. Not living a respectful life. [Dan dichotomizes respect and fun as mutually exclusive options.] "They want to go out without you; go to girl friends and get drunk. With my girl friend she wants to see an American movie, and I want to see an Arabic videotape. I don't want anyone to put my country down. I'm not very religious, but I want my kids to be Muslims. I want to meet one of my own people. I want to marry someone who won't cheat on me. If I have a child I want him to be mine and not be gone after five years." (as happened to his Jordanian friend after divorce). "I'm not going back to Jordan to marry (he was returning for the first time in thirteen years in July) but I'm keeping my options open." **Are you going to stay and work in Jordan?** "No. Now this is my country. I am a citizen. My girlfriend—I cook and she won't even wash the dishes. I supported her and she spent it on make-up and clothes. We Jordanians have real good traditions. If I go to (an American) bar, I'm suffering. I believe in sitting down with people who share my values. The purpose of getting married is to be happy."

ATTITUDES AND IDEOLOGY: What do you think the good and bad points of Americans are? "I like American freedom, civilization. We had an image of American society as perfect. People are nice, God-loving, peaceful, nice, helpful. On the negative side, first, the foreign policy has no basis; it is built on blindness; (2) there is crime; in a great country (like this) they should solve it; if people are good, the government is good; (3) family ties are weak; I have a lot of American friends; the (American) man couldn't care less what the members of his family are doing; if a daughter or a son has a problem, he won't help; if the daughter needs money for an apartment, he won't help."

What is your view of the army? "Ninety-nine percent positive. I'm proud I served; it taught me principles: to be a tough man with good morals. I still think of myself as a military man. I have the discipline to start something and carry through with it. I believe I can achieve anything I want to. The only thing is, I don't exercise. I work twelve to fourteen hours a day. I get only Sunday off."

What is your view of birth control? "It is necessary these days. If a child can't grow happily and healthily, they shouldn't have it. Creating children without preparing for them is a disaster." **By what methods, I asked?** "As long as science approves, I'll go with it."

What of abortion? "Fifty-fifty. Killing a baby, I feel real bad about that. Why couldn't they plan beforehand? It's a moral problem. It depends on the circumstances."

What is your view of Jordan's unemployment problem? "It is serious. King Husayn will take care of it. Jordan is a third-world country. I feel there is a light in the future. The U.S. is serious about peace."

What is your view of tribal law? "It is very old. We have a new life to live. We should take some good parts of it. It is no longer good for us." **What about the *maḍafa* (guest house)? I asked.** "The *maḍafa* is no longer effective. It receives no respect from people. In the past what was said (by the elders) in the *maḍafa* was law. It is negative because by belonging to one of the influential families you can get what you want (in the *maḍafa*)."

What is your view of TV? "TV is a vehicle to get your point across. TV is the main factor now. (On the negative side one sees) a boy talking to his dad in a rude way (on TV). Would I ever address my dad, (by his first name)!"

What is your view of your own upbringing? "It was a good thing. I was brought up to be a good child, to respect (others); (I was taught) to be a good person, religious, encourage education. On the negative side, I never had a chance to be a child at home; (the upbringing) was too disciplinary, too strict; they didn't give a boy the chance to make his own decisions. My father wanted me to study, and it was my dream to be an officer."

GULF WAR VIEWS: Did the War lead to any changes in your life here in Arlington? "None."

Did the war lead to any changes in your relations with Americans? "No."
Did the war lead to any changes in your relations with other Arabs? "I lost my respect for Saudi Arabia, but that doesn't mean I won't go and work there. They never gave a chance to the Arabs to solve their problems first. Iraq was willing (to have an inter-Arab solution), but it did exactly what the United States wanted them to do, i.e., provoked a war. The greatest disgrace was that if they (Saudi Arabia) are so rich, why not do it on their own? Why, they are the richest (country) in the world! All they had were mercenaries (*murtaziqa,* meaning American troops). I'm not for Iraq occupying Kuwait. But what happened after that is a crime."

Did the war lead to any change in your views of Americans and American society? "No. I was expecting the U.S. to go into the Middle East a long time ago."

Did the war lead to any changes in your own feelings about yourself, your country, the Arab World, the Middle East? "I lost my confidence in the Arab World. I believe they will never be united. They've never been (united). We should work to create a new leadership to take care of the people before they (the leaders) take care of themselves."

What are your views of George Bush and Saddam Husayn? "Bush was unfair. I like him for everything he's done except for the Gulf. He wasn't honest and sincere; he did what the Israelis wanted him to do. Saddam is one of the traditional leaders who has the sincerity but does not have the political genius to play—to know how to put the U.S. on his side."

What do you think of all the American flags and yellow ribbons? "It was foolish. You are a superpower plus thirty-two countries (are on your side). Who are you fighting? An out-dated army. Like you fight a little child and beat him up and make him a hero."

What was the most surprising thing to you about the way Americans reacted to the War? "I was surprised about how the politicians played it. People who arranged for the parade (in Dallas) yesterday. For what? What did you do (that was so great)?"

6/9/91 (from my diary based on conversation in car) I asked Dan how he compared Ohio and Dallas. He said he liked the latter. He said that here they have a Jordanian society outside Jordan. He said that opportunities in Texas are also greater—one can either pursue the management of restaurants or accounting or combine them. Ohio was not favorable for his economic opportunities: he was first dependent on the Jordanian family and then went into the business venture that went awry. The old Jordanian gentleman riding with us in the car said that the topography and climate of Texas was like Jordan, flat, sandy, and hot. Dan said that Ohio was hot in the summer and very cold in the winter. [Perhaps Dan invited the old man to make the Sunday get-together more like home, a *madafa* with elders?] Dan said he wanted to go back to school and get a CPA degree and get a PhD in political science and teach in a college.

He said he wanted to retire to Kufr al-Ma, to die there. I want my partner (wife) to go with me. I want to hear a girl speaking Arabic again, I yearn for that. I want a friend, first. I want to introduce her into the culture. I want to come home and complain to her. [The wife is viewed as partner, friend, and comforter.]

6/10/91 (reflections from my diary) Dan's apartment was by far the most cramped, though he had an upstairs-downstairs arrangement. He said he had sent money home when he graduated (1984). He has a home in Kufr al-Ma that is empty north of the village preacher's house. Dan was very critical of the preacher; he called him, *jiddi* (young goat), and laughed and said that as a young shepherd he stole a sheep and then denied it. He said that the preacher was not sincere and was using his preaching position simply to make a living.

6/10/91 (reflections from my diary on the day I left Dallas) Dan wrote down his address and telephone number in my diary, referring to himself as Dan so-an-so, an anglicized, shortened name. He could be reached in his apartment mornings until 3 p.m. and on Sunday. He worked until 9 a.m. and got up around 1 or 2 in the afternoon today to prepare *maqluba* ("turned-over") for us, so-called because the lamb meat is cooked on the bottom of the pan and the rice on the top and is then tipped upside down for serving. The roasted chicken was placed on top. Dan's best friend, a Jordanian, is living with him (perhaps as Dan had lived with the friend when he first came to Texas). His friend had come back to Texas from Los Angeles after divorcing his American wife, after three years there. He had come back to Dallas to be near his daughter, whom he loves dearly—he used to come back and forth from California. He didn't like the smog in California, and the life was costly.

Zayd
Interview in Kufr al-Ma: 1986

Zayd attended primary school and junior high school in Kufr al-Ma. In 1979 he finished Irbid Trade School (in the nearby market town), which he attended for three years. On the 16th of December he arrived in the United States. He had proceeded to the U.S. immediately after spending twenty days in Abu Dhabi where his father helped him get a visa. He went to Houston, Texas. Amid-East (an educational placement agency) picked Houston; they picked a language institute in Houston and (as a follow-up) a college in another state, Ohio. He refused to go to Ohio since his patrilateral cousin (*ibn 'amm*) was in Texas. He stayed only two months at the language school and got accepted at San Antonio College in engineering. He switched to Trinity University in San Antonio and got his BA from Trinity. He came back to Jordan to see his family and returned last summer to the U.S.A., where he is going to school and studying for his MA.

(When he first came to Houston) he went to ELS (English Language School) for eighteen days; it was very costly and they taught "elementary stuff"; he took a test and they put him on the second level. In the Spring of 1980 he took one course at the University of Houston; it was a good course and the professors were very helpful. In the summer of 1980 he studied civil engineering at Blinn College, Branham, Texas, one hundred miles from Houston. He learned about it from Jordanian friends who were there. He went there because he got an easy acceptance that didn't require the TOEFL (English language exam). He stayed there two semesters, unsuccessfully; there (in Jordan) they didn't teach enough math and science to learn engineering. "I gave it a shot, and I didn't succeed."

The Irbid school he went to was a German school where he learned carpentry; "it was okay, not too great. I was good and liked it—carpentry; but academically, it was weak." He was never too fond of math. His average was 68.3 in high school in the government test. He attended Blinn College in the summer and fall of 1980. He knew he couldn't make it in engineering.

He returned to Houston to attend flying school to become a commercial pilot; he learned about this from his Jordanian friends: he went to the Air Academy, Hobby Airport, Houston. They required 250 hours to become a commercial pilot. He studied about 150 hours, and he changed his mind again. It was okay. The only work in Jordan for pilots was with ALIA (the national airlines)—and they had so many pilots, there was a waiting list of three years just to have one's application considered! He found out about this because one of his friends went to Jordan and came back to the U.S.A. One of his friends is working as a waiter in the U.S.A.; a second is in the Jordanian army and will go into his family's farm. [I presume the two friends were at the airport academy with him.]

What is your evaluation of the instruction at the Air Academy? "It was fair only. The airplanes were not the newest; the instructors—some were competent and some were not so good. Some treated us as if we knew nothing; a British instructor treated him as a dummy—kept saying he needed more (training) on the same procedure, and he came back and he preached to him for two more hours, and got ten dollars an hour for ground school instruction; he felt they took advantage of him. The owner of the school had a sign, 'Foreign students will be charged for two hours flying and one session ground school.' Even if you didn't go to the lesson you would still be charged $20 a lesson; you paid $63 an hour for dual flying with the instructor. If you reserved a plane and you were sick, you had to call or you still paid. You had to go twice a week. It was not fair." [Zayd understood piece-rate compensation, pay for service, but not payment for (appointment) time which he construed as non-service. Note, the only blatant charges of discrimination against foreigners have been from migrants in the U.S.A. and England.] In August of 1983 he returned to Jordan after three years' absence to visit his family and see what was going on. He stayed a month. He returned (to the U.S.) in September 1983. He found out that in Jordan there was a demand for computer training. In the fall of 1983 he didn't study. In the spring of 1984 he began studying data processing at Houston Community College—some of his Jordanian friends were studying there. He had one friend from (the nearby village of) al-Husn (in Jordan). In December 1985 he got an associate degree in data processing. He took one more semester. He is still thinking of going back and getting a BA in Business Computer Information Systems—he would go to the University of Houston, Down-Town College. Or else he'll serve his two-year army duty and have another job on the side in the afternoon and live like everyone else here (in Kufr al-Ma)—he hasn't decided where. My family wants me to stay here.

What was the cost of your education? "In 1979 it cost $900–1,000 a month; at Blinn College $2,000 for the summer semester plus expenses of $100–150 a month or $600. The fall semester was also $2,000; i.e., for the full academic year including summer it was $9,000. Data processing school was good and the instructors were good, and they had enough computers, and the schedules for using them were okay. I didn't study much for a 3.0 average."

Why didn't you study harder? Because he was working.

What jobs did you hold while in the United States? In 1980 he worked at McDonald's while at the English school; he went for the first week and quit after three days. "I wasn't raised to believe I was supposed to do this kind of job. I felt humiliated when someone asked me to pick up the mop and clean the floor. (I) didn't feel comfortable. The wages were okay, $3.25 an hour." He didn't work again till he left Blinn College. He went to work at an Italian restaurant as a busboy in Houston. He worked there for a year; they promoted him to cocktail waiter [he worked as a busboy for four months]. "The first time I served iced tea to a customer I felt humiliated. Then I got used to the idea, and it was okay." He worked eight months as a cocktail waiter, taking drinks from the bar and serving customers. The busboy's minimum wage was $3.25 an hour, and the waiter gave him 10 percent of his tips. His weekly schedule as busboy was three days a week, three dinners and lunches or twenty-five to twenty-six hours a week: $150 a week as busboy or $600 a month. At the cocktail bar he got only tips. As cocktail waiter he made $800–1,000 after taxes. His job was okay and he got a scholarship from Abu Dhabi of $500 a month; he had the scholarship four years, 1981–1985. His first full-time job was while he was going to flying school, which he did on Thursday and Saturday. He went to another French and Italian restaurant in Houston, serving as waiter for seven months in 1982. He made $1,000 a month full-time. He never saved any money from his jobs—just enough to live; he lived like his other Jordanian friends who worked hard—not like those who got money from their families. [There were two classes of students: those who got just enough for school and a "plain student life" vs. others who had to supplement their status by working.] As bartender from the restaurant he was paid $1,200 plus the waiters gave them a percentage of their tips for a total of $1,500 a month full-time.

Did you own automobiles? In six years he bought and sold six cars. He bought his first car in 1981, a 1973 Dodge, four-door, for $550. He bought and sold his second car in 1981, seven months later, a 1973 Monte Carlo for $500. He sold the first for more than he paid for it after he had it for more than a year. He bought his third car in 1982, a 1979 Ford Mustang for $6,000; the financing charge was 24 percent—he paid $250 a month; the insurance ran out after the first year, and he had to pay insurance of $50 more a month for a total of $300 a month. He bought his fourth car in the summer of 1984, a new car, a Grand Prix Pontiac, after he had paid the other one off—it cost $11,000; he gave his Ford as a trade-in for $2,800 and paid installments of $285 a month. He said that he got Americanized (buying on the installment plan). He said the weather was hot in Texas. If you drove a used car, it cost so much to fix it. He kept the car six months. He found out that they sold him insurance just for the car and not for himself, i.e., no personal liability insurance. He trusted them and he was ripped off. (This pertains to the question of difficulties he encountered.) He thought that if he had an accident, it would be a disaster. [This incident shows his intelligence and awareness of the new environment.] After two months of his not paying he said, "Come pick up the car, and do what you want to do." He bought his sixth car, a 1975 Toyota Celica for $1,000. [Note the progression from an unstylish secondhand car to a new car to a secondhand economizing car.] He said he had to have a car. The Metro system in Houston was not great. It took an hour to get to school or work on it, and it took fifteen minutes in the car. The gas was $1.00 a gallon and went down to 75 cents.

[I noticed he was smoking.] He said he went to the physician's clinic in Houston to ask about how to quit smoking; they said they would give him medicine to make him physically nondependent, but psychologically he might still be dependent. He says he still smokes two packs a day.

At this point in the interview his village relatives and friends, including the Shaykh who taught Zayd English in the village, came to visit his father.

What kind of housing did you have in Houston? Zayd lived with his cousin for two weeks, and then he moved to San Antonio and lived with a roommate who was from Damascus, Syria. He lived there six months, paying $100 for a one-bedroom apartment. His (the Syrian's) customs were the same, but his roommate lived a different style-of-life since his father was a lawyer. In Damascus they lived in a nice house and had a nice car, and the roommate's father visited them in Texas. Zayd acted like all this was no big deal even though his family didn't have much (materially) in Kufr al-Ma. He and the Syrian and another Jordanian moved to a three-bedroom apartment in another area because he said the groups who lived in the area were not good—they were homosexuals and liked sexual relations. He was shocked by the public acceptance of homosexuality—he saw two guys kissing. He said (to his roommates), "Tomorrow we're moving." "I didn't want any of my friends to know I was living in that area."

Did you have girlfriends? I had many girlfriends from different nationalities—Mexican-Americans, British, South Americans, and Native Americans. **Where did you take them?** To dinner, dancing, to the park. He had a steady girlfriend at different times. The first was an "all-American girl" from Chicago from a good family; her father was a judge, and she was seven years older than me; her mother was a teacher. She was a good girl. He visited her aunt and aunt's husband in Houston. **Did you think of marrying her?** He liked her but never thought of marrying her. It was inside me that she would not like it here (in Jordan), and I don't want someone who can't speak to my mother. I don't want to do that to my parents. I met her at a night club, disco. The second girl was from Wales—I met her at a disco. My friend, an Arabian from Qatar who was dating her friend, fixed me up with her on a blind date. She was young, beautiful, energetic—I was thinking of marrying her—they had some customs in Wales similar to those in Jordan. But we never got to that point. I liked her, but not enough to marry her. We went dancing, and she asked me whether I wanted to dance, and I said, "Not now," and when I got back (from talking with other fellows) she was dancing with another guy. "I got mad; I was jealous; I called her off the dance floor, and she got mad." [I assumed they broke up after that]. The first girlfriend had to leave Houston, and she asked him if he wanted to go with her and start a business in St. Louis. [He didn't want to go]. He met his third (and current) steady girlfriend at Houston Community college. She was an American from Texas; very nice and educated and studying to be a CPA. "I told her that if I came back to Houston (from Jordan) we would pick up where we left off or I'd write her." **Did you think of marrying her?** "No. She isn't an ideal woman for a wife; it is not beauty I want; she is too committed to her work; to work in a bank; she takes her work too seriously, thinking of promotion and the prestige of work."

What roommates and housing did you have in Houston? He stayed at his first place six months; he stayed at the second place with the two roommates above-mentioned in the three-room apartment one year. At the third place he lived with another Jordanian friend for a year—the others had to move; the rent was $130 a month; he didn't cook, but ate at the restaurant where he bartended. When he was with the three roommates, the Jordanian from Irbid cooked—he cooked Arabic and Italian-style—(till) he finished civil engineering. The fourth place he moved in by himself, a one-bedroom apartment, in order to have more privacy. Then he went to Jordan. At the fifth place he was with another Jordanian friend for six months. Then he moved to a house with his Jordanian friend and a Jordanian-American, a house they rented for $200 a month. All his roommates were Jordanians.

What is your view of American customs? "Some are good and some aren't. In the city it was hard to make American friends. When I went flying it was cold (weather), and people came out with a coat and hot coffee. It is not too friendly in Houston—they are too busy with themselves, yes. When I moved to a house we met neighbors and made them Arabic food and they were pleased and invited them back for barbecue and beer (this was in the housing before the last where they stayed five months). They had difficulties with the Jordanian-Americans—they are all money-minded; they (Americans) do anything for money. He (the Jordanian-American) got a house for no money at all; (then) he told his partner (to-be), 'Give me $5,000,' to be the partner of a house for which he had paid nothing—he just had to make payments on the house. He (this Jordanian-American) told the Jordanian guy, 'I paid $5,000 for the house and let's be partners.' He got into partying and drugs, and brought people with drugs (to the house), and we decided we didn't want this (and left)."

How did you adapt to American life? "I did adapt to American life. I was homesick, and when I go back here (the village) everything was (is) different. There is no hot water in the morning; I have to heat the water. There is no phone; my father applied for a phone years ago. It is not easy to get a car because of high taxes. Public services are bad. Roads are bad. I wouldn't drive on these roads. I drove seven years in Houston with no problem, and didn't hear a horn blowing. I got a 1983 car for $3,000, Nissan control, and here (Jordan) my brother got a 1969 Mercedes that I wouldn't look at for $2,000. In the capital (Amman) there are palaces; in the States you don't find them. These people (in Jordan) got a position in government and ripped off the people, and have bathtubs and Mercedes, and a Jacuzzi (bubble-bath), and we don't have hot water! They should do more—there is aid coming from the U.S.A., and we don't see a fraction of it—it's all going to individuals: a guy in the local government takes some and contractors take (some). If the government is good, they'll educate the people. If they levied taxes on the people (for services) I'd go for it—two or three dinars won't hurt the family. Everyone needs a leader; if the leader is good … it's ridiculous to elect a taxi driver as mayor (in Kufr al-Ma); there are many more qualified (men)."

What is your view of the unemployment problem in Jordan? "The government should say what kind of jobs are needed and distribute the people (accordingly). My father wanted me to be an engineer and I started in that (occupation) and I changed (my mind) so many times. But if the government says what technological changes are occurring, (one) can act accordingly."

I asked Zayd about ethnic discrimination and he referred to the "rednecks" from Pasadena, Texas. **Would you meet them often?** "Yes. They would pull up their cars alongside ours and then just look at you and say, 'Look at that Saudi shaykh—that dumb camel jockey.' I think they think of Arabs as shaykhs with a lot of money and wives and camels and someone who has found gold and doesn't know what to do with it. I got to know (more friendly) curious Americans and girlfriends (introduced them). I would explain about Jordan if a teacher asked in class."

What did you like about the U.S.A.? "The freedom. Nobody gets in your business. You can do what you want to do. If you want to be lazy and lie back you will die starving (in America). They do more for their citizens there. What are accessories here (in Jordan) are rights there, i.e., welfare, social security. They help other people and other countries."

What didn't you like about the U.S.A.? "(1) There is too much freedom; the law is not strict. Some individuals get away with murder; (2) If you have a good lawyer, money, power, you can override the rights of victims. Money can get you in politics. If you hurt someone, a good lawyer can get you out of it. My government teacher told me that. (3) The way they treat this part of the world—the Arab World."

Would you go to the U.S.A. again (if you had to do it all over again)? "If I knew I was going to feel this way, frustrated and confused between my country and the U.S.A., no. My roots are here (Jordan), but I like the things over there. People in Jordan (meaning people in the village), people walk in (on the spur of the moment) and expect to see me, and I was at my sister's (house). I saw my brother on my way back. (When he returned home) his father said (accusingly) 'Where were you?' I said, 'Do you expect me to sit and wait for them?' Sometimes you're doing something and people come in and disturb you. Now if I go to someone's house, I'll send word ahead."

"The last job I had for one year, for a company, I earned $600 a month, variably. I loved (the money) there. The last job I had was as a limousine driver. People wanted (you) to be at the restaurant on time at 7:00. I liked the money. I never liked any of the (other) jobs—all of them were service jobs. I've grown up working with people, but not serving as their servant."

What is your view of your childhood? "It was happy compared to other people. I was well taken care of, loved." **You never felt the presence of constraint?** "No. Because I didn't know any better, I accepted it the way it was. I knew later there must be something better when I began reading books."

Did you receive physical punishment as a child? "My father used communication. I loved my father very much. From a young age he told me my education was important: 'Look at so-and-so, he's an engineer, a doctor. I was (village) mayor (*mukhtar*) at seventeen. You should be good,' my father told me. He made me good. And now I do everything possible to fulfill that picture. In the States, the first person to come to my mind is my father. He said, 'I'm watching your studying; I'm working for you; I want to be proud of you.'"

Is there competition among kinsmen now? "My cousin was headmaster of the school so they pointed to him (as a model); 'its his cousin,' (they'd say). I feel obligated (by this fact). We are going to be good (in the sense of achievers) because others look at us with expectation. I can't disappoint my family. While I'm doing that, I'm serving myself. Later when you're an adult.... My mother never punished me physically."

What are your views of women working outside the house? "They should, now especially. A man now can't provide enough (economically). Now fifty-fifty is good. It is good for the woman to go out of the house where there is only preparing food and (being) with kids, so that she can come into contact with society. I find it very disturbing to find an educated man marrying a ninth or twelfth grader. I don't know how they will relate to one another."

What kind of jobs can women take? "There is no problem with jobs. Anything within range: not dancing (but) like teaching, nursing, a secretary, a professor or anything." [Note, only actual physical contact with the opposite sex is ruled out in jobs.]

What are your views on birth control? "I'm all for it. I nag every one of my relatives when I see them. Someone thirty-five years old with seven kids—that's ridiculous. My brother is like that with his salary of 150 dinars a month and his wife is working. How is he going to support these kids when they grow up?"

What methods are possible? "I know there are side effects (to certain birth control methods). Birth control in any form—it should be used. I won't bring any children into this life unless I know what I'm going to provide and where they're going to go."

How do you view tribal law? "I don't think it's good. I'd leave it to the State to decide. I don't think it's (tribal law) based on good judgements. A lot of times they (tribal reconciliations) don't work. Not everyone is satisfied. I want rules to be based on fairness and education; to consider a lot of things. I don't want one guy deciding for five thousand people. Let's be fair to everybody and solve the problem intelligently."

What is the effect of the army on society? "The army is good, but it should give more to individuals. They take his youth and don't give him much in return. The salary is minimal. It isn't good enough. The draft. I'm not for it. I think people should become acquainted with it (the army) for three months. I don't see any reason to take two years of my life and give me only twenty dinars a month. I don't think that's good. And, once again, I'll have to be dependent on my father for money. I'll feel awkward."

What's your view of television? "In Jordan it's not too great. They don't provide good programs for kids. They don't go into the details of the news in the (Arab) states. The King goes to visit the President of so-and-so; they don't talk in detail about why he's going. I don't know why they want to keep the news away from the public; or (is it that they) just don't know better? I feel deprived. I can't read the paper over a cup of coffee and I don't get much out of it and I don't enjoy it. The TV is the same. They don't talk much about the world. The times of showing are limited—only six hours a night. One should be able to watch the news any time and not just what the government wants you to hear."

"Sometimes there are (village) customs that aren't good at all. People give their opinions (about how you should act) when you haven't asked for them. In the U.S.A. no one gives their opinion unless asked. Here they judge first and don't listen to you. They (villagers) pick on one another. They say, 'Look at that person, what he is doing.' They don't say, 'Whatever makes him happy, that's good.' [Individualism and hedonism are endorsed.] Another thing. Respect for elders, right or wrong. I don't like that. It bothers me from the inside. I think people should be honest with one another. Sometimes people don't see someone for a year because they've heard gossip—why don't you go and see the person and discuss it. Some don't like one another, perhaps between Beni Yasin, Beni Amr, and Beni Dumi (the clans of the village) because of a lack of understanding. Sometimes relatives stick together, right or wrong. I don't like that either. I should know the facts. I should listen to anyone's opinion even against my brother, if he is wrong."

Interview in Houston: 1991

5/29/91 (phone conversation, Binghamton, NY), I gleaned from a phone call to Zayd in the spring of 1991 that he had finished his BBM and now works part-time for a limousine company. He lives in the heart of Houston in the Galleria area. He said that he finished his degree and was going back to Jordan, but his father told him to stay in the U.S.—that the economic situation in Jordan was not good yet.

6/3/91 I spoke to Zayd over the phone again to confirm my visit to Houston. He said that he had received word from his father that he had to serve in the Jordanian army for two years including three months of basic training. He didn't want to do that or, alternatively, pay $6,000 to the government—he thought that excessive.[6] So now he had to mull it over and make a decision before August. He came to Texas two months after the first transnational migrant from Kufr al-Ma (his cousin). They were the first two in Texas. Dan was already in Ohio studying business accounting, but he didn't know about him.

6/5/91 (in Houston) Zayd said that one learns in one week in the U.S. what one learns in a year in Jordan. He had told his brother and his father to give him $50,000 and he would invest it in a small business and double or triple the money. He also tried to encourage his brother to come to Texas and see the investment opportunities. His brother had been working as a nurse for thirteen years in Abu Dhabi and had saved a lot. He had also just finished a law degree by correspondence with the Arab University in Beirut, and was fighting a lawsuit over a piece of property in Irbid. He said he will do well as a lawyer; he is aggressive. But neither his father nor brother would give him money to invest in Texas. His other brother had gone to school in Pakistan from 1983 to 1986, studying at the Pakistan International Airline Training Center; he got a degree in Aviation Maintenance Technology and came to Texas in January of 1987, leaving in August. Zayd's brother liked it in Houston, but they would only give him sixteen credit hours here so that he had to retake courses. He has served in the army two years. Then ALIA (the national airline) hired him. This brother was taken by his father to Abu Dhabi at age fifteen. He was brilliant and got a 98 in math. His father feels guilty about his going to Pakistan (for an education). Zayd said that in Jordan if you're age thirty and don't have a government job and aren't married with children you are a failure. He said, "I'm doing as well as Abdullah, son of Shaykh Qasim (an influential in Kufr al-Ma). One needs to make 1,000 dinars (ci. $1,400) a month to live a middle-class life."

[Zayd suddenly changed the subject, discussing another Texas migrant's ('Isam) father.] 'Isam's father went to Abu Dhabi originally on a teaching mission for three to four years and then decided to stay. 'Isam's father was a big spender in Kufr al-Ma on a 40–50 dinar a month salary and had gone into debt—maybe that's why he went to Abu Dhabi. He said that some say that 'Isam's father is still in debt in both Abu Dhabi and Kufr al-Ma because of his generosity. 'Isam's father probably played the role of "Shaykh" in Abu Dhabi for the people of Kufr al-Ma and Al-Kura (i.e., he offered regular hospitality to them). He was the pioneer (migrant there). Neither 'Isam nor his brother finished their studies in Texas. 'Isam has only been here (in Texas) five years. He couldn't finish his degree between learning English and working. For the last six or seven years 'Isam's father has come to Kufr al-Ma every other year. He is approaching age sixty. 'Isam's father was very patriotic (about Jordan); people couldn't understand him going away for such a long time. When Zayd visited his brother in Al-Ayn (Abu Dhabi) 'Isam's father was living close to his brother's house. Zayd went to visit 'Isam's younger brother, who got a degree in engineering in a short time from the University of the Emirates in Abu Dhabi. He is working in Abu Dhabi with a private company.

6/5/91 (from Zayd in Houston) "In Kufr al-Ma it was pathetic. They have nothing. My mother doesn't wear a $500 dress. When I finished (my studies) my father said, 'Hurry up, come back; we want to get you married and get you a car and build you a house.' I don't want that average living. I guess that was one of the bad things that happened to me here (Houston). You drive down the street and see a Mercedes-Benz, and millions have…. And I'm going to go back to…. At the end of my life I want to be close to God. I'm not practicing my religion now, but later…."[7] He doesn't like what he sees. Most of his friends (in Houston) are under the thumbs of their wives; (sometimes) the wife (suddenly) runs off with the kids. If I get divorced my wife is going to take the kids. He said he married a girl from 1983 to 1986. He said he married an (American) girl to try it (marriage) out and to get citizenship.

6/5/91 Before, he had told me that his life was very empty here; lonely. When he went back to Kufr al-Ma in 1983, he asked his father if he could smoke and he said, "Okay." In 1986 he was asked by his father if he drank. He replied (in front of some guests) that he had done everything (in the United States). His father later said, "I wish you hadn't been so frank." From that time on he got along well with his father. And he is very close to him, unlike some other (migrant sons). In reply to my question he said that his father knew of his marriage and divorce of the American girl. He said that she was into drugs. He placed her in two jobs and she lost both. So they were divorced. Fortunately, they had no children. He said that a Jordanian (his best friend now in Houston) from the village of al-Husn was his roommate from 1983 to 1985. On the question of marriage to Americans he said that his cousin had been here eleven years and had just married. 'Isam got married a few months before that. He married a doctor's daughter. Zayd's cousin met people through a school principal with whom he lived in San Antonio. The principal had ties in the church; he befriended him.

Zayd was thinking of starting a limousine business with one or two "limos." He wants to work until March (1992) to save up money for a business. Perhaps he will work five to seven years and make money and sell it (the business) and go back to live comfortably over there (Jordan). He wants to marry there (in Jordan) and return to the U.S. with his wife. I raised the question of whether she would be happy here. He replied, "The Arab woman—her life is her home and her husband." He will teach her and give her the benefit of his experience; he would send her to school. He fears bringing up children here (U.S.A.); there are drugs and (pretty soon) you can't distinguish them (Jordanian children) from American kids. "I want them to turn out my way." He would not want his children to be brought up in the United States.

6/6/91 In his bedroom in his Houston apartment Zayd has a painting of a full white-breasted nude reposing with a loosely draped negligee on a bed next to a very long scenic photograph of the Muslim quarter of Jerusalem with the Dome of the Rock and the Aqsa Mosque prominently featured. On the other wall was a collage of family members. In the living room was a picture of his (brilliant) brother and a picture of that brother and his father after the former's graduation from the University of the Emirates in Abu Dhabi. [I noted that in this picture Zayd's father is bareheaded, considered a violation of the modesty code in Kufr al-Ma.] In December 1990 Zayd was offered a possible job in Saudi Arabia with the Modern Industries Company in Jidda. They sold cooking oil, soap, toothpaste, and cleaning products such as shampoos. He filled out an application form, but then the (Gulf) war broke out. Representatives of the company had come to the Saudi club in Houston and a Saudi friend had told him about the job and brought him a form to fill out.

He told me about the case of honor concerning the son of an elder from his clan having an affair with the daughter of his uncle. They were discovered by the brother of her husband. He saw the act and beat him up and broke his arms. They were divorced immediately. Her father came to his father and asked him what to do. His father said, "Get out, you're not a man." If he were him, he would have killed his daughter (and preserved his and his kinsmen's honor). But her father had spent many years in Zerqa (the largest city in Jordan after Amman), and the girl walked around bareheaded (and was not enculturated into the mores of the village).

Zayd knows all the marriage ties of his brothers: The oldest, forty-one, a policeman (two stars) finished high school and married the daughter of a clansman. He lives in the adjoining village of Deir Abu Said. The next oldest, thirty-five, B. Nursing, Tripoli, 1974–77; B. Laws, Arab University of Beirut by correspondence, 1987; lives and works in Al-Ayn, Abu Dhabi in a hospital. He married the daughter of a villager from the clan of Beni Yasin. He will return to Kufr al-Ma in the summer of 1991 after thirteen years in Abu Dhabi. The next-to-youngest, twenty-seven, studied at the Avionics Institute, Karachi, 1986–89. He has worked for ALIA, the national airline, since 1990, in Amman; he is unmarried. The youngest, twenty-four, is a high school graduate and works in a retail clothing shop in Deir Abu Said. He married his patrilateral cousin.

We looked at Zayd's photo scrapbook and he explained the identities/situation of each picture. There were pictures of him in Jordan; photos of him as a restaurant waiter in Houston; a photo of him all dressed up—a prominent visiting Jordanian took him to the symphony with other Americans in Houston. There was a photo of migrants from Kufr al-Ma in Pakistan: one who studied journalism in Karachi and now works with the Ministry of Development; a second who studied food technology; a third who studied food technology and agronomy and now works in Irbid with a canning company; a fourth who studied avionics in Karachi and now works with ALIA. There was a second photo with three students from Kufr al-Ma who studied English in Pakistan and another who studied journalism. Zayd has in mind starting a club for those who want to travel to places and want to ask someone questions before they go [note his entrepreneurship mindset]. He said his father sent him to someone in Deir abu Said who had gotten a degree in biology in the U.S.A. before he went to Texas. [Note how the father attempted to prepare him psychologically for migration.]

I noted that Zayd still chain-smokes. He had an ashtray in the bathroom. I noted also that he doesn't handle the Quran as a sacred thing—doesn't kiss it despite his childhood piety.

6/6/91 Zayd's coming to the United States was his first trip out of the country. He remembers the first apartment he ever stayed in on 1407 West Alabama and the first night he spent in a hotel—Sheraton Downtown, Room 2525. He said he listened to a tape on the car radio about a rich person who had many friends and then lost all of them (when he fell on hard times) except the core who would give him their soul. He said there was a "king" (*malik*) of Inbe (a nearby Jordanian village) who discovered gold and was subsequently seated in the place of honor in the guest house (*madafa*) whereas before he used to sit by the shoes near the door (a place of low status-honor). [Note the strong theme of money as the road to status, but not loyalty.] He said that when he worked at the French and later, Italian restaurant, Trace, he made good money; in addition he had a grant from Abu Dhabi (to live on).

6/6/91 (in the car) Zayd said that when he gets "down" or bored he drives through Allen Parkway to see how the dregs of society (the blacks) live, and then through River Oaks to see the clean and beautiful area, and he imagines living there. [During the driving tour we visited four areas: downtown; Allen Parkway Village (poor blacks, dingy houses, proliferation of small churches and lodges); Montrose, drugs, prostitution and the gay area that looks more respectable; River Oaks, average house costs 3–5 million dollars.] He said that he would like to have a house (in Jordan) on Abu Kharrub (a high point overlooking the village), above the house of a retired army officer and village notable. If he started with ten cows (in Kufr al-Ma) he could make as much (in income) as three salaried employees.

[Zayd gets to know different social strata through his chauffeuring job.] He doesn't like his River Oaks clients; they are arrogant and demanding, particularly the women. A lot of people are intimidated by them.

Originally, he got an I-20 form from his school to get a visa. I took a picture of 1407 W. Alabama Street where Zayd first lived with his cousin for two months. He first went to school at the private English language school run by Americans. He spent $350 a month for a couple of books and lousy teaching. He saw it was a scam and took a term of intensive English at the University of Houston, downtown in Montrose. He lived with his cousin and a Syrian fellow for 2½ months. He said, "We came home one night and found two guys on the corner kissing one another." Immediately they moved ten miles away.

[We spent the afternoon in the Galleria section including the huge shopping mall.] Zayd said he participated fully in aspects of American life: dancing, drinking, and bars; but he is ignorant of other aspects of American society—American family life. He sees the life that he formerly led now as silly. He said that he could have gotten a job with an American company after graduating in December at $300–400 a week or $1,500 a month. After twenty years, if he kept his job he'd be making $100,000 a year. He figures to make that long before then. Some of his classmates are working with Lockheed and NASA. At 6 p.m. I took a picture in the Galleria of the McDonald's where he got a job twenty days after coming to the U.S.A. He was bored at home—he was taking an English class. He worked 3½ hours at McDonald's; then, when the owner asked him to mop the floor, he called up his roommate and asked him to take him home. He saw Robin Williams in (the film) *Moscow-on-the-Hudson* about a (Russian) saxophonist who deserted his band in New York City and also worked at McDonald's and as a chauffeur. [He already sees his early migrant experience with some objectivity and in relation to similar strivers.]

6/7/91 Zayd said yesterday that he didn't gain citizenship till 1989; he didn't apply till 1988. He was married in 1983 and lived with his wife for one year. Then he bought her a ticket to California and said, "I don't want to see you ever again." He did see her by accident several years later and she came up to him and greeted him effusively, but he ignored her. There is a rule that you can't apply for citizenship until three years after marriage or five years after marriage, if divorced. He was separated for five years and neither he nor his wife cared. She still doesn't know she's divorced. I said that he ought to tell her. He said that he didn't know where she lives.

His best Jordanian friend has just bought a house in Houston. Zayd said he really didn't want it; his Hungarian wife wanted it. They have two children, one a few months old and the other 2½ (years). Zayd said that his friend could have taken the money, the 10 thousand dollar down payment on a 40 thousand dollar house, and invested it in a business and within a few years made enough money to buy a house too. He said that his friend had a job as an inspector of cars for a gas station; the job had no future. [Zayd is oriented toward the future as well as investment, and deferred gratification.] He could be fired at any time. His friend works from 8 to 5 p.m., and he asked me how the schools were in Hopewell, New Jersey near Princeton where his friend's wife and in-laws live. He said his wife was concerned about schooling for his children in southwest Houston where there was an increasing crime and drug problem. He was thinking of moving to New Jersey.

Both Zayd and his best friend feel the same way about refusing to serve in the army. They said they thought about getting all Jordanians in the same situation in the United States to petition to Jordan, not necessarily under their own names, saying that they would never return to Jordan or spend or invest there until the law was repealed. The buyout was originally $10,000 and has been reduced to $6,000. They were hoping it would be reduced again or abolished. Yesterday Zayd told me in the interview that he had had his hardships in the U.S.A. and doesn't want any more (in the army). He said he was going to pay the $6,000 now allowed to buy your way out of army service. This law was passed a year ago because of Jordan's economic situation. It is very unfair and shameful. But he will take advantage of it. Zayd has to decide by August. He will work in Houston till next March (to earn the money). Zayd's friend is a sports fan and insisted on watching the Lakers-Bulls game.

When he returned to Jordan in 1986 Zayd couldn't fit in. He yearned to return to Houston. He said that his father knew of his marriage and divorce. He has an unusual relationship with his father: he can tell him anything; when he thinks of his family, he thinks of his father.

1/7/91 Zayd's father would reason with him, tell him, "If you don't study, you'll be eating dirt; you'll go into the army." Then, if that didn't work he'd say, "Get out of my sight, you good-for-nothing (*ya hamil*)." His father was very authoritarian and acted as the head of the family although he was the youngest sibling. He would discipline the wives of his brothers and his brothers never objected. His father's mother was a Zaydan, a notable family in the district, and his father was opposed to the Zaydans and saw the villagers as ignorant in not standing up to them.[8] Abdullah Zaydan was his grandmother's first cousin. Perhaps by becoming mukhtar (village mayor) his father acted out that independence. But Abdullah Zaydan respected him. In 1986 Abdullah Zaydan's grandson was getting married, and Zayd's father was the only one from the village invited to the wedding celebration. And he got special treatment there.

198

His father spent twenty years in the army; he had become master-sergeant by the time he left. His father had to pay an intermediary (*wasṭa*) to get into the army. Today, (1991) again you have to pay an intermediary to get in [though not in the intervening period, i.e., the 1980s–90s decline in oil economies and migration has again made the army a secure occupation in an insecure world]. In 1976 his father's maternal cousin (*ibn khal*), a Zaydan, had a brother in Germany with connections in Abu Dhabi who wanted to open a car dealership in Abu Dhabi, and they wanted his father to manage the dealership (and so his father went to Abu Dhabi, but the dealership didn't work out) and so his father returned to Jordan. A few months later a group from Abu Dhabi intelligence wanted army intelligence officers to train their own intelligence. In the middle of his army service his father had switched from regular army to army intelligence. They paid him a good salary, 400–500 dinars or about $1,400, and in addition gave him free living quarters and gave him a 100 percent increase later; his father stayed in Abu Dhabi eight or nine years. When his father went (to Abu Dhabi) he became the oldest villager there, but he lived in the army intelligence headquarters and couldn't maintain a guest house there. [This was the explanation for why his father never became a "shaykh of *maḍafa*" in Abu Dhabi as 'Isam's father did.] Zayd's father asked him (at the time he was preparing to go to the U.S.A.) if he wanted to join the intelligence service of Abu Dhabi for 700 dinars a month as a beginner. "I regret that I didn't join now, but my father didn't push it because he knew I wanted to come to the United States." (In the days of my school in the village) when parents took their children to the school they told the teacher, 'To you is their flesh and to us their bones, (*ilak al laḥm wa ilna al 'aTHm*),' i.e., we entrust you to discipline them as long as they learn.

Dan got a green (residence) card by marrying and applying for it. Zayd got a green card 2½ months after applying for it in 1983. But, beginning three years ago, a three-year wait after marriage was instituted before getting a green card. Alternatively, one can come on an immigrant's visa and wait one or two years to get a green card. There is a new law: (1) you have to have a joint bank account (with your spouse) or (2) a joint lease agreement or mortgage payment because there were so many cases of fraud marriage. Zayd got married in January 1983 and got his green card in March or May; when they interviewed him for a card they stamped his passport, "Employment authorized," and gave him a receipt that acted as a permit. He has dual nationality. He can't afford to lose his Jordanian citizenship since a house and land are in his name (in Jordan). If he had to make a choice between citizenships, he would remain Jordanian.[9]

Zayd's father had schooling through the fifth grade, but he writes excellent Arabic. Every one of his letters has a different message. And his father knows some English; he knows that because he spoke a few words of English at the American Consulate in Abu Dhabi when Zayd came there on the way to the States. Zayd says that he still remembers the exact date he came to Houston (it was so traumatic), December 16, 1979.

After studying civil engineering at Blinn College, flying at the Aero Academy in Houston, and taking courses in government and economics at Houston Community College, Zayd registered at Texas Southern University, Spring 1989, to work for a bachelor's in business administration, concentrating in management, and he received his degree in December 1990. There he took overloads, eighteen to twenty-one hours. He was a 100 percent (fully enrolled) student, devoting 50 percent of his time to work. He said he loved it (his study program); he finished with a 3.2 average. He worked all that time in the limousine service.

MIX OF EDUCATION AND WORK: The limousine people called him, and he said that he would work on condition that his school would come first, so that he could arrange his schedule to take time off to study for his exams. He made $800–1,000 a month. He got a scholarship of $600 his first semester at Texas Southern. He had received no financial help from home since 1981.

How do you evaluate your education at Texas Southern? Texas Southern was good, but it could be better. It could be more organized: there were delays in registration; some classes were not available; he took some courses out of order. He charmed them (the administrators) to get it done. Some of his professors were poor.

Did you ever suffer discrimination (in classes)? There was one senior professor who criticized everyone. He pointed to foreign students in class and said, "You come here to get an education which we taxpayers pay for." Zayd said, "My blood was boiling. I was really angry, but I knew this senior professor was the only one who taught the course. I was playing with fire (if I said anything)." Nevertheless, he went to the professor's office and said:

> "Professor, I need to speak to you. We're not coming to beg. We got a visa. Your government allowed us in. We're doing our share. We're paying our tuition." The professor replied, "You know I didn't mean you. Those Nigerians steal books." Zayd replied, "As of now, I don't respect you." The professor replied, "I like your guts."

Subsequently, Zayd increased his participation in class, bought the professor a book, and got an A in the course.

I asked whether there was give and take in his classes. There was more give and take in the advanced classes. The classes averaged thirty to fifty students. He jumped in, in all classes and participated and stood out. That was the only way— "Hit at the beginning, the first impression was important," and then one could coast in the middle part of the term.

What courses did you take? His first year he took college algebra, management information systems, behavioral organization management, marketing, finance, statistics, managerial economics, speech—he enjoyed giving a talk on South Africa—and executive communications, which he enjoyed. It was mostly common sense (this latter course) but some cases were taken from real life. He said he couldn't get practical experience during the summer in a cooperative program with a company because he had to work.

In reply to my question, he said that about 50 percent of his social network who went to school finished; another 50 percent dropped out and worked; he (himself) studied electronics (just) six months. Very few finished their education and went back to Jordan immediately. Five percent were composed of those relatively wealthy who never worked. Almost all went to school, but about 50 percent finished. Of the ten in his basketball circle, four finished in engineering, one finished in business, four dropped out, and one never went to school (his best friend).

WORK HISTORY (compare with 1986 interview): For two years he worked part-time in a limousine service, Houston Luxury Limousine, twenty to twenty-five hours a week; the owner was a Palestinian.

WORK CYCLE: His daily work cycle was unpredictable; sometimes he worked four to five hours, sometimes ten hours. Usually, he worked from 6 p.m. to two to three in the morning (when it was a busy day). Then he would go to bed; get up around 10 a.m.; go to the exercise club; read the paper, see friends. His weekly work cycle was also unpredictable: he could work eighty hours a week for three weeks over one period, but the average was forty to fifty hours a week.

INCOME AND INCOME SPENT: He got $5 an hour plus 15 percent of the total paid plus extra tips. He spent $4,000 for two years at Texas Southern, $3,000 for Blinn College, and $3,200 on Houston Community College for a total of $15,000 or 5,000 dinars including gold and the airplane ticket. At the present time he is not in debt though he has borrowed previously from his friends, $2,000 four months ago to lease a limousine and work on a business deal on his own; $600 at the beginning of the year when he was being squeezed by bills; he said that he had financed two cars before, but he won't do it now. At present he spends $320 a month on an unfurnished apartment with bedroom, kitchen, and living room; $50 a month on electricity; $200 a month on a car; $150 a month on the phone; and last term he was spending $1,000 a semester on tuition and books. He is saving $600–800 a month now.

DIET: Mostly, he went out to restaurants; he proposed going out to breakfast the first day—we had coffee and then lunch at around noon; it was a special treat on the morning I left, that he arranged a Jordanian breakfast: "foul" (cooked broad beans with lemon and olive oil), "lubany" (a yogurt derivative with olive oil), olives, thyme, eggs, and Arabic bread.

AUTOMOBILES: He has two automobiles, a Volkswagen and a 1985 Nissan. Two years ago he bought and sold three cars in one week. He got an engine from a junkyard and bought a car for $800 and paid $400 to install the engine in the car. He bargained down the dealer of the third car from $4,500 to $2,700. [Note this continued fascination with cars together with the continued entrepreneurship with respect to cars; automobiles have been a testing ground for his entrepreneurship as well as a romance and a comfort—he goes out driving when he is down; at present both his emotional satisfaction and his income are related to cars.]

TIES WITH VILLAGE OF ORIGIN: He visited twice, in 1983 for one month and in 1986 for 2½ months.

REMITTANCES: He has not sent remittances until recently; he has sent small amounts to his younger brother and a sum to his older brother for a house deal; he also sent his father a small amount to help with the purchase of furniture.

INTERACTION WITH HIS VILLAGE MATES ABROAD: He has seen one cousin only ten times in eleven years and his other cousin, 'Isam, only five times in five years. But he meets with his basketball circle every week, and has borrowed money from that circle twice—and sizeable sums ($600 and $2,000) twice in the last six months.

ATTITUDES AND IDEOLOGY: What did you like and dislike about life in America? "I missed Houston in 1986 (when I went back to Jordan for the summer). At other times I've felt it's not worth it. Now that I have accomplished my objective, getting a degree, I feel empty. I have no concrete goals. I might marry; it might not happen. I want to open a business; it might not happen. I didn't attend my graduation; it was no big deal, though I got the cap and gown." [He has a slight feeling of anomie after getting his degree—but not the same sharp ambivalence as in 1986.]

What is your view of the (Jordanian) army? "It is a waste of time for me; not that the army is bad; for the very young discipline is good, but I've learned all that here."

What is your view of birth control? "One should use it when there is a need to. Now you can have a vasectomy. It (birth control) can cause problems for the woman. The man won't have any problems with a vasectomy. I'd probably do that after having kids; after having four kids." [He is a rare Jordanian who is willing to bear the onus of birth control himself by having a vasectomy.]

What is your view of Jordan's unemployment problem? "Diversification is one of the solutions. Everyone wants his son to be an engineer (when) a computer science major can be more efficient." Better management of foreign aid. (One must) work on the work ethics of the employees. (We) have to produce.

What is your view of tribal law? "As far as I'm concerned tribal law has no place in our society. We've had some bizarre crimes, and the perpetrator got off because his family had influence and begged a shaykh (to intervene). If justice had been rendered crimes wouldn't be repeated. These shaykhs who render decisions don't necessarily have knowledge, only wealth." I interjected, "Your father supports it." "My father was *mukhtar* (village mayor)," he replied. "Life is much more complicated now." I replied that people understood the system of tribal law, and the victim felt that his feelings were addressed by it: a man comes and asks forgiveness. Zayd's rejoinder was that often the victim feels shame (*yastahi*) or weak in the presence of the shaykh (tribal elder) who makes him climb down from the (just) verdict.

I asked what his view of TV was. In both the U.S. and Jordan it should be more constructive. In the U.S. it is a private company, and (one can) pay for twenty-four hours. In both countries more quality programs are needed, whether comedy or educational. The best of channels (in the U.S.) is the Discovery channel with documentaries and PBS—they don't overdo it with commercials. In Jordan (we) need more commercials to pay for TV, and need more variety. In Jordan he watched Middle Eastern television from Cyprus and "Twenty-Twenty" in Jordan, and some comedy shows in English. He found the Arabic programs very simple, silly, and poorly done for lack of funds or expertise. Maybe they should privatize the TV industry in Jordan; it would have to be sold to business to sponsor programs.

What is your view of rural-urban differences in Jordan? [He had told me about the case of honor involving the daughter of a villager earlier and explained it partially on the basis of rural-urban differences (she had been reared in Zerqa and had always gone bareheaded).] In the city they have health, education, and shopping (opportunities). In mentality there is no significant difference between Irbid and Kufr al-Ma and even Amman. Life is much cleaner in the village (as far as noise and pollution). The major (Jordanian) cities are now witnessing an increasing influx of foreigners from Egypt, Lebanon, Syria, and Pakistan and are seeing more crime. And they (the foreigners) are introducing certain lifestyles: more open and liberal lifestyles are being introduced by the Lebanese including food and music.

What is your view of your own upbringing? "I think it worked okay. I think there could have been a little more democracy in the family. When I was growing up as a kid, if financially possible, we could have been introduced to more experiences." **Like what?** "Here in Houston kids participate in arts and sports, and the family pays for it. I don't remember having any toys when I was very young. They (toys) have to do with mental and social development. Teaching was left up to the mother who was illiterate; she could have added to what we know now. In those days a youngster was not listened to or allowed into the guest house. I am angry about it. All the kids could do was serve coffee and tea (there). Here (U.S.A.) you can talk with kids at an early age, and they will talk confidently; now it's changing some." In his first year in Houston Community College he didn't want to give an oral report for fear of making a fool of himself; he was encouraged by his girlfriend to do so. When he was a child his father would wake him up at 5 a.m. when he got up for prayers, and he would relish the early morning and the birds and take his books out to the fields and study; he memorized things so clearly that he could recite chapter and verse in the classroom that morning.

ATTITUDES PERTAINING TO THE GULF WAR: Did the Gulf War lead to any changes in your life here in Houston? "No, not really. I tried to be less visible as an Arab. I limited my going out. I avoided Middle Eastern nightclubs and belly-dancing places where I used to go once every two months." He thought the crazy Americans would bomb them. Someone asked him at a gas station, "What language are you speaking?" He replied, "Turkish." It was better to avoid those problems. [Note, he was defiant in the University when he met discrimination, but on the national scene in a crisis he remained passive and practiced dissimulation.]

Did the war lead to any changes in your relations with Americans? "I don't have that many American friends." A few asked him questions in school his last semester; they asked his opinion; he told them the causes of the conflict and the reality of it as opposed to the TV images. The majority were interested, the professors especially. One professor called him to her office after class and asked, "Who is Saddam Husayn?" He replied that Israel had a hand in (the war). Israel got Americans to do their dirty work, and Americans fell for it. He had about thirty friends at Texas Southern (more accurately, acquaintances); and five good friends.

Did the war lead to any changes in your relations with other Arabs? "The phone was busy during the war; we didn't visit more; we were (all) glued to TV."

Did the war lead to any changes in your view of Americans and American society and culture? "Not the average person. But it affirmed my belief that there were forces behind the public display. I've always known the U.S. government was not free. It was manipulated by outside forces or inside forces to do what they did. Any person who had any sense knew this display was to move (people) emotionally. It confirmed my belief that the government wasn't operating properly." He has read Paul Findley's book, *They Dare To Speak Out.* If you see the numbers, money spent, it's mind-boggling. The message of the book was that everybody has a price, from the President down. This after I said that the Arabs ought to spend their money in the same way. He said that during the political campaign it happened accidentally that Reagan was going to speak on the same platform following Findley; they arranged to have Reagan speak separately.

Did the war lead to any changes in your own feelings about yourself, your country, the Arab World, the Middle East? Not about himself. Jordan could have taken a better stand, but it had to do what it did to ease pressure from the inside. But between the United States and Saudi Arabia, they okayed for King Husayn to be pro-Iraqi. Two weeks ago Bush called Husayn and said, "We need you." I would have liked to see the scenario managed by the Arabs. It would have given them more credibility in the world arena.

What do you think of all the American flags and yellow ribbons? "On the part of Americans it was patriotism in their own way, even though it was manipulated by the media and government statements. It was massive marketing to sell the idea of war to the American public."

What was the most surprising thing about the way Americans reacted to the war? "That so many people that were for war without knowing about it. They were so ignorant and being driven by the media. I thought that people would be more critical."

I asked about Zayd's social network in Houston. With Americans he worked on projects (with them) together; they would go to lunch between classes. He has been to their homes very briefly—to do assignments, not for social activities. [Apart from girlfriends, Zayd, as he said, knows little about American home life.] After school, his good friends are Arabs, mainly Jordanians. "They are more reliable; you can count on them; you need something—they're there for you: money, you can borrow $1,000, and he'll give it and trust you (to repay it). The American won't give you $20. I never asked them, but that's my perception of it." (On the other hand) he lent another foreigner, a Nigerian, a couple of hundred dollars, and it worked out okay. "I don't know whether it's my pride or not in not asking (Americans for money) or (the anxiety of) not knowing the answer. I can pick up the phone and get my friend in Dallas and ask for money, and he'll send it." (He said he had just joined a health spa to cut down smoking as he lit up a cigarette.) Most of his friends are Jordanians. Good friends, he has ten, two from al-Husn; one from Salt; four from the Jordan Valley, Deir 'Alla; he has one or two Palestinian friends with whom he has worked, and a Palestinian acquaintance; he has three or four Lebanese friends and would borrow and lend from them; and one Iraqi. Or if I need to move, a friend will help me; they will invite me to their parties. Every Sunday we play basketball, we visit parks, we go to restaurants together. They call each other once a week and check on how everything is going.

What about helping find jobs? Zayd replied that they would help with that too. The network now as (opposed to 1986) is closer. Then, everyone was struggling with school and work; now everyone has graduated. [The Arab student network has evolved to another stage in educational status, skills, and emotional closeness].

"I want to have friends more than before. In 1984–85 it was a lost period." He has only one friend who was born here, a Lebanese—who wanted to be 100 percent Arab. The network now is closer, not bigger. "We are more mature. Most of us are over thirty or approaching thirty; we want to identify with a group. It's helping."

BAHHAR

6/17/1991 (from my diary, day of arrival in Seattle; conversation mainly in the car) Bahhar met me at the airport. I wouldn't have recognized him. [He told me earlier when I phoned him in Nebraska at his in-laws in North Platte that he remembers me; I used to hand out candy to the children.] He told me that he went to the Merchant Marine Academy in Greece for two years and qualified as a radio officer. He then worked as a radio officer and first officer (next to the captain) for seven years for a Greek cargo company plying the Mediterranean and other areas.

COURTSHIP: (from Bahhar) He met his wife, R, when she came as a tourist to Jordan, and she took the ship (he was on) from Aqaba to Romania. He was the first officer and, alternately, radio officer on the ship, and they became acquainted over ten days. Then he stayed with her a few days in Romania. Then she went to Greece; he gave her the address of his brother (Migrant Two, Chapter four), who was doing medical studies there. She stayed with him, apparently, while Bahhar went back to Jordan where his oldest brother was coming back from Saudi Arabia on a visit. He stayed a month in Jordan, and then went to Greece and spent two weeks with her there. (After corresponding with R for a year) he asked if his Greek company had ships going to the U.S.A. They said, "Yes," and he flew to St. Kitts and then sailed around the Caribbean till he got to Savannah, Georgia. Then he called R from there, and she came. He said that she had many relatives in Georgia. They saw one another off-and-on over the next year while he was shuttling around the Caribbean, and they were married at the end of the year. [They were married in Galveston, February 1980 and went to Jordan in June 1980 where the village preacher wrote a Muslim wedding contract. The wedding celebration was on the ship off Venezuela in March 1980.] His brother-in-law, a pathologist, got him a contact with the Halliburton Company in Galveston which did seismic geophysical research in the Caribbean, as well as sometimes prospecting for oil. It was a worldwide company. He said that, not being a citizen, working for the University of Texas, Galveston, in their research ship was an advantage to a foreigner since he didn't have to meet all the regulations about hiring foreigners that private companies did. Till he got his citizenship he couldn't be a captain (on a U.S. ship). His brother-in-law also had lots of property and investments and headed a well-known real estate agency in the city. Then R's brother-in-law moved to Nebraska and took his wife's mother with him; he went to establish a clinic there. And Bahhar bought his brother-in-law's condominium, which was near the university. It was a good neighborhood, but it got run down in real estate value and style-of-life when a bunch of apartments opposite were converted to public housing. And so he sold the apartment back to his brother-in-law and decided to leave for Seattle. His wife didn't like being left alone in the neighborhood. They moved to Seattle in December 1990. Bahhar said there was a lot of flooding in Galveston, and it was too hot, and the district had run down. Answering my question, he said he liked Seattle, but he doesn't know much about it since he has been out to sea.

He says he is thinking about going back to school or getting another job—he doesn't know what—so he can spend more time with his family. He has a child one year old and another coming in January. He said he loved the sea, but now he wants to come home more.

TIES WITH VILLAGE OF ORIGIN: Bahhar said that his older brother, Migrant Two (chapter 4), put him through school and then, immediately after he finished, Bahhar put his younger brother, in turn, through college at Yarmouk in Jordan. The younger brother now teaches in Jordan. He said he has also begun sending money home. He has been back to Jordan several times, twice with his wife, who loves it there. He sent his mother a ticket to come (to the States) after the Gulf War but it aborted twice, and now she'll wait till he goes back, and maybe she'll come later. He was in the village in 1988 after I left.

6/18/91 Bahhar has returned to Jordan four times since 1980 when he came to the United States. He goes back once every 2½ years and stays a month, except last time when he stayed three weeks in Jordan and ten days in Greece. He always stops first in Greece to see his brother, and Migrants One and Three (Chapter 4). His last trip was in 1988. Before, he sent remittances to his younger brother and to the whole family ($100 a month) and $100 a month to his brother in Greece. He told me later that he didn't think he'd go back to Jordan to live. He said the stability of Jordan was not good. "I'd rather be back with my family, but I look at the people there, and they all want to get out." He said that R would rather live in Jordan. But what's the point of living there if you can't make a living. If she gets sick she can't get the same medical care (she gets in the United States).

TIES WITH SONS OF THE VILLAGE ABROAD: He says that he first came to Galveston and not to Houston or San Antonio where the other Jordanians from Kufr al-Ma lived. He came to his wife's family (and socialized with them). The only Jordanian he had contact with was Zayd. The latter was changing addresses and telephone numbers so often that he lost touch with him. He has talked to Dan in Ohio a few times on the phone. He hasn't seen Dan since he left Jordan. He talks to 'Isam's brother every time he comes back on shore leave, but not to Zayd. The last time he talked to Zayd was "when the three came and visited me in Galveston—'Isam (my cousin) and Zayd came and spent a day with me in Galveston in 1986"; he did see 'Isam once in San Antonio in 1989. Bahhar said that last Sunday he had talked to both Dan and his cousin on the phone. The latter had said that he enjoyed being with me, but that, "he looked quite different."

6/18/91 Last night we went to a French-style restaurant by the sea and had red snapper fish; then we walked along the Puget Sound shore a bit. The sun was setting and it was cool with lots of people coming to the park and walking along the shore. The conversation last night at the restaurant indicated the independence of Bahhar's wife. When I came to autograph my book on Jordan for them, R said she was called "Hanan" in Jordan. She said one of the reasons for coming to Seattle was that she had a degree in audiovisual studies and film production and she had produced a film at the University of Texas, and there was no opportunity to do anything like that in Galveston, Texas. In Seattle she is going to look into such opportunities and perhaps go back to school at the University of Washington. She noted that they had an Islamic Center at the university. She calls herself by a hyphenated last name, the first part of which is her maiden name. She said she wanted her children to carry her name. They tried to change Bahhar's name to "Abu Hadabi" (his lineage name), and they had a lawyer about to set up the change, and then Bahhar changed his mind. [Note that names are an issue in this family and indicate a concern with social identity.] She said "Ali" was the last name on Bahhar's passport, though being the fourth after his patrilineal pedigree. Bahhar recounted the altercation with a cousin on a visit to Jordan: there were two brothers from his lineage in Kufr al-Ma who lived in the city of Zerqa. One of them became a fundamentalist and married a fifteen-year-old girl, and kept her in purdah inside the house and veiled outside; she couldn't even talk with her own brother or her husband's brother. He came on strong to R and told her she had to be obedient and that man was superior and in charge, and that women should stay in the home. He said that God was male, and the husband was the vicegerent of God. So R said, "How do you know God isn't a woman?" His face got red, and he got up abruptly and left the room and started praying. Bahhar said that R was well-respected in the village, and many people came to visit them when they came. They talked about R's insisting on shaking hands with Bahhar's brother (on entering the house) while he was praying, and he ignored her, and she insisted, and he smiled and finally shook hands with her even though the handshake nullified his ritual ablutions and his prayer.

R studied biology at the University of Texas. Before that she worked in London for one term researching red tide, an algae that devours fish. In response to my question she said she didn't like the English; she found them uninteresting. On questioning, R said she makes some Arabic dishes.

They talked of the constant stream of visitors when they last visited Kufr al-Ma: D, 'Isam's father, 'Isam's uncle, and their brother. [Note, that apart from the latter these are educated men or men who have had contact with western culture.] So many people came that they had to go off to Petra for a few days for a rest. She said she wore native dress in the village. Bahhar told her how to behave—modestly.

REARING OF CHILDREN: Bahhar said he wanted to teach the children Arabic. They have heard of an Islamic school where they teach Arabic in Seattle, and they're thinking of sending their one-year-old son there. R took classes from the Ferneas (Middle East specialists) at the University of Texas. She said that she had read my book, *Arab Village*.[10] R said she was tired of working as a technician in a biomedical laboratory. She had just gotten a degree at the University of Texas when the fundamentalist told her to stay home.

COURTSHIP: She met Bahhar on the cargo ship when it came into the Gulf of Aqaba. She always wanted to marry someone from an exotic place. Bahhar didn't talk to her the first day (he said on another occasion that he spoke only broken English then). He sat opposite her at the table, and she thought he was Greek.

SAILING: Bahhar talked of wanting to take another set of exams so he could double the tonnage of the ships on which he was allowed to be an officer. Now he is limited to five hundred tons. He took an exam only once before—for captain, though there are other exams for first mate. The exam he's going to take involves knowledge of firefighting, first aid—this has to be repeated each time—and emergencies. He said that when he was working for the Greek company they went everywhere, but not to China—he refused to go there because they would not allow the sailors to move freely on shore, it being a communist country. Nor has he been to India. The ship was diverted from Bombay to Karachi once. He has gone to Australia and the Caribbean.

SOCIAL STRUCTURE OF THE SHIP: Bahhar said that to be the radio officer of the ship was an advantageous role to play. The harbormaster in Greece advised him to become a radio officer. [Note how he interacted from the beginning with native Greeks.] He said the radio officer was indispensable to the men—the only indispensable person on the ship. Everyone treated you well to get immediate access when they wanted to send a message. And it was a well-paid position, almost as much as first officer. He talked of the difficulty of working on a seismic geophysical ship (as he did in the U.S.A. after he was married). There was the danger of hitting vessels in the straits. He said on the seismic ship he had a crew of eight and the remaining sixteen were "seismics." The crew included three officers, two cooks, and two or three able-bodied seamen. The work on the seismic ship was boring. He enjoyed working on the cargo ships a lot more.

GREEK ETHOS: The Greek sailors were happy—they liked sailing; they regarded it as a fortunate profession. The American sailors seem always to have problems that they bring on board with them. One has to be careful how one treats them, i.e., they were temperamental.

6/18/91 (11 a.m. from Bahhar in my motel room in Seattle) Bahhar said that on the Greek ship there were twenty-eight men—all crew: three officers (captain, first officer, and second officer); three engineers (chief engineer, second engineer, and third engineer); one cook and two messboys; five to eight able-bodied seamen or "ABs"; and three oilers (who cleaned the engine room). On the U.S. geodetic ship there are only eight crew, and the rest are seismic (computer) specialists and technicians who can't take life at sea. So there is a constant turnover, though there is a core group. Also the "seismics" have different specialties and don't have much in common among themselves. Many are young kids trained in a computer program who suddenly find themselves on a ship. [Thus the social structural tensions on the American ship are based on age, super-specialist training, opposition of crew and seismics, and American personality structure, and not least important, constant turnover.] Then Bahhar gave me a more accurate breakdown of the structure of the American "crew" on the geodetic ship: three officers, three engineers (one chief and two regular), three able-bodieds, two cooks, and one galley hand. He said that you could gain some understanding of the seismic group who had been out to sea for at least a year. The University of Texas research ship sometimes carried thirty-three and even forty-five men as opposed to twenty-four. Years ago when he first started he had more crew on the geodetic ship, but now he has more advanced equipment which performs many functions automatically.

SAILING WORK CYCLE: Bahhar said that he had been on shore leave for two months now, and he knows his work-leave schedule for the next six months. He will now go sailing out of New Orleans for one month and then will get a month shore leave. Then he will work for two months and get one month off. During the last year he has always sailed from New Orleans. Every four weeks they have a crew change, and they stay overnight in New Orleans. They are flown by helicopter to the ship from the airport. They change ½ to ⅓ of the crew every month. The helicopter takes them to the ship while it is still going. "As a single person I enjoyed every minute of it—the merchant marine. Even after the first two years of marriage I enjoyed it because R used to come with me on the ship. (For land-lubbers) even when they work overtime they still come home at night. The month we get off goes so fast, and the month at sea drags so long. I have fun at home and (get restless) on ship. The company gave us an extra month; we used to get four months off; now they give us five. This year I'll take six months off. They have a new sea bonus program: for every day at sea, we get ½ day of shore leave."

When he worked for the University of Texas, 1981–87, they had a lot of short contracts of a week to ten days' duration, maximum three weeks, and then go back to port for repair and maintenance; often they had month-long breaks from sea duty; some years they were only out to sea three months out of the year. In the last two years the exception was the Japan trip when they went for four months. With Geosource Company his shore leave cycle was work two months and one month shore leave throughout the year. With Halliburton he worked 7½ months a year and was off 4½ months a year. When he worked for the Greek Rousanto Company as both radio officer and first mate, the radio officer worked eight hours a day, but actually there was only two hours of work sending out telegrams; the rest of the time the radio officer just listened to the radio. The first mate's job was to go up and stand and watch on the bridge for eight hours.

GALVESTON: Bahhar said he didn't like Galveston from the day he got there. It was flat and without greenery. He bought a palm tree and put it on their patio (because there was no greenery), and it grew very large. But once he got the job at the University of Texas he couldn't leave.

VIEW OF SAILING: I asked Bahhar if he had to do it all over again, would he go into the merchant marine? He repeated his view about the life being wonderful for a single man but not for a married man with a family. It (sea-life) drags on him now that he has a family. R went with him the first two years. She went on a trip to Venezuela and then the Dominican Republic for one month; she went on another trip from Delaware to Houston. She loved it. She liked ships. She didn't have to do anything. The messboys came in the morning to fix the room. The galley fixed her coffee. She just sat and watched. In port they would go out all day.

I asked if they had talked about how the children would be raised. Bahhar said that he wanted the children to be Muslims and have Arabic names. R said that was okay as long as she raised them properly (according to her values) and as long as they had her maiden name in their name as well as her husband's, and as long as they had a Christmas tree and an Easter basket.

6/19/91 (my reflections on the plane flying home from Seattle) Bahhar's evaluations of Americans (on the attitudinal questions) were almost entirely negative. The American seamen he interacted with got off the ship and went straight to the bars and stayed up all night and got drunk and came back in the morning and slept it off till the afternoon. Bahhar, on the other hand, would go off and tour all day in the port and do it again the next day. One guy (sailor) even asked him to pick up a kimono for his wife in Japan since he went into the bar day after day and drank. He told him he didn't even know his wife's size. He regarded Americans as temperamental; one couldn't build up a friendship with them or depend on their reactions. They brought their troubles with them onto the ship. They spent all their money by the time they came back on the ship after shore leave. Many of the seismic specialists were young kids who were trained in computers, and put straight on the ship; there was a high turnover as a result. So the group of Americans he interacted with were transients, temperamental, and "not fun people" (as the Greeks were), without saving or planning habits.

BAHHAR'S FAMILY: Bahhar, age thirty-eight, was married in 1980; he has a wife, R, and a son, Amir, one year old; he is expecting a child in January; he says the sex of the child doesn't matter as long as it's healthy.[11] His oldest brother first worked in a Jerusalem hospital as a nurse for four years, and then went to Saudi Arabia in 1963; they gave him training at an American hospital in Jerusalem; the oldest brother has been in Saudi Arabia since 1963, working for the Ministry of Justice as a translator and/or clerk/typist. His brother in Greece, age forty-two, married a Greek. His three sisters all married village men at an early age. His younger brother, thirty-three, is unmarried; he is a schoolteacher in Kerak who teaches Arabic; he graduated from Yarmouk University in 1987. His father was a *fellah* who retired after the oldest brother started working; then Bahhar took over and started supporting the whole family.

WORK HISTORY: 1976, Radio Officer, Edek Eteir Company, Greece (stayed six months), earned 25,000 drachmas or $850 a month plus overtime.

1977, Rousanto Shipping Company, Greece. He worked for them around three years and made $1,200–1,400 a month. They gave him the opportunity to serve as chief mate as well as radio officer, giving him experience and an increased salary and saving them money since they didn't have to hire a separate first mate. After his first mate shift (eight hours a day) he went and did his radio work; sometimes he worked ten to twelve hours a day.

1979, Dalex Shipping Company, Greece (worked for them fourteen months) for $1,600 a month. He liked working for them best (of the three Greek companies); their ships were new and they worked in the Caribbean area and Gulf of Mexico.

1981–87, Chief Mate, University of Texas, Galveston, $32,000 a year and in the last two years, $38–$46,000 a year with overtime. For the first five years they used to work from one week to ten days, a maximum of three weeks out to sea and then come back to port after finishing the contract. Generally, they had a lot of short contracts with a month break in between. Some years they were only out to sea three months of the year; the rest of the time they worked in port on call doing repair and maintenance. The University of Texas was very strict. Whenever anything went wrong, they immediately went back to port to fix it. Most of the time they were in the Gulf of Mexico. In the last two years he went to Costa Rica, Hawaii, and Panama and on a separate trip to Japan for four months (this was unusual). The University of Texas had a cooperative research endeavor with Tokyo University. Mostly, they studied geological formations on the ocean floor, looking for volcanoes and earthquake fissures; sometimes they had contracts with oil companies checking for oil; they got samples. They also had a contract with the National Science Foundation. Their schedule was as follows: carry out a contract for a few days or a week and then lay off for a month, except for the last two years when they went to Japan. On that trip they were on ship for four to five days and then went back to port to wait for new equipment or supplies. He spent his shore leave as a tourist, going to Yokahama, Tokyo, small towns, and cities and later, they went to Fiji.

1988–89 Chief Mate, Geo-Source (Houston), $35,000 base salary plus paid vacations. The work cycle in this job was two months work and one month off. He had this job for four months.

1989–91 He is now a Chief Mate or Captain (a ship's officer in the merchant marine with a radio officer's and captain's license) with Halliburton Geophysical Services at $37,000 a year with a paid vacation and transport to his place of residence anywhere on the continent on the occasion of every shore leave plus 80 percent of all medical benefits for himself and his family. Halliburton has its headquarters in Houston, Texas but it has offices worldwide in South America, London, and the Far East. With Halliburton he has been out to sea 7½ months a year and home 4½ months. He had the regular base salary regardless of time served at sea until a year ago when they instituted the sea bonus program which provided a 20 percent increase in salary for time spent at sea. Now if he spends the 4½ months at home he'll make less. With Halliburton if there is a problem with the heavy equipment they send a helicopter or a small boat to repair it immediately—they don't go into port.

HIS TRAVELS ON THE GEODETIC SHIPS: Japan was the best country he'd ever seen. They were nice people and very clean; the only thing was that it was very expensive. They would leave the ship for shore in the morning and come back at night. They had excellent transportation, and you didn't have to speak Japanese. Afterwards they went to Australia (with the University of Texas). They went for three weeks to the Northern Territory, Port Darwin, and to northeast Queensland. They had to make repairs. They lost one of their propellers. They had to wait two weeks. "In Australia I liked the Great Barrier Reef; I went snorkeling." They sailed through the reef for 550 miles. He and the captain navigated through it. It wasn't easy because there were reefs on either side, and they only had radar and visual capacity—to note the buoys and lights. All the other ships had special pilots to get them through. They did it for three days. They only used one engine since the other wasn't working. They went to the South Pacific (in the geodetic ship), to Panape, Palou, and Truk. "They are the most beautiful islands. So far in the middle of the ocean. The water was crystal clear. You could still see Japanese tanks and ships sunk in the sea bottom and planes shot down—these were now tourist stops." When he was working with the Greek company they once ran aground on the Red Sea near the Gulf of Suez at 3 a.m., and he sent an SOS. They had a new captain. He wasn't watching the radar. In Spain his ship hit the dock.

EDUCATION: (For his earlier education see Chapter Four.)

1985: He studied for a Captain's license in Galveston, Texas. He studied at home, but he also went to a refresher school for three months called the Navigation Training School. If he had questions he would go to the training school to brush up. He took an exam all written, for two days and obtained the "Master's license," as it was called. He never took a radio officer's exam in the U.S.; they took him at the University of Texas because of his experience. The radio officer's course (in Greece) included navigation, electronics, and Morse code.

1985–88: He took extra training in Radar Enforcement, Firefighting, First Aid, and Sea Survival (to upgrade his captain's license). The latter two courses he took in a special course of studies in Philadelphia. The Geosource Company sent him there and paid for the hotels in Philadelphia and the courses in Houston; he was even allowed to bring his wife. They don't allow drugs or alcohol aboard ship. To get the captain's license (and to renew it) one had to take a physical test and a drug test. If one had worked at sea one year out of the last five, one didn't have to take the general exam again. The captain's license is only good for five years; one has either to renew or upgrade it then. If one wishes to upgrade it, then one needs more courses and training. He hopes to take the test next year.

The Coast Guard will inform him which (grade) license he can go for. He has applied to be tested as captain for 1,600-ton ships and as second mate for ships of unlimited tonnage. [Note, he is constantly motivated to achieve more and upgrade himself in his profession.] The Coast Guard has to check his papers.

EVALUATION OF GREEK VS. AMERICAN MERCHANT MARINE: The

Greek Merchant Marine Academy was better. The Greeks taught you exactly what you needed to know. When you finished the school you were able to do the job. The U.S.A. may have more advanced equipment. On the Greek ship each officer has his own big bedroom, and one doesn't have to deal with anyone else (e.g., a roommate). One could go to port a lot—one was happier. One could make phone calls (from port). "The ship I'm working on now is small; the quarters are smaller; they have to have room for the equipment." The training he got with the Halliburton Company was good; he has no criticism of it.

ETHOS OF GREEKS AND GREEK MERCHANT MARINE VS. AMERI-

CAN: Americans make a lot of money at sea and spend it at home in a few months. [American quick-make, quick-spend, in-debt complex.] The Greeks saved more. They went into port more often [Americans as notably uninterested in the world—insular], but they didn't spend as much. The wives in Greece went to the company each month and took the paycheck. The seamen were given (only) $100 a month at sea to spend in the ports. [Greek families practice compulsory economy through the company.] Greek men would go nine to eleven months without seeing their families. They wanted to save the money. "The Greeks are easier to get along with. The environment of the Greek ship is different. In the U.S.A. there is more pressure; all they (Americans) want is profit." The Greek ship had no contact with the company; the ship sailed all over the world without contact. "In the U.S.A. you're involved with the company every day. If the ship is damaged, they do everything possible to fix it quickly."

AFFINAL RELATIONS AND RELATIONSHIP BETWEEN THE SEXES IN

THE USA: What about relations between the sexes (and dating) in the United States? "I got married before I came to the States (i.e., before he got a job here or knew anything about the society). I came to Houston, and had a lawyer draw up the marriage contract with her family, and I left the same day on the ship. Only R's brother and sister were there (at the contract drawing-up). Her mother was in Georgia. [This was in February 1980.] A month later R flew to the Dominican Republic and stayed with me on the ship as we proceeded to Venezuela, and the Captain married them on the ship and they invited people from the mainland (of Venezuela) and the ship's officers and crew, but not her family, to the wedding celebration. They remained together on the ship one month.

Bahhar said, "R (his wife) is a very nice person, and if I didn't trust her 100 percent I wouldn't go out to sea. And her mother is a very nice person. And her sister is a doctor and her father was a doctor; he died in 1976. And her older brother is a very nice person. I get along with her family very well. I spent a long time in the house with her mother. For six months we were in her mother's rented house." He saw her brother a lot. Her sister was in Alaska, now in Tennessee, and her brother was in Kentucky (now in Nebraska). They visit her brother and sister every one or two years. "They know about my culture, and I am not (a) strict (Muslim). I've traveled so much that I must accept people the way they are."

Then nothing shocked you about American life? "On the ship we were coming to different places all the time. I was all over Europe. When the ship came in to a new port I used to get excited. It doesn't mean that much to me anymore. When we arrive in a new country, I sit and relax on the ship's deck the whole day. Only on the next day do I venture off the ship to the port."

EXPENDITURES: What did you spend your income on? They had no debts; only a credit card. "I've never been in debt." If he wants to buy something like a camera which costs $1,000, he makes certain he will pay the debt back in a month or two. On housing they spend $675 a month on a one-bedroom apartment; all utilities come to $850 a month; on R's education at the University of Texas they spent $10,000 for 1½ years (this included the rent for a small apartment in Houston); he sent his younger brother to Yarmouk University (in Jordan) giving him $2,000 a year for several years; they have paid off the car installments which were $360 a month. They had savings before they had the baby, but now they have no regular savings plan. He saves 11 percent of his salary with the company every month at a good interest. They spend $3,000 a year on recreation; every time he comes home they go on a trip—sometimes in the U.S.A., to Disney World a few times; they've gone camping; they visit her family in different states; sometimes they take a trip abroad—the Cayman Islands or (this year) the Bahamas; they average three trips a year, each costing $1,000. R worked as a real estate agent (for a short while) and as a lab technician in Galveston for five years, making $16–$18,000 a year.

QUESTIONS ON SOCIAL ATTITUDES AND IDEOLOGY: What are the good and bad points of Greeks? "The Greeks, if you know them very well, they accept you, and they are fun people. But when it comes to religion, if you come close to them they want you to convert. I worked with Greeks more than others—others knew them as students (only). I was the only officer on the ship who was a foreigner. They never called me by my (Muslim) name; they called me "Jordanus," from the Greek name for the Jordan River. I was treated like a Greek—not as an Arab. (But) I never drank but went to the bar and sat with them for a few minutes, and then left."

What are the good and bad points of Americans? "They are a lot easier to understand." "The people I work with, when you try to come close to them, they change. They become distant the next day. For instance you sit and become friendly with someone for a couple of hours; the next day he doesn't want to talk to you at all. I found a lot of Americans not as friendly as Greeks or Arabs. I say, 'Hi,' to someone here in the apartments and he won't reply. They're not warm, friendly, especially if they know you're Middle Eastern."

What do you like about Americans, you married one? He replied, "R is not a typical American. I hear stories from friends about their (American) wives. She's different."

What is your view of birth control? "It's good." Under what conditions and by what methods would you practice it? "The condom, the diaphragm." What about an operation? "Not for the male, but for the female, if she wants it, and we have all the kids she wants, it's okay."

What about abortion? "I don't think so. Except if she's raped or to save her life or if the baby isn't going to live."

What is your view of Jordan's unemployment problem? "The government hasn't provided enough jobs in the last few years. You see, years ago the army was the largest employer. It gave security to the individual and his family. But the economy and life has changed. People in the army wanted to get out and do independent work. A lot of people got an education and couldn't find a job. Everything's limited (in Jordan), like teachers. A villager from Jdeita has to go to Deir Abu Said (another community) to high school; the same for a villager from Sammu'; there should be more schools. We had less doctors than needed because they weren't being paid well. So everyone tried to go to Saudi Arabia or Kuwait or the Emirates. That was bad because then, Jordanians started hiring Indians and Egyptians and foreigners who took the jobs of the (native) blue-collar workers. They worked for less than Jordanians, 1/3 less. We should look after our own people."

What is your view of the Jordanian army? "The army was really good. In the last six to seven years the officers wanted to get out. They did everything possible to get out. They were not getting enough money to live." He wouldn't advise anyone to join the army (because of the salary).

What is your view of tribal law? "I used to witness its operation; it's good for small problems, but not larger problems. Most of the time you get the older people (together) and they make a decision, but they don't do it in the right way. Take (that honor) case, for instance. It wasn't fair for her to get killed and him to get away. The Wazir's (a family) themselves did all that."[12] What happened to the culprits? "I don't think they did anything to those guys."

What is your view of television? "It's bad. It's good in certain points. For Jordanians it's a lot different. There is more selection of channels, educational channels (in the U.S.A. than in Jordan). But mostly (in Jordan) you're dragged to watch for hours and hours without thinking." Bahhar says he's addicted to baseball. "I don't go and stand and watch them (in person as I should). If I turn the TV off, R will come and turn it on something else. When I go off to the ship, I don't get TV there—we have only videotapes."

What is your view of rural-urban differences in Jordan? "There are still differences between villages and towns." But most villagers work today in towns. "In the last ten years it's changed a lot more."

What is your view of your own upbringing? "It was simple. I didn't have much. My father and my family raised us as good children—respectful of them and everyone else. We were quiet—not like other kids, fighting."

Was there anything bad about your upbringing? We didn't have much to show. We were not open to the other world. I always, when I was a kid, I had a dream. I wanted to get out of Jordan one day, (to know) what's going on outside. My (oldest) brother left (for Arabia). Even my (next oldest) brother left (for Greece). (I thought to myself) I'd probably do the same thing. If they had stayed in Jordan, I'd probably had done the same—maybe joined the army or gone to a university in Jordan. (Migrants One and Seven) went and my brother went. My family said, 'Go to your brother (in Greece).' It was cheaper to send me there than elsewhere."

ATTITUDES ABOUT THE GULF WAR: Did the Gulf War lead to any changes to your life? "Not much. I don't work with anyone in Seattle, and people who work with me understand where I come from. They know I'm Jordanian, not Iraqi. They knew I wasn't supporting the war, anyway."

Did the war lead to any changes in your relations with Americans? "No, not on ship. We always talked there. But I never argued with them. There was no point to talking to someone who doesn't understand what's going on. I just watched the news. If some understood, I'd talk. People didn't distinguish between Iraqis, Jordanians. I tried to avoid all that."

Did the war lead to any change in your relations with other Arabs? "No, I don't even have contact with other Arabs."

Did the war lead to any changes in your own feelings about yourself, your country, the Arab World, the Middle East? "Right now I have a job. It's okay, no problem. If I start looking for another job (as he's anticipating doing), I don't know how they'll look at me. As an Arab? People look at you in a different way (when you're an Arab). They don't want to get to know you at first. Because you're an Arab you lose a lot of points. Unless they need your body."

What are your views of George Bush (the father) and Saddam Husayn? "I think Saddam is stupid." Why? "Because he tried to get more power for himself under the pretext of doing it for the Palestinians. It wouldn't get him anything even if he took Kuwait. It was wrong. To throw someone from their house and take over. He got too many chances to take himself off the hook. And Bush said he'd have serious talks about the Palestinians, if he pulled out before a war. He would have saved his own soldiers' lives and be more famous in the Arab countries and in his own. Bush played a game with him. They (the allies) just cut him off and let him starve and got him really weak. Bush was more concerned with saving his own people's lives. Saddam wasn't concerned with his own people's lives. Bush wants to win the election."

In 1991 what did you think of all the flags and yellow ribbons? "I don't really care what they (Americans) do. It's not my culture. They overdo things here: all the parties for the troops. In Seattle they're going to do it in August!"

What was the most surprising thing to you about the way Americans reacted to the war? "Americans were with Saudi Arabia (as allies) but they talked as if they were waging a war against all Arabs. Americans take one leader and extend (the animosity) to all nationals. They assumed all Jordanians are pro-Saddam. All Iraqis are seen as guilty."

Interview with wife, R
6/18/91

FAMILY: R's father was a doctor born in Macon, Georgia; he attended Emory University and the University of Georgia. During World War II he served with Public Health in New Orleans; he met the wounded in an ambulance (as they came off the ships). He specialized in internal medicine and heart and chest disease. He practiced medicine in Florida, Tennessee, and Texas. He contracted tuberculosis from his patients and was sent to New Mexico for one year to recover. Her mother was born in Claxton, Georgia. She went to nursing school. She contracted rheumatic fever and met her husband while in nursing school.

R, age thirty-four, was born in Statesboro, Georgia and lived in Tallahassee, Florida, West Palm Beach, and Paris, Kentucky. She went to high school in Lexington, Kentucky and graduated in 1974, graduating after the eleventh grade. Then she went to Tyler, Texas to live for one year. Her father died, and she returned to Florida with her brother.

EDUCATION: 1974–76 Tyler Junior College (southeast of Dallas), a science major who never got the associate's degree; she was undecided about her career plans (then).

1976–77 University of Texas, Austin; she got sick with mononucleosis for six months and dropped out.

1978 Huntington, Long Island, one month; they offered an overseas travel program; she wanted to go to Kenya, but her family went crazy, and she settled for going to England.

1978 Lowestof's Fisheries Lab (London); independent studies in marine biology, three months.

1978 Friends World College (London), arranged to do Red Tide Research on her own and to write her own journal for one semester. Her idea was to link up with Yarmouk University and to do work in Aqaba on the red tide (an algae that destroyed marine life); this did not work out. She said that she did not like England. She liked challenging cultures. "I always wanted to marry a foreigner," she said. She went to Aqaba and became a tourist, enjoying the sunning and diving until she ran out of money, and she had to head back to Europe.

1982–83 Galveston College, took business courses—accounting and business law. During 1983 she saw Bahhar every two or three weeks.

1984–85 University of Texas, Austin; in August 1985 she received a Bachelor of Science and Radio and Television Film. She had taken courses in photography at Tyler Junior College to get the skills in editing. They had an Institute of Photography in Santa Barbara, California where she wanted to move. In 1990 they visited it, but Bahhar wouldn't go (because of the lifestyle there). She said she was going to join the Washington Film and Video Association. To explain her liking for foreign countries, people, she said that her father once worked in a hospital in Florida that had a lot of foreign doctors who had foreign children—Cubans, Turks, Filipinos, English—and she got her liking of foreign ways from that.

COURTSHIP: R said that they had similar interests: both loved ships; both liked to travel and were interested in other cultures; she was a cave explorer, spelunker, in Mexico. After she left Greece they communicated for a year by letter till Bahhar came over. He called once or twice by telephone from Greece. She had relatives in Claxton, Georgia, a grandmother and aunts. They spent one week together in Georgia before he had to leave with his ship (which had come in to Savannah). She came to New Orleans three times to meet his ship between July 1979 and February 21, 1980. She remembers the name of the ship, the *Mcamdis*. She applied for a fiancee's visa in preparation for an old-fashioned wedding (because he couldn't enter the States). His ship came into Galveston harbor in February. It was illegal for an American to go on to a ship, or even to make radio contact with it. The ship couldn't come into port because of the fog. After waiting a day or two she got a supply ship captain to go out and find the ship. They spent seven hours out in the bay searching, but couldn't find it. The next day her brother said, "Let's hire an airplane," and they went out the next day and located it through a break in the clouds. They had to maintain radio silence and couldn't talk to the ship. She then went out with the supply captain again; the day was rough and cold. (They found the ship), and she spent a week on the ship till it came into port. Her brother at that point said, "Let's get your blood tests" (he was a doctor), and he lined up a justice of the peace, and they got married (only her brother and sister were in attendance). Two hours later Bahhar had to return to his ship. She then left for her grandmother's house in Claxton. A month later she went down to the Dominican Republic. She got a wedding gown in Savannah and flew down to the Dominican Republic with decorations for a wedding celebration. She talked to Bahhar by radio from a sailboat; Bahhar saw her with his binoculars. (She did not want to wait until the ship came into port to see him.) A few days later the ship left for Venezuela with her on it. She found an Italian baker in Venezuela's port to bake a wedding cake, and she got flowers. They had a reception on the ship with the captain and the crew as invited guests. Her brother liked Bahhar and wanted to speed the process of his coming to the United States; and perhaps he wanted to stop supporting her, she added with a smile. He thought it was crazy for her to fly back and forth across the Caribbean meeting his ship in various ports. Her brother had called Texas senator John Tower when they were hassling Bahhar in Amman (that next summer when they visited Jordan) as he was trying to get permanent residency status (i.e., with the green card); they were already married, and she couldn't understand why they weren't facilitating the process of his getting the green card. She also talked to an officer in the State Department about it.

'ISAM

5/29/91 (phone conversation from Binghamton) 'Isam is a comanager of the Red Lobster restaurant in Midland, Texas, one of four comanagers. He has been in Texas five years. Midland is about three hundred miles west of Dallas, and it takes four hours to get there by car from Dallas.

6/8/91 (Saturday morning in Midland) 'Isam's reference group first formed in Abu Dhabi where he began to date and interact with English and American girls (one each) while still in high school.[13] [His political opinions are right-wing as befits the Texas oil culture of Midland, Texas: adulation of free enterprise, hard work, no sympathy for the poor, competition for women as well as money and jobs—he endorses the dating system. He has set goals for himself: (1) he will set aside 10 percent of his income for his parents beginning this year; (2) he will "retire" in seven years (by that I assume he means he will become an independent entrepreneur by then).] 'Isam already has two businesses he runs on the side, marketing and advertising, in addition to spending long hours managing the restaurant.

'Isam said that one big problem in this country is the difficulty of establishing credit. He bought a car and made a big down payment and got an installment payment set up. He said they won't give you a good apartment unless you've established a line of credit. He lived with a friend and had no credit. The company for whom he worked no longer exists (to act as a credit reference). If you're a student you have to make a 2½ month down payment to the bank and then pay it off (to get credit).

'Isam said that he could sell his advertising business today for $15,000. He wants to hire a couple of people to work on the marketing and advertising side to release him for other independent enterprises, e.g., a booklet on gourmet menus. The way he gets people to take his advertising boards is to ask, "What do you sell? To whom, housewives or businessmen?" If it's businessmen he'll say, "Then we'll put it up in 'The Bar'—young businessmen between age thirty and forty hang out there" and he'll tell them he'll give them a 10 percent discount for putting it up somewhere else. They are also asked to give a 10 percent discount to customers—who must mention the ad to get it. That way, he can monitor how many saw it. He also suggests to the proprietor that he jack up his price and then give the 10 percent discount. 'Isam says he wants to buy a classic car, a 1958 Chevy (with fins); he says he's going to buy a bigger luxury-class car soon. He joked that he might have a whole stable of them sometime. He said that if he bought a house and he moved from Midland, his company would sell the house for him. Midland was the only town where most of the business people dressed informally except in the big banks and companies downtown. This reflected the large number of wealthy independent entrepreneurs who dominate the town's society (and don't have to dress up to impress people).

FATHER: His father, age fifty-five, is a junior high school principal in al-Ayn, Abu Dhabi. He has been in Abu Dhabi for fourteen years. He went in 1970 with a five-year teaching contract to teach junior high. He stayed for one year in Abu Dhabi unemployed; he worked four or five months with the Ministry of Agriculture; then he taught for one year again.

EDUCATION: 'Isam graduated from high school in Abu Dhabi at age eighteen in the science track. In San Antonio he entered Incarnate Word College to study English. This was arranged through a high school teacher (Brian). He paid $3,000 that semester; he was late registering. He stayed there one year, studying English the first term and calculus, biology, and physics the second term, tending toward a science degree. The next year he registered at San Antonio College, paying $600 tuition per semester. He studied basic science, history, literature, psychology, sociology, chemistry, physics, and calculus, aiming at engineering. He already had two jobs and he had started dating, but he was 3.75 Dean's List at Incarnate Word. The two jobs he held during this period were dishwashing and cashier. His second year he studied math and science and he completed that year. He didn't finish his third year. He finished sixty-eight hours and still needs thirty-eight toward a degree.

I asked him how he evaluated his education at San Antonio College. It was a community college; there were a lot of minorities; they didn't have as good quality teachers (as expected). No one could understand the Iranian professor. The professors weren't good. He didn't like many of the Middle Eastern students; they were a bunch of socialists; they were always talking politics; "they weren't here to learn, mostly to discuss: talking about society, Karl Marx and solving (political) problems." [Whereas his brother simply avoided Arab students for pragmatic reasons (the need to learn English), 'Isam condemned/avoided them for ideological reasons.]

HOME: one-bedroom apartment.

AUTOMOBILES: He made a $6,000 downpayment on a $13,000 1988 Dodge Diplomat; they bought it on installments, $228 a month. In 1989–90 he bought a 1986 Chevrolet for $8,000; he had bought a small Fiaro Chevrolet; after six weeks it was stolen. When he moved out of Brian's house he used his brother's old 1977 Monte Carlo for one year. He said he is going to buy a Chevy Suburban.

"**Why?**" They are a nice comfortable car; they are safer. I don't need a trunk, i.e., storage space; a lot of the time he takes business people for dinner, and there is room for his advertising boards.

WORK HISTORY: In the Emirates he had a Lebanese friend from Beirut. His father died and left him a construction company. 'Isam helped him finish out a contract for fencing on a hospital. He answered phones and talked to clients and drove the company truck. His friend's mother loved him even though he was a lady's man. He drove a Mercedes. 'Isam said, "There are people who go to management school (like Zayd) and only make $18,000–$20,000 a year—what I make now." **I asked him if he'd go back to school.** He replied, "I'm not going to invest my money in something I'm not going to get a lot out of."

He's held the following jobs in reverse chronological order:

Manager, Red Lobster restaurant (1990–91) ten months, in Midland, $27,000 a year plus $4,000 bonus four times a year;

Manager, Coco's, five months, in San Antonio, $23,000 a year;

Manager, Raffino's, eight months, in San Antonio, $25,000 a year;

Waiter, TGI Fridays, one year, in San Antonio, $18,000 a year;

Manager, Pizza Hut, six months, in San Antonio, $6.50 per hour, forty hour week, $18,000 year;

Washing Dishes, Pizza Hut, six months, in San Antonio, forty hours a week;

Washing Dishes, in the morning, Incarnate Word College, five months, $4.00 per hour, thirty hours a week;

Cashier, San Antonio College, $4.50 per hour, twenty hours a week; these last two jobs gave him an income of $22,000 a year. Previously he cashiered at the International Student's Office at San Antonio College at $3.35 per hour, the minimum wage. He couldn't work off campus because his work permit restricted him to on-campus work for one year. He asked for a release from immigration to work off campus every six months for a couple of years till June 1988. He made friends with the immigration officer, and he told him not to worry about it. [Note that 'Isam remembers the exact wage paid and the time spent—these were traumatic formative years]. He just got his green card last year (1990); he never bothered to apply for it. He wanted to be a citizen; it's good for two years; then you need an interview, and have to apply for a passport (i.e., citizenship).

HOUSING: He stayed with his brother in Brian's house for 1½ years; it was an old house in a million-dollar home area in San Antonio. 'Isam helped with the bills. Brian lived by himself and was divorced. He just took what they ('Isam and his brother) could afford. He was divorced and lonely. The home was built in 1890; there are all antiques in the house. Then he lived in a one-bedroom furnished apartment close to the school for $250 a month; he lived there for eight months, eating in restaurants (where he worked to cut expenses); he never ate breakfast. He lived with a Palestinian from Abu Dhabi for six months; 'Isam was supposed to mentor him; the apartment cost $400 a month; it was hot, old, huge; they were both in good neighborhoods on the north side.

On May 12, 1989 he was married. He then got a one-bedroom apartment, unfurnished, in San Antonio for $295 a month; they rented furniture and lived in it for seven months. The last month that he was in school he went back to managing Ruffino's restaurant. Then when he went to work at Coco's he got an apartment for $310 a month. In Midland they got a one-bedroom apartment with a six-month lease for $320 a month; it is on the north side. They got to Midland on December 1, 1990. The apartment is four minutes away from the Red Lobster restaurant by car.

SPENT INCOME: What did you spend your income on? He says he has a $5,000 credit card debt. He saves $200 a month or 12 percent of his income. He piles up $800 in monthly credit card debt. He spends $3,500 on housing a year or 20 percent of his income. Payments on the bed, furniture, and electronics are $70 a month. He spends $3,600 a year on his car. He says he gives money to the Catholic Church.

BUSINESS ENTERPRISES: He has an advertising business, A&L Enterprises. It requires no capital. Others invest; he gets the printing and framing done for free. He started on April 15, 1991. He has an advertising board up at the airport for which he gets $300 a month; one up in the men's bathroom of "The Bar" for which he gets $200 a month; and one up at the Mail Center for which he gets $100 a month. Ten percent of the profits go to the people who make the frames. The total costs are $800, and he made $1,000 the first month, and he paid himself back for everything he used.

The marketing business involves hooking people up with manufacturers and suppliers, e.g., office supplies for a professor. "Why don't you order from this manufacturer?" he will ask (potential customers). 'Isam gets a percent of the volume from the manufacturer up to 25 percent. He has done it for one year. He has six or seven households or businesses as customers. He makes $200 a month doing nothing (he is not counting his own labor and time) off of five or six people. It was set up some time ago. He says he plans to make $36,000 in the advertising business by next December; and $8–$9,000 from marketing. He has another business enterprise in mind: providing gourmet food from fast-food suppliers.

WORK CYCLE: In the restaurant he averages forty-five to fifty hours a week; in a crisis, e.g., losing a manager, seventy-two hours. For the marketing he takes two nights a week. His daily work cycle is from 8 a.m. to 6 p.m. Tomorrow he is going to Dallas or San Antonio to work on marketing.

Have you ever had any failed investments? He replied that he was always careful. He had thought of providing a delivery service for restaurants. He would distribute a booklet with menus free to different people, and from home they could order (anything on the menu). The restaurant would reduce the price by 15 percent. He would make five to ten dollars from each order. When I said that that was an ingenious idea, he said, "I'll never starve, that's one thing."

Have you had any ties with other Arabs, Middle Easterners? In his restaurant he sometimes sees someone who looks Iranian; he will go up to him and ask, "Are you enjoying your lunch?" Most are engineers. He doesn't usually meet them. Once a Saudi Arabian invited him to go to the mosque. He called him a couple of times; 'Isam didn't go. In San Antonio he helped the foreign students get squared away.

TIES WITH VILLAGE OF ORIGIN: He hasn't returned to Abu Dhabi or Jordan since he came five years ago. **I asked whether he sent remittances.** He says he sends to his parents now and then. His goal is to set aside 10 percent of his income for his parents. He calls his older brother (in Abu Dhabi) three or four times a month.

What interaction have you had with other sons of the village in Texas? He has seen his brother twice since he moved to Midland (December 1, 1990, i.e., twice in six months). He says he has seen him five times in the last two years. He has seen Zayd four times in the last five years, once every six months. He has never met Dan [and he had the opportunity to, but did not meet him in his visit to Dallas this weekend].

'Isam came to the United States in August 1986. He may go for a visit in a couple of years. His father said he could go and come back and get a better job. His father paid his expenses for his schooling for the first two semesters. His mother sold her gold bracelets later, and sold stock in the Bank of Islam worth $4,000 and his father gave him $1,000 (all for his education).

Interview with Wife, L
6/8/91

L, age twenty-one, was born in Corpus Christi, Texas and moved to Laredo at the age of one year. She went to high school in Laredo, Texas and to the University of Texas, San Antonio for 1½ years; she was working for a general BA. She would work for a teaching degree if she went back to school.

WORK HISTORY: She worked for her sister and brother-in-law in a CPA firm as a clerical. After she was married in 5/10/89 she worked as a cashier in a restaurant for three months; then in Saks 5th Avenue department store in San Antonio for fourteen months. They came to Midland in December 1990; in Midland she works for J.E. Borron, Men's Clothing for $6.50 an hour plus a commission of 8 percent.

ETHNIC-RELIGIOUS AFFILIATION: She is Roman Catholic through her mother. She attends church on religious holidays—Christmas, Easter, Ash Wednesday, July 4. (Her father) is a Mexican/American of Scotch-Irish background from Iowa.

COURTSHIP: How did you meet 'Isam and your courtship start? "He was a waiter at TGI Fridays during the day and went to school at night. The first time I saw him he was as a waiter dressed up as Dracula at Halloween." At first he annoyed her—he kept coming around. Her parents came to eat there when they came to San Antonio. The first week of February he asked her out. They were married three months later.

Where did you go out together? They went to bars and parks and out to eat. He embarrassed her by hanging around. "What's the matter, L," he would ask, "You don't like foreigners." He told others he was Greek. He said he had to be careful. "I really liked him by the time I got to know him. He dated lots of girls. I was one of those girls who said I wouldn't marry till I was 26."

What happened when you found out he was Jordanian? "It didn't make any difference. I didn't know the politics of it. I got to know his Palestinian roommate. The different thing about 'Isam was that he detached himself from other Arabs. Their apartment was full of Arab men watching TV, smoking, playing cards. 'Those are the Arabs that give us a bad stereotype,' he said." "The guy he was rooming with, 'Isam was doing (him) a favor by rooming with him. He was new (in the U.S.). After 'Isam moved out (of the apartment with Arabs), he went backwards on his Arabic. 'Isam knows people everywhere; he is a very sociable and likeable person. I liked him because he was so much more outgoing and ambitious." The first apartment they lived in they had no furniture; they rented furniture; they bought a couch and a bed on their respective charge accounts. They got most of the furniture at auction in San Antonio. They got married to forestall the opposition to her marriage from her father; he wanted her to finish college and didn't want her to marry a foreigner. Her father said the marriage wouldn't last more than six months. He knows that 'Isam treats her well.

PROBLEMS OF INTERETHNIC MARRIAGE (from L): Were your problems due to your interethnic marriage? She said that in the beginning she was perhaps infatuated more with the situation than in love with 'Isam. They had troubles their first year. "I had never lived with another man," she said. His first job was seventy to eighty hours a week. His Persian employer kept talking about loyalty to him, and then he laid 'Isam off in the first year. He had no savings. She was working at Saks 5th Avenue. The problems were more related to personality than to ethnic background. His father pushed religion on him quite a lot and

'Isam resented it. "'Isam says he's an atheist, but there's more Muslim in him than he realizes."

"I tell him my position, and he tells me his (and as a result of this frank exchange) 'Isam sometimes becomes defensive." She sometimes asks 'Isam for advice, and she likes him because he won't tell her what to do. She said that 'Isam sometimes cooks, but not much Arabic food. She doesn't like to cook.

Did you talk about how to bring up your children? They talked about raising children in a religious tradition. 'Isam says he has no hang-up about bringing children up as Catholics, but she doesn't believe it. 'Isam drinks alcohol. She says he did in Abu Dhabi—he kept bourbon hidden under his bed. She said they are both against drugs. They were married by a Lutheran pastor. Brian, the high school teacher with whom he lived, was a Lutheran. They decided to be married at Brian's church in a small chapel, a private marriage; there were eleven people there. Her parents did not attend. The reception was at Brian's home. Brian had visited 'Isam's father in Abu Dhabi. They were married on May 12, 1989.

L said that 'Isam's brother was angry that 'Isam didn't consult him before getting married. The problem (between the two brothers) came when 'Isam found his brother basically living off Brian, and 'Isam started working in the cafeteria of the university and a restaurant to pay off some of his brother's debts. Later, 'Isam hooked on to the restaurant business and his brother felt jealous at 'Isam's success and greater enterprise and ambition. "The battle continues," she said. 'Isam has decided to stay here (the U.S.), and he has told her that he had a scholarship to the University of the United Arab Emirates. He was ranked eleventh or twelfth in the country, and he didn't use the scholarship. He said the opportunities were greater here.

'Isam is very generous; he sent money to his other brother, who had to pay $5,000 to get out of the Jordanian army during the Gulf War. 'Isam is very homesick, but can't go back to Jordan due to his army obligation. 'Isam told his parents in Abu Dhabi that he wasn't going to come back. When 'Isam was laid off he went to work as manager at Coco's restaurant in San Antonio; he had previously managed the Pizza Hut and Jim's Coffee Shop. Coco's gave him a recommendation. She said that 'Isam's father is probably disappointed that he has not finished.

'Isam (again)

'ISAM ON COURTSHIP: (How they met and courted): "I was going through my address book one day and I found twenty-eight (women's) names, and I said to myself this is too much"; some had gotten married. He had gone out with a German girl, a model, for eight months; they had thought about getting engaged; then she went to New Zealand to model and they broke up, and he didn't date for five months. At TGI Fridays where he worked, he used to go out with customers. "L asked me out," he said. "Many girls asked me out. I liked L. She was quiet. At that point I would have married a girl from the Middle East. I got tired of the wild girls who would be here today and gone with someone else to-morrow or partying or drinking"; he was uncomfortable with students smoking pot. [Note 'Isam and Zayd react the same way to the extreme freedom, unpre-dictability, and partying of American girls; but Zayd's solution is to go back to Jordan and marry a Jordanian girl; 'Isam's is to marry a non-party, family-bred, traditional American girl.] She was a homey girl. She didn't come to the restau-rant with her girlfriends. She only came with her parents who brought her when they visited her. (On the first date) he took her out on a Friday, and they stayed out all night. They went to a college bar; then they picked up a video and talked all night. She was a very proud person. She had big dreams. She wanted a better life; wanted to live in a nice home; to travel; she doesn't want to work for the rest of her life. She has two sisters: one works as a CPA and makes a million, but works a lot. The other sister has a college marketing degree and is not making money. L was dating a guy for three or four years and continued dating him for three or four weeks (after we started dating). We met at the end of January 1989 and dated seriously every day. He helped her with her studies. In early May her father wanted her to go back to Laredo. L said to him, "Let's get married." He said, "You must be crazy. I wait on tables. I make just enough to cover my own expenses." The plan was to elope. They talked about eloping. Brian loved L. A German girl, Michel, said she (L) was the best thing for him. They got more committed. They began to plan. They called Brian and said they wanted to get married. He said the pastor would come to the house (to marry them). He had gone to the (Lutheran) church before with Brian and sometimes by himself. He enjoyed the friendly atmosphere (of the church) and breakfast. Over three years he went to the church about twenty times.

What are your feelings about Christianity and Islam? "I respect both. Nei-ther is wrong. (There are) people who misuse religion. I'm an atheist." His father never brought up the question of marrying a non-Muslim. He talks to his older brother (in Abu Dhabi) all the time, three or four times a month. In a letter his father said, "Don't forget why you're there—to get a degree. Don't become irre-sponsible; pay off your debts." He sent $300 to Abu Dhabi when they needed it early on. He called his father and said, "I'm thinking of getting married." His fa-ther said, "Do you know what it's going to take?" His father said, "God bless you. I wish you were here."

He told L, "I'm not going to go back. This is my home." He did date a girl his last year in high school, a Lebanese girl, and she kept calling him in the States. His father knew about her. His father didn't like it that girls called him up in Abu Dhabi, but his grades were high. He said that he was a little brat in Abu Dhabi.

What did you agree on regarding the raising of children? He said that he had said to L, "I don't care. I'll go with you (to church) some of the time, though I don't believe in it. I'll raise them (children) with the same ethics I grew up with." He does want to take the children back to Abu Dhabi/Jordan for three or four months to know their Middle Eastern origins. "I've become very Americanized, but if I go to Jordan I must become Jordanized."

VIEWS OF ABU DHABI: 'Isam said he was in Abu Dhabi between the ages of nine and eighteen. "I don't like the foreigner-non-foreigner distinction there. I don't like the weather (there). I liked the modernity; you can buy oranges all year around; I liked the convenience—dishwashers and dryers are available. I didn't like the fact that I didn't have friends to play with; you weren't allowed to go out in the neighborhood and play; it wasn't safe." There were lots of people from Pakistan and India; there was kidnapping or raping of boys and girls. Sometimes he had to drive twenty miles to see a friend.

VIEW OF RELATIONSHIP BETWEEN THE SEXES: "I had girlfriends in Abu Dhabi. I had several. I started dating at twelve or thirteen." He went to an all-male school, but there was another girls' high school, and they met in the park. He also saw the Lebanese girl in her house when the father was away; the mother would arrange it. He didn't go to the cinema. They would meet at the park, say on the occasion of a friend's birthday party. They would meet on the beach. Their kids had a car, and sometimes they would go with the family and walk on their own on the beach. For 2½ months he dated an American girl and an English nurse; they went dancing at the disco several times. He would ask a girl out, and they would be accompanied by her mother, and she wouldn't let him kiss her. He once went to a pool party where he was surrounded by girls (apparently he was the only male); the girls were touching him, and he thought that their fathers were going to beat him up. The dating system in the United States was good. "In Jordan, whoever my family picked, that would be it"; he wouldn't have found L.

SOCIAL VIEWS AND ATTITUDES: In the U.S.A. there is too much socialism. "They give welfare to people who don't deserve it. They sell their food stamps and buy beer. They spend more time investigating people who get welfare (than actually benefiting people)." The only thing he doesn't like about the American system is that there's too much lobbying. Everything else he loves. "There's too much favoritism towards minorities—so many seats reserved for Blacks; if he's the right color (and he comes along) at the right time (he gets the job); he should deserve it. The Spanish come across the border; they want to be supported. I like having choices. Getting a lot of support from a lot of people. There are a lot of good people who'll help you succeed if you want to exert yourself. There's no limit (to what you can achieve)."

What is your view of the Army? "In the Emirates it's a job; you get paid for it; there are no risks; no loyalty. In Jordan, they're dropouts. Parents say to children, 'If you don't get your act together you'll wind up in the army.' It's physical; it's nice. You serve your country. (But) what if Jordan gets in a fight against Israel? I have loyalty to Jordan, but not to King Husayn. I'd like to advertise for free for Jordan; make it (attractive) like Spain.

What is your view of birth control? "It's great." By any methods? I asked. "Yes, basically."

What is your view of Jordan's unemployment? "There is a lack of direction and responsibility of the government. There are no counselors to say to prospective students, 'Don't become an engineer.' It's hard to start a business there now for Jordanians."

What of the government of the Emirates? "It can't be any worse. A shaykhdom! One thing I love about them (however): they take care of their own people—they get free medicine; we pay $10. I don't know any citizen there who doesn't have a home and a living. They are simple and trust you."

What is your view of tribal law? "It's great," he said. **Do you have tribal law in Abu Dhabi?** "Yes. A kid was killed by an automobile. My father and twenty people came and stayed at the victim's house and stayed till he promised to relent on the punishment. People come to ask the father to relent if it is a case of drunken driving."

What is your view of TV? In Abu Dhabi it's entertainment. The soap operas are watched, the cowboy movies. American TV is good. People can do without it (however). He never forgave Roseanne for insulting the flag.

What is your view of your own upbringing? "I had a great time in Kufr al-Ma. It was fun. Going around school. Playing marbles. Going with my Dad; I loved social gatherings. *Mansaf*.[14] My Dad always treated us as adults. We sat next to him in the *sidr* (place of honor of the guest house) and drank coffee. (As a result) I can stand in front of thirty thousand and talk. Beni Dumi was best [he has pride in kinship affiliation]. I left (Kufr al-Ma) at age nine for Abu Dhabi. It was hot and the house burned and I ran outside and hid under the Jeep. I think back of dating ages and high school buddies; I wrote poetry in the (school) paper. I was active in politics. At age sixteen I was rebellious; I wrote about lazy Arab presidents and spending $5,000 for wedding celebrations." All his friends scattered in the summer. "It (Abu Dhabi) wasn't your home. We always leased a home, and couldn't bang a nail in the wall. I didn't like being treated as a foreigner.[15] My father taught for twenty-five years in Abu Dhabi, and all of a sudden a young kid comes back (from abroad) and gets twice as much in salary as my father."

ATTITUDES TOWARD THE GULF WAR: Did the Gulf War lead to any changes in your life here in Midland? "I was afraid my last name or looks would turn people off—you know, Red Necks. In San Antonio I knew a lot of people. In Midland he was referred to as "This guy, 'Ali." He was harassed in the Dallas airport. Too many questions were asked, and they went through his suitcase very thoroughly. They went through his shoes. I was mad. "Can I speak with your supervisor?" I asked. He (finally) said (to the baggage inspector), "I'm going—if you want to keep the baggage, stuff it!"

Did it lead to any changes in your relations with Americans? "No, I don't think it did."

Did it lead to any change in your relations with other Arabs? A number didn't like him because of his political stance. His ex-roommate, a Palestinian, got turned off.

Did you get into arguments over the war? He was not the arguing type.

Did the war lead to any changes in your view of Americans and American society/culture? "Not in any way. I didn't have a problem with the war. The idea was good. The purpose was good: protect your oil. I love what's going on with the Kurds. They destroyed civilian places and didn't get Saddam. Now they're fixing it (by intervening to aid the Kurds). If there had been more involvement by the UN it would have been better."

Did the war lead to any changes in your feelings toward yourself, your country, the Arab World, the Middle East? "No. About my country I feel King Husayn did wrong by siding with Iraq. It was a war between the world and Iraq. Like Israel. Instead of losing the export business (by siding with Iraq)."

What are your views of George Bush and Saddam Husayn? "I respect Bush a lot more. I thought he was a loser. He did what he promised. Maybe he didn't have to destroy Iraq. Saddam Husayn got too carried away. He thought the Arabs would be on his side. He's not as bad as Khomeini. He's just like Saddam Husayn—no democracy."

What do you think about all the American flags and yellow ribbons? "I have one on my car. I have American friends in the war and two friends from the emirates in helicopters there. My best friend's fiance was over there. I still have a yellow ribbon. They're (Americans) very patriotic. It was nice to see it. They came and wanted to put up a sign in the restaurant, 'Free Kuwait.'" He told them, "Sure, put it up." He left it up a week. He bought a TV due to the war. L was alone a lot. I made my point clear about wanting Saddam stopped. I wore a name tag (with those sentiments) most of the time.

Analysis

Let us begin with the last migrant to arrive, the youngest, and the one who stayed the shortest time (five years), 'Isam.[16] His adjustment to Texas was facilitated by his older brother and the latter's good friend and mentor, a retired school principal, Brian. His brother tutored him in English when he first arrived, found him housing with his mentor, and lent him his car. In addition to providing him with free housing, Brian suggested his initial college training, and later he was instrumental in arranging 'Isam's elopement marriage in a difficult situation (his future wife's father strongly opposed the marriage). Yet 'Isam moved out of Brian's house at the earliest opportunity, and did not consult with his brother on various important matters including dropping out of college, working at various jobs, or his own marriage, which his brother opposed. When I interviewed him in Midland, Texas, a four-hour drive from Dallas where his brother worked, 'Isam said that he had seen his brother only twice in the last six months and five times in the last two years. He had seen his cousin, Zayd, who lived in Houston four times in the last five years, and had never met Dan, the other co-villager living in Texas. On the other hand, he maintained cordial telephonic communication with his father and mother, who provided him financial support for his first year of study, and with another elder brother in Abu Dhabi; he had lent the latter $5,000 to secure a waiver from army service in Abu Dhabi during the 1991 Gulf War. 'Isam had a collage of his family in his apartment in Midland.

Besides sibling rivalry and independence—both of mind and from close kin ties—the interview in Texas revealed his entrepreneurship, high ambition, and preoccupation with and capacity for work. He had held ten jobs over five years, beginning as a dishwasher, then waiter, and ending as a manager of the Red Lobster Restaurant in Midland. In addition to the manager's job, he was currently engaged as a middleman in marketing arrangements and as a producer and seller of small-size, high-quality advertising boards. Up until his marriage, his social life was as hectic and frenetic as his work life: one day he looked at his address book and counted the names and telephone numbers of twenty-eight past and future potential girlfriends!

Of all the migrants, 'Isam was the one who had consciously and decisively opted for assimilation, telling his wife on marriage that he would not return to Abu Dhabi or Jordan to work or live. He was the only migrant who supported the patriotic fervor that swept the United States during the Gulf War, displaying a sign in his restaurant, "Free Kuwait," a name tag with the same sentiments on his person, and a yellow ribbon on his car. Even before the war he had condemned the television comedienne, Roseanne, for her insulting behavior toward the American flag at the All-Star game in San Diego. 'Isam had also acculturated more rapidly than any Texas migrant with the exception of his brother: he and his wife hardly prepared or ate Arabic food, they had almost exclusively American acquaintances in and out of work, and he had knowledge of American Protestant religious ritual and custom through occasional attendance at Brian's Lutheran Church and some knowledge of American Catholicism through his wife's religious affiliation.

We have already discussed in previous chapters the concept of "preadaptation": experiences migrants had either in their home countries or in other countries that prepared them in some fashion for the new way of life in the country they finally chose for study. 'Isam's case illustrates another process I shall term "misadaptation": negative experiences migrants undergo either in their home countries or other countries before arriving in the country of study. These experiences also predispose them to embrace or at least accept the way of life of the new country. Although he had favorable memories of his early life in rural Jordan, they were not deep-rooted. Furthermore, if 'Isam were to return to Jordan, he would have to serve in the army.

He grew up in Abu Dhabi in a society that was concerned and equitable with regard to its own indigenous population, but not to foreigners regularly employed in the country (like Jordanians), who were treated as strangers and mercenaries. Although his father had lived and taught in Abu Dhabi for nearly twenty years, his seniority of service was not recognized, and he was not compensated even to the level of much younger Abu Dhabians who had far less service. Moreover, foreigners were not allowed to own property, even their own home. Neighborhoods were segregated by ethnicity and class; as a child 'Isam had no neighborhood children to play with. Thus 'Isam embraced the relatively open society of the United States, not only for its economic opportunity but also for its social freedom. This is not to say that his assimilation was smooth; he disguised his Arab identity to his future wife, and he was hassled at the Dallas airport during the Gulf War. Full assimilation is dependent on the host society's acceptance of ego as much as his/her acceptance of the host society.

By contrast, Dan, the first student to arrive in the United States, the oldest, and the one who stayed the longest period and lived in two different states, was, counterintuitively, the most decisive in rejecting assimilation to American society.[17] Although he had acculturated through his anglicized first name change, early and abortive marriage, his many dates, his more serious live-in relationship, and most of all his jobs (e.g., his telemarketing job improved his understanding of various American accents and his own fluency in English), which took up almost all his working hours and required constant contact with the American public, he stated clearly that he had fundamental reservations about American society and culture. After working for a period of time in the United States, he planned to return to Jordan to live.

Like 'Isam's, Dan's adjustment to American society in Ohio was facilitated by an American mentor, a professor in Cincinnati who first led him to the college where he received his degree in business management and later invested with him in his first venture as owner-manager of a restaurant. But unlike 'Isam, Dan's first mentor was collective: a Jordanian family in Cincinnati that provided him employment, commensality, constant sociability, and a loan.

In contrast to 'Isam, Dan maintained his Arab identity, specifically in a political context. He was by far the most concerned with and agitated about the Gulf War: he condemned American foreign policy during the war; and he condemned in even stronger terms Saudi Arabia for its mercenary policies and the Arab world generally for its lack of unity.

Dan's unique (among the Texas migrants) identification with the Arab world and its political problems was matched by his conscious adherence to his own language and Arab Jordanian culinary preferences, to which he gave full play the one day of the week when he was not working, Sunday. Language was as much a stumbling block to assimilation as his Arab political consciousness. This fact was revealed in his agitated condemnation of the "uncivilized" Americans who objected to the owners of Denny's restaurant about the loud Arabic speech of Dan and his friends. Notwithstanding, Dan preferred Texas to Ohio (he had spent about the same amount of time in both) because in the former, as he said, "There is a Jordanian society outside Jordan" in which he could control acculturation and affirm his Jordanian Arab identity. Although he worked with Americans six days a week, he said that 99 percent of his friends were Arabs or Arab-Americans.

After thirteen years of living, studying, and working in the United States, Dan's decisive anti-assimilationist stance revealed itself in a series of emotionally charged statements:

I want my kids to be Muslims. I want to meet one of my own people. I want to marry someone who won't cheat (on me). If I have a child I want him to be mine. [His closest friend had married and divorced an American woman who had taken custody of their children.] My girlfriend—I cook, and she won't even wash the dishes. I want to hear a girl speaking Arabic again.

These statements demonstrate his rejection of American social culture as he experienced it mainly through his brief marriage and the dating scene. In general he regarded American society as impersonal and dehumanized, a society in which "the American man doesn't care what the members of the family are doing" and is unwilling to help them (the children) in need.

On the other hand, and surprisingly in light of many of his comments above, Dan took pride in his American political identity, saying, "I am a citizen" and "This (the U.S.A.) is my country." He intended to return to the United States, after marrying in Jordan, to live and work, exercising his political and economic rights. But his planning did not end there. Dan had already determined to retire to Kufr al-Ma where, despite his self-styled spendthrift ways, he had saved the money to build a house, and to die there, a decision diametrically opposed in both its intent and finality to that of 'Isam.

If 'Isam provides a clear case of independence, sibling rivalry, and pronounced acculturation and assimilation, Bahhar and his brothers represent an example of close economic cooperation and social support over three continents. Bahhar's oldest brother, a migrant clerk in Saudi Arabia (see Chapter Two) provided constant financial support to Bahhar's brother in Greece (Migrant Five in Chapter Four); the latter provided constant economic and social support for Bahhar while he was studying in Greece. After Bahhar finished his education he, in turn, put his younger brother through college in Jordan. It was also the example of his older brothers who went to Saudi Arabia and Greece, respectively, that inspired Bahhar to realize his dream of leaving Jordan and exploring the world outside. He literally realized this goal by joining the Greek merchant marine and sailing around four continents. As a result of these experiences he was exposed to the widest variety of foreign cultures of any migrant described in this book, and he developed a stance of cultural relativism as attested to by his remark, "I've traveled so much, I must accept people the way they are."

This breadth of multicultural exposure was matched in Greece by a depth of acculturation and assimilation seldom attained by other migrants. Bahhar worked cheek-by-jowl with Greek sailors on small ships confined at sea for a month at a time or even a year before returning to home port. The way of life and ethos he learned during the four years he spent on these ships made an indelible impression on him and served as a measuring rod of all that he would observe and experience in the United States. To a large degree this experience formed the basis of his "misadaptation" to the United States.

His response to this intimate contact with Greeks was overwhelmingly positive. He found Greek sailors happy; they liked sailing; they regarded it as a fortunate profession. They were eager like him to explore the world and they took an interest in the foreign cultures they discovered in each port town. In all his experiences with his sailing comrades he was treated like a Greek, and he strove to act like one.

Even before joining the merchant marine during his student days in Greece he became accustomed to and enjoyed the public collective sociability of Greek life, going out in the evening on collective dates or with members of the Greek family he came to know well on weekends. The public life of the taverna and the plaka suited him as much as the life of the sailing ship. Of Greeks generally he said, "If you know them well, they accept you," and in another context, "They are a fun people."

His experience on American geodetic ships provided a sharp contrast. He discussed his relations with American sailors in the following way:

> The people I work with, when you come close to them, they change. For instance, you sit down and become friendly with someone for a couple of hours. The next day he doesn't want to talk to you at all.

Besides being moody and temperamental, he found the American sailors unsophisticated and uninterested in world affairs or even the different cultural milieus they visited. They would go into the port town and spend all day drinking, day after day. Before the end of the month they would be in debt. By contrast with Greeks, American sailors followed a quick-make, quick-spend, in-debt pattern that was the opposite of programmed decision-making. More important, in contrast to the fun-loving Greeks at the end of a mission after their return from shore leave, the American sailors brought their troubles on to the ship with them. Most astonishing and bothersome was the emotional shallowness and insensitivity of American sailors. He cited the example of the sailor in Japan who told him, Bahhar, to go shopping for a kimono for his wife while the sailor went into a bar day after day and got soused—and he didn't even know his wife's dress size!

More generally, although Bahhar did not personally suffer occupationally from ethnic discrimination in the U.S.A., he sensed it, particularly during the Gulf War when he feared that he would be discriminated against if he quit his present job and sought another, saying:

> As an Arab, people look at you in a different way. They don't want to get to know you at first. Because you're an Arab you lose a lot of points.

More generally and without regard to the Gulf War situation, he commented, "I found Americans not as friendly as Greeks or Arabs. They are not warm, friendly, especially if they know you're Middle Eastern." Bahhar's is the most pronounced case of misadaptation I recorded.

Paradoxically, Bahhar was also the best integrated, social structurally, of all the Texas migrants. He held the steadiest, highest-paying job, and he was an accepted member of an American family with strong consanguine ties. His affines were a relatively affluent professional family: his brother-in-law and sister-in-law were doctors, as was his deceased father-in-law. His brother-in-law had been instrumental in getting Bahhar a job and housing in Galveston, and, initially, a green card in Jordan. He also personally facilitated and arranged Bahhar's marriage, and Bahhar and his wife had lived for a time in his mother-in-law's apartment.

Untypically, then, he had a firm social base in, and also an insight into American family life that none of the other Texas migrants possessed. Yet neither his acculturation nor his integration at the familial (in sharp contrast with his earlier abortive relations with the Greek family of the Greek woman he courted) and occupational level led to a change of his Jordanian Arab identity. The maintenance of this identity was clearly an issue for Bahhar and was reflected in his naming choices: his refusal to change his name in Greece as the price of marriage, his hiring a lawyer to change his name to reflect his lineage in Jordan (an act never executed), and his giving his two children Arabic names.

Bahhar's case demonstrates an important point: acculturation, social structural integration, assimilation, and change of ethnic identity are not mutually implied processes; they are separate processes and may often be quite independent of one another.

His experience on the ships in the two societies/cultures may explain the peculiar combination of Bahhar's successful acculturation and integration into American culture and society, even his partial assimilation from the point of view of the host society, with his own refusal to identify with it. The ships are metaphors for the two cultures. The American geodetic ship with its young crew of somewhat temperamental technical specialists, high crew turnover rate, cramped quarters to make room for equipment, constant monitoring from shore and instant repair, and short period at sea was the American business venture guided by the profit motive afloat. The Greek ship with its more spacious officers' quarters, its older, more stable crew who viewed sailing as a delight and a profession and not a job, its long unmonitored voyages to exotic lands, and its high esprit de corps, was the sociable Greek taverna and public square (*plaka*) afloat.

Of all the Texas migrants, indeed, of all migrants from Kufr al-Ma to any place, Zayd was the one whose experience abroad was marked by the most persistent and pervasive change. Over his eleven-year stay in the United States he changed professional goals three times, attended six different schools, held six different jobs, bought and sold at least eight different cars, lived in at least nine different domiciles, went on numerous dates, had three steady girlfriends, and was married and divorced.

His arrival in the United States represented the most dramatic "turning" in a life and a career of any Jordanian student abroad.[18] This fact was marked by his being the only migrant who remembered the exact date of his arrival abroad, the room number in the hotel in which he stayed in Houston his first night there, and the address of the first apartment he rented. He was also a migrant who suffered a high degree of stress at the same time that he acculturated and thoroughly enjoyed aspects of the U.S.A.'s open society. He is an introspective migrant who has reflected upon his living between two worlds and, after some effort, worked out a satisfying modus vivendi in a way few other migrants have enunciated or even contemplated. He has accommodated pervasive change by engaging in a unique reinterpretation of the rural Jordanian tradition of family life and conjugal roles.

In considering this reinterpretation it is necessary to call attention to other aspects of his adjustment: his focus on social status, his remarkable accommodation of Jordanian and American norms, and his relation with his father. His reference group in 1991 combined Jordanian and American circumstances and personalities in a peculiar, fragmented, and yet coherent way. He had already complained in 1986 that rich Jordanians (by implication members of the political/economic elite) lived in luxurious places in Amman while in his home village the people did not have hot water. When I asked him in 1991 what his opinion of tribal law was he framed his negative reply in terms of a resentment of the power and status of the "shaykhs" (tribal elders/leaders) who rendered decisions without having either knowledge or wealth: "Often the victim feels shame or weak in the presence of the shaykh, who makes him climb down from the (just) verdict." Later he spoke of the power of political influence and money spent to influence American foreign policy including the attempt to silence the ex–United States representative, Paul Findley for pronouncing anti-Zionist sentiments. At one moment he spoke with irony of the sudden elevation of a common peasant in a Jordanian village to be "King of Inbe" after he discovered a treasure trove. In the next breath he spoke of the arrogance of the rich people living in River Oaks (a wealthy Houston suburb) whom he often drove about the town for the limousine service for which he worked. However, he pronounced against having the "average living" of marriage, house, and car suggested to him by his father (not at all an average living in Kufr al-Ma) as the marks of a satisfying life because his horizons had been widened by his American experience. On the other hand, he spoke about having a house in Kufr al-Ma on the top of the hill opposite a wealthy retired army officer and municipality official (D in chapter one) whose son had become a highly successful business manager in Saudi Arabia (Migrant 4 in Chapter 5). There he would retire comfortably off the income provided by ten cows. However, he stated in 1991 that the income of his present job of limousine driver compared favorably with the income of the son of an influential in Kufr al-Ma who had returned from Pakistan with a degree in animal husbandry, suggesting that his reference group was still the village of Kufr al-Ma where, he said, it would take an income of 1,000 dinars a month to live comfortably. But then he spoke of first driving through Allen Park (where the poorest of Houston's society lived) and then through River Oaks and imagining the life he avoided on the one hand and the life he aspired to on the other, suggesting that his reference group was the status hierarchy of Houston. The fact that he could constantly switch back and forth imaginatively between the reference groups of Kufr al-Ma and Houston and make acute observations about his own present and future position in each indicates that he had very much come to terms with a life between two worlds, or as I have phrased it, a "life on the border."

Zayd's attempt to resolve his ambivalence about these two worlds did take a psychological toll. Zayd was a chain smoker when I met him in 1986 and though he tried to quit, continued to be one in 1991, having an ashtray in the bathroom of his apartment. He said in our conversation in Kufr al-Ma in 1986 that the most difficult thing to adapt to in the United States was the constant pressure. He had said then, "I can't disappoint my family," and regarding the prevailing norms of kinship in the village, "Sometimes relatives stick together, right or wrong, I don't like that. It bothers me from the inside."

Certain aspects of American life and the values underlying that life had been embraced. In 1986 Zayd laid out the American work ethic: "If you want to be lazy and lie back, you will be starving (in America)." His own student and work life in Houston reflected this ethic, combining study and work for nine of the eleven years, and ending in the last two with a course overload. This achievement was not easily come by since Zayd had, early on, evinced a distinct repugnance to manual and service labor. Zayd also learned programmed decision-making in Houston: he planned securing his green card through marriage and perhaps citizenship (though motivation is always mixed in these matters), and he was aware of the other avenues by which they could be procured. He planned to invest in a business *before* investing in a house and to postpone marriage till he had resolved the obligation of Jordanian army service, which he planned to do by saving enough money by working as a limousine driver till the spring of 1992. He planned to devote two years to getting his bachelor's in business management degree by working in the limousine service a certain limited number of hours a week and taking course overloads, and he received the degree as he had planned. He now planned to return to Jordan, marry there, return to the U.S.A. with his wife, and raise children in Houston, but only until they reached school age, when he would return to Jordan to work. By the late 1980s he had also acculturated to the Texas college scene and knew how to present himself and to play on the foibles of professors and get good grades.

Sorting out his beliefs and feelings with respect to cross-sex interpersonal relations and conjugal roles in Houston proved much more difficult than acculturating to either the university or the work world. His ambivalence on this subject was pronounced in 1986. On the one hand he embraced many norms that indicated preference for the conjugal family, saying in various parts of our conversation:

> I don't want to tell her [his future wife] what to do. (I want it to be) a two-way street. I want someone to be able to argue with me and tell me when I'm wrong or right. I want someone who is educated and intelligent. I don't want to marry a seventeen-year-old and baby her and have kids every year. I want to be able to sit down and talk and see how the person feels.

When I asked him in 1986 about whether he approved of women working outside the home he replied:

> A man can't provide enough (today, economically); now 50–50 is good. It is good for the woman to be out of the house where there is only preparing food and being with kids, so that she can come into contact with society. I find it very disturbing to find an educated man marrying a ninth or twelfth grader. I don't know how they'll relate to one another.

But all these statements were framed by others that suggested that the conjugal family and relations within it were to be viewed within a consanguine family structure and a patripotestal authority structure:

> "… I don't want someone who can't speak (Arabic) to my mother. I don't want to do that to my parents," said to explain his unwillingness to marry his first steady girlfriend in Houston. "She is too committed to her work (for me to marry her) … she takes her work too seriously—thinking of promotion and the prestige of work," said about his third and last steady girlfriend in Houston. "If she loves me enough to agree to do the things that please me, I can marry her." This was the statement that definitively ended our conversation on the subject in 1986. In 1991 when I asked Zayd whether a Jordanian wife would like living in Houston, he replied, "The Arab woman—her life is her home and her husband."

Zayd had inserted and accommodated strong and egalitarian conjugal family themes within a consanguine family model in a reinterpretation of social tradition. He had assimilated the American view of courtship, the American view of marriage as a partnership, and the American "yuppie" view of educated, intelligent spouses who would construct their own guidelines for their life together. Pleasing his wife, allowing her to work outside the home, discussing problems and exchanging thoughts with her about a variety of matters to lead to a compatible life were important. But they had to be done within a consanguine family structure of pleasing the parents, and in doing so, the self, including the husband's making the critical household decisions.

In his adjustment to life in Houston, Zayd's relations with his father were critical. The importance of a close father-son tie in the struggle to maintain an identity after extended exposure to a foreign culture has already been discussed in chapter three with respect to Ali and in chapter four with respect to Migrant Four. Zayd's father, like Ali's, had a powerful impact on his son, not only as a model but also as a social and emotional support in the diaspora. Zayd said about his father in 1986:

> I love my father very much. From a very young age he told me education was important. "You should be good," (he told me); he made me good. In the States the first person to come to my mind is my father. "I'm watching you studying. I want to be proud of you," (he said).

In a way Zayd was living out his life in Houston vicariously in the style his father would approve. The father had supported education in the village by establishing the first school there and had said, "Sitting without work, there isn't any." This is the father who had pioneered ahead of him by seeking employment in Abu Dhabi after his army retirement in order to earn money to provide higher education to his sons. Zayd's confrontation with the professor at Texas Southern was very much in the pattern of a proverb his father had recounted to me, "Straightforwardness is the essence of honor."

If Zayd strove to please his father and if his values reflected those of his father, his father also responded with sensitivity to his son's aspirations and feelings. In 1979 although his father would have much preferred that he take a position in the army or study in Abu Dhabi and suggested that he do so, he deferred to his son's wishes and supported his study in the United States (unlike Dan's father, who adamantly opposed his son's study there). In 1983 on the occasion of Zayd's first return visit to Kufr al-Ma, he asked his father for permission to smoke in his presence, and the latter assented. He had told his father about his marriage and subsequent divorce.

In 1986 when Zayd disappointed his father and revealed his immorality, by rural Jordanian standards, in Houston (he drank and dated there), revealed it even to the elders of the village when they questioned him about his activities in Houston, his father did not turn against him (as Yusuf's did for a time when he insisted on continuing his studies in England). He said only, "I wish you hadn't been so frank." But then, again, Zayd was following his father's own straightforward dictum/practice. From that time on his father was not only a model and social support but a confidante as well. Zayd said that he could then tell his father anything. And when I asked him about his view of his upbringing in the village in 1991, Zayd replied that he saw the image of his father waking him up for prayers at 5 a.m., heard the sound of birds in the first light, and remembered taking his schoolbooks out to the fields in the early morning, and he relished all these memories. When he thought of his family, the first person he thought of was his father.

Few fathers and sons had such a close relationship as Zayd and his father. Some (e.g., Yusuf) had ambivalent and others (see Migrant G, the fitter mechanic in chapter one) abrasive relations. As the next chapter will point out, even within one tight-knit family, the relations of fathers and sons and the reinterpretation of family traditions can vary considerably. Here, the point is that Zayd's close relations with his father were instrumental in both his social integration and his grappling with his own identity in Houston.

His last four years in Houston Zayd participated regularly in a ten-person basketball group made up of, as he said, "more mature individuals," all Arabs, mainly Jordanians, most over thirty, who had survived the initial period of adjustment and struggle with schooling (many had their degrees) and had "sown their wild oats." Zayd referred to the pre-1986 period in Houston as a "lost period." He said in our 1991 interview in Houston, "I want to have friends more than before," and later, "We want to identify with a group. It's (the friendship circle) helping now." Friends would help him move, lend him money, and invite him to parties. Once a week friends communicated by telephone to inquire about one another's welfare. The basketball group would meet regularly on Sunday morning to play and, afterwards, go out to a park or a restaurant. That this was not simply an occasion to play basketball but a commitment seriously undertaken was indicated by Zayd's telling me that once he had driven to Galveston late on Saturday, got delayed, and nevertheless started back to Houston at 6 a.m. Sunday morning in order not to miss the 10 a.m. game. The basketball group provided mutual reinforcement for a group of "sojourners" (rather than immigrants or exiles), that is foreign students who, after a long period of exploration and struggle, were determined to maintain their cultural identity and were at that stage in their life/career cycle when they had both the time and the strong desire to develop a mechanism to do so.

In the five years between the first and the second interviews Zayd's odyssey had been profound. If he could not assimilate in 1991, nor yet wholeheartedly embrace the culture and society of Jordan, and while he harboured feelings of loneliness, even anomie after finishing his degree, he had definitely moved beyond the dilemma that he had clearly articulated in 1986: "My roots are here, but I like the things over there." Unlike Ali and Yusuf, Zayd finally had come to terms with "life on the border." He had repudiated the view that his life would be focused on having an average living (upon receiving a degree he had rejected a job in Houston paying $20,000 a year with regular expected increments). He would return to Kufr al-Ma, marry and build a house there. But he would return again to the United States, this time with his Jordanian wife and work. He would raise a young family in Houston. But then he would return again to Jordan when they came of school age so that they could learn the values he prized. However these values now included freedom, striving, hard work, and marriage as a two-way street as well as honour, modesty, respect for the consanguine family, patripotestiality and the serenity of religion.

240

Comparative Considerations

It now remains to reflect comparatively on the modes of social structural (as opposed to cognitive) integration of migrants in the countries considered in the preceding chapters, as well as to compare the migrants treated in this chapter. In the United States integration into a social network usually occurred through a key mentor, with that mentor differing widely. Dan was embraced by a Jordanian restaurant owner and later an American professor, Bahhar by his affines, particularly his brother-in-law who mediated for him with government officials and businessmen. 'Isam's mentor, through his brother, was a school principal; what was remarkable in his case was his ignoring both his brother and his mentor as he developed his own aspirations and way of life, values and mode of assimilation. Only Zayd lacked a key mentor; his steady girlfriends certainly aided his acculturation, but they did not provide domicile, financial aid, or help in securing jobs or dealing with the government. Later his basketball group provided his significant cultural reference group as well as his social network. The wives of these migrants all acted as mentors in some sense, but the social structural implications of the marriages were quite different and tripartite: Dan and Zayd's wives were unimportant for social integration, 'Isam's important, and Bahhar's wife was critical, as will be elaborated below.

If one is to consider the relative ease of social integration of Jordanian migrants in the four societies dealt with at length above—Saudi Arabia and the Gulf, Greece, Pakistan, and the United States, it is not difficult to place them on a continuum. On the continuum Saudi Arabia and the Gulf are the most difficult into which to integrate and Greece is the easiest, with Pakistan and the United States occupying the center, the former closer to the Arabian side and the latter closer to the Greek side.

MOST DIFFICULT INTEGRATION		*EASIEST INTEGRATION*	
Saudi Arabia	Pakistan	U.S.A.	Greece
Gulf			

This counterintuitive conclusion is based on the following facts. In Saudi Arabia and the Gulf it was impossible for migrants to gain citizenship; in Greece it was not difficult to do so. Jordanian marriage with Saudi Arabian women was de facto excluded. In Greece it was not excluded; indeed, six of eight long-term migrants married Greek women! In Arabia there was no regular neighborhood interaction between migrants and Arabians; in Greece there was. In Arabia all migrants worked, but the work was usually ethnically segmented with migrants seldom dealing directly with Arabians. Many student migrants in Greece worked alongside Greeks. In Arabia migrants did not recreate with Arabians whereas in Greece migrants engaged in leisure activities with Greeks in public spaces on a daily basis. Arabia and Greece are the ends of the continuum.

In Pakistan there were no regular neighborly interactions or work relations (not because they were prohibited), but there was regular contact with Pakistanis within the university, though mainly in class; outside the university there was some dating, though it was resented by Pakistanis. Only one of twenty-seven Jordanian migrants married a Pakistani, but among the populace generally Jordanians were respected for the religious charisma they carried with them as Muslims from the holy lands, the heartland of their religion. Since no Jordanian migrants sought Pakistani citizenship, it was not an issue.

The other intermediate case is the United States where dating was open, courtship occurred, regular work relations were possible, and all four migrants married American women. But in the United States two of the marriages ended in divorce, and there, although citizenship was possible, it was not easily attained, requiring long waiting periods, and then only after certain contingent statuses, e.g., marriage to an American or the securing of an immigration visa. In Texas the migrants did not have regular neighborly relations in the urban quarters in which they lived—in most cases no neighborly relations all—and they rarely spent leisure time with Americans, if at all.

A closer comparison of the differences of migrant social integration in Greece and the United States is instructive. First, one should call attention to the fundamental social structural similarities of the migrants in Greece and the United States. They all came as single, young (with one exception) men whose own Muslim legal culture allowed marriage of Muslim males with non-Muslim women (but not vice-versa). There were no religio-legal impediments to their marriage with Greek or American women.

Only one social-ecological factor favored integration in the United States as opposed to Greece: the migrants in Texas were scattered in separate cities with relatively long distances separating them—Galveston, Houston, Midland—whereas in Greece they were all concentrated in one city, Salonika. Otherwise, all other social factors favored integration in Greece when compared with the United States. Greek government policy favored foreign students from Jordan by affording them easy university entrance at low tuition and with the easy possibility of working to supplement their income. Dating in Greece was often collective so that Jordanian men got to know Greek women together with Greek men in a relaxed atmosphere. In terms of status, aspirant Jordanian professionals of tribal origin were good matches for upward mobile rural Greek women. In addition, the dowry given by Greek women (or their families) to their husbands made marriage a release from an economic burden for Jordanian men, who often had to pay their Jordanian wives a substantial marriage payment. In the United States courtship was more individual, government policy more restrictive, the economic burden of marriage for the male greater—'Isam's first reaction to his sweetheart's suggestion of marriage was that it was preposterous—and the attractiveness of educated Jordanian men less in a dominantly middle-class American society.

Two other factors facilitated social integration in Greece and retarded it in the U.S.A. The first relates to the public culture of the society at large and the other to the culture of the family. In the United States and particularly in Texas a business and consumer ethos prevails in which work absorbs most of one's energies and time and in which, after paying for the necessities, one's income is spent on consumer goods such as cars, stereos, videos, sports paraphernalia, and home conveniences. In Greece a premium was placed on enjoying oneself in the presence of others, visiting, eating, and drinking with kinsmen and friends in private and public gatherings that often went on far into the morning hours on weekends. This kind of social life accelerated integration into a social network as well as acculturation.

As or more important, in Greece courtship and marriage and even longtime acquaintanceship (as in Bahhar's case with his landlady and her family) involved absorption in a consanguine family structure: the courting or married couple were as a matter of course absorbed into the families of the parents of the Greek partner, spent their leisure time with them, and received their aid and mediation in dealing with daily problems or sudden crises. This absorption into the Greek consanguine family seems to have occurred for Migrants One, Two, Three, and Eight and was well documented for Migrant Two in Chapter Four. In the United States, on the other hand, only Bahhar was absorbed into the consanguine family of his wife and afforded the sociability and practical help that Jordanian migrants could expect when they married Greek women. 'Isam's wife's father opposed their marriage, and the life the young couple led in San Antonio and Midland was quite separate from that his wife's parents led in Laredo, though 'Isam saw them on their occasional visits to San Antonio. Dan never spoke of any significant relationship or support on the part of his parents-in-law in what was any case a very short and conflictful marriage. Zayd's only mention of his in-laws was buying his wife an airplane ticket to her mother's home in California when they broke up, and there is no evidence that he had any significant relation with or even knew them. With one exception the Jordanian migrants to Texas were not absorbed into the consanguine families of their spouses because no such family existed either normatively or actually within a geographical distance allowing regular interaction.

It is appropriate in ending this chapter to comment on the roles wives played in the acculturation/integration of migrants or their retardation in that regard. Because the marriages of Dan and Zayd were conflictful and resulted in divorce they probably had as much negative as positive effect upon acculturation and integration since the marriages highlighted the lack of agreement on certain mores and folkways and because the supporting consanguine families were absent. However, the marriages did result in the acquisition of the green (residence) card and eventual citizenship. Since I have very little data on these two spouses I shall focus on the roles played by the wives of 'Isam and Bahhar, whom I interviewed and whom I have designated "L" and "R." These wives played a critical role in advancing acculturation and social integration.

The wives differed in many important respects. For instance, L was the only one to defy her parents' wishes and proceed to marry 'Isam—indeed, she proposed to him! She was also the only spouse to indicate that she had no interest in returning to school to complete her college education. Both L and R worked, e.g., as sales clerk and lab technician, but they lacked fully professional work skills and earned relatively low incomes. R was the only spouse who had any academic or personal knowledge of the Arab world. After marriage she had returned to the University of Texas and finished her BA degree, taking courses in Middle Eastern studies. She had read my book, *Arab Village,* which described in detail her husband's home community as it existed in 1959–60. Moreover, at the time of the interview she had visited Jordan twice—and in 1994 visited a third time. R was also the only spouse to come from a professional family including three doctors. In status, professional skills, family presence and support, and ethnic origins the wives differed.

In three other important somewhat interrelated respects, however, they were similar. They were both (at least temporary) college dropouts; R had returned and finished her degree. Their romantic inclinations accounted in part for their dropping out, i.e., their whirlwind courtships and marriages and/or their desire to travel abroad. R was the most romantic, meeting her future spouse on the Gulf of Aqaba and sailing with him up the Red Sea and through the Mediterranean and later around the Caribbean. L's romantic desires were focused on the whirlwind three-month courtship she had with 'Isam that ended in their elopement and marriage.

This romantic element in their makeup was related to an important aspect of their marital accommodation with their husbands and to the latter's integration/acculturation. Their love-marriages propelled them to form genuine "conjugal families," that is, families focused on spouses sharing responsibilities and on a give-and-take basis. All the spouses worked outside the home, R stopping only after giving birth to her children, and in the absence of her husband who was at sea much of the time. Bahhar shared in child care when he returned; indeed, he was eager to do so. 'Isam and L both cooked, though neither liked to do so.

Perhaps more important, their love-marriages led both spouses in each marriage to accommodate to the cultural background of the other with respect to naming, child-rearing, solving daily problems, and future travel, residence, and work. L and 'Isam discussed the religious education of their yet unborn children and the latter, a self-confessed atheist, agreed "to go with her to the Catholic church some of the time, though I don't believe in it." L agreed to take the children to the Middle East for a visit so they could become acquainted with their origins. L said that when they had a difference they would exchange views: "I tell him my position, and he tells me his," though 'Isam didn't always like to hear what she said. L continued that she went to 'Isam for advice on various matters, and she liked him because he never told her what to do, leaving the decision to her.

R was enthusiastic about her children being exposed to her husband's language and culture, and she took her children to Jordan and Kufr al-Ma in 1994 while her husband was at sea expressly for that purpose. She called me before she left, asking my advice on obtaining videotapes in Arabic that could be used to teach her very young children the language. Bahhar had supported R financially and emotionally in her desire to return to college and finish her degree, an opportunity she seized upon to widen her knowledge of Middle Eastern culture and society. She had agreed to giving the children Arabic names as long as her own family name was attached to their surnames, i.e., her children carried both the mother's and father's family identity.

It should be clear that these accommodations, practical and involving the household, and ideological and involving ethnic and personal identity of self and children, were not easily made for any of the parties. All of the men were firm in their desire to maintain their family identity, and three were firm in wishing to maintain their ethnic identity, though in different ways. The two women had strong views, and one was a feminist: R told the startled fundamentalist in Jordan that God could have a feminine identity! L, the spouse who did not espouse feminist views during the interview, was the one woman who defied her father's wishes in the critical matter of marriage.

The fact that they were able to work out not only a practical household accommodation, but also a cultural and cognitive accommodation was instrumental in the maintenance of their cross-ethnic marriages and as a result, the acculturation of their husbands and their integration into American society. Many of the solutions the couples devised for themselves and the scenarios projected for their children in the future may appear to be fanciful. The important fact is that the mutuality implicit in a conjugal family structure allowed them to frame questions and provide tentative answers in a way that respected the traditions of both spouses.

Notes

1. The "conversation-interviews" on which I have based my analysis in previous chapters tended to be more conversations than interviews since the great majority took place in the informal atmosphere of the home in a still somewhat multiplex village community, often with others (fathers, mothers, uncles, brothers, cousins) present. The latter knew me from my several previous research trips. The "interview-conversations" recorded in this chapter were held in the more formal atmosphere of the informants' apartments in Houston/Arlington/Midland, Texas and in Seattle, Washington. With one exception, Zayd, whom I interviewed in Kufr al-Ma in 1986, I had never met the informants before my visit to Texas/Seattle in June 1991, although all had heard about, and some had seen me as children many years before. The interview-conversations are presented in the order in which the migrants arrived in the United States, the first in 1978 and the last in 1986. Bracketed text refers to my own comments and interpretations of the interviewees' statements.
2. The present time referred to is 1991 when the conversation-interviews took place.
3. Note the universal status symbol of the luxury car for Jordanian migrants.
4. This substantiates his statement that he spends his money on cars. But the "cars, food, women" statement omits the fact that Dan has built a house in Kufr al-Ma for his future residence and

retirement. This fact indicates that he did save and that his reference group is still his village in Jordan.

5. Although he defines his social network as 99 percent Arab, Dan has taken a stand-offish attitude toward his Jordanian relative and co-villager. He ignored this villager's request (they had similar naval training in Pakistan) to let him know when he came to the United States so he could come too. He admonished his cousin who came to the U.S. as an illegal alien, leaving his wife and four children in Jordan, and told him to go back. The illegal had sold his truck to come. He was illiterate (a school dropout), knew no English, and had no credentials to make good. Dan doesn't have his address in Chicago. He had come to Arlington along with a Mexican migrant coworker.

6. Due to a chronic shortfall in the Jordanian state's treasury (Jordan is a poor country without an industrial base, oil, or rich agricultural river valleys) the Jordanian government allows males of draftable age to buy their way out of military service.

7. The dots indicate a gap and/or indecipherability in my notes.

8. This family name is a pseudonym.

9. I have omitted one very short section of the interview here.

10. R is the only wife to have prepared herself academically for life in the Middle East; she is the only one to have gone there—she went twice; L knows nothing and isn't really interested; note, R will be going back as "Mother of Amir"; note also that R is the only consciously feminist wife. R is also the most clearly upper middle class since both her father and her brother were/are doctors, as is a sister; L's father is a doctor.

11. The interview was conducted in 1991; therefore all ages are as of that date.

12. See *Arab Village*, Chapter One and "On the Modesty of Women in Arab Muslim Villages: An Accommodation of Traditions," in the *American Anthropologist*, Vol. 70, No. 4, August 1968 for details of this case of honor.

13. By reference group I mean the social group or category with which one compares oneself in terms of style-of-life, aspirations, and values. Often, it is not one's own kinship, ethnic, class, or neighborhood group. See Robert Merton, *Social Theory and Social Structure*, Chapter 9, for details.

14. *Mansaf* is the Jordanian national dish composed of several layers of thin bread on a huge tray on top of which is piled a mound of boiled rice. On top of the rice are chunks of boiled lamb meat covered with a sauce of cracked wheat and yogurt, and occasionally roasted pine seeds. It was usually served only on special occasions such as marriages, funerals, or the entertainment of a very honored guest. The adult men of the neighborhood guest house usually came together around the tray to eat the *mansaf. Mansaf* therefore, symbolized both customary hospitality and the collective camaraderie of the community.

15. The status distinction between natives and foreign nationals who came to work and suffer the various disabilities is widespread on the Gulf.

16. The names of all migrants in this chapter are pseudonyms. I have given the pseudonym, 'Isam, meaning "self-made man" in Arabic to the youngest migrant because his workaholic work habits, his entrepreneurship, and his interview statements indicated his tremendous drive and high aspirations regarding occupation, income, and style-of-life.

17. I have chosen the pseudonym, Dan, for this migrant because he himself had changed his Arabic name to an anglicized American short-form that was somewhat similar to the original. He had done this because some Americans were referring to his Arabic name in a shorthand pejorative version.

18. For the concept of "turning" I have drawn on James Freeman's excellent life history, *Untouchable;* Freeman in turn drew on David Mandlebaum's "The Study of the Life History: Ghandi," *Current Anthropology*, Vol. 14, No. 3 (June): 177–96. Freeman defines the turnings of a life history as those points that "mark major changes that a person makes and thus demarcate periods of his life" including the introduction of "new sets of roles," "relationships with new people," or "new self-conception(s)."

7
FATHERS, SONS, BROTHERS, AND
THE VILLAGE COMMUNITY
AFFIRMATION OF THE MORAL
SOCIETY IN THE SHADOW
OF ITS DECLINE

I have been describing the migration experience in terms of the pursuit of higher education, work, or army training, exploring, elaborating, and critiquing such concepts as assimilation, acculturation, and societal integration while introducing the concept of the reinterpretation of tradition as a significant process in coping with change. In analyzing the migration experience I have taken into account the effect of such diverse contexts as the societies of Saudi Arabia, Greece, Pakistan, and the United States.

The intermingling of the voices of the informant and the investigator or, viewed in another way, of the indigenous native and the prying foreigner, become much more conscious in this chapter where I turn to the specifically interpersonal implications of migration for family relations, particularly between fathers and sons and between brothers.[1] Although most of the fathers discussed here did not leave the Jordan-Palestine-Israel area, and all the sons did, the former had served in positions in the Jordanian army or bureaucracy that had brought them into more than casual contact with the world outside the village and, indeed, with persons and ideas emanating from beyond the borders of Jordan. Yet the generation of fathers was brought up in a multiplex peasant village where the norms of extended kinship and community identity and loyalty, to which they were still significantly though not uniformly attached, prevailed. The generation of sons, on the other hand, although they almost all regarded their upbringing in the village in a positive way, were very selective in accepting such institutions as tribal law, the etiquette and obligations of extended kinship, and the modesty code.

In addition to assessing the importance of both transnational and intranational migration for changing interpersonal relations within the family and the village community, a primary goal of this chapter is to document both the supportive and the conflictive aspects of father-son relationships in Kufr al-Ma and to document as well the variety of reinterpretations of family traditions that can be held by brothers within a close-knit extended family. This chapter is an extension of the recent anthropological attempt to focus on the family and household as the proper locus for an examination of the process of the reinterpretation of tradition from one generation to the next.[2] In addition, the chapter will discuss aspects of modernity reflected in the careers of mobile fathers that predisposed their sons toward similar values. Finally, as a result of all the mobility that has taken place, both within and outside the country, the chapter will describe and analyze the decline in the "moral community" that has occurred in the village since I initiated my field work in 1959.

Before proceeding, it is necessary to specify the relationship of the author to the informants of both generations, particularly to the family of Muflih al-Hakim and his sons who provide the core data for this chapter and who are the centerpiece of analysis. By 1986 when I gathered the great bulk of data used for this book I had returned to Kufr al-Ma six times over the previous twenty-seven years, had a good knowledge of the community, was known at least by reputation by all but the very youngest generation, and had good rapport with nearly all the migrants interviewed.[3]

My relationship to Muflih al-Hakim, one of the two village mayors, was quite close.[4] He acted as my friend, mentor, and key informant. He alerted me to important village events such as wedding celebrations, family gatherings, and mediation attempts, introduced me to village notables and local officials, checked on my welfare from time to time, taught me politeness formulas, and even took me with him when he was deputed as *wasṭa* (go-between) in the preliminary negotiations for the contraction of the marriage of a village man to a woman from another village—a delicate and usually private, indeed secret, process. As I reflect on my relationship to him in comparison to that with other village figures including the other much younger mayor whom I regarded as far less knowledgeable and as opportunistic and self-seeking, I regarded Muflih as a kind of rustic hero: a poor man, he sacrificed for the community interest, and was loyal and generous to his kinsmen, forward-looking in his plans to modernize the village, just in his opposition to double-dealing, and a skillful mediator and troubleshooter. I was also partial to his personality: he was gregarious, a good storyteller, pious in religious devotions, and a patriot—he had fought in the 1936 rebellion against British rule in Palestine.

His sons, particularly the three oldest, X, A, and N, who were in their early teens during my initial field trips, appreciated the closeness of our relationship but, as I realized during our conversations in 1986, were somewhat jealous of this relationship. They saw their father in a different light. What emerges in the following description and analysis are the two sides of filial and sibling relationships in a consanguine family: the ambivalence of sons for their authoritarian father and the self-sacrifice and mutual support of brothers for one another in pursuit of education and marriage. On the other hand, the conversations with Ali and Zayd (chapters 3 and 6), migrant 4 (chapter 4), the son of D (chapters 2 and 7), and the son of E, migrant 7 (chapters 1 and 5), demonstrate the positive emotional ties between fathers and sons and the continuance of the father as a role model for sons, both significant factors in the adjustment, indeed survival, of sons in the diaspora.

Analysis

Before dealing with the conflictful and ambivalent aspects of family relations I must stress again the persistent themes of mutual love and support by fathers for their migrant sons and of sons patterning themselves on their fathers through the diaspora period.[5] The son of E (migrant 7, chapter 5) said of his father, the retired army dental technician, "My father is a great one; he spent his life so his sons could get an education." And Q, interviewed below, who was the most successful of the village migrants in Arabia in terms of income and occupational status (he owned shares in a company in which he was business manager), commented, when I expressed surprise that he gave much the greater part of his earnings to his father to invest as he wished, "The main thing is I just want my father to be happy." When I asked migrant 4, the doctor who had returned to Jordan with his Greek wife to practice medicine in the nearby market town of Irbid, how he regarded his upbringing in Jordan, he replied that his father had placed responsibility on him when he was young, had treated him as a mature person, "and that was good." He was more open to outside influences as a result of his father's work as a customs inspector in town. On the other hand, his father kept him in the house and did not allow him to attend wedding celebrations at night. He concluded his reply to my query by saying, "I don't gamble, I don't smoke," crediting his father for this fact. "I'm glad (of my upbringing)." He viewed his father as providing wise guidance and a middle way so that he could benefit from the town's environment without becoming addicted to its vices. As recorded in chapter three, Ali received constant moral guidance and emotional support from his father while studying in Germany through his father's letters. Father and son expressed mutual sensitivity to one another's likes, dislikes, and idiosyncrasies. Ali's selection of medicine as a profession and his persistence in his career goals over fifteen years in the diaspora could, indeed, be considered a vicarious fulfillment of his father's aspirations, a father who died many years before Ali returned.

The most intense case of identification and emotional support in the diaspora and in Kufr al-Ma was Zayd's. "In the States the first person to come to my mind is my father...." he said. "I love my father very much.... 'You should be good,' he told me; he made me good." Zayd said he could tell his father anything, and he did so, even in public to the point of embarrassing his father. When he reflected on his upbringing in Kufr al-Ma the dominant image was his father waking him up just before dawn for prayers, and the dominant remembered feeling was the serenity of the early morning.

Zayd's relationship with his father was probably atypical in its open communication, emotional intensity, and mutual trust. But other migrants pointed to the key positive role their fathers played in their socialization, a role that continued into the diaspora. A migrant, speaking in Dallas in 1991 said, "My father exposed me. Knowing so many people.... He used to take me with him when he was invited out for meals (to the homes of important people), to Irbid or Amman. He put me in a play in the village.... I played the role of Omar ibn al-Khattab in the school play." His father not only encouraged his early artistic tendencies which later flowered in San Antonio, but also set up his upward-mobile social aspirations which he expressed in San Antonio by saying, "It is honorable to be with cultured and educated people, not trash." In addition, his father instructed him in the strategy of acculturation to pursue in the United States when, on the verge of his departure from Abu Dhabi, he told him, "Try not to be antisocial, but stay away from Arabs; become friends with Americans; you'll learn faster." He took this advice to heart, leaving his Arab roommate, rooming with American families, and bonding himself to his American mentor, Brian, who introduced him over a nine-year period to the various aspects of the middle-class culture of San Antonio.

His brother, 'Isam, on the other hand, certainly was not a model of filial piety, apparently having engaged in clandestine dating and drinking in Abu Dhabi as well as rejecting his father's religious piety. But if he was a rebel in Abu Dhabi and proclaimed himself an atheist in Texas, he still prominently displayed a collage of his family in his Midland, Texas apartment, lent his brother in Abu Dhabi $5,000, probably at the behest of his father, so he would not have to serve in the army during the Gulf War, and received his father's blessing for his marriage, though the latter admonished him to finish his studies and pay his debts. His father and mother provided financial support for his first year of studies in Texas, the latter by selling her gold jewelry. Although 'Isam had left Kufr al-Ma for Abu Dhabi at age nine, he still remembered his life in the village as "a great time," the outstanding image remaining with him being sitting alongside his father in the men's guest houses of the village on the occasion of public feasts. This early public exposure gave him confidence to pursue his public life of salesmanship and business in Midland.

Even with the mayor, Muflih al-Hakim, about whom his sons expressed considerable ambivalence and, in one case, anger in the interviews below, one of his sons, "A" expressed empathy, gratitude, and identification. "A" said that his father had never had a life of gaiety or ease (he was a poor peasant who died in debt), but he left his sons "a sweet reputation," (he was "the face of the clan") as his inheritance and taught them the traditions of the village and the tribal culture, a fact which elevated them above their peers in the subdistrict. A internalized his father's patriotism and religious piety: he was a staunch defender of the army as a way of life and he named his children after religious figures or symbols, as his father did before him. He supported tribal law—his father and grandfather had achieved a reputation as effective tribal mediators in the villages of the subdistrict. And A, like his father, much preferred the life of the countryside to the life of towns.

The dominant themes of father-son interpersonal relations, then, are affection, communication, support, and mutual sensitivity; the father was a role model followed and a positive image sustained through the diaspora.

On the other hand as a minor mode, some conversation-interviews indicated conflict with fathers, chagrin at their lack of empathy and understanding, anger at their authoritarianism, and disapproval of what were considered their anachronistic ways. Two migrants, Yusuf and Dan, had become estranged from their fathers initially, over higher education and career selection (see chapters 3 and 6). Yusuf's father had in mind for his son a religious education and a follow-up job in the Jordanian government, either as a bureaucrat in one of the religion ministries or as a professor in one of the state universities. Accordingly, he had sent him to Nablus in Palestine to finish his secondary school education in preparation for entrance into the religious university of Al-Azhar in Cairo. I never engaged Yusuf on the matter of his estrangement with his father, but, by his own account, he defied his father, refused to return to Jordan after finishing studies at Al-Azhar, and went to England to continue his higher education. His father cut off correspondence and financial support for him for two years, resuming only after he had been accepted to study for his PhD in linguistics (not religious studies or Islamic law) at Leeds University. Yusuf was reconciled with his father on his return to Jordan, accepting a position as a professor at Yarmouk University in the nearby town of Irbid. He visited his father, a village notable, in Kufr al-Ma from time to time, but he never stayed overnight; he was alienated from village kinsmen whom he had not invited to his wedding and from village society generally.

Dan's father had wanted him to pursue university studies and, presumably, to undertake professional training, but Dan dreamed about becoming an army officer. When Dan was severed from the army during his service as a security officer at the Jordanian embassy in London, his father could not have been pleased. And when he went to the United States the estrangement with his father was solidified, particularly after he married an American girl. In a brief conversation with me in 1986 his father refused to speak about him, counting him as lost to the family—he had not returned to Jordan for eight years; and when I interviewed Dan in 1991 in Arlington, Texas he had still not returned after thirteen years. When I asked Dan whether he planned to return to Jordan to work he replied, "No, now this (the U.S.A.) is my country. I'm a citizen." He said that he had never written to his father for financial aid (at a time when he was working at two jobs as well as studying) because his father was mad at him. And so he had "to do it on my own." He had "to make good to show people."

Despite the long-term estrangement from his father, his American citizenship, and long-term separation from his family and home community, Dan's reference group was still his native village. He had built a house there, and despite his disavowals, wanted to marry a Jordanian woman from the area who would speak his language and refuse "to cheat (in marriage)" on him, and to whom he could complain (in his own language) when he returned home at night. Although he was estranged from his father, he was not alienated either from his village community or from Jordanian society and culture at large. This conclusion was conveyed dramatically in his statement, "I want to retire in Kufr al-Ma; (I want) to die there."

The strongest condemnation of a father's behavior toward his sons was by G, the master sergeant and air force fitter mechanic who had been sent on army training missions to England, France, and the U.S.A. (see chapter three). When I asked him what he thought of his childhood upbringing, he replied, "Money there was not. Fear used to kill us. He who takes a beating just before going to school, can he learn anything?" He said that the old men of the village (including his father) only thought about how their sons could help out in ploughing or shepherding or bringing in money. They were not for educating children or thinking about their future. "We still live in fear of them," he said. "Very few looked forward. A man only thought of marrying his wife so she could help him plough." He climaxed his discussion of his past upbringing by saying, referring to his father, "They killed us! They killed us (with blows)!" When I asked him why he was beaten he replied, "If one asked him for money for pencils or school pads, he beat us—perhaps because he didn't have the money." G's account of his village childhood and his patriarchal socialization are filled with images of corporal punishment, niggardliness, reactionary attitudes toward work and education, and unhappiness. However, his account of his father's treatment and its evaluation, as well as his general unhappiness with his village upbringing was quite atypical of migrant accounts, as the previous chapters attest.

Muflih al-Hakim and Sons: The Multivocality of Family Tradition

We now come to the family of Muflih al-Hakim and his seven sons, who present the most complex view of interpersonal relations and the most diverse reinterpretation of family tradition. This case demonstrates the necessity of approaching the problem of the transmission/reinterpretation of tradition at the family level of analysis as well as the importance of noting the multivocality that emerges when attention is paid to the views of the members of the family, individually and collectively.[6] The sons of Muflih are listed in Table 1 below in order of age:

TABLE 7.1 • *Sons of Muftib al-Hakim*[1]

Name	Age	Marital Status	Children	Spouse's Kin Relationship	Years Studied	Highest Degree	Military Service (Years)	Place of Residence	Present Occupation	Countries Worked/Studied	Time Spent (1986)	Occupation in Arabia	Frequency of Visits	Kinship Relations Abroad	Monthly Income (1986–1989)
X	45	M	10	Same Village	12*	High* School	20	KM	Shopkeeper Irbid						180D[3] 180D
A	38	M	7	Same Lineage	9	Junior High School	19	KM	Shopkeeper Deir Abu Said	Abu Dhabi	5 Yrs	Soldier, Signal Corps	1 month twice per year	Co-Jordanians	1,800D 245D
N	35	M	2	City but Village Origin	13	High School	0	KM	Gas & Electric Specialist, Dept of Educ Deir Abu Said	Saudi Arabia (Jauf)	9 Yrs	Airport Lighting Specialist	3 weeks twice per year	Co-Jordanian	583D 125D
O	32	M	2	Next Vill Outside Tribe	12*	High* School	7	Tabuk, Saudi Arabia	Business/Circulation Manager, Newspaper	Saudi Arabia (Jidda, Tabuk)	8 Yrs	Cargo Supervisor, Marketing Agent, Business Manager, Newspaper	1 month once per year	Co-Jordanians	600D 600D
9[2]	27	UM			16	B.Sc. Agriculture	2	Shawback, Jordan	Teacher, Agric College	Pakistan	6 Yrs		Twice in 6 years, 3 months each time	1st year, Co-Clansmen; 5 yrs, Co-Jordanians	$\overline{165D}$
P	25	UM			11	Junior High School	2	KM	Assistant Shopkeeper, Irbid						70D 100D
22[2]	23	UM			15		0	Lahore, Pakistan	Student[4]	Pakistan	3 Yrs				—

[1] Unless otherwise indicated, all information relates to 1986.

[2] Numbers refer to migrants to Pakistan previously listed in Table 1, Chapter 5.

[3] D=Jordanian dinars. In 1986 the Jordanian dinar was worth ci. $2.50.

[4] This son eventually received his dental degree in 1988 and now (2001) practices dentistry for the Jordanian army.

*Passed High School Equivalency Exam

Before analyzing the multivocal character of the reinterpretation of family tradition, I must call attention to the broader kinship context within which Muflih and his sons operated during the 1960s and 1970s. This context was the *luzum* or close consultation group.[7] The close consultation group of which the mayor and his sons were members was composed of a group of first patrilateral cousins (see Chart 1, generation C following). The fathers of these cousins formerly lived in the same house as one household. Members of a *luzum* had to consult one another when arranging marriages of their daughters, consult before selling agricultural land to outsiders, and contribute truce and blood money to members in cases of honor. The pressure to live up to ethical obligations such as reconciling kinsmen, showing respect for elders, and contributing to the wedding expenses of close relatives was much greater among the members of the close consultation group than among the patrilineage at large.

Muflih al-Hakim was the leading member, the eldest member of the *luzum* (the group of paternal cousins)—and one of the two village mayors—which was responsible for enforcing traditional norms of kinship behavior as well as consulting in economic, social, and political matters. Although the *luzum* was supposed to operate with solidarity as a cooperative group, the very matters that were the focus of cooperation were also often the focus of controversy and ill-feeling, particularly in a situation of occupational mobility and household differentiation.[8] In the early 1960s six of these ten cousins including one of Muflih's brothers had enlisted in the army and received regular salaries. Muflih's own children were still too young to enlist, and he himself was a poor peasant with very little land.

By the 1980s occupational, household, and economic differentiation had proceeded among the three wings of the close consultation group: Hakim's (B2 on Chart 1) sons and grandsons included three in universities, four as migrants to Saudi Arabia, and five in the Jordanian army; Muhammad's (B5) sons and grandsons, on the other hand, included ten in the army and none in the university or in Arabia; and Ali's (B7) sons and grandsons included two in the university, one in Arabia, and none in the army. As occupational differentiation and mobility proceeded and the independence of separate households increased, it became more and more difficult to hold together the members of a *luzum*. As the senior member of the *luzum*, Muflih, until his death in 1972, played the key role in maintaining its integrity.

Although he had settled down to the life of a peasant, householder, and village mayor in the 1950s, Muflih had previously led a diverse and peripatetic occupational, military, and cultural life. He had first gone to Palestine in 1926 at the age of sixteen. He ran away at harvest time with a friend from the village and secured a job in Tiberias where he helped build the house of a wealthy Jew. Two months later he returned to Kufr al-Ma in time to attend the opening of the school term. A year later he walked to Haifa, a distance of about fifty miles, and worked as a watchman in the garden of a Palestinian Arab. He received the equivalent of

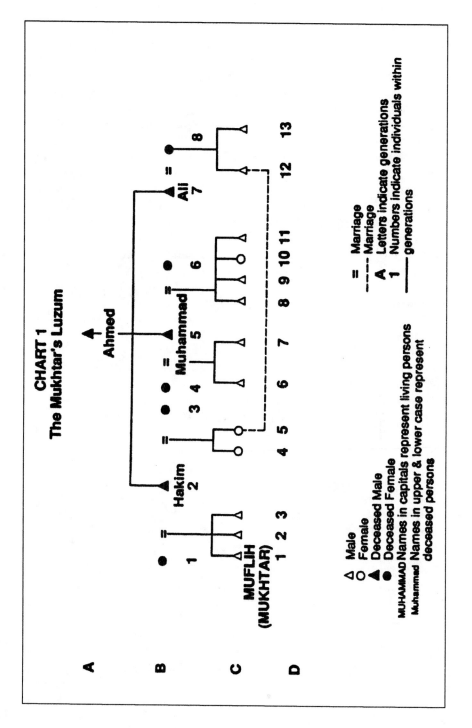

CHART 1
The Mukhtar's Luzum

three dollars a month in addition to room and board. He returned once again to Kufr al-Ma to finish his third and last year of formal schooling. During the following three years he worked as a plowman on his father's land. In 1930, after a poor agricultural year, he returned to Haifa where he worked as a fisherman and plasterer. From 1931 to 1933 he worked in Beisan, a small Arab market town overlooking the Jordan Valley, bringing his mother and two brothers to live with him after his father had married a second wife. While in Beisan he worked in the banana orchards for 24 cents a day and later, for a year, as helper to a blacksmith. Then, he left his mother and brothers in Beisan and for the next three years, 1934–1936, he worked in Jaffa and Tel Aviv as foreman of an Arab construction gang employed by Jews. During that period he learned Hebrew and, in fact, courted a Jewish girl, all the while posing as an Iraqi Jew. The courtship was abruptly ended when his father threatened to disown him. In 1936 he returned to Beisan to enlist as a recruit in the first Arab rebellion against the British. He was placed in an ordnance unit whose duty was to supply rifles, horses, ammunition, and money to Arab guerillas. Carrying out his duties involved a fair amount of smuggling, extortion, and thievery. In 1939 he was jailed by the British authorities on the charge of smuggling guns from Damascus and participating in a terrorist organization known as "The Black Hand." On his release in 1941 he worked as a laborer in the construction of the Eden Line, a military defense line stretching from Umm Qays in Jordan to Haifa, and later he worked in Haifa for the British Army loading ammunition onto ships. Thereafter, he worked for several months in Umm Qays as a builder of houses. In 1942 he married, and from 1943 to 1948 he lived in Kufr al-Ma, working as a plowman. With the outbreak of the Palestine War, he enlisted in the Arab Legion and saw action in the Jerusalem and Nablus areas. In 1951 he left the Legion and returned to Kufr al-Ma where he worked as plowman until 1957, when he was chosen unanimously by his clan to represent it as *mukhtar* or village mayor.

Muflih's occupational history is atypical in the number and variation of jobs held, in the length of time spent away from his home community, in the involvement with cultural strangers in arenas outside the immediate urban occupational context, and perhaps, as a result of all this, in the empathy he possessed for a way of life other than that of his native village. In other respects, however, the *mukhtar's* work history is completely typical. Many other villagers spent long periods in Palestine, worked under Jews and Englishmen, participated in the national struggle, and returned to the village in their middle years to marry and take up traditional occupations.

After his death Muflih's sons, particularly the elder two, X and A, undertook a remarkable corporate consanguine family enterprise, later carried on by their younger brothers.[9] Each had already enlisted in the Jordanian army in the early 1960s, the former transferring to the air force in the 1970s. They began contributing to their brother N's high school education in the town of Irbid and thereafter to their other two brothers' (O and P) high school educations. In

1986 A outlined the vicissitudes of the family's collective fortunes in the following way:

(1) He and his older brother sacrificed their own education and went to work to keep the family afloat. (2) N was sent to high school in Irbid, and they wanted to help the next, O, but he twice failed his high school exams. Finally O went into the navy, served in Aqaba, learned English there, then got a good job in the port of Jidda (in Saudi Arabia). N got a job in Saudi Arabia, and the fortunes (of the family) changed. Then (3) the brothers sent Nine to Pakistan (for an education) and wanted P to go too, but he failed his high school exams three times. But they sent 22 (the youngest brother) to Pakistan when 9 said, "Send him to us." Then (4) A went to Abu Dhabi and (as a result) built a house and N built a house (both of the new type of smooth-cut stone and cement). And they will probably marry off Nine next; they had already married off O.

During the 1960s and early 1970s the aid to their siblings had been funneled through their father, who, as household head, disbursed the funds from the collective family enterprise. After their father's death A and N disbursed aid directly. After A went to Abu Dhabi in 1981 he became a major contributor to Nine's and thereafter 22's university education in Pakistan, contributing 5,000 dinars to the former's and 5,000 dinars to the latter's education over five and seven years respectively. Until 1975 all the brothers lived together. At that point N left the joint household and in 1977 O left. However, N and O, as Arabian migrants, remained the major contributors to the education of their younger brothers until A went to Abu Dhabi in 1981.

The building of a house and marriage were also viewed as collective family enterprises, although in the case of the Arabian migrants the income came from them. In the late 1980s Nine's marriage was arranged in a similar fashion as for his brothers before him, but this time also financed collectively by them; Nine had just begun earning a salary as a junior college teacher, and with a regular income marriage had become appropriate and expected. It is clear that education, marriage, and house-building were viewed as collective family entailments. But work was also of this character. P has been engaged as a junior partner in his brother, X's, Irbid shop for nine years, and on his return from the army, A's shop in Deir Abu Said was both organized and capitalized by his brothers, this time by the oldest and the youngest.

The sons of Muflih al-Hakim were not the only siblings maintaining a collective consanguine family enterprise. Migrants Two and Five, the doctor and the naval officer trained in Greece (chapter 4) together with their older brother, a pioneer migrant who worked as a clerk in Saudi Arabia (chapter 2), and their youngest brother who was receiving a university education in Jordan, supported one another consecutively and financially in their quest for higher education. This consanguine educational family enterprise was remarkable in its continuance for eighteen years and its spanning three continents (Europe, North America, and

Asia). I do not wish to suggest that all male sibling relations are harmonious. The case of 'Isam and his brother in Texas indicated that sibling rivalry can also mark relations between brothers. Nevertheless, the consanguine family enterprise of the sons of Muflih for over twenty years, although atypical in its length and multi-functionality, is not unique in kind and demonstrates the resilience of family ties in a period of rapidly changing economic and social circumstances.

The Reinterpretation of Family Tradition

Robert Hefner (1985) has pointed out in a pioneering fashion the critical role individual life history plays in the passage and reinterpretation of tradition between priestly fathers and adept sons in hinterland Java (see chapter 9). He demonstrated that whether family (in this case religious) traditions were passed on, and if so in what form, depended very much on the knowledge and inclinations of family heads as well as the penchant of their heirs for religious learning. But Hefner suggested that the differences in the passage/reinterpretation of tradition were attributed, by and large, to different household traditions of transmission. However, differences of the order he suggests and greater can be found *within* a single consanguine family.

The sons of Muflih did not disagree on all matters of general social import or on all aspects of their father's life and cultural legacy. For instance, with the exception of N, they agreed, generally, that their father's public life as village mayor, mediator, and troubleshooter provided a positive legacy: "The village used to respect my father (Nine); ... he had a good name (X); he left us with a sweet reputation (A)." With the exception of A, who endorsed it without reservation, they regarded tribal law as a mixed blessing, strengthening social ties and providing insurance against misfortune at the same time that it unjustly made the individual responsible for crimes he did not commit and sidetracked state law, preserving an anachronism. The brothers generally agreed on the appropriateness of the code of modesty for women and on the view that women's primary role was as wife, mother, and homemaker. And they were certainly united on the value of education, which they pursued themselves (two passed high school equivalency exams while in the army) and which they supported in an unstinting fashion over a long period for the brothers who pursued higher education.

But they differed sharply on some social issues, on the implementation of others on which they agreed, and on their father's legacy in both its personal and collective aspects. For instance, although both O and Nine held that women's place was in the home, the latter stated that he wouldn't allow his wife to work as a secretary even if she didn't have children and the former advocated reducing male unemployment by sending women back to their homes. In fact, the former not only allowed his wife to work (after having children), but also took her to Saudi Arabia with him where she was employed on a five-year teaching contract. Nine condemned his brother for his permissiveness. Nine also condemned his eldest brother, X, in no uncertain terms for not practicing family planning, and P was nearly as enthusiastic and supportive of army training as N was sharply critical and derisive of it.

The differences between brothers emerged most dramatically in their view of their father. The second oldest son, A, took by far the most favorable view of his father, seeing him as "the face of the clan" who taught them tribal traditions and left them with "a sweet reputation." It was A, the least educated and the sibling who had spent the longest period in army service (twenty-five years) who internalized his father's views on "the moral (rural) society (see discussion below)."[10] That is, his behavior endorsed religious piety (in names as well as worship), family and community sociability (he complained that he saw his older brother only four times in the month's vacation he spent in the village), and the superiority of the countryside to the town as a way of life and an ethos: the air of the village was as free from social pollution (mixing of the sexes and cinemas) as it was from chemical pollution.

I recall that many years before, in 1960, I had taken his father on a trip to visit a Christian townsman in the relatively sophisticated Palestinian town of Ramallah. We had stayed as guests of this townsman and his family for three days, during which time we were fed delicious (in my view) meals with meat and rice, a rarity in the diet of the village at that time, and were offered comfortable (in my view) sleeping accommodations—beds with sheets and blankets—rather than mattresses placed on the clay, mat-covered floors as was common in the village. I thought this interlude in Ramallah would be an experience the *mukhtar* would treasure long after. I was surprised when, on returning to the village several days later, and on reclining on the floor mattresses in his guest room, the *mukhtar* breathed a deep sigh of relief. "How good it is to be back home," he said. I suddenly realized that despite the amenities of the town, he much preferred the countryside's way of life. He had been uncomfortable sitting in the straight-backed chairs in Ramallah. There were chairs in the village at the time, but the few who had them did not sit in them. And the food had been too rich for Muflih's palate. In 1986 A did have chairs in his house—and tables and windows as well as crockery and silverware. But he also kept a separate room, empty of furniture, where he could spread out mattresses and pillows, recline on the floor in the style characteristic of the guest room, *madafa*, and entertain family and intimate friends. But even A, who spoke empathetically about the lack of gaiety in his father's life and its poverty, spoke with some ambivalence about his father's behavior. If he left them a sweet reputation it was at the cost of leaving the house at 9 in the morning and not returning till 9 at night. The children seldom saw their father, and as A said, "The people of the village missed him more than his family (when he died)."

His eldest son, X, spoke of his father somewhat less positively, but still with favor and empathy: "My father wanted to educate us, but he had all he could do to feed us. My father had been around, and he had connections and he had a good name and, as they say, 'Like us, like others,' [i.e., in terms of economic status and opportunity for education all the peasants shared the same lot].

Rather than simply accept his peasant lot fatalistically, O placed a positive construction on his upbringing in the village while at the same time elaborating its flaws: "I saw mistakes I can benefit from—the treatment of the small child; if he was smart they didn't open the opportunity for him to enter studies. Childhood had harshness (*qasawa*); material conditions weren't so good. I went to school and had no money. I couldn't move along with my friend," i.e., O's friend would invite him and he couldn't reciprocate. But O concluded this evaluation of his upbringing by saying, "It was difficult, but I benefited from it."

Nine was not positive about his village and family upbringing. Indeed, he criticized it at length: "We have made an error in Jordan. The father comes and says to his son, 'You study medicine'; he won't let the child choose his studies." And he elaborated later:

> They used to socialize by striking (the child).... Some (children) flee from school. When I hit him and say, 'Go back (to school),' he goes back in fear. This is the last method I'd use. The father should try and convince the child and only use force as a last resort. I'd even give him money to go; and tell his brother that he's no good [i.e., use psychological pressure as a tactic].... When I was small there was in my upbringing a mistake. They would treat us with severity. There was poverty in those days.

But although Nine did not regard his childhood as having positive latent functions, like O, he did not regard it as having a long-term negative impact, and he expressed even a hint of a positive impact, saying: "I did not grow angry over my upbringing. The customs of the village did not have an (ill) effect on me. The village used to respect my father. Why shouldn't I be respected too?"

There was a much more negative interpretation of Muflih's legacy to his children than the positive one indicated by X above. This appraisal was triggered by my quoting to X a proverb his father had recited to me regarding the value of having male progeny: "A house of men rather than a house of wealth."[11] X replied:

> A saying differs (in import) from one situation/environment (*bi'a*) to another. The person living in the desert had to have men (supporting him) because he was open to raiding (*ghazzu*). But Richard, in Boston you take your rights without (the need of) men. If I'm in the desert I need men to protect my sheep; I don't need money. That proverb was 100 percent true then; now it is 50 percent true. Women at that time didn't vote. At the time you were here (in 1960) women couldn't vote or be elected to Parliament or as head of the municipality. (In the past) they collected money (for any collective cause or need) from each patrilineal kinship group (*'ashira*), saying, "Collect according to (the number of) peckers (males)."

X regarded his father's wisdom as of little use today. The traditions which A so valued as a legacy were for X anachronistic.

On another occasion X told me that his father was a strict disciplinarian. His motto was, "Hit first and explain later." By contrast his own children couldn't believe their eyes when their father returned from work in the evening, and they rushed to greet him. He and his brothers were afraid of their father and actually loved to see him leave the house because then they could go out and play. X capped his evaluation of his father by saying, "He was good with you (the anthropologist)," and by implication not with them. This remark was like A's above, a commentary on his father's absorption in and endorsement of the moral society of the village: one always gave preference to the guest (here, the anthropologist) over and above one's conjugal family, whether in time spent, food offered, or favor curried.

The longest conversation, indeed, dialogue I engaged in regarding the legacy of their father was with N. It expressed the most sharply negative view of Muflih and was, perhaps, fueled by my own positive view of his father. N's initial response to my query about his view of his village childhood was a derisive olfactory response:

> It was very bad. I still smell it. I don't know why more people didn't die (of dirt and disease) in those days.... When there was no road to Irbid (the nearest market town) how could they (villagers) know about soap (cleanliness). People's minds were small then. No one dreamed of having a car.

This statement places blame on the central government for its lack of material modernization of the countryside. But N's reference to the smallness of people's minds was inclusive of his own father. The image of their small house and his father's division of space within it—eight children and their mother crowded into one room while the other room was reserved for his father and his daily guests (he was after all the village mayor)—an image reflecting his father's affirmation of the moral society was an image he hated. The first thing he did after saving money from his earnings in Saudi Arabia was build his own house and move out of the family homestead. The animus for his father was reflected symbolically in the fact that he never introduced himself by his patrilineal pedigree (with his father's first name as his surname) as was common, in order to avoid being recognized as his father's son and to avoid hearing the praised lavished on his father by those who knew him in the district. He simply introduced himself by his own first name.

The full range of N's reinterpretation of family tradition emerged in his reply to my question, "Why didn't your father buy land?" The following dialogue was the result:

> "He had no ambition; he didn't think of saving money to buy land. My father could have been a government employee (*muwaTHTHif*) in Irbid. He could have been more than a village mayor (*mukhtar*). He had learned reading and writing. Yusuf's father (a kinsman of his father's own generation) became a government employee and court

clerk and his children are doctors." I replied that his father sacrificed his own interests (as mayor) for those of the village, and that every society needs individuals who work for it rather than their own interests. N said that his father could have been balanced—had ambition for himself and his family as well as the people. "My father—it was 99 percent for the village but not for himself." "Your father was like his father before him, generous, hospitable, a successful mediator," I replied. "But every epoch has its (unique) conditions and changes," he said. People come to X, his older brother and a shopkeeper in town, and say, "Come be head of the municipality (of Kufr al-Ma)." "Why should I?" his brother replied. "For one hundred dinars, when I have ten children (to support). I must work." I said, "If your father were alive today, he'd go to Saudi Arabia [i.e., I suggested that there was no economic opportunity in those days]." N replied, "In those days Irbid (the closest market town) was Saudi Arabia! Every age has (to be judged by) its own standards (*kul 'asr 'endha mustawa*)." He said that his father used to take off for the capital, Amman, and stay a week—he had many friends there and indulged their hospitality. They had asked X to become head of the municipality in 1981; he had just started his job in Irbid. Still, if X decided to run for office today, he would succeed. "First you establish a foundation for yourself and afterwards the town," he said. He would not allow his wife and ten children to live in one room and the guest to sleep by himself in the other. He continued, extending the criticism to himself, "If I had bought land instead of building a house I would have reaped 100,000 dinars and built three houses. Civilization (*haḍara*) changes. They used to go to Haifa and Jaffa (for employment instead of Beirut and Amman). Mahmoud (a kinsman also of his father's generation) has six children. He used to have a shop and was doing well. He quit it and has gone back to being a cultivator (*fellah*); he has retrogressed. His son works as an employee of the local municipality; his second son is an officer in the army; his third son is a warrant officer in the army; his fourth son serves in the army of Abu Dhabi, making only 180 dinars a month; his fifth son is in the army. Why didn't he send *one* to the university? N's own father never said, "We want to send him (a brother) to the army so he can study abroad and be sent on a mission abroad at state expense." When N was in Irbid studying in trade school he used to sleep there (in the school). It was discipline like the army—he didn't like it. Three months before the final exam N felt his study time was being constricted (by the school regimen); he wanted to study longer hours (than permitted); he wanted to study later and get up earlier (than was allowed). His father refused his request to be allowed to rent a room in town a few months; he thought he would become heedless (away from the school). N said that if he had more time he would have scored 90 (and not in the 80s) and perhaps have secured a (state) scholarship to study abroad.

In his long response to my question about buying land N outlined the bill of particulars against his father: He lacked ambition; he was not an entrepreneur; he did not become a bureaucrat as he could have; he preferred the company of the village and the company of his friends in other places to the company of his own conjugal family; and while he was at home he spent most of the time in the guest room and not with his children. He refused to give his son the minimum economic support to complete his high school education with distinction. In general, he was lacking in foresight and affection; he was not a modern man.

He capped this dialogue with his indictment of the army as a career. I asked him what he thought about the army as a profession:

"Soldiering is charity (ṣadaqa) from the state. I consider any soldier a failure." I replied, "But your older brother, X, went into the army for sixteen years and came out and is now a successful shopkeeper." "He was in the air force and he mixed with people—he was different." He elaborated that A, his older brother who was then soldiering in Abu Dhabi, would fail in the outside world. That the present head of the municipality (of Kufr al-Ma) should be prohibited from holding office. (He was a former soldier.) "The soldier always says, 'Yes sir' (naʿim sidi). The army teaches fear of the superior and the retired soldier carries fear around with him. If the governor (of the district) says something to the head of the municipality or yells at him, he will say, 'Yes sir.' My paternal uncle (a soldier)—he looks like a wild animal (fearsome), but if a corporal comes, he says, 'Yes sir.' Look at so-and-so [he was referring to H (see interview, chapter 3), a villager who was an officer in the army, spoke excellent English, and was working for his university degree], he will clam up as soon as you begin to talk politics, and he is a major. I was once in the guest house and observed him change his opinions completely as soon as he learned that there was an officer in civilian clothes in the guest house that outranked him. The soldier, even with his children, he gives orders—no please or thank you, no human treatment." At this point I observed that some men did seem to come out of the army and take up other occupations. N replied that if the soldier leaves the army and stays in civilian life for the same number of years as army service, the effect of the army would wear off. "If the order comes from the governor," he said, "and he demands that the villager get up in the middle of the night and drag someone out of bed, the civilian will reply, 'Farts on the governor' (tuzz ʿala al-muḥafiTH). (On the other hand) the head of the municipality will run off and get the guy out of bed."

N's condemnation of the army was based on the fact that it trained failures for the world. That is, its inculcation of discipline, respect for authority, and automatic obeisance eliminated the possibility of training for the entrepreneurial and innovative skills needed in a rapidly changing modern world. His own father, though he was never a regular army man (he served in the guerillas), reflected army values in his treatment of his own children, his excessive use of politeness formulas to government officials in town, and his admiration of military heroes: four of N's brothers including himself were named after military heroes who led the Muslim armies out of Arabia and into North Africa and Spain in the seventh and eighth centuries.

In these seven brothers we have the full range of reinterpretation of family tradition, specifically, their father's own legacy to them: from A who praised his father, empathized with him, and named his own children according to the same principles as his father, to N who denigrated him, sharply disagreed with his view of the moral village society, regarding it as anachronistic, and even refused to introduce himself by his father's name. It would be a mistake, however, to view N as a thoroughly modern man, just as it would be a mistake to view A as a thoroughly traditional one. A unstintingly supported his brothers in their quest for secular higher education outside the country. And N contracted his marriage in a way that was utterly in accord with the moral village society. This observation leads to a more general discussion of the meaning of modernity in a rapidly changing Jordanian rural society.

Modernity, Mobility, and Education

In chapter three modernity was defined as the social, cultural, and psychological framework which facilitates the application of tested knowledge to all branches of production: the unhampered search for knowledge, a positive stance toward innovations, a fostering of social mobility, and an achievement ethic that channels rewards to high performers. It entails commitment to continuous self-improvement and programmed decision-making. Modernity has been associated with professionalization and bureaucratization and the values they represent: universalistic standards of expertise, recruitment, and promotion; an ethical system of self-control associated with a corporate body, a routinization of tasks through rules, roles, and files implying planning and discipline; impartiality and affective neutrality in dealing with the public; and a sense of responsibility that goes along with performing a service essential to society. Modernity is associated with the dominance of the modern nation-state, education as an elixir, and the values of individualism and cultural relativism.

There is some evidence to indicate that the migrants most reflective of modern values, those who relentlessly pursued higher education and work and their entailed mobility, were those whose fathers had been "in the world" before them. These fathers had either served in the Jordanian bureaucracy or as officers or noncommissioned officers in the Jordanian army, or they had served or worked in Palestine, and, though they had not ventured outside the Arab world, had come into contact with men who did.

The army dental technician, E, is an interesting example of such a father. He had served for two years in Palestine, including Ramallah, one of the most sophisticated towns on the West Bank, and the rest of his army career had been spent in the capital, Amman. As a dental technician in these locales he had been exposed to a wide variety of educated and traveled persons. He had learned his vocation in the army and had taken an examination at the Ministry of Health after retirement that qualified him to practice it in civilian life. He always wore trousers and a white shirt and never the usual rural headdress (shawl and headband). He supported family planning. Three of his sons were college graduates, a fourth was a junior high school teacher; one daughter was a junior high school teacher and two other daughters were attending junior college in the nearby market town. Two of his sons had gone abroad for their higher education, the elder earning an MSc in London after a BSc in Pakistan.

When I asked E why he supported family planning he commented that Jordanian friends he knew in other towns no longer counted the numbers of men in their clans (as an index of status) but rather only the number of educated men. He was one of the few village men I ever talked to who took pride in the fact that he had called the police when his neighbors blocked the public road near his house rather than defend his honor by ousting them personally (presumably with other family/clan members) by force. He stated outright, "In matters of honor the West is better," and proceeded to outline the more enlightened way the Hungarians dealt with alleged rape—without forcing the male or female involved to marry one another, i.e., without a shotgun marriage. On the other hand, E still favored the preservation of tribal law. But it was valued for honoring the person and giving him dignity as well as respecting the group (of which he was a part). E's commentary on tribal law and the treatment of rape paid attention to the individual and his/her rights and feelings.

D, who had enlisted in the army in 1946 as a private and retired as an infantry captain after 23 years of service (see chapter 1 for details), is another father of migrant sons who had been "in the world." As a child he had attended the religious kindergarten (*kuttab*) in the village for two years, a kindergarten taught by a Palestinian *shaykh*. After finishing the fifth year of study in the nearby primary school of Deir Abu Said (there was no education available in the subdistrict after grade five at the time) he joined the army and was sent to Palestine where he spent half of his army service. He married a Palestinian woman from Jerusalem in 1950, and Five (Q), the son who received a university education in Pakistan (see chapter 5) and later became a highly successful business manager in Saudi Arabia, had his primary school education in Jerusalem.

When he left the army in 1968 D opened a grocery shop in Kufr al-Ma and was almost immediately elected as head of the village council, a position he held without salary for five years. In 1976 he left the village for the port of Aqaba where he worked for five years in the demanding job of shipping supervisor (his family remaining in the village) in order to earn enough money to support his son's university education in Pakistan. When I left the village in 1986 he had another son studying for his MA degree in English at Sind University in Pakistan, and a daughter who had married E's oldest son, the veterinarian with a MSc degree from London.

When I asked D, "What do you think of women working (outside the home)?" he replied, "It hasn't happened here yet," and quoted a Tradition of the Prophet: "It's never occurred that a man and woman who are strangers get together except that the devil is the third party (*ma ijtama'a rajalu wa imra'a illa wa kana al-shaytan thalathihim*)." But he proceeded to say that teachers and nurses were okay, but that "we don't like secretaries in offices." But my own observation of his household indicated that his family was the most egalitarian in the village regarding cross-sex interpersonal relations. On two occasions when I visited his home and found him absent, D's Palestinian wife came and stayed with me alone, engaging me in conversation till he returned while other visiting village women sat on the veranda. His nubile daughter wore pants with a covering dress unlike the usual long full-length dress most village women wore. His Pakistani daughter-in-law was called out of the back room to come out and shake my hand, something that had never happened in any other village household. Instead of waiting by myself I was asked if I would like to come into the inner room and join the women in watching television! On another occasion when D was present and a tray of food was brought out at supper time, D's daughter-in-law was asked to come out and join us around the tray. All of this interpersonal interaction with a stranger was highly unusual.

When I asked D about birth control he replied, "It has its appropriate circumstances in Islam (*fi ilha THuruf fil islam*)." He then quoted the Quran: "There is not a creature on earth except that God provides for it." Then he quoted another Quranic verse: "Don't kill your children fearing want (hunger), we will provide for them and you too (*wa la taqtalu awladakum khashyata imlak; nihnu narziqahum wa ayyahum*)." "But," he continued, "from a human point of view, if the mother is ill or has given birth to many offspring and it hurts the mother's life, then you can use birth control." "Where will the jobs come from for future graduates?" I asked, coupling the population problem with unemployment in Jordan. He replied that religion did not contradict itself. Jordan still didn't have overpopulation, but he said, "Our income is restricted. One is perplexed as between (the demands of) religion and (the demands of) modern life." But he said, finally, returning to the earlier theme, "God's earth is wide (*ard allah wasi'a*). One doesn't have to stay in Kufr al-Ma (to pursue a livelihood)." He said the constitution of Jordan supports birth control in emergencies.

D is another highly mobile army man who was promoted through the ranks and was even more profoundly affected by Palestinian urban culture through the marriage with his Palestinian wife. His commitment to education was attested to by his willingness to sacrifice the comfort of his village in retirement to work in a demanding job to support his son's higher education abroad. This was the son who married the Pakistani wife and brought her to live in the village in his father's house; her father was a university professor in Pakistan. This culturally exogamous marriage was consistent with his father's exogamous marriage before him, and it fit the pattern of more egalitarian cross-sexual relations that characterized the household. D's answer to my question on birth control reflected two tracks and two points of view that seemed to be vying with one another with neither dominant: on the one hand the Quran clearly ruled against it; on the other hand modernity demanded it. His last comment to the effect that the Jordanian constitution supported birth control in certain circumstances is significant for its recognition of the legitimate intrusion of the nation-state into matters that others might have regarded as private and religious.

Although the mayor referred to above had not been a Jordanian army officer or a member of the Jordanian bureaucracy, he had fought in two wars, been up and down Jordan and Palestine as well as southern Syria, had worked in an astonishing variety of jobs for Jews, Palestinians, and British, and had even learned some Hebrew in an attempt to court a Jewish girl in Tel Aviv. After his death three of his sons went to work in Arabia and two pursued higher education in Pakistan. Two of the sons who did not pursue higher education, X and O, passed a high school equivalency exam many years after they left school, a highly unusual achievement. As X pointed out to me, O's occupational history in Saudi Arabia was highly opportunistic and entrepreneurial: he changed jobs four times, each job being different occupationally than the previous one. Although this work pattern may seem to be more like ad hoc than programmed decision-making, it was guided by consistent principles: a person without professional skills had to optimize income in a volatile work market. The job changes not only increased O's income, they increased his range of contacts (for future jobs) and also moved him from a blue-collar to a white-collar environment (e.g., from port cargo supervisor to marketing agent to newspaper business manager). When I asked O about his upbringing in the village he regarded it as harsh, difficult, impoverished, and closing off the child from education. But he summed it up by saying that it benefited him as a learning experience—one learned from mistakes. And X, the eldest child who was also shut off from an education ("My father wanted to educate us, but he had all he could do to feed us"), was emphatic in his regarding it as an elixir and social stratifier: "Look at the difference between the educated and the uneducated. In America all Americans regard others equally. Here in Jordan there is still a distinction between (the) educated and (the) uneducated; there is "Yasin" and "Dr. Yasin." Education has social value. What pushes me to educate my son (his eldest son was studying at Yarmouk University).... I work as a shopkeeper; he will work in a government office." If education had social value it also had moral value, as expressed by X when he said, "Better a merchant with a doctorate than an ignorant merchant."[12]

And N enunciated the preadaptive link of Islam with the modern view of education more fully when he said, "The religion of Islam is a religion of knowledge," referring to and embracing in that statement what non-Muslims would refer to as secular education. Finally, N expressed explicitly in a village/tribal proverb the commitment to an achievement ethic that the fathers and sons above-mentioned all would have agreed with when he said: "A man will be rewarded for his acts despite himself."[13]

If the above-mentioned remarks of "in-the-world" fathers and their largely migrant sons endorsed such values as education, social and occupational mobility, achievement, and the recognition of the dominance of the nation-state, attributes associated with modernity but also capable of accommodation with religious and tribal norms, a number of remarks reflected an acceptance of cultural relativity, a value at odds with such norms. N's statement, "People's minds were small then," (because there was no road to Irbid to afford both knowledge and provision of soap) to explain the lower standards of village cleanliness in his childhood, contextualized village affairs within a space as well as a time horizon. And X's evolutionary interpretation of the irrelevancy of his father's proverb, "A house of men is a house of wealth," to the situation in Kufr al-Ma in 1986 did the same thing. N made the statement of cultural relativism in its diachronic aspect explicit when he said, "Every age has to be judged by its own standards." A few transnational migrants were also explicit about the necessity to tolerate the customs of other societies and ethnic groups. When I questioned Yusuf how he was able to accept with equanimity the public "mixing of sexes" in England that was at odds with both his own tribal/village background and his religious commitment, he replied that he had seen it all in Germany before, and to a lesser degree in Egypt. H, the army lieutenant sent twice to England for training, also took things in his stride. When I asked Bahhar, the merchant marine officer who had studied in Greece, married in the United States, and traveled around the Mediterranean, Caribbean, and the Indian Ocean, the same question, he replied, "I have seen too many countries, peoples; I must accept...." A few men, then, had not only accommodated values associated with modernity to those within their own, village/tribal milieu and to their own religious worldview/ethos, they had also accepted some values that were at odds with that milieu/ethos.

The Decline of the Moral Community

In his book *The Moral Economy of the Peasant: Subsistence and Rebellion in Southeast Asia,* James Scott, describing the peasants of Viet Nam, has referred to the "moral economy of peasants." This phrase refers to the moral contract entered into by peasants with their landlords. The contract is based on the peasantry's weak power position and its consequent high valuation of security.[14] The arrangements entered into by the peasant with the landlord were not fair or equitable by any stretch of the imagination, but they did provide security. If the landlord was willing to accept the right of the tenant to a livelihood, the latter would concede the right of the landlord to rent. Peasant rebellions, Scott argues, are not against the class system, but rather against the landlord's infractions of the moral contract. When such infractions do occur, the peasant reaction is rebellion widely construed, e.g., to cheat on rent, to deceive....[15]

Analyzing the moral aspect of relations in a peasant society provided Scott new insights in the analysis of economic and political relations. It is important to investigate the moral aspect of social relations in Kufr al-Ma not for the purpose of analyzing economic relations between patrons and clients or the form/functions of peasant rebellions, but for the purpose of understanding the changing character of social relations in a tribal/peasant community, a change that underlies much of the behavior and many of the attitudes of migrants and their elders described in this and preceding chapters. The discussion of the "moral community" in Kufr al-Ma, then, focuses much more generally than Scott on the norms of kinship and community social control involving wide-ranging reciprocity with implications for day-to-day visitation, hospitality, interpersonal relations, sacrifice of conjugal life for clan and community interests, gift-giving, joking, and tribal law.[16]

The extension of transport and education, occupational differentiation, growing differences of wealth, and most recently the impact of transnational migration and television has changed the moral aspect of social relations in Kufr al-Ma and resulted in the decline of what I have termed the moral community. This process involves the village, including its component kinship units. I do not wish to indicate that the values underlying such a community—sociability, reciprocity, sacrifice for the larger kin group, regard for the in-group (family, clan, village) as the proper locus of social control, respect for tribal law, and obedience to authority—have disappeared. The evidence of this and previous chapters suggest that norms reflecting such values continue in force, if not for all, for many, and if not in all situations, in some. More important, the evidence suggests that a reinterpretation of traditions has occurred in a way to accommodate these values with the new situations spawned by the forces of change referred to above.

Nevertheless, there is no question that the ethos and worldview of villagers as I perceived it in 1986 was not what it had been twenty-five years before. Then, there was no question that village life was considered superior to town life and that the village community was the proper arena for social control. In 1960 men were criticized for settling their disputes in court when they should have settled them within their extended families or within the guest houses of their clan. And they were particularly criticized for raising cases in court, civil or religious, that involved exposing the women of their families to strangers. It was expected that kinship disputes would be kept hidden from non-kin and resolved within the kin group. Ceremonial visits on the occasion of the two religious festivals of Ramadan and the Great Sacrifice were paid by family members on the three festival days consecutively to close kin, friends and covillagers, and distant kin.

In 1960 the village numbered about two thousand in population, a size that allowed the approximately three hundred households to recognize the identity of one another's family members on the streets and in public places such as shops, schools, and mosque. Indeed, it was assumed at that time that all villagers including the members of the three separate clans and the independent families had some kind of kin relation with one another, if not by descent, then by marriage, even if that tie could not be traced. Any adult male felt free to reprimand any child or adolescent misbehaving in the public way, regardless of family of origin or economic status. The village was regarded as a web of kinship, and life in the village was perceived by its inhabitants as warmer, more secure, and more satisfying emotionally than life outside it. Individual jokes might be made about covillagers (and reflected in nicknames), but collective jokes about other villages, which were frequent, always accentuated the moral superiority of one's own.

The comments of many migrants in the 1980s still reflect an adherence to the ethos and worldview that was dominant in the 1960s. With respect to knowledge of local and family traditions and kin pedigrees, A stated, praising his father, it was "a family preserving traditions ... more than others." Knowledge of traditions is still connected to knowledge of and respect for tribal law and the norm of the solidarity of patrilineal kinsmen. A's brother, Nine, the returned Pakistani migrant, stated, "One of the good things (about tribal law) is that it gathers together family ties. I know all of my father's brothers' sons.... (see chart 1). On the festival day we all go to visit the oldest person of the kin group. And A stated, "It (tribal law) still preserves the ties of people with one another." The teacher who migrated to Saudi Arabia (chapter two) associated tribal law with peace-making, forgiveness, and magnanimity, and the plasterer working there stated, "If I quarrel with so-and-so (another villager) better that we (villagers) settle it.... The government (only) jails and fines." Many migrants who were ambivalent about tribal law saw as its positive function, the maintenance of solidarity and harmony among kinsmen and co-villagers.

The countryside is still preferred over the town/city as a place to live and raise families by the great majority of village residents, although the village is no longer the locus of work. Indeed, there is evidence that the growth of Kufr al-Ma from a village of two thousand in 1960 to a municipality of ci. five thousand in 1989 has not all been the result of natural increase of population; there has been a reverse flow of rural-urban migration because of the spread of urban amenities (electricity, piped water, and paved roads) to the village as well as because of the sporadic political insecurity in urban areas. A reflected the still positive evaluation of rural life when he said in 1986, "The air is free from pollution; there is no cinema, (nor) mixing of sexes (in public); ties are more numerous in the countryside; they are guardians of custom there." When I asked "I," the army migrant who served in Washington, D.C., why he chose to live in the village rather than Amman (where his father lived) he replied that he preferred the countryside, that it was his birthplace, it was quiet, and there was fresh air.

This attachment to and preference for the village community must be seen against the background of a steady and cumulative decline in sociability and reciprocity and an increasing unwillingness to sacrifice for the larger group, be it kinship unit or community. A's father, the village mayor, epitomized this norm in the 1960s when, according to his son, he was totally involved in dealing with the affairs of the village to the neglect of his own conjugal family: "My father left home at 9 a.m. and didn't come back till 9 p.m. and the people missed him more than his family (when he died)." This was the same son who referred to the "sweet reputation" that his father left his family by acting as "the face of the clan," i.e., by being "good to the world" rather than to his wife and children. N had condemned his father for this very sacrifice, and he and his brother, Nine, had condemned their father for his authoritarian attitudes.

The changing attitudes toward sacrifice for the larger group is exemplified by two sets of fathers and sons. D, the retired army officer, served five years as head of the village council in the late sixties and early seventies without remuneration.

His son, Q, the successful businessman in Saudi Arabia, found it painful even to have to replace his tie and suit for more informal clothing on visits to the village. And Muflih al-Hakim served as mayor of the village for many years with a minimum of compensation and in spite of his own poverty. His eldest son, X, refused to consider being head of the new municipality of Kufr al-Ma because of his economic obligation to provide for his own large conjugal family.

The decline in sociability has also been noted by many migrants and nonmigrants. This decline was at all levels—within consanguine families, between close kinsmen, and between distant kinsmen, clansmen, and covillagers. A complained that he saw his older brother, the head of the family, only four times in five weeks during his Ramadan visit from Arabia. Seven, the veterinarian trained in Greece, complained that "they (his patrilineage) all used to meet (nightly) in the house of the elder. Now, no one does." He said that now he visits his brother once a week. "People are tired; they come home at 5 and watch TV." The decline of the moral community even within the consanguine family was indicated by his remark: "The people used to be good-hearted; there was no double-dealing or deception [undoubtedly, this statement represents an ideal, nostalgic reinterpretation of the past]; today, no one likes the good for the other, even for his brother." The changing ethos of visitation between close patrilineal kinsmen is reflected in G's remark, "Visiting is not like it used to be; I won't visit Luqman, and he's the son of my father's sister, unless I have an invitation." Yet Nine made a point of emphasizing the ceremonial visitation on the occasion of religious festivals of the elder of his patrilineage (above), perhaps, in part as a kind of insistence on the continuing symbolic importance of such ties.

The decline of sociability and reciprocity and with them the norm that the community/kin group is the proper locus of social control is indexed by the decline in the prominence of the guest room (*madafa*). In 1960 the village guest rooms/houses were a nightly focus of gatherings of adult men for exchange of information, gossip, entertainment through storytelling, and marriage negotiation. Most important, it was to them that disputes were taken for resolution, and in them that formal peacemaking (*sulha*) took place with all the concomitant noble gestures of hospitality and generosity. In 1960 there were fifteen men who "curtained the village," i.e., who maintained hospitality in their homes in a room set aside for guests. In this room, furnished with mats, pillows, mattresses, and an enclosed, solid grate holding charcoal and brass pots for holding coffee, members of their own clan, villagers, and travelers passing through would be offered tea and coffee, lively conversation, and accommodation for the night, if necessary. I was told in 1986 that there were three men in the village who maintained a guest room, but after five months of research I could verify the existence of only one. By 1986 nearly every house had a television set (some had two) and men (and some women) commuted every day from work in town or other villages. The attractions of the *madafa* paled in relation to the television screen (which broadcast in Arabic and English). Men came home tired from work and commuting and

271

like their counterparts in the western world wished to relax in comfort with their conjugal families and be entertained without effort rather than take part in the repartee of the guest room, which in the new age had become palaver rather than an education on the world. Men had said in that previous time, "Our (guest room) social gatherings are our schools (*al majalis madaris*)." In that time the heads of households saved/withheld whatever surplus in flour, figs, or animals (sheep/goats for slaughter) was available for guests on appropriate occasions—rather than expending/lavishing them on their own conjugal families. If the extension of transportation, occupational mobility, and international migration had weakened the *maḍafa*, television had provided its coup de grace.[17]

Although many villagers were addicted to television, and others such as G regarded it positively, saying, "Our children benefit from TV; my son and I, we came upon civilization together; there are programs in English," still others, albeit a minority, regarded television with some hostility and ambivalence: "TV is good, but it spoiled our social life" (A). "Foreign (English-language) TV disturbs our children, (and) films are a moral disturbance" (P). The ambivalence with which television is regarded by some and the nostalgia with which the old-time *maḍafa* is regarded by many reflects a Janus-faced double-minded lifestyle. A furnishes one of the rooms of his house in a western style, complete with sofas, soft chairs, settee, and rugs; and he leaves another room bare of furniture, with mattresses and pillows piled in the corner so that they can be quickly laid out if appropriate guests, i.e., of the adult or elder generation come to visit.[18]

The impact of occupational mobility and growing differences of wealth, conspicuous consumption, education, and migration have resulted not only in the juxtaposition of different styles of life within single households and ambivalence toward the products of modernity, but also in a cynical attitude toward those who do maintain politeness, courtesy, amiability, and sociability among one's kinsmen and village mates. This cynicism was captured by the term, *mujamala*, used by G's first cousin as we were discussing the decline of sociability in the village in 1986:

> Today there is *mujamala*. People make friends with you, but rarely are honest with you. I'll laugh with you but I'm really not with you. People make friends with you to get the money you have, and after it's finished, they leave you. The poor fellow—no one talks with him.

G's cousin construed amiability and politeness, the denotations of *mujamala*, with false flattery and hypocrisy, its connotations under certain circumstances. The decline in the multiplexity of village relations had resulted in an instrumental pecuniary interpretation of kinship relations. People were being used rather than enjoyed/entertained.

This interpretation was made even more explicit by Z, a retired army sergeant who, by dint of hard work and entrepreneurial skills, had a prosperous cinder block workshop and small confectionary shop just outside the village:

272

"Today if you have money, people will respect you and say, 'Welcome (*ahlan wa sahlan*).' If not, they won't." He was fifteen when his father died. No one paid attention to him. (They said), "He has no weight; no (kinship) ties; he doesn't have a house; he doesn't have (agricultural) land (*ma fish illu wazan; ma fish irṭibat; dar ma fi; arḍ ma fi*)." This (treatment) continued until he opened his workshop. After two or three years he made a little money. "People began saying, 'Father of Muhammad (a term of respect), please come in, Father of Muhammad (*abu muḥammad tafaḍḍal abu muḥammad*).' And they got up and gave me a seat of honor (in public gatherings). Why, because I had money." One day he was working in his workshop when a message came from the chief officer of the subdistrict asking him to come to his office. "I wondered, what's this for? What have I done (wrong)?" I took off my dirty clothes and put on clean clothes and went. The chief officer (*mudir*) was sitting behind his desk like a prince. The chief officer said, "Your relatives from Beni Dumi (his clan) have signed a petition nominating you as village mayor (*mukhtar*)." I laughed. The chief officer got upset. I said, "When I was born from my mother's womb I was named Yusuf Ahmed (his given name) Muhammad, after my father, Abbas, after my grandfather, and my relatives erased all these names and said, 'That's the good-for-nothing (*hatha al-hamil*).' Today after I've opened a workshop and am making money they want me to be mayor. But my name is the same, Yusuf Ahmed Muhammad Abbas. I have a cinder block workshop. I have children to take care of. I don't have the time (to be mayor)." The chief officer said, "Okay." The Arabs for me are in this mode—if a person has money all will respect him, esteem him; if he has no money, this man will have no esteem (*al-'arab 'endi fi sura hayy; izza 'endu massari al-kul yuhtirmak wa ya'tibrak; izza ma 'endak massari, ma fish hatha 'endu 'itibar*). At this point I (the anthropologist) interjected, "This is true in every country—the rich are respected and not the poor." "But," Z replied, "God gave wealth (blessing, livelihood, nourishment), much or little, it is in the hand of God (*allah 'ata al-rizq; al-kathir aw al qalil bi yad allah*). If you have money I sit you on the top of ten mattresses (in the guest room); if not on the ground."

Z's attitude toward his close patrilineal kinsmen was not simply negative. It was scornful with a note of bitterness in it, and he extended it to cover his whole ethnic group, a far more sweeping condemnation than that of G's cousin.

Z's repudiation of kin and village reciprocity and sociability was extended to cover relations with the State when, later in our conversation, we began to discuss the relations of villagers with the police:

Today, if someone picks the fruit off my trees I go straight to the police. Before, the mounted policeman was a strange/rare sight in the village. He would treat the village as a bunch of monkeys and hit them in the doors of their houses. Today there are many soldiers and police personnel around.

This statement is significant for two reasons. First, it established that some villagers (see also E above) spurn intravillage kinship ties for the bureaucratic arms of the state in resolving many matters, something avoided in 1960. Second, it demonstrates a shift in the behavior of both the police and the villagers and a change of the ethos governing their relationship. The State's agents were no longer to be feared and avoided, but utilized to defend one's interests. The concept of the rights of the citizen has taken root among some villagers. This change also reflected the closing of the gap between urban and rural styles of life—the policemen no longer regard the villagers as monkeys because the village had become much more like the town in its material modernization, administrative status (it was now a municipality), occupational structure, and educational aspirations. The quest for diplomas (which were hung on the walls of village homes as soon as they were attained) and bureaucratic ratings was as avid among many villagers as among urbanites.

Zayd's remarks about wealth and its impact on social relations, coming from an entirely different milieu, Houston, Texas, have remarkably the same thrust as those of G's cousin and Z. Listening to the popular song on his car radio describing a rich person who had many friends and who suddenly lost all of them when he fell on hard times reminded Zayd of the "King of Inbe" (a nearby Jordanian village) who discovered hidden treasure and was suddenly elevated to the seat of honor in the guest house. This sense of the division between rich and poor was sharpened into a more elaborate sense of status difference as he cruised around the neighborhoods of Houston, neighborhoods varying greatly in economic and social status. In an earlier interview in 1986 Zayd had complained about the fact that "in the capital (Amman) there are palaces; in the States you don't find them. These people (in Jordan) got a position in government and ripped off the people, and (they) have bathtubs and Mercedes and a Jacuzzi (whirlpool hot tub), and we (villagers) don't have hot water." His moral condemnation, unlike most villagers, extended all the way to the highest governmental level.

Although they differed in the societal scope of their remarks, what is particularly interesting about the three evaluations of the morality of village social relations, G's cousin's, Z's, and Zayd's, is that they did not differ substantially in their thrust: a negative view of kinship and village behavior as well as the pecuniary instrumental attitude that underlay it. The negative views of those who had never left the country—G's cousin and Z—were as strong as that of he who did. Indeed, the strongest condemnation of kinsmen was by Z, and not the transnational migrant to the most culturally foreign nation, the United States. This fact demonstrates that the decline of the moral community in Kufr al-Ma is not just a reflection of migration but of the much wider range of changes discussed above.

The negative views of kinship ties described above, however, portray only one side of the changing moral community. The other side, demonstrated again and again in the previous chapters, is a continuing intense attachment to such ties and a nostalgia about the village past. In a conversation in 1986 the head of the village municipality, a retired army sergeant and taxi driver, demonstrated the yearning for the past (at least in the historical imagination) when he said, speaking about the time when all the houses were of mud brick and the narrow unpaved streets only permitted the passage of animals:

"Life was good then. First, there was (plenty of) land; only a few hundred souls lived here. Second, there was much rain and only agriculture, and every house had animals, and there were no state-protected woodlands (i.e., there was plenty of wood)." Then he turned to the social dimension of the past. "Formerly, children weren't allowed into the guest room. Now my son sits there and contradicts me in front of others. There used to be a sense of honor (*nakhwa*). Today everyone is preoccupied with himself (*al-yawm kull wahid balshan bi halu*)." He returned to the theme of the former self-sufficiency of the village in subsistence: "If there was a war now, we'd die from hunger. The land is too little for us and the rain is meager." However, he ended his remarks by an affirmation of one aspect of the modern age: "Before, government knew only the Wazirs (the family of the Pasha who formerly dominated the subdistrict in a semifeudal fashion since the nineteenth century). In the 1967–68 elections we didn't support the Wazirs (and they lost). With knowledge the district emancipated itself."

The other significant aspect of the decline of the moral community is the troubling ambivalence felt by some returned migrants (a minority) who have been exposed to other societies and other ways of life for long periods of time. Q was one of the most liberal migrants in allowing for and encouraging the education of women and their work outside the home. He found nothing wrong with women working as engineers, nurses, and secretaries in business offices, something opposed by the great majority of migrants. He opposed tribal law without citing any virtues associated with it, and advocated its total cancellation. And he supported birth control without conditions. All these positions were quite discrepant with prevailing village opinions, including those of other migrants. But for a highly successful businessman with a degree in English literature, a professor's daughter as a wife, and an exposure to western culture in Saudi Arabia itself (he worked in the Canadian embassy for over a year) and in trips to Europe and the United States, his views on social issues might be quite expectable.

Q was also highly critical of his kinsmen and their behavior in Saudi Arabia:

People who go abroad are going and competing with others (back home). Most of the people (back in the village) are jealous of each other. These people (in Saudi Arabia) who just stay in the company compound—they are counting every single penny. When I went to Riyadh I called the people from Kufr al-Ma on the telephone and invited them to come to the hotel (to socialize and to offer them hospitality). Do you know they didn't come because they didn't want to pay the taxi fare of ten riyals. There is a competition between cousins and close relatives; there is an intense competition.

As well as their behavior in the village:

"If I go one or two days to Kufr al-Ma, I can't bear it. Everyone looks at me in a different way. Even my relatives think that my working in Saudi Arabia (has made me different). I have a car—they think I'm too proud of myself; I'm not at their level. Some haven't even come to see me. I throw my business away when I come to Kufr al-Ma (by taking time away from the office). I don't even wear a necktie to fit in." I (anthropologist) interjected, "You don't feel constricted by village customs?" "No, in fact I respect all these things." "It didn't retard you?" I asked again. Q's reply was sharply different in tone from that immediately previous: "In fact, I see so many things wrong, and I want to correct it. But I overlook them since they'll think I'm arrogant (if I give my opinion)."

Q's remarks bring out an aspect of the decline of the moral community unstressed by others: the envy and intense competition of migrants among themselves and, particularly, among kinsmen of different economic status, and in Q's case of conspicuously different social status. Yet the egalitarian norms of the village have not been lifted, and Q felt it necessary to dress down when visiting the village. He clearly resented his kinsmen for not accepting him or his generosity in the way he wished to dispense it: with a display of conspicuous hospitality in a classy hotel in Riyadh.

The strained relationship between Q and his close relatives is explained by the decline in the norms of reciprocity that prevailed in the village in 1960. Then, a migrant or other person who absented himself from the village for a long period of time always brought gifts for his relatives, and they in turn always visited and welcomed him on his return and invited him to their guest room for a sumptuous meal (of rice and meat), a considerable expenditure in those days.[19] With all the comings and goings of a large number of migrants to Arabia after 1973 this expenditure was no longer possible. Reciprocity broke down at both ends. The migrant could no longer afford to bring gifts to all his relatives on a continuing basis because he, himself, was now more concerned about providing for his own conjugal family, including the building of a house, the education of his children, as well as the establishment of a commercial enterprise in and around the village. These relatives who remained in the village were equally committed to educating their own children beyond junior high school and to establishing their own commercial enterprises in a village economy in which dry-cereal farming was disappearing as a mode of livelihood. They were not willing to expend resources on lavish meals for their kinsmen.

What is most significant, however, is not the decline in reciprocity and the rise of jealousy and competition among close kinsmen. This development may be overstated by Q since other families like those of the mayor and the sailor, Bahhar's, have demonstrated kin solidarity over a long period of time, at least among male siblings. Rather it is the fact that although Q seems thoroughly alienated from the village style of life and many of the values that underlie it, he continues to seek praise and affirmation from close kinsmen. Or as I have phrased it in previous chapters, he continues to seek "the village's compassion." His education, his work, his marriage, and his travel demand disassociation from the village in a way, for instance, accomplished by Yusuf.[20] But his continuing view of the village as a reference group whose approval is important has led to deep feelings of alienation and ambivalence.

The decline of the moral community does not result in the sloughing off of its migrant sons, even those most acculturated to other ways of life. Such sons do not resolve their existential dilemmas in the way done by Yusuf (withdrawal and avoidance) or even in the way done by Zayd—and that done only after many years of striving and difficulty—by agreeing to "live on the border," i.e., in and between two worlds. For some, alienation and ambivalence are the lot of the returned migrant, as attested to by Q's successive statements: "I respect all these things (village customs);… I see so many things wrong (about village life) and I want to correct them."

But this ambivalence did not threaten the father-son bond. Q, the business manager who had spent five years in Pakistan and six in Saudi Arabia and the most successful of the current crop of migrants to Arabia, was deeply attached to his father, to whom he gave the bulk of his substantial earnings. When I asked him why he did this and why he didn't give his father advice on how to invest the money (his father invested most of it in agricultural land) he replied, "The main thing (is) I just want my father to be happy."

Notes

1. In fact, although as an anthropologist and an American I was a foreigner in Jordan, my presentation of self and the villagers' perception/reception of me was much more complex since I was of Arab origin, spoke Arabic, and adopted the headband and shawl as my everyday dress. However, I was Christian in origin and not Muslim as were all villagers. My marked status in the village and the constant negotiation of identity between anthropologist and the people studied is an important subject of study to which I hope to devote a separate essay in the future. For a stimulating discussion of how all life history accounts necessarily involve two voices—that of the biographer and that of the subject see L.L. Langness and Gelya Frank, *Lives: An Anthropological Approach to Biography,* 1981. This chapter is not an attempt at life history, biography, or family history, but Langness' and Frank's discussion applies to all anthropological research that depends on lengthy accounts elicited from informants including this study.

2. See Robert Hefner's *Hindu-Javanese: Tengger Tradition and Islam,* 1985, for a pioneering attempt to examine the passage/reinterpretation of tradition at the family level from one generation to the next.

3. Only one migrant living in the village (who had gone to Saudi Arabia for education and later work as a teacher) refused to be interviewed by me. Although the younger generation of men were eager to talk to me, many were rather aggressive in attempting to convert me to Islam. This aggressive attempt at proselytization was quite unprecedented (for me) and was an aspect of the religious resurgence that took place in Jordan in the 1980s. The resurgence and the bureaucratization of religion in Jordan deserve separate analysis and are the subject of a future publication, "Fundamentalism and the Bureaucratization of Religion: A Jordanian Case Study." I have written more generally about religious resurgence at the end of the twentieth century in another book, *Understanding Fundamentalism: Christian, Islamic and Jewish Movements,* AltaMira Press, New York, 2001. In particular, see chapter six for details of a conversation with a Jordanian fundamentalist.

4. See my previous analysis of local-level politics in Kufr al-Ma, *Low-Key Politics: Local-Level Leadership and Change in the Middle East,* 1979, for the important political role played by Muflih al-Hakim as one of the two village mayors.

5. As in previous chapters the analysis will focus on "action," that is, it will move back and forth between a discussion of the social relations of individuals and groups and the meanings attached to those relations by the individuals themselves. See Vernon Reynolds as quoted in L.L. Langness and Gelya Frank, *Lives: An Anthropological Approach to Biography,* p. 33 and Bruce Kapferer, editor, *Transaction and Meaning: Directions in the Anthropology of Exchange and Symbolic Behavior,* 1976, for a discussion of the relationship between behavior, meaning, and action.

6. In this account the women's voices are missing, specifically Muflih's wife and daughter. As a young, single, foreign, male observer and researcher in a tribal culture with a strong code of modesty I was barred in my earlier field work from interviewing women. By 1986 that code had been relaxed somewhat and had been reinterpreted, as the previous chapters indicate. However, in 1986 the code of modesty was still persuasive, in reinterpreted form, at the normative level and was still influential at the behavioral level. Today a number of professional women, both foreign and native to the culture area, have conducted anthropological field work. For the first time since the exceptional field work of Hilma Granqvist in Palestine in the 1920s, the voices of women are being heard. Among the social anthropologists conducting field work in the Middle East who have accentuated the voices of women in a number of remarkable studies see, Leila Abu Lughod 1986, Carol Delaney 1991, Elizabeth Fernea 1965, 1976, 1985, Erika Friedl 1989, Mary Hegland 1983, 1986, 1995, Suad Joseph 1978, 1999, and Seteny Shami 1990.

7. See *Arab Village,* chapter 2, pp. 56–69, for a discussion of the close consultation group in Kufr al-Ma.

8. See *Arab Village,* chapter two, cases 3 and 4, for examples of such controversies among the members of various close consultation groups.

9. I use the term "consanguine family" in Linton's sense of a family focused on parent-child and sibling relations rather than husband-wife ("conjugal") ties. See Ralph Linton, *The Study of Man,* 1936.

10. My concept of "the moral (rural) society" has been influenced by Max Gluckman's (1955) discussion of multiplexity, James Scott's (1976) discussion of the moral economy of peasants and Robert Hefner's (1985) discussion of ritual reproduction, but is unlike them in that I focus neither on the moral contract between landlord and tenant nor on the reproduction of a ritual system through the patterned mobilization of people and resources. The discussion below focuses on the norms of kinship and community social control involving wide-ranging reciprocity with implications for day-to-day visitation, hospitality, interpersonal family relations, sacrifice of conjugal life for clan and community interests, gift-giving, joking, and tribal law; and the effect of migration, occupational differentiation, extension of transport, education, and the introduction of television on the reinterpretation of such norms and their underlying values.

11. Muflih quoted this proverb in response to my remark that a father should be much happier with a surplus of daughters over sons because each daughter received a substantial marriage payment from her husband (to be) whereas each son had to pay a marriage payment to his wife (to be). In the 1960s these payments were commonly provided by the father; or conversely he was the recipient.

12. It should be remembered that education was not the elixir that many villagers believed. During the 1980s there was a white-collar underemployment problem in Jordan, particularly in professions such as engineering and medicine. The pursuit of and spending on education can also be abortive: O and P, the mayor's sons, on whom their brothers had expended resources failed their senior high school examinations several times.

13. Although the achievement ethic is rooted in tribal as well as Islamic norms, when I posed the question of its relative value to villagers in the 1960s, only one person, Yusuf's father, the civil court clerk, was willing to defend it (against the more accepted ethic of role ascription). See Antoun, *Local-Level Politics,* 1979, Chapter 7.

14. I wish to thank my colleague Richard Moench for clarifying certain aspects of Scott's argument.
15. See James Scott, *The Moral Economy of the Peasant,* for the details of the argument.
16. For a detailed account of how the process of social control unfolded in the guest houses of the village with regard to a case of marriage/divorce in the 1960s see Antoun, "Institutionalized Deconfrontation: A Case Study of Conflict Resolution among Tribal Peasants in Jordan," in Paul Salem, editor, *Conflict Resolution in the Arab World,* American University of Beirut Press and Syracuse University Press, 1997.
17. The most popular weekly television show in Kufr al-Ma during my five-month stay in 1986 was the "professional" wrestling matches that are regular Saturday morning entertainment in the United States; they were televised in Jordan in the evening.
18. See Linda Layne's interesting 1994 discussion of the symbolic significance for the construction of ethnic identity of the fact that in the tribal society of Jordan the guest room/tent must be re-constituted on the occasion of the arrival of every guest (Layne, *Home and Homeland: The Dialogics of Tribal and National Identities in Jordan*).
19. The rice was imported and the meat was expensive. Alternatively, the host slaughtered one of his own animals, a considerable loss of capital since sheep yielded wool and goats milk, and both could be sold at a good price for their meat on the open market.
20. His wife lived in the village in his parents' house, and in that sense one could argue that he was tied to the village. But she was Pakistani, and at any time he could have taken her with him to live in Saudi Arabia (as many migrants there did) or in Amman where he now lived. His marriage had not resulted in an alliance with another village family, a tie that would have bound him to the village.

8
COMPARISONS AND REFLECTIONS ON THE GLOBAL SOCIETY

Having described and analyzed transnational migration in detail in one case study in Jordan, it is time to place this case study in a comparative perspective and reflect on its general significance. Transnational migration for work and higher education is part of a worldwide phenomenon whose complexity is just becoming understood along with its cultural and economic consequences in a variety of diverse fields such as music and industry! Anders Hammarlund, a producer at the music department of the Swedish Broadcasting Company conducting research on Turkish music in Sweden, at the behest of one of his Turkish friends, helped to organize a folk music ensemble composed of three "Turkish" musicians—the Turks in Sweden are themselves divided between Turks, Kurds, and (Christian) Assyrians—one Argentinian, and three Swedish musicians. The ensemble was to play "syncretically," i.e., juxtaposing rather than integrating, pieces and instruments from a variety of musical traditions including Swedish and Turkish.[1] Hammarlund argues that the labor migrants to Sweden, and by implication Europe, are best labeled "migrants" and not "emigrants" or "immigrants" because they were "literally and symbolically" "oscillating" "between ... old and new countries," i.e., they were "precisely" on the move.[2]

Rothstein in describing the attributes of the "global factory," i.e., the new industrialization at the end of the twentieth century, emphasizes "the overlap in people, things, behavior, and ideas between the First and Third, core and periphery, or developing and developed worlds ... are so great that the categories are useful only if we see them as points in a continuum...."[3] "Not only capital and products but people are also increasingly on the move...."[4] She adds, "Wherever we are in the 'developed' world, we are increasingly likely to encounter people from" the developing world and vice-versa.[5] And she concludes, "The global factory *is* composed of local actors and events, but the stage on which they play is the world."[6]

This study has amply documented the degree of transnational mobility in the pursuit of higher education, work, and military training. But it is worthwhile emphasizing the character of that mobility along with some of its implications. Before Migrant Two went to study medicine in Greece he had already studied Arabic in cosmopolitan Beirut, and after his brother spent four years in Greece studying naval science, he sailed around the world in the merchant marine for four years before going to the United States. Before the officer, H, received military training in Sandhurst, England, he had gone to visit his uncle for several months in urban, modernized, tribal Kuwait, and he was later sent for military training to the United States. Before J's oldest brother went to fundamentalist Medina, Saudi Arabia, to practice medicine, he studied for four years in secularist Turkey where he married a Turkish woman whom he took to Arabia. J, himself, was twice sent on short military training missions to Los Angeles, and later served as an engineer attached to the United Nations in Croatia and Bosnia. Before Migrant Seven went to study veterinary medicine in Greece, of which he was critical, he spent a year studying geography in Baghdad in secular, nationalist Iraq, which he loved. And directly after migrant four finished studying English literature in Hyderabad, Pakistan, he went to Saudi Arabia to practice business management, a follow-up of his contacts and work for Saudi businessmen in Karachi. He soon returned to Pakistan to marry the daughter of a Pakistani professor whom he took to live with his parents in Kufr al-Ma.

But to describe the succession of countries studied/lived in is misleading because, as Rothstein has suggested, life in the global society is necessarily local. H did not just go to the United States for military training, he went to Columbus, Georgia, and Four did not just go to Saudi Arabia, he went to Riyadh and then, completely different Jidda. Zayd did not just go to Texas, he went to Houston whereas 'Isam went to San Antonio and Midland. Their different degrees of involvement in local, American cultural and artistic life were not simply a reflection of their personalities and previous life histories. Nine did not simply go to Pakistan for an education in agronomy, he went to Peshawar to attend a secular university in a tribal and refugee area whose ethos was fundamentalist. Peshawar was as different from overcrowded, multiethnic Karachi, as Karachi was from Feisalabad (where the majority of migrants went) in the heart of the fertile Punjab. It was also not accidental that students who studied in Russia, though they never entertained communism as an ideology or questioned their own religious orientation, came back complaining of the lack of planning in Jordan.[7] The variegated, discontinuous, contradictory implications of these educational experiences are perhaps best reflected by Yusuf's preadaptation in Egypt (where he studied Islamic law and educational psychology) and Germany to nontribal secular societies; his exposure to cosmopolitan London in an encapsulated fashion; and his absorption into a religious life with an increasing fundamentalist orientation (through Pakistanis) in Leeds (where he gained a PhD degree in descriptive linguistics). Yusuf returned to Jordan as a much more committed Muslim (with a neat, trimmed beard) than when he left.

The fact that all the migrants to Greece went to the same area, attended the same university, tended to study the same subjects, and formed a network of mutual aid in the beginning years of their immigration, may explain the broadly similar results of their study-work experiences: acculturation, marriage to Greeks, reinterpretation of tradition, but maintenance of ethnic identity.

One, Two, or Many Worlds

Gupta and Ferguson argue against the view that regards "cultures as discrete, object-like phenomena occupying discrete spaces," and for the view that "spaces have *always* been hierarchically interconnected, instead of naturally disconnected...."[8] They add that "cultural difference is produced and maintained in a field of power relations in a world already spatially interconnected...."[9] They are protesting here against the "conventional accounts of ethnicity ... [that] rely on an unproblematic link between identity and place," whether the reference group is the tribe or the nation-state,[10] rather than recognizing "the increasingly tenuous links between people and place."[11] At the same time they recognize "the profound [imaginative] bifocality that characterizes locally lived lives in a globally interconnected world...."[12] That is, they recognize the powerful human cognitive drive, regardless of circumstances and often in spite of them, to divide the world between "us" and "them." To avoid this dichotomization they argue for focusing research on hybridity and interstitiality or what they term, "borderlands," which they regard not as intermediate topographical sites, but rather as "an interstitial zone of displacement and deterritorialization that shapes the identity of the hybridized subject."[13] They are referring here to the social psychological states not only of people who suffer bodily displacement—migrants, refugees, exiles, and expatriates—but also to native members of host societies who while in their "ancestral places find the nature of their relation to place ineluctably changed," and the "essential connection between ... place and ... culture broken."[14] These "hybridized" and "interstitial" individuals they now regard as the majority of the world's inhabitants.

Lisa Malkki, also reflecting on the relationship of people to space and culture, argues that the dominant metaphors linking people to place are biological, and metaphorically equivalent: soil=tree=[home]land=kin.[15] She argues that "the rooting of peoples" has not only become the dominant metaphor to describe political and social relationships, but it has also taken on moral and metaphysical meanings and power.[16] But territorial displacement is fast becoming a common mode of living at the end of the twentieth century, and, given the dominant metaphors, is regarded as pathological, with refugees as the principal example of rootless immorality, threatening the integrity of nations and cultures.[17]

Su Zheng in describing parts of the Chinese-American community also refers to the fact that "more and more data suggest that culture is volatile and people mobile, and that we are in [quoting Said] 'a generalized condition of homelessness.'"[18] However, she reports a new theme replacing that of rootlessness: "a transnational migrant circuit."[19] Three separate nodes comprise this circuit or, otherwise viewed, imagined community: the place of origin, China; the place of migration, the United States; and the far-flung distant territories of the Chinese diaspora across the Pacific and throughout Southeast Asia. Instead of emphasizing rootlessness, Zheng emphasizes the "interconnections, interactions, intercommunications" made possible by modern transportation and communication: nonstop, trans-Pacific jet flights, long-distance telephone calls, faxes, and the face-to-face and voice-to-voice encounters the former make possible.[20]

In discussing Haitian immigrants in Miami, Gage argues that their imaginative community has four "nodal points": the host society (U.S.A.), the society left behind (Haiti), the Haitian diaspora (Haitians in Canada, Boston, and New York City), and the African diaspora—since Haitians are descendants of Africans displaced by the slave trade—which itself has four nodal points (Europe, Africa, the U.S.A., and the Caribbean.[21] Gage argues that out of this complex imaginative universe and extended geographical frame, new forms of nationhood are being born in the diaspora focused on both subcultural pride as immigrants and pride in the country of origin (Haiti).[22] This new identity is being constructed through "disembedding mechanisms," that is, "social relations ... constructed outside of the realm of face-to-face encounters and localized contexts," through audio and video cassettes, radio broadcasts, affordable air travel, mailed remittances, and circular migration.[23]

Hammerlund has analyzed the music of immigrants in Sweden, on the other hand, in terms of four "social subfields," the subfield being "the social locus of ... transmission and interpretation of a tradition."[24] Hammerlund assumes that "the acceptance of tradition implies continuous interpretation and reconstruction."[25] The four musical subfields of the Turkish musician in Stockholm on whom his research focused were as follows: the Turkish republic; the Turkish village in which the musician was born and lived till age fourteen; Swedish society; and "the transplanted Anatolian village in Sweden," i.e., the multiethnic immigrant suburb on the northern outskirts of Stockholm in which the musician performed and most Turks lived.[26] Each of these subfields is in turn complex; the musical tradition of the Turkish republic, for instance, is composed of western art music on the one hand and Turkish (state radio) folk music on the other, though rejecting Ottoman art music, which was cultivated by urban intellectuals in nightclubs.

All of the scholars mentioned above have been wrestling with the relationship between people (on the move), place, and culture/tradition, and seeking to develop more useful concepts to analyze that relationship. What is obscured in these discussions and what needs to be clarified is what the terms for description

284

and analysis suggested actually refer to. Sometimes they refer to geographical loci (nodal points), sometimes to social relations (subfields), sometimes to social psychological states (homelessness, borderlands), sometimes to imaginative/cognitive constructs (bifocality), and sometimes to some combination of the above, e.g., "transnational migrant circuit" refers to both ongoing social relations and an imaginative universe, and "nodal points" are imaginative universes as well as geographical loci.

All of the transnational migrants from Kufr al-Ma were involved in a "transnational migrant circuit" in an imaginative and cognitive sense, variously entertaining, reflecting on, and reorganizing images of life in their homeland and in the diaspora. But only the migrants for work to Arabia were frequently involved social relationally in coming and going between homeland and place of immigration. After an initial adjustment period, social psychologically, very few migrants suffered/endured "a generalized condition of homelessness," "rootlessness," or "an interstitial zone of displacement and deterritorialization."[27]

Those who did, for instance Zayd and Dan in the U.S.A. and to some small degree Yusuf in England, are very interesting cases and reveal much about the process of integration/assimilation or the lack of it in the diaspora. Their problem of identity was that they were at the same time, "self" and "other." Dan was very proud of being an American citizen, but he wanted to die in Jordan. But these migrants are the prominent exceptions to the rule. The great majority of migrants maintained a strong identification with and attachment to their culture and their village. Over 90 percent returned to Jordan, and, again, the great majority continued to maintain domiciles in the village.

It is interesting that Jordanian migrants to the United States were not able to build new forms of nationhood based on subcultural pride as an immigrant group and pride in country of origin in the way that Gage describes for Haitians in Miami or Zheng describes for Chinese in New York City. Although Zayd's basketball team and Dan's Sunday gathering were strong efforts to maintain and develop ethnic identity, the circumstances of international relations which made the U.S.A. and the Arab world enemies (or so it was imagined by many Americans) and the internal state of Arab societies made this reinterpretation of nationhood impossible. During the Gulf War Zayd said, "I tried to be less visible as an Arab." And Dan commented, "Here [in the U.S.A.] you are an Arab and a Muslim," this after saying that he and his friends got into an argument at Denny's because a Texan sitting in the next booth complained loudly to the proprietor about their speaking in such loud voices in Arabic.

But even Zayd and Dan, exceptions that they were, constructed a clearly bifocal imaginative/cognitive universe, and not a more complex trifocal or quadrafocal one as suggested for the Chinese in New York City, the Haitians in Miami, or the Turks in Stockholm. Dan's bifocality focused on women: He said about dating, "I think it's neat ... I really liked it ... But marrying (an American)!... All they (American women) care about is having fun and getting drunk." Later he said, "I want to hear a girl talk Arabic again, I yearn for that." Zayd's bifocality focused on religion: "I'm not religious, but "I want my kids to be Muslims." And again, "I'm not practicing my religion now (in Houston), but later [when he returns to Jordan] (I will)."

Social scientists such as Harold Isaacs in dealing with ethnic differences and their future in the postmodern world, and not just in the diaspora, have painted an extremely pessimistic picture: "great jagged irregularities of uneven development of societies, economies, technologies," "crippled cultures,... besieged traditionalists,... deracinated modernists," suffering "alienation and anomie," surging to find refuge in "the ruins of their many Houses of Muumbi" (i.e., in traditional tribal and ethnic ties), and "the collapse of empires and the proliferation of states" with the superpowers unable to control their clients.[28]

My own research on the transnational migration of Jordanians to four continents does not support such a scenario. Rather, migrants impressed me as resilient, coping with their problems in the diaspora through effective social networks, and in the most difficult cases such as Zayd's, after a long period of stress and trial (as well as edification), reinterpreting their traditions to incorporate much of the new and retain much of the old in a scenario that encompassed both worlds. It may be useful to remember that living in two worlds has ancient roots in rural-urban migration and more recent roots in industrial societies, where, for instance today in India an elaborate classification of and attachment to Hindu subcastes, rural occupations, village neighborhoods, sects, and legal and philosophical systems is accommodated to working in modern factories where dress, time, technology, working environment, and working regime are completely different.[29]

The Grand Variety of Human Experiences, Interpersonal Relations, and Social Constraints

This case study challenges certain notions about migration cited in the literature on the Middle East and provides an in-depth investigation of a completely neglected aspect of transnational migration: the quest for higher education.[30] The literature does not at all suggest the grand variety of experiences, occupations, and residences enjoyed/endured/occupied by migrants for work and higher education. It suggests that workers in Arabia were/are strictly confined in terms of work contracts, could not stay for long periods of time, and usually came without their families. Jordanians from Kufr al-Ma seconded by the government to Arabia as teachers certainly had little choice as to occupation or residence, and those hired by companies had their roles and their residence determined for them. But company workers were hired in a variety of circumstances and places (in the Jordanian capital, in the village, in Arabia, through face-to-face contacts, through intermediaries (*wastas*), through answering advertisements), and they sometimes moonlighted to augment their earnings. Although teachers and soldiers had narrowly defined job-specific roles in specific locations for a given time period, many other nonprofessional migrants switched jobs as soon as a higher-paying one (or one with more perquisites) appeared on the horizon.

Both teachers and nonprofessional migrants to Arabia as well as students seeking higher education in Europe, Asia, and North America enjoyed/tolerated/suffered a highly variable experience in their relationships to the native residents of their host countries. This complex and variegated experience is well illustrated in terms of degrees of multiplexity, i.e., in terms of the degree to which migrants established multiple strands of interest, other than the job-specific one, with natives and other migrants. The schoolteacher on the Red Sea who commuted up to the mountains to teach had a highly multiplex relationship in the hamlet where he taught, the residents constantly inviting him for meals and sociability, but he had no significant social relationships with neighbors or residents of the village in which he lived. The woman who taught in the Bedouin hinterlands of the interior oasis of Wajh, though suffering through the difficult physical circumstances (meager housing, winter cold, and mosquitoes) was treated even more cordially by the inhabitants, as though the teachers were "kinsmen of the town." The plasterer along the northern border developed a limited, targeted multiplex relationship with his Jordanian manager and his Saudi boss, but otherwise he had little contact with Saudis or non-Jordanian migrants at either the personal or the administrative level.

On the other hand, the school administrator on the Yemen border developed the most multiplex relationship with Saudis on a day-to-day basis, but he was sharply aware of the discrimination that he and all foreigners were subject to in terms of job rewards, promotion, and tenure. The interpreter, become translator-administrator, become personnel manager, had a series of unusual multiplex relationships with foreigners, beginning with his residence with an English family in Great Britain, continuing with his residence for over a year with a group of American managers on the Gulf, and ending with the exceptional circumstance of his managing Saudis in Riyadh. In this latter relationship he exercised his authority through developing a joking relationship with them and by distributing largesse. However, many other migrants in Saudi Arabia never interacted with Saudis or, for that matter, saw them on the job or off.

Students pursuing higher education abroad ranged in multiplexity: from the highly multiplex relations Jordanians established with Greeks, extending to marriage and permanent residence in Greece; to the trifocal social relations in the United States, socializing almost exclusively with Arab males, dating American females, and attending school with a mixture of Americans and other foreigners; to the encapsulated life most Jordanians experienced in Pakistan, studying, living, and dining among themselves on campus, though they got to know non-Pakistani students on sightseeing trips through Pakistan, especially during student strikes.

In the diaspora migrants were subject to various economic, political, and social constraints which varied according to country, location, and circumstance. The varying involvement of sending/receiving governments in recruitment/termination of migrants is obviously important as a constraint. The maneuvering space of migrants also differed with occupation: teachers and soldiers had no opportunities to moonlight as compared with business managers, translators, and foremen; oil rig workers had no time, energy, or opportunity to moonlight as compared with salesmen, drivers, and restaurant workers. Moonlighting seems to have been much more prevalent in Saudi Arabia where guarantors were more subject to bribes than in the other Gulf countries.

Economic opportunities differed in different countries with Saudi Arabia providing ample high-paying opportunities, the U.S.A. and Greece providing many low-paying opportunities for students, and Pakistan and Egypt providing few of any kind. Whereas opportunities for work were ample in Arabia, political, social, and legal rights were restricted for migrants, who were subject to expulsion and lacked the possibility of gaining citizenship as opposed to Greece and the United States where study, work, marriage, and citizenship were linked in the realm of potential programmed decision-making.

Another constraint is the prestige of migrants in the host country. This prestige differed in different regions (within countries) and among different categories of the host population. Yet, overall, the Jordanian migrants to Pakistan had the highest prestige due to their religious status (coming from the holy land) and their higher economic status—which placed them on a par with Pakistani professors rather than Pakistani students. In spite of the differences of religion and language, Greece was surprisingly hospitable to Jordanians, who were treated as guests and aspiring professionals. Migrants in the U.S.A. and Britain had relatively low prestige and, once outside university grounds, suffered discrimination on the basis of their ethnic origins including their physical type as well as their association with rich oil shaykhs. As one migrant to the U.S.A. put it, "Arabs lose a lot of points here." The Arab countries are intermediate in this regard. In Egypt, Jordanians were treated as unsophisticated tribal people; yet they were treated openly and cordially. Arabians felt a kinship with Jordanians on the basis of a similar language, culture, and tribal background, but they often treated them haughtily, referring to them as mercenaries and beggars, alluding to their lower economic status and the necessity of their having to leave home to earn a living.

The order of migration is also a constraint upon the success of migrants in the diaspora. As opposed to the Turks who arrived in Germany after all the other Europeans, the Jordanians came to Arabia relatively early and, equipped with many white-collar skills, including literacy and fluency in English (unlike the Yemenis who came at the same time or earlier), they were among the preferred migrant populations until the Gulf crisis of 1990.

Coping in the Diaspora: Styles/Degrees of Integration, Acculturation, and (Mal)Adjustment

1. Social Relations

I have already discussed in general terms the factors that bear on acculturation of immigrants to their host countries/communities such as language, religion, policies of receiving governments toward migrants, structure of receiving educational/military institutions, and time spent in the diaspora. Interestingly enough, time spent abroad, though it seems to bear a clear positive relationship to acculturation, seems not to be critical in achieving assimilation, with some of the longest-term migrants in the diaspora (Dan, Zayd, and Yusuf) becoming the most critical of the host culture.

If one examines "integration," i.e., emphasizing economic and social adaptation comparing Greece and the United States, the Greek consanguine family, the Greek ethos welcoming the stranger seeking education, the custom of collective courtship, the status/culture match of Jordanian tribal men and Greek rural women, the custom of the dowry, as well as the Greek government's policy of simplifying foreign student admission and allowing work, all operated to facilitate integration of Jordanian students into Greek society. In the United States the conjugal family—often broken by divorce or spatial separation—individual courtship, a business ethos emphasizing profit and work but not sociability, particularly to foreigners, and more complex procedures to receive work and residence permits, retarded integration of Jordanian students in Texas.

If one compares integration of migrants in Greece, the United States, Pakistan, and Saudi Arabia, on the other hand, Greece and the United States allowed more integration than Pakistan. There, no regular neighborly interaction took place between natives (outside the university) and students, who were encapsulated within university grounds; dating by Jordanians of Pakistani women was resented; work was too low-paying to be lucrative for students; and a language barrier separated Jordanians who spoke the educated lingua franca, English, but not Urdu or any of the regional or tribal languages of Pakistan. But Jordanians in Pakistan were more integrated there than they were in Saudi Arabia, which offered work, but segregated workers from the rest of the population, residentially, almost invariably preventing neighborly interaction, common recreation, marriage, or citizenship.

One Muslim marriage norm potentially worked for integration of all Muslim males in the diaspora: Muslim men are allowed to marry non-Muslim Christian and Jewish women in patri-oriented societies where the children assume the affiliation of the father. Greece is one such society, accounting for the largest number of marriages in the diaspora. Marriages were also contracted by all migrants in the United States, but two ended in divorce, and the reluctance of these Jordanian men to remarry was partly on account of fear that their children might be taken away from them by their American wife. Counterintuitively, marriage rates were lowest in the Muslim countries of immigration: only one in Pakistan where differences of economic status, culture, and language assumed importance, and none in Saudi Arabia or the Arab Gulf countries where a de facto social and economic status bar, implementing the norms of tribal societies, prevailed.

2. The Constraint of Language Difference, Religion, and Custom

In accounting for the different degrees of acculturation many factors need to be considered. I will consider only two here, the similarity of language and religion, and the prestige and status of the immigrant group vis-à-vis the host society.

In considering migrants pursuing higher education it seems that the most effective cultural learning contexts and the most rapid acculturation were in those non-Muslim countries providing formal training in language and culture in the first year of study. Three countries did this: Greece, Russia, and Germany. In Russia all foreign students, regardless of subject studied, were required to study Russian language and culture exclusively during their first year, and during that year they had to live with a Russian roommate. The Jordanian students interviewed, freely dated Russian women—one married a Bulgarian student who returned with him to Jordan—and none complained of ill-treatment by Russians inside or outside of university contexts.

A second language-culture learning situation is in those non-Muslim countries where the language of instruction is other than Arabic, and formal language training is not initially mandatory for the first year: England, France, the U.S.A., Yugoslavia, and Rumania. This language learning situation applied to most Jordanian army soldiers sent on military missions abroad.

A third language learning situation applies to those who study in a Muslim country where no formal language training is provided and the language of instruction is not Arabic—Pakistan. In the U.S.A., England, and Pakistan, Jordanians were able to build upon the fact that the second language of Jordan is English. In Pakistan the learning situation was complicated by the fact that the language of instruction (English) was not the language of the nation (Urdu) or the language of the regions (Sindi, Punjabi, Pushtu).

Another cultural learning situation prevails for migrants who work in Arab Muslim countries for a company in which the majority of white- and blue-collar workers are non-Arabs—Saudi Arabia and the Gulf emirates. In these countries there is linguistic uniformity among the indigenous population, but that population is not the one with whom the migrants interact most. At the white-collar level they interact with Europeans and North Americans and at the blue-collar level with Asians as well as other Arabs. The indigenous language situation differs between the Gulf countries and Saudi Arabia. The former have a non–Arabic speaking population of some antiquity coming from along the Arabian Sea and the Indian Ocean. Many Gulf families from Abu Dhabi and the United Arab Emirates are composed of an Arab father and an Iranian or Indian mother whose children—before they enter school—speak the language of the mother, and not that of the father and the nation-state. This is the language situation in which many retired Jordanian soldiers going to the Gulf for further military service, such as A, found themselves.

Next are those student migrants, relatively few, who went to Arab Muslim countries—Egypt, Saudi Arabia, and Iraq—to study in a totally Arabic-speaking and Arabic-reading environment. Finally, are those few migrants who went to the Arabic-speaking but dominantly Christian environment of (Beirut), Lebanon.

If one constructed a continuum of cultural exposure for Transjordanian migrants based on linguistic and religious similarity, adding the factor of similarity of tribal culture, it would look as follows with Iraq being closest and the U.S.A. being farthest from the native culture of rural Jordan.

DIAGRAM 1
CONTINUUM OF CULTURE EXPOSURE

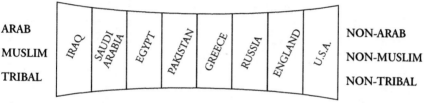

ARAB   IRAQ   SAUDI ARABIA   EGYPT   PAKISTAN   GREECE   RUSSIA   ENGLAND   U.S.A.   NON-ARAB

MUSLIM   NON-MUSLIM

TRIBAL   NON-TRIBAL

If one considers the question of the relative prestige/status of Jordanians in their host countries, a quite different continuum emerges. Migrants to Pakistan had the highest prestige overall because of the religious aura attached to them by the generality of the population due to their coming from "the holy land," and because of their superior economic status within the university—their student living allowances were the equal of a Pakistani professor's salary.

At the opposite extreme, in the U.S.A. and England their status was low compared to most Americans and English; their culture and religion was not honored; on the contrary it was sometimes maligned; and their dark physical type sometimes led them to be classified with "Asians" in England and Blacks ("sand nigger") in Texas. Greeks, on the other hand, seemed to regard Jordanian students positively as aspiring professionals in spite of their Arab Muslim identity. The Russian government went to great lengths to treat Jordanian students well, but this positive treatment was not always matched by the population at large.

England is the country where the discrepancy between the treatment received inside the university and that received outside was widest. Sometimes students were able to reverse the status situation usually applied to their ethnic group by virtue of their occupation (e.g., Yusuf taught Englishmen Arabic and Islamic law) or could affirm their superiority by virtue of it: Bahhar was an officer on a merchant marine ship composed of Greek sailors.[31]

3. The Varying Content of Acculturation

The content of acculturation differed from one migrant to the next within particular countries and within regions within these countries. To use the United States as an example, 'Isam, partook very little of the high cultural life of Texas, but immersed himself in American business culture and its ethos with a vengeance (aiming to make a million dollars by the time he was age thirty), whereas his brother devoted his time and energy to participation in local operettas and other artistic activities. 'Isam had established a conjugal family on the American pattern with both spouses working. He was exposed to American Protestant religious practices through his American mentor. Of all the migrants, only 'Isam supported the American prosecution of the Gulf War and placed yellow ribbons on his automobile. 'Isam's friends were all non-Arabs; he had deliberately cut himself off from the community of Arab students after moving out of an apartment with a Palestinian from Qatar at the end of his second year in San Antonio. Bahhar and R also established a conjugal family and had just celebrated the first birthday of their son in Seattle. They had jointly decided to move to Seattle from Texas, to visit Jordan, to give their children Arabic names, and later, for R to visit Jordan alone with their two children so they could maintain contact with their cultural roots. Recall that Bahhar and R went back to Kufr al-Ma the summer following their justice-of-the-peace marriage in Galveston to be married by a Muslim shaykh. R is the only spouse who had taken a formal university course in Middle Eastern Studies and who consciously expressed the importance of maintaining their children's Jordanian heritage. However, 'Isam and Bahhar and their spouses hardly ever cooked Arabic food, and seldom went out to Middle Eastern restaurants.

Zayd and Dan, on the other hand, ate Arabic food whenever possible in restaurants or, occasionally, at home. Home-cooked Jordanian food was the centerpiece of Dan's Sunday social gathering. Both Zayd and Dan acculturated through buying, selling, refurbishing, and riding in automobiles, though Zayd's romance with the automobile had more profound dimensions. They both led a bifocal life in Houston-Arlington, working or studying with Americans during the day and socializing with Jordanians and other Arabs in the evenings and over weekends. Both had married, had divorced, now frowned on dating, and in general criticized American family life or the lack of it.

If 'Isam was the only patriotic defender of the United States' role in the Gulf War, Dan was its most vociferous critic, and if 'Isam had accommodated to

American Protestantism, if not embraced it, Zayd is the only American migrant who repeatedly asserted his Muslim (and not just his Arab) identity.

There is a continuum with respect to attachment to Arab culture, but its content is variable: Dan affirmed his Arab Jordanian identity in a culinary, social, and political context; Bahhar affirmed it through naming his children in the U.S.A. and refusing to change his own name in Greece, and through visits to family and kinsmen in Kufr al-Ma; Zayd affirmed his Arab identity through sport and sociability, but in doing so widened its meaning by brushing elbows with Lebanese and Saudis in Houston; 'Isam, on the other hand, not only avoided Arabs, but also consciously cut himself off from his Arab heritage which was in any case inchoate, having left Jordan at age nine and never having fitted into the segmented patrilineal, multicultural milieu of Abu Dhabi thereafter.

There is also a clear-cut continuum of behavior and acculturation regarding work. 'Isam is a workaholic who spends most of his working hours including weekends reflecting on and juggling various business ventures, quite apart from his demanding regular work as a restaurant manager. Dan spoke proudly of working in a restaurant in Ohio during student days, cleaning chili machines in a room where the temperature was 140 degrees; and he was currently "daylighting" as the manager of a 7-11 store, after finishing his work as night auditor at the Dallas–Fort Worth airport. Zayd began his stay in Houston by fleeing a McDonald's restaurant after the manager told him to mop up the floor, but, thereafter during his eleven years in Houston he took a succession of jobs to support his student and social life, stating, "If you don't work, you'll die starving in America." Bahhar, on the other hand, always worked in the merchant marine, but he praised his early life in the Greek merchant marine by saying—in contrast to Americans—"Greeks are a fun people"; "Greek sailors were happy; they liked sailing."

4. Programmed Decision-Making

A specific aspect of socioeconomic change is the widening scope of programmed decision-making in the diaspora. Michalak has defined programmed decision-making in describing the experience of Tunisian migrants in France and on their return, in terms of the development of a budget and a timetable: he notes that as Tunisians moved from the status of unmarried new migrant (sowing their wild oats) to married veteran migrant they tended to develop a daily budget, stipulating the amount needed to save/invest and a timetable for savings and return.[32] In studying returned Yemeni migrants from Saudi Arabia, Tutwiler has spoken of the move from "deferred to programmed decisions" in terms of "calculations of costs, risks, and probable benefits ... well in advance of initiating action" and accepting a greater degree of risk in expectation of a greater return; as opposed to seeking to defer decisions till they have to be dealt with, allocating resources on an ad hoc basis, and maximizing subsistence security, and reducing risk and uncertainty by following tried-and-true methods and social arrangements, i.e., investing in social relations: in kinsmen, friends, neighbors, and co-villagers.[33] Tutwiler attributed the growth of programmed decision-making among returned Yemeni migrants to the change in the socioeconomic situation which provided much more money for investment, more investment opportunities, and the knowledge that if one failed, one could always return as a migrant to Saudi Arabia to recoup savings.[34] Michalak's explanation of the growth of programmed decision-making emphasizes the difference in the life experiences of stay-at-homes vs. migrants in the diaspora, changes in the family cycle of development, and generation differences; whereas Tutwiler emphasizes the growth of economic opportunities.

Both explanations are pertinent to migrants from Kufr al-Ma. Almost all migrants to Greece and the U.S.A. endorsed and/or practiced family planning (though not birth control) as did many to Pakistan. Many migrants went to Saudi Arabia to save money so they could build and furnish a house. Migrant Two spoke of building a garage for her husband, who was a mechanic, to work in after completion of a house. Migrant Four said he would work in Arabia for two more years to finish his house and an additional year to pay off installments on his car. Migrant Six figured that he and his brother would have to save for two more years to earn 10,000 dinars to build a cinder-block-cutting workshop.

N returned from Arabia after he saved enough money to marry, build a house, and purchase a small plot of land in the village as his brother, A, did before him and his brother, O, planned to do after him. I have no data as to whether migrants had or adhered to daily budgets; I doubt that migrants to Saudi Arabia had them, but students pursuing higher education abroad may have been forced to have and to follow them.

The most pronounced programmed decision-maker is Zayd, who applied such decision-making to his education, his work, his pursuit of citizenship, his future marriage, and his circulatory migration. He would first save enough to build his business; then he would return to Jordan to marry (and not vice-versa as his friend did); then he would return to Texas with his wife to work for five to seven years; then he would return to Jordan to enculturate his children in a Jordanian context. During his later years in Texas he allotted two years to getting his degree in business management while working as a chauffeur. Early on he was aware of the different strategies (marriage vs. immigration visa) one could pursue to obtain permanent residence and a green (working) card and subsequently citizenship; and he knew the time it would take for each strategy. His opposition to early marriage, children, and house purchase were consequences of his programmed decision-making.

Quite apart from the goal of achieving professional and academic degrees, the pursuit of education fit into the planning process and signified the enhancement of technical skills as well as self-improvement. The many military men who took various training courses attested to this fact. J is the exemplar in this regard, taking seven courses. The many men who attended the two-year institutes in Irbid following graduation from high school were well aware that their graduation certificate translated into a certain bureaucratic rank and salary, if hired.

Deferred decision-making, reflected in the extension of hospitality to kinsmen, friends, and co-villagers, was the dominant mode in Kufr al-Ma in 1960. It diminished after 1973, but continued at both a normative and behavioral level at different times and in different contexts after that. For instance, new migrants such as the successful business manager, Q, and the butcher and refrigerator salesman, expended considerable hospitality on their co-villagers in Arabia, but later, particularly after returning to Kufr al-Ma, they became parsimonious and more planning conscious. Migrant 6 extended hospitality to Saudis throughout his residence in Arabia, but he also engaged in programmed decision-making as indicated above. Others such as Migrant 7 never extended hospitality while in the diaspora, saving every penny to meet the debts and obligations his two families (wives) contracted in Jordan.

5. Orientations, Styles, and Degrees of Migrant Discourse and Adjustment

In considering styles and degrees of migrant adjustment, adaptation, and acculturation in the diaspora, it is useful to distinguish three migrant orientations: the exile, the assimilator, and the sojourner. These orientations refer to the social psychological state of the individual (and are not therefore wedded to a particular place such as the home or host country). These terms also have implications for the imaginative/cognitive universe the migrant constructs as well as the social relations he/she pursues. Though these orientations may be related to economic goals, they are unrelated in any patterned way to economic investment behavior or its locale. Both the hydrology supervisor and the refrigerated meat salesman in Saudi Arabia were free spenders in Saudi Arabia, but savers/investors back in their home communities in Jordan.

Most of the migrants from Kufr al-Ma reflect more than one orientation, at different times and in different situations. However, one mood and attached imaginative/cognitive construct seems to dominate the interview-conversations, and the pattern revealed by these conversations is consistent with the information I gathered about these same migrants and their social relations in the diaspora and in Kufr al-Ma. However, since I gathered neither social psychological data nor cognitive/semantic data by any formal investigative techniques the following discussion should be regarded as suggestive only.

"Exiles" define themselves as foreigners and strangers in the diaspora with the implication of not only non-acceptance by the host population, but also their own rejection of key (but not all) aspects of the host culture. They look forward to some future time when they can be reunited with their own culture through marriage and/or eventual return to their homeland. They construct the most sharply bifocal imaginative universe. Zayd and Dan are the most pronounced in demonstrating the exile's orientation, but N, the airport lighting technician in Saudi Arabia, before his marriage and before he brought his wife to live with him in Arabia, demonstrated this orientation to some degree, as did his brother, A, in Abu Dhabi. Both Zayd and N are highly critical of their own societies generally, as well as of certain aspects of the behavior of their fellow-villagers. Q also seems alienated from his co-villagers, perhaps even more than N and Zayd. The exile feels at home neither in his place of origin nor in the diaspora. Yusuf cetainly rejected the style-of-life of his native village and cut off relations with it, but he had settled comfortably in town.

Not all exiles are cut off social relationally from their place of origins; some visited and communicated regularly, e.g., N and A, but others were cut off for long periods from their homes, e.g., Zayd visited Kufr al-Ma only once in eleven years and Dan had not visited for thirteen years. Migrant Two, the doctor in Greece, had not visited Jordan for more than seven years, not because he did not wish to, but because the Jordanian government prevented his doing so after he had taken Greek citizenship without informing it. Non-visitation, in and of itself, is not evidence of the exile orientation. The lack of necessary connection between exile orientation and place is demonstrated by "exiles within the gate." A man banished by the government to Kufr al-Ma, his home village, for political activity had been living there for many years, raising hundreds of chickens in a "scientific fashion"—no other villagers did so. Although he was a son of the village, born and bred in it, he did not associate with his fellow villagers in any forum; he did not visit them nor was he visited, even by his own brother; he did not attend the Friday mosque prayers; he did not marry. He regarded his fellow villagers as ignorant and uncivilized, and he was totally alienated from them and their ways. He was an exile within the gate.

The "assimilator," on the other hand, is one who accepts as a proper reference for his own behavior the standards of the host society.[35] Rather than imitating the ways of the host society in order to get along, to fit in while working/studying there, he does so because he accepts those standards as proper. 'Isam, the student-become-entrepreneur in Texas, is clear in his own mind that neither the societies of Jordan nor Abu Dhabi were for him. He married an American, sought U.S. citizenship, and enthusiastically supported the American effort in the Gulf War, unlike most Jordanians. 'Isam stands alone in his wholehearted up-front assimilationist orientation.[36]

Other migrants had assimilated with respect to certain aspects of the host culture, e.g., Ali accepted unreservedly the German standards relating to medicine, health, hospital organization, and science, but he rejected the norms of German family life and personal morals. And Yusuf appreciated and accepted as superior the English norms of higher education, but he too rejected English norms of family life, as well as what he considered English racial prejudice and cultural arrogance. The educational administrator in Arabia had assimilated to the social life and standards of the Saudi population on the Yemen border among whom he lived and worked; or, perhaps, assimilated is not the proper word, since he regarded their norms of sociability and reciprocity as close to or the same as those of his own native village. And he wholeheartedly approved of the religious norms applied by a state influenced by religious fundamentalism. But he rejected the particularistic bureaucratic norms which refused to reward merit.

The educational administrator after his first few years in Arabia, like the great majority of migrants, was a "sojourner." The sojourner is working for a particular economic or educational goal, biding his time in the diaspora while doing so, working, studying, or training with no expectation of absorption in the host society. The task of coping in an alien society over a long period of time is not an easy one, and necessitates a substantial degree of acculturation, i.e., learning the ways of dress, language, study, politeness, sense of time, and food preference.

Although all sojourners acculturated, they did so in very different ways, pervaded by different moods and motivations, and from quite different economic bases. Some sojourners were firmly positioned in occupations that provided considerable economic security, such as the educational administrator and the doctor in his later years in Germany, the merchant marine officer in Greece and the U.S.A., the telephone operator and secretary of the Saudi prince in Riyadh, the clerk in the Department of Justice in Riyadh (the first migrant to Saudi Arabia), and the circulation manager of the newspaper in Tabuk. Yet the tenure of those in Arabia was/is contingent on political circumstances as the 1990 Gulf crisis attested. Other sojourners were firmly positioned, but "temporaries," e.g., those seconded on five-year teaching contracts. Some sojourners operated as entrepreneurs in Saudi Arabia, moving from job to job as different economic opportunities opened up.

Other migrants were romantics of various types. One is the merchant marine officer who placed a high priority on adventure and traveling the high seas and observing different people and cultures, culminating in his romance with an American woman he met in Aqaba, wooed in Greece and the Caribbean, and married in Texas. There is a romantic aspect of Yusuf's stay in London, when, according to his own account, on weekends he would just get in his car and drive wherever his fancy led him, exploring different parts of England.

Then, there are a number of "affable acculturators," migrants who knew quite well the instrumental character of their residence and work abroad, took the lumps they received from the host society in their stride, and acculturated, sometimes with pleasure, and, in any case, without major difficulty or protest. Migrant Four, the translator-turned-supervisor in Saudi Arabia, seemed to thoroughly enjoy the time he spent with the English family, the American managers, and the Saudi employees. The attitudes these affable sojourners expressed ranged from that of the "pragmatic raider," the plasterer on the northern border—"I only want their material possessions, not their friendship"—to that of the supervisor: "While I'm working, I don't think of home." But he too quickly set the practical limits on his acculturation by saying, "Why should my wife become a foreigner too (by coming to live with him in Riyadh)?"

Neither the plasterer nor the translator-supervisor had the edge in his voice of the educational administrator when the latter said, "Don't think the foreigner has any value in the bureaucracy," and "Foreigners will work harder in the diaspora; they can send them home any time," and again, "I have fifteen years' experience; a Saudi can come without experience and be put over me (in the administrative hierarchy) ... as soon as a Saudi comes, they put him over me." They did not have an edge in their voice because, unlike the latter who brought both his wife and mother to live with him in Arabia, they had no expectation of settling in the country. This is the edge that betrays a trace of the exile. Neither the supervisor nor the plasterer spoke of their stay in the diaspora as an ordeal and a sacrifice (unlike the army corporal in Abu Dhabi, who continually worried about his wife and children in Kufr al-Ma and frequently telephoned home to ascertain their welfare).

The attitude of the sojourner, and not the attitude of the assimilator on the one hand or the exile on the other, is the dominant attitude of the transnational migrants from Kufr al-Ma, whether pursuing education, training, or work.

Related to the three orientations described above, but not coincident with them are three migrant "discourses," that is, oral statements and stories by migrants recounting their experiences according to a pervasive theme.[37] In analyzing Tunisian migrants to France, Michalak has referred to the discourse of suffering and the discourse of success.[38] I add a third, the discourse of happiness.[39] The discourse of suffering incorporates themes such as discrimination, boredom, loneliness, dirt, poverty, self-sacrifice, and the devaluation of one's culture. The discourse of happiness focuses on romance, freedom, learning, self-esteem, discovery, cars, and women. The discourse of success, less important for the migrants interviewed, focuses on the attainment of professional degrees, a job with a good salary, marriage, the building of a house, and the attainment of the significant items in a growing consumer culture: cars, clothing, refrigerators, and electronic equipment.

A discourse can be country and region-bound. The discourse of Q in Pakistan is a mixture of suffering and success, but in Saudi Arabia, it is one of happiness and success. Migrant Six, the educational administrator (chapter two), recounted a dominant discourse of happiness and success while in highland Abha and one of suffering in lowland Jizan. A discourse can also be arena bound. N evinced happiness in his work at the Tabuk airport but suffering in his living quarters in town until a later stage in his sojourn; and Yusuf and the students in Pakistan evinced happiness about their life inside university gates but suffering outside them. The discourse can also be time bound, as suggested with N above. Yusuf described his student days in Egypt in nostalgic terms, but his description of Egyptians on his return trip was not flattering to them. Similarly, his early years in London he described in somewhat carefree terms, but his later years in Leeds were loaded with responsibility to both university studies and mosque obligations. The same person can engage in quite different discourses at different times in the same milieu, as attested to by Zayd, Dan, Yusuf, and the educational administrator.

N's conversation-interview (chapter seven) was dominated by the discourse of suffering. He spoke of the ignorance of villagers in the days of his childhood, their narrow worldview, including that of his own father, the prevailing dirt of his surroundings, and the lack of sensibility to children and their welfare. G, the air force fitter mechanic (chapter three), also spoke about his childhood in derisive terms, citing the behavior of his own father who administered physical punishment and invective when his children asked for the money to purchase school supplies. A complained of the boredom of his life as a soldier in Abu Dhabi and his chronic attacks of anxiety about his family back in Jordan. Zayd suffered from loneliness in Houston, and the educational administrator was agitated about the occupational discrimination he received as a foreigner. Others were able to cope with discrimination pragmatically, accept it (Migrant Seven), or transform it as did the doctor (Migrant Eight) in Greece who said, "The Greek favors the Greek, but if you are gentle, they treat you like one of them." Both Dan and Zayd in the U.S.A. and Yusuf in England reacted to the fact that many Americans and Englishmen devalorized their Arab culture.

The discourse of happiness is similarly complex and has many different aspects. N received a sense of self-esteem from his work at the Tabuk airport where he met many businessmen and officials who treated him with politeness and respect, as did Q in his business dealings all over Arabia. H received self-esteem from his army career and officer's training abroad, and Yusuf and Ali along with most students in Pakistan, from their pursuit of higher education abroad. Romance was a prominent element of the discourse of happiness of the radio officer in Greece and, thereafter, on the high seas, as it was with the hydrology supervisor among the Jordanian Bedouin. The freedom of life in the diaspora figures in the discourse of Zayd in Houston, Yusuf in London, and the hydrology supervisor in the desert. In the early part of their migrant careers hedonistic concerns including dating women and driving cars appeared in the discourses of Zayd and Dan; and wine and women in the discourses of Dan, Q, and the refrigerated meat salesman. But for Zayd, the automobile represented freedom and refuge as well as enjoyment. A final element in the discourse of happiness is that of enlightenment, discovery, and learning. N found this at the airport, the radio officer on the visits to the ports of Asia and Africa, Migrant Nine in his mission to Afghanistan, the hydrology supervisor among the Bedouin, Yusuf in weekend trips all over England, and Zayd in his daily experience in Texas: "In the U.S.A. you learn in one day what you learn in one year in Jordan." The natural environment was also a source of gratification, particularly in Greece and was part of the discourse of happiness: "I liked everything in Greece: the sky, the sea, the forests, the good treatment." Just as the oppressive heat was part of the discourse of suffering in Pakistan.

Nearly all migrants for higher education talked in terms of the discourse of success, valuing their professional degrees, their well-paying jobs, their marriages, and their building of a house or shop. But this discourse was not as pervasive or significant in the context of the interview-conversations as those of suffering and happiness. Migrants for work to Arabia talked more in terms of the indices of success, but success, even in their discourse, was interrupted and often dominated by the ethos of exile and/or happiness.

The Reinterpretation of Tradition

Controlled acculturation, preadaptation, impression management, core identity, (previous) misadaptation, symbolic ethnicity, reidentification by alter, the pluralization of private belief, and the relativization of public value—all these are concepts discussed in previous chapters to explain the processes/mechanisms by which migrants coped with life in the diaspora as well as life on their return. But the concept crosscutting all chapters and the principal cognitive process/mechanism for coping with change is the reinterpretation of tradition. The reinterpretation of tradition is a cultural-cognitive process by which customs and beliefs are reinterpreted in the light of new local circumstances in the changing world. The assumption made here is that all "tradition" is constructed, that is, that even when the cultural content of the tradition is the same, the new circumstances make its meaning different.[40] So, for instance, even if the American flag were exactly the same in shape, color, form, materials, and symbols (in fact it changed with the addition of two new states to the union after World War II), its meaning to the American people was quite different after World War II, after the Vietnam War, and after the Gulf War, as evidenced by the fact that flag-burning was not an issue after World War II, was resorted to during the Vietnam War, and was reacted against by the time of the Gulf War.

In the preceding chapters the reinterpretation of tradition has been discussed with respect to such issues as birth control, women's work, tribal law, and Islamic penal norms (the *ḥudud*). These reinterpretations are not responses to alienation or anomie, but to new demographic, technological, social structural, and economic circumstances.

One argument of this book is that such reinterpretations are best approached by focusing on the family or, even better, the subfamilial level. Anthropologists have long focused on the analysis of societal processes through the family. In the 1950s Leach argued the necessity of focusing on the local descent group rather than on generalized kinship systems.[41] In the 1960s Fortes and Goody urged the necessity of focusing on the household as a unit of production and consumption.[42] And in the 1980s Hefner urged the necessity to focus on the family as the intergenerational transmission unit for the reinterpretation of tradition.[43] This book argues, particularly in Chapter 7, that one must submit the family itself to scrutiny (and not assume its unity) and investigate the individual reinterpretation of tradition within it. One can then discover a variety of reinterpretations (including [of] the family tradition itself), i.e., the multivocality of family tradition.

Since I had devoted considerable attention to the status of village women, particularly their public behavior and the attitudes toward that behavior in the early 1960s, I began to reflect on how changes in occupational and residential mobility in general and the diaspora in particular had led villagers to reinterpret that tradition, what I had earlier called "the modesty code."[44]

I discovered that the startling new circumstances had indeed led to a considerable reinterpretation of tradition without eroding the mores that underlay it, i.e., the continued belief in (an amended) sexual division of labor and the honorable deportment of women in public. Quite often in interviews the reinterpretation would be initially denied and later admitted through a series of qualifying phrases I have termed, "hedges." For instance, the educational administrator in Arabia, in replying to my question, at first stated he did not believe women should work outside the house, and then he went on to cite all the circumstances that would allow them to do so.

When I reviewed the various interviews pertaining to women's work and compared them (in particular in Chapters 3, 4, and 6), I noted that the reinterpretation of the tradition of modesty and honor composed a discourse that was logically articulated: women had the freedom to work outside the home as long as the woman's honor, the integrity of the family, and the welfare of the children were preserved. This result could be achieved by a variety of different mechanisms: sexual segregation in the work situation, avoidance, accessible monitoring, restrictive work hours, work proximity to the home, safe transport (to work), and responsible white-collar employment. Birth control (*tahdid al-nasl*) was similarly reinterpreted so that what was never a matter of public discussion or permission in the village in the 1960s became so in the 1980s, by distinguishing between birth control and family planning (*tanTHim al-nasl*).

Attention to the relationship of space and gender further illuminates how the reinterpretation of tradition works in both the village and the diaspora. Garner has pointed out the critical relation of space and gender in analyzing agoraphobia in the United States.[45] She has pointed out that much public space is regarded as a male domain and that private space is often regarded as a female domain. In the village in the 1960s one could argue that women and, particularly married women, suffered from collective agoraphobia because the norms of modesty, both tribal and Islamic, frowned upon their movement, unaccompanied, in the public ways. Yet my observation in the 1960s was that women filled the public ways in the course of their carrying out both household and agricultural duties. There existed in the village, then, a kind of institutionalized contradiction between economic necessity (to fetch water and wood and to tend animals) and the mores stipulating confinement to courtyard and, more generally, to village quarter. On the other hand, no women were veiled in Kufr al-Ma;

nor have I ever seen veiled peasant women in Jordanian, Egyptian, or Iranian villages; that space is defined as relatively close, home, and private, compared to the towns and cities of these countries.

When women from Kufr al-Ma began going to Saudi Arabia as teachers, they were entering spaces that were defined by the denizens of the village as distant, foreign, and public, and, thereby, exceedingly dangerous. How could villagers deal with this new situation and at the same time preserve the mores of modesty and honor? Garner has pointed out that when venturing out into public space, one can have either an animate or an inanimate protector.[46] The veil is an inanimate protector of women in public space whether in Amman or Arabia. But there is another additive or alternative "cover" that is equally if not more effective, an animate cover, a male companion falling within the categories stipulated by the Quran, i.e., beyond the bounds of eligible sexual relations and marriage, e.g., father, brother, son; or oppositely, a legitimate sexual partner, i.e., husband. Women working in Saudi Arabia are always accompanied by one of these men for the duration of their stay. Therefore, when the pursuit of economic opportunity required the violation of collective norms of modesty and honor by departure of women from the village, they were safeguarded by the reinterpretation of tradition referred to above that allowed the woman occupational mobility, and by the provision of animate and inanimate protection in public space.

The Persistence of Community in the Global Society

This book is about the bursting of the bounds/bonds of nations on the one hand and the persistence of local community on the other. The migrants described have spent long periods of time pursuing education and work in seventeen different countries. But their nondiscursive practice indicates the continued "naturalized identity between people and place"[47] as attested to by the amazingly high rate of return of migrants to build houses and to live in the village; or if not to live there, to marry and have their children there; or if not possible, to continually visit their relatives, friends, and properties; or if not possible, to die there. The village community still makes marriage and fatherhood/motherhood critical for the achievement of maturity, and residence within the arc of visitation critical for happiness.[48]

A comparison here between migrants from Turkey to Europe and Jordan to Arabia is edifying. The result described by Keyder for returned Turkish migrants from Germany—the severance of "the remaining ties to traditional community values" … leading to "an alienated modern life" does not obtain in Kufr al-Ma. Rather, visits, remittances, communication through emissaries, telephone calls, letters, and local investments maintain a transnational migrant circuit and all it implies.[49] The "disintegration of the household" and by implication the family through the absence of one or more members, their dispersion inside or outside the country, and "the role incompatibility arising from the changing status of women" and increased divorce is the result Keyder posits for the nonmigratory family members remaining in the Turkish village community.[50] Jordanian families in Kufr al-Ma certainly experienced absence of key members for long periods and their geographic dispersal over vast distances, but I have no evidence that role incompatibility or substantive emotional stress is widely experienced by women remaining in the village. Although the family structure in Kufr al-Ma, like that of Turkey, is dominantly composed of conjugal families, in Kufr al-Ma these families exist within the framework of a larger consanguine family, that is, patrilineal and matrilateral relatives assume responsibilities of departed family members and usually act as protectors and confidantes.

But there is another explanation of the lack of role incompatibility and emotional stress on the part of the wives left behind in Jordan: the normative family structure described by Gluckman as "estrangement in the family."[51] In many societies affective interpersonal relations are not expected between spouses, but rather between parents and children and/or between siblings. Brink, reporting from rural Egypt on the effect of emigration of husbands on the status of their wives, states the situation as follows:

> I found no evidence of psychosomatic illness or sexual unfaithfulness among the wives in the sub-sample. The women do not seem to suffer emotionally because of the long separation from their husbands. In part this lack of display of emotion occurs because public mention of love or affection between spouses is taboo for village couples. Rural Egyptian marriages are not based on love, and any display of this emotion between husbands and wives is considered shameful. However, I was able to get to know some of these women well enough to explore beneath the public facade, and I believe that separation from their spouses was not as difficult as it would be for a couple whose marriage is based on romantic love. In fact, some of the women thought it amusing that I would expect this to be a problem. Their marriages had been arranged by their parents, and most of the women had only seen, and had never spoken to, their husbands before their wedding. Their marriages were begun in extended families where ... leisure time was spent with entire extended families or in unisexual groups.[52]

Brink's observations in an Egyptian village are consistent with my own in the Jordanian countryside. Circulatory migration, the existence of a consanguine support network (if not a consanguine family), and the continuing pertinence of the normative frame of estrangement in the family that values the emotional and social relational closeness of parent and children and siblings rather than husband and wife, may explain the continued strong family and community ties of migrants from Kufr al-Ma despite their long periods of absence.

To be sure, continued residence abroad, marriage abroad, investment abroad, the birth of children abroad, and, particularly their education abroad as well as the change in the lifestyle of the migrant and the move toward assimilation—and not acculturation—and away from living in two worlds, diminish the ties of the migrant with the local community, and eventually sever them. I have only one such migrant case, and that after over twenty-five years of residence, work, and marriage in Germany. This fact indicates the continuing power of the local community to hold its members, imaginatively, if not residentially and social relationally. However, counterintuitively, unlike the Turkish case, there seems to be no systematic relationship between length of time spent abroad and severance from the local community and its norms. The great majority of migrants who have spent seven or more years abroad in Arabia, Pakistan, Greece, and the U.S.A. are still imaginatively linked to the village as the source of their identity and their home.

Although the village community continues to be a social relational and imaginative focus for migrants, there is no question that it has declined in its moral power, as the last chapter has demonstrated. However, transnational migration need not have the result of unfastening tribal ties and weakening community norms of social control and sociability as the Yemeni case described by Tutwiler demonstrates.[53] Reporting on the rural province of Mahwit in the early 1980s, Tutwiler describes the building of roads, the emergence of vehicular traffic into the interior, the development of a commercial market in Mahwit town, and the proliferation of retail enterprises there—all this in conjunction with a massive circulatory migration of Yemenis to Saudi Arabia and the regular sending back of remittances. This migration and its economic impact has not resulted in undermining tribalism, i.e., the norms that support sociability, reciprocity, sacrifice for the larger kin group, and the proper resolution of disputes within the pertinent tribal group. In Mahwit the development of the market is an outgrowth of tribalism as well as migration: the market is controlled by tribal people and operated according to their own norms. Money made from commercial ventures is invested back into gift-giving and into the ethos of generosity and the tribal social control system, which provides protection from the relevant threatening groups. In Mahwit to hoard money is still considered shameful, and the remittances from transnational migration have allowed Yemenis to become better tribesmen. Morality there lies not in your occupation (migrant), but what you do with your money: help relatives get married, give gifts to kinsmen, provide financial aid to the needy, make entertainment and charitable expenditure on religious holidays (Ramadan), pay litigant expenses for family members and tribesmen, or help in the opening of a shop.[54]

But Jordan, although Arab, tribal, and a major participant in transnational migration, is not Yemen, and Kufr al-Ma is not Mahwit. Like the town of Mahwit, Kufr al-Ma in some respects has evolved into a small town with its essential amenities (piped water, electricity, and paved roads) as well as its legal status (municipality). And this fact may account in part for its continued attraction to its migrant sons. But sociability has declined at all levels, the guest house as a focus of social control and enculturation has all but vanished, tribal law is questioned by many, ceremonial visiting on the occasion of religious festivals has declined, the rate of village exogamy has increased, and the existence of the village as a unitary web of kinship with everyone knowing/recognizing everyone else has ended. Although the norms of reciprocity among close kinsmen remain, economic differentiation, status differences, and the partial replacement of an egalitarian ethos with the skeptical one of *mujamala,* have produced strains among some close kinsmen (but not among others) and resulted in the curbing of gift-giving and hospitality.

In writing about the anthropology of justice and law from a cultural perspective in Islamic society, Rosen has pointed out that several cognitive changes have taken/are taking place in the Middle East that have implications for social relations.[55] One of these changes relates to the idea of causality. He states, "it has commonly been assumed in Moroccan culture that human or divine agency lies behind all events. To know how something happened you mainly need to know who made it happen.... Now, ... one sees instances in which chains of events are themselves seen to entail their own natural or probable consequences."[56] The process of long-term reciprocity that has long prevailed in Kufr al-Ma as the guiding principle underlying gift-giving and the offering of hospitality to kinsmen, neighbors, and friends is based on the belief in intimate chains of personal agency. One's offer of hospitality triggers another's offer or a gift or a visit at some later stage in a never-ending series of personal transactions. Somewhat sophisticated migrants like Q still cannot emancipate themselves from viewing causality in terms of chains of personal agency rather than chains of circumstance. The notion that "events at times take a course of their own"[57] has not yet replaced the notion that by offering hospitality, giving gifts, or witnessing, i.e., vouching for the reputation of human agents, one can thereby predict their (presumably favorable) behavior. But in Kufr al-Ma, unfortunately, given the new socioeconomic circumstances e.g., economic differentiation, occupational mobility, the wave of transnational migration, and the drive for higher education and the concomitant need for savings, it is not possible for hospitality and gift-giving to continue at a rate that sustains tribal and community norms. Whereas tribalism prospers in Mahwit, it is being replaced by the ethos of envy, self-interest, and *mujamala* in Kufr al-Ma.

The ultimate impact of transnational migration on Kufr al-Ma is, however, still in the future and unknown. In this book I have documented the pluralization of private belief in every chapter about a great variety of subjects including tribal law, birth control, the state and its bureaucracy, women's work, the (village) past, television, the army, education, and the Quranic stipulated punishments. But very few migrants have proceeded to the relativization of public value, i.e., to assume a live-and-let-live posture which endorses the different ways of others, but not for themselves.[58]

Nonmigrant villagers still lack awareness of the range of pluralization of beliefs among village migrants, and returned village migrants still lack awareness of the pluralization of belief among nonmigrants. One explanation of this circumstance is the disappearance of the *madafa*. The guest house was the arena, par excellence, where information was exchanged, discussed, and evaluated, in an ongoing evening-long free give-and-take atmosphere. The one guest house that remains in the village (in 1989) is on many evenings sparsely attended. Or, could it be, on the other hand, that many avoid the guest house precisely because they know that kinsmen and neighbors would be in disagreement over interpersonal norms and the vital social issues of the day? When questioned about whether they discussed many of the matters of vital import to themselves and their nation with other villagers, a number of transnational migrants replied that the villagers were ignorant (so how could they discuss these matters with them). This reply indicates their anticipation, at once, of uniformity (of their opinion) and disagreement (with it).

It will take time before the young men educated abroad in the 1970s and 1980s move up nearer the top of their respective hierarchies—business, governmental, military, professional—and exert an impact on their peers, increasingly on their subordinates, and on policymaking.

The question of tradition and its reinterpretation by this younger generation had already begun in the 1970s, and it did not require leaving the country to initiate it. Evidence of this questioning and reinterpretation was presented to this anthropologist in 1979 during a question period at Yarmouk University, located in the heart of the formerly peasant and now post-peasant society of northern Jordan. After the lecture comparing the nontribal Iranian village I had studied in northern Iran with the Jordanian village of Kufr al-Ma, a student asked me, "What do you think of the *madafa* (as an institution)?" I repeated what I had said in lecture: the guest house was an institution serving a variety of social, quasi-legal, educational, and ceremonial functions. A few minutes later I was asked by another student, "What is your view of the *madafa*?" I was puzzled and replied in the same way, saying that it was a multifunctional institution. After a few minutes a third student asked, "What is your view of the *madafa*?" I suddenly realized that I was being asked to evaluate the guest house as to its moral worth—good or bad. I was taken aback. For anyone to have asked me this question in 1959 when I began my research was unthinkable. The students were well under way with reinterpreting their tradition, and the anthropologist's input was grist for their mill.

Transnational Migration and the Diaspora

Many anthropologists and social scientists have recently described the condition of global society at the end of the twentieth century and posed important questions about the implications of this society for peoples and cultures in their local settings around the world. The importance of such recent scholarship has been attested to by the formation of three new journals, *Cultural Anthropology, Diaspora,* and *Public Culture* in the last decade. How does my own in-depth research following migrants from a single community around the world illuminate these findings on the global society? How does it inform us more fully about transnational migration and life in the diaspora as well as life in the hometowns of the world? I will answer these questions by focusing on four authors and two works: Linda Basch, Cristina Szanton Blanc, and Nina Glick Schiller's (1994) book, *Nations Unbound: Transnational Projects, Post-Colonial Predicaments and Deterritorialized Nation-States,* and James Clifford's (1994) article, "Diasporas," in *Cultural Anthropology.*

Basch's, Blanc's, and Schiller's groundbreaking book on East Caribbean, Haitian, and Filipino migrants in New York City defines transnationalism in terms of "the processes by which migrants forge and sustain multi-stranded social relations that link together their societies of origin and settlement."[59] They argue for a new conception of a nation-state that includes as citizens "those who live physically dispersed within the boundaries of many states, but who remain socially, politically, and culturally and often economically part of the nation-state of their ancestors."[60] Drawing on Rouse, they emphasize the existence of transnational migrant circuits which involve "continuous circulation of people, money, goods and information" such that "the various settlements have become so closely woven together that, in an important sense, they have come to constitute a single community...."[61]

At the family level they have emphasized that transnationalism involves a constant coming and going involving many roles (grandparents, uncles, aunts, parents, children, siblings) for many purposes (visit, vacation, schooling, work, child fostering, wedding) and involving consanguineal and affinal ties. The aim of this coming and going is to maximize chances for family members to survive in a situation in which neither home nor host country has offered legal, economic, or cultural security.[62]

They point to a counterintuitive fact about transnational migration: "Familial, social, economic, and religious ties to Haiti have increased as Haitian immigrants have become fully established in the United States."[63] This observation they find generally applicable to the Filipino and East Caribbean cases. In all four migrant populations (from the Philippines, Haiti, Grenada, and St. Vincent) they emphasize that transnational migrants simultaneously "develop projects in home countries at the same time that organizational activities also absorb them within the U.S."[64]

I am simplifying here the authors' complex argument that embraces issues and relations of nationhood, class, race, and domination. In relation to my own research their key point is that it is no longer possible to speak simply of "emigrants" and "immigrants" or "assimilation," "acculturation," or "nation-state" because migrants are simultaneously involved, interactively in a "transnational world network."

There may be some basis for arguing that the Jordanian migrants to Greece formed "transnational communities" in the sense that they were residentially focused in the diaspora in a single city and single university in northern Greece. But there was no coming and going of family members between Jordan and Greece of the kind suggested above. Moreover, in Greece six of eight migrants married from the native Greek population, suggesting a high degree of acculturation and some assimilation.

Similarly, it could be argued that the Jordanian students in Pakistan attending Feisalabad University formed a transnational population since they were residentially and commensally focused, and, unlike Greece, nurtured their own language and culture in the diaspora. But there was no coming and going of family members between Jordan and Pakistan and the Jordanian students singularly failed to establish multiplex ties with Pakistanis, apart from the one migrant who married and the other who became involved in athletics.

The Jordanian migrants who went to the Arabian Peninsula for work, particularly those who went to Saudi Arabia, could be counted as the one convincing case of a transnational migration circuit, but this circuit was highly restricted on the Arabian side since there was no opportunity for permanent economic or political integration into Saudi society. Even on the Jordanian side the movement of people was restricted since family members did not go back and forth in a visiting pattern—and only spouses were allowed to live as residents, and that on a selective basis. In sum, the interactional transnational circuit does not characterize the Jordanian case.

What of the ideological, affective, and imaginative side of transnationalism? Clifford begins his essay by outlining the "essential features" and "diacritical" approaches to defining "diasporas." The former approach emphasizes a discrete set of attributes: expatriate minority communities; dispersed to at least two peripheral places; maintaining a vision/memory/myth of a homeland; believing they cannot be fully accepted in the host country; seeing the ancestral home as a place of eventual return; committed to maintenance or restoration of the homeland; with the group's identity defined by this continuing relationship to the homeland. The diacritical approach defines diasporas against the norms of the "other": the nation-state or the indigenous aboriginal (tribal) community claiming continuous habitation of the land.

Clifford rejects both approaches and defines diasporas in terms of a shared experience and ethos of displacement, suffering, adaptation, or resistance (rather than return to homeland) and in terms of "a loosely coherent adaptive constellation of responses to dwelling-in-displacement."[65] Clifford's diasporas have both positive (association with world historic forces, e.g., Islam) and negative (discrimination and exclusion) aspects, and diaspora culture is both utopic (selectively preserving and revitalizing valued traditions) and dystopic (focusing on uprooting and loss).

At the core of Clifford's view of diaspora is the notion of "a changing same," "a collective identity maintained over long stretches of time; attempts to conceive the continuity of a people without recourse to land, race or kinship as primary grounds of continuity."[66] For Clifford the "diaspora world-view" is (or should be) a positive one in which the "practice of dwelling differently" by deferring return (to the homeland) indefinitely is cultivated through connection (with other peoples in the diaspora) rather than through separation.[67] From this perspective the Geniza Jewish culture of Cairo and the Ashkenazi Yiddish culture of Europe represent the positive aspect of diaspora culture. They were composed of populations that did not return but defined and cultivated their differences through constant interaction with other diaspora peoples/cultures as well as with the host society.

Although one could argue that in a sense Zayd and Dan in Texas had cultivated a sort of diaspora worldview accommodating work, education, and a future family life with living in two worlds (Jordan and the U.S.A.) interactionally and imaginatively, as well as in time and space, they in no way fit Clifford's diaspora worldview and ethos. Their dreams and visions of the future always focus on a return to the homeland even when that homeland falls short of diaspora life in terms of technology, efficiency, or political rights and justice. "I shall return" is the message delivered by Dan's construction of a house in Kufr al-Ma after thirteen years of residence in the U.S. and in Zayd's membership in his basketball group and his plans for marriage and family life after eleven years in Houston. Both Zayd and Dan were "dwelling differently" in the U.S.A. but that dwelling was neither relished nor cherished.

Even the migrants to Greece who learned Greek, married Greek women, and took up residence and work in Greece were not, in Clifford's terms diasporic in worldview, though they were probably so in ethos, having adjusted, it seems rather easily, to the sociable and genial public life of Greek consanguine families and friends. Most, perhaps all, would have returned to Jordan if employment in their chosen fields was available—and some did, even when it wasn't. And all but one were married in a Muslim ceremony and gave their children Muslim names. Even migrant Two, the doctor who was almost totally acculturated to Greek ways, assimilated into his Greek consanguine family, and integrated into Greek society generally, insisted on maintaining a distinctly separate code of modesty and honor for his daughter, and he was planning to return to Jordan for a visit even after his disputation with the Jordanian government. Two's Greek citizenship like Zayd's and Dan's American citizenship did not signal an imaginative leap into either a diaspora or a transnational universe.

More important than the question of return to the homeland, however, are the imaginative dimensions of land and kinship. More than 90 percent of the Jordanian migrants studied did return after long stays abroad, and that is a significant fact. More significant is the fact that with very few exceptions all migrants, whether at home or abroad, continued to envision their past, present, and future by reference to their families and their village of origin. The village was the "primary grounds of their continuity": visions of their past, their childhood filled with security, sociability, reciprocity, and serenity; visions of their fathers and mothers; visions of present decline—of the village as a moral community; visions of their present status in the diaspora compared to other sons of the village still there; and visions of the future—a marriage, a white-collar position, a burial!

How can one account for this non-transnational, non-diasporic interactional and imaginative reality? I shall hazard three educated guesses. First, although Jordanian students and workers spent long periods abroad, they went there, and by and large remained, sojourners rather than exiles or refugees on the one hand or immigrants aspiring to assimilation on the other. Second, it can be accounted for by the continued resilience of a peasant and tribal worldview and ethos (rather than a national and global one) in a particular ecological niche in a post-peasant global society. The people of Kufr al-Ma are not just Arabs and Muslims. They are tribal Arabs and Muslims with a strong tradition of reciprocity and indigenous conflict resolution from an area of Transjordan inhospitable to commercial agriculture or industry.[68]

Finally, perhaps the heuristic model of transnationalism and diaspora offered by Basch, Blanc, Schiller, and Clifford does not capture an essential aspect of the reality of the (origin country) global village. That global village is a world of coming and going, of communication by phone, letter, newspaper, radio, television, e-mail, audiocassette, and videotape, and of continuous circulation of people, money, goods, and information. Training of future local and national elites in foreign educational institutions, foreign military establishments, and foreign bureaucracies, no doubt, has profound implications for the direction of future national and transnational integration, as does training of third world nationals in their own countries by visiting foreign advisors/experts (including United Nations personnel).

But in much of the world the family and the local community—not the national community—continue to fill the imagination and the emotions of sons and daughters whether they are found in the diaspora or at home. The question asked by the Haitian migrants in New York City, "In which country does my future lie?" was never asked by Zayd or Dan in Texas, by Yusuf in England, Ali in Germany, or Jordanian students in Feisalabad or Karachi, Pakistan or those in Salonika, Greece. Geographically and spatially they were part of a diaspora and a transnational existence, interactively they were part of it in a restricted sense, but imaginatively and affectively they were tied to another world of childhood, family, and local community.

Notes

1. See Hammarlund's stimulating description and analysis of "Migrancy and Syncretism: A Turkish Musician in Stockholm," *Diaspora,* Vol. 3, No. 3, Winter 1994.
2. Opis. cit. p. 310.
3. See Frances A. Rothstein, "Conclusion: New Waves and Old—Industrialization, Labor, and the Struggle for a New World Order," in *Anthropology and the Global Factory,* F. Rothstein and M. Blim, editors, 1992, p. 239.

4. Opis. cit. p. 241.
5. Opis. cit. p. 239.
6. Ibid.
7. My interviews with (four) migrants to Russia were too few and not extensive enough to ana-lyze, thus their omission from the book. I hope to analyze them in the future after gathering more pertinent information.
8. See Akhil, Gupta and James Ferguson, "Beyond 'Culture': Space, Identity and the Politics of Difference," *Cultural Anthropology,* Vol. 7, No. 1, February 1992, p. 7 and p. 8.
9. Opis. cit. p. 17.
10. Opis. cit. p. 7.
11. This phrase is Su Zheng's paraphrasing of a theme pursued by James Clifford in *The Predica-ment of Culture,* 1988. See Zheng's "Music Making in Cultural Displacement: The Chinese-American Odyssey," *Diaspora,* Vol. 3, No. 3, Winter 1994.
12. Gupta and Ferguson, p. 11.
13. Gupta and Ferguson, p. 18.
14. Gupta and Ferguson, p. 10.
15. Lisa Malkki, "National Geographic: The Rooting of Peoples and the Territorialization of Na-tional Identity Among Scholars and Refugees," *Cultural Anthropology,* Vol. 7, No. 1, February 1992, pp. 28ff.
16. Malkki, p. 31.
17. Opis. cit. pp. 31–32.
18. Zheng, p. 275.
19. Opis. cit. p. 276.
20. See Zheng, pp. 276ff.
21. See Averill Gage, "'Mezanmi, Kouman Nou Ye? My Friends, How Are You?': Musical Con-structions of the Haitian Transnation," *Diaspora,* Vol. 3, No. 3, Winter 1994, p. 254.
22. Gage, p. 268.
23. Gage, p. 268.
24. Hammerlund, p. 311.
25. Ibid.
26. Hammerlund, p. 312.
27. For a discussion of these matters see Su Zheng, "Music Making in Cultural Displacement: The Chinese American Odyssey," *Diaspora,* Vol. 3, No. 3, 1994; Lisa Malkki, "National Geo-graphic: The Rooting of Peoples and the Territorialization of National Identity Among Schol-ars and Refugees," *Cultural Anthropology,* Vol. 7, No. 1, February 1992; and Akhil Gupta and James Ferguson, "Beyond Culture: Space, Identity, and the Politics of Difference," *Cultural Anthropology,* Vol. 7, No. 1, February 1992.
28. See Harold R. Isaacs, *Idols of the Tribe: Group Identity and Political Change,* 1989, pp. 106–7.
29. See Milton Singer, *When a Great Tradition Modernizes: An Anthropological Approach to Indian Civilization,* 1972 for details.
30. See the literature cited in the Introduction.
31. I have already discussed in chapter 4 how the Greek sailors redefined this relationship in a more egalitarian direction by renaming Bahhar, "Jordanus."
32. See Lawrence Michalak, "The Impact of Continuing and Return Migration from Tunisia: Case Studies from the Tunisian Northwest," paper delivered to the conference on International Mi-gration of Middle Easterners and North Africans: Comparative Perspectives, Berkeley, May 1988.
33. See Richard Tutwiler's "Tribe, Tribute, and Trade: Social Class Formation in Highland Yemen," PhD dissertation, State University of New York at Binghamton, 1987, Chapter 7 for details of the argument.
34. Tutwiler, Opis. cit.

35. See Teske and Nelson for a detailed discussion of the process of assimilation in contrast to the process of acculturation.
36. Note, however, that an assimilationist orientation does not necessarily or even usually involve cutting oneself off from one's family. 'Isam had a collage of his family sitting in his living room, he remained in communication with them, and he had lent his brother money to avoid military service in Abu Dhabi during the Gulf War.
37. I am not following Michel Foucault's use of the term, discourse, here, suggesting relations of power and domination. See Foucault's *Discipline and Punish*, 1977 and *The History of Sexuality*, 1976 for examples of his usage.
38. See Michalak, p. 28.
39. The discourse of some migrants was not dominated by suffering, success, or happiness, but by other themes. For instance, the discourse of Ali in Germany and to a certain degree, Migrant Nine in Pakistan, was dominated by religious duty, and that of Migrant Seven in Greece by cynicism (applied to both Greek and Jordanian society). But these were the rare exceptions and not the rule.
40. See Handler and Linnekin for the pursuit of this theme in French Canada and Hawaii.
41. See Edmund Leach, "The Structural Implications of Matrilateral Cross-Cousin Marriage," *Journal of the Royal Anthropological Institute of Great Britain and Ireland*, Vol. 81, 1951.
42. See Jack Goody, *The Developmental Cycle of Domestic Groups*, 1958.
43. See Robert Hefner, *Hindu-Javanese: Tengger Tradition and Islam*, 1985.
44. See Antoun, "On the Modesty of Women in Arab Muslim Villages: A Study in the Accommodation of Traditions," *American Anthropologist*, 1968.
45. See C.B. Garner's very interesting analysis in "Out of Place: Gender, Public Place, and Situational Advantage," in *Nowhere: Space, Time and Modernity*, edited by Roger Friedlander and Deirdre Borden, 1994.
46. See Garner, pp. 342–47.
47. The phrase is Malkki's, p. 26.
48. See Antoun, "Social Organization and the Life Cycle in an Arab Village," *Ethnology*, Vol. 6, No. 3, 1967 for a detailed account of the importance of marriage and how it was contracted in Kufr al-Ma in the 1960s.
49. See Keyder, Opis. cit., p. 89 for details of the Turkish case.
50. Keyder, Opis. cit., pp. 119ff.
51. See Max Gluckman, *Custom and Conflict in Africa*, chapter 3, 1960.
52. See Judy Brink's "The Effect of Emigration of Husbands on the Status of Their Wives: An Egyptian Case," *International Journal of Middle East Studies*, Vol. 23, No. 2, May 1991.
53. For the details of the argument see Richard Tutwiler's "Tribe, Tribute, and Trade: Social Class Formation in Highland Yemen," PhD dissertation, State University of New York at Binghamton, 1987.
54. See Tutwiler, Opis. cit., particularly chapter 7.
55. For details of the argument see Lawrence Rosen, *The Anthropology of Justice: Law as Culture in Islamic Society*, 1989.
56. Rosen, Opis. cit., p. 77.
57. Rosen, Opis. cit., p. 78.
58. Zayd and Bahhar are the exceptions, recognizing other contrasting ways of life as legitimate, and Yusuf adopted this stance with respect to some aspects of English and Egyptian life but not to others.
59. Basch, Blanc, and Schiller, p. 7.
60. Basch, Blanc, and Schiller, p. 8.
61. Rouse as quoted in Basch, Blanc, and Schiller, p. 29.
62. See Blanc's discussion of Haitian transnationalism, pp. 164–69.
63. Basch, Blanc, and Schiller, p. 147.

64. Bach, Blanc, and Schiller, p. 249.
65. Clifford, p. 306.
66. Clifford, p. 320.
67. See Clifford's discussion, pp. 321–23.
68. For a detailed description and analysis of the tribal mode of conflict resolution in its community setting in 1960 see Antoun, "Institutionalized Deconfrontation: Tribal Conflict-Resolution, A Jordanian Case Study," in *Conflict-Resolution in the Arab World,* Paul Salem, editor, American University of Beirut and Syracuse University Presses, 1997.

BIBLIOGRAPHY

Abadan-Unat, N. 1986. "Turkish Migration to Europe and the Middle East: Its Impact on Social Structure and Social Legislation," in *Social Legislation in the Contemporary Middle East,* ed. L. O. Michalak and J. N. Salacuse. Berkeley: Institute of International Studies, University of California.

Abu-Lughod, J. 1977. "Recent Migrations in the Arab World," in *Arab Society in Transition,* ed. N. Hopkins and S. Ibrahim. Cairo: American University in Cairo Press.

Abu-Lughod, L. 1986. *Veiled Sentiments: Honor and Poetry in a Bedouin Society.* Berkeley: University of California Press.

Ahmed, A. and Donnan, H. 1994. *Islam Globalization and Modernity.* London: Routledge.

Alba, R. 1990. *Ethnic Identity: The Transformation of White America.* New Haven: Yale University Press.

Antoun, R. T. 1967. "Social Organization and the Life Cycle in an Arab Village." *Ethnology* 6: 294–308.

_____. 1968. "On the Modesty of Women in Arab Muslim Villages: A Study in the Accommodation of Traditions." *American Anthropologist* 70: 671–697.

_____. 1968. "On the Significance of Names in an Arab Village." *Ethnology* 7: 158–70.

_____. 1972. *Arab Village: A Social Structural Study of a Transjordanian Peasant Community.* Bloomington: Indiana University Press.

_____. 1989. *Muslim Preacher in the Modern World: A Jordanian Case Study in Comparative Perspective.* Princeton: Princeton University Press.

_____. 1997. "Institutionalized Deconfrontation: A Case Study of Conflict Resolution among Tribal Peasants in Jordan," in *Conflict Resolution in the Arab World,* P. Salem. Beirut and Syracuse: American University of Beirut and Syracuse University Presses.

_____. 2000. "Civil Society, Tribal Process and Change in Jordan: An Anthropological View." *International Journal of Middle East Studies* 32: 441–463.

_____. 2001. *Understanding Fundamentalism: Christian, Islamic and Jewish Movements.* New York: AltaMira Press.

Banuazizi, A. and M. Weiner. 1986. *The State, Religion, and Ethnic Politics: Afghanistan, Iran and Pakistan.* Syracuse: Syracuse University Press.

Barber, B. 1980. "Toward a Definition of the Professions," in *The Political Influence of the Military: A Comparative Reader,* ed. A. Perlmutter and V. Bennett. New Haven: Yale University Press.

Barth, F. 1969. *Ethnic Groups and Boundaries: The Social Organization of Culture Difference.* Boston: Little Brown.

Basch, L., N. G. Schiller, and C. S. Blanc. 1994. *Nations Unbound: Transnational Projects, Postcolonial Predicaments, and Deterritorialized Nation States.* Amsterdam: Gordon and Breach.

Be'eri, E. 1970. *Army Officers in Arab Politics and Society.* New York: Praeger.

Berreman, G. 1962. "Behind Many Masks: Impression Management in a Himalayan Village" (monograph). Lexington, Kentucky: Society of Applied Anthropology, University of Kentucky.

Blau, P. and W. R. Scott. 1980. "Professional and Bureaucratic Orientation," in *The Political Influence of the Military.* New Haven: Yale University Press.

Brill, E.J. 2002. *Encyclopaedia of Islam* (new edition). Leiden.

Brink, J. 1991. "The Effect of Emigration of Husbands on the Status of Their Wives: an Egyptian Case." *International Journal of Middle East Studies* 23: 201–211.

Cerase, F. P. 1974. "Migration and Social Change: Expectations, Delusions, and Reflections upon the Return Flow from the United States to Italy." *International Migration Review* 8: 245–300.

Clifford, J. 1988. *The Predicament of Culture: Twentieth Century Ethnography, Literature, and Art.* Cambridge: Harvard University Press.

_____. 1994. "Diasporas." *Cultural Anthropology* 9: 302–338.

_____. and G. Marcus, ed. 1986. *Writing Culture: The Poetics and Politics of Ethnography.* Berkeley: University of California Press.

Courbage, Y. 1994. "Demographic Change in the Arab World: The Impact of Migration, Education and Taxes on Egypt and Morocco." *Middle East Report* 24: 19–22.

Day, A. D. 1986. *East Bank/West Bank: Jordan and the Prospects for Peace.* New York: Council on Foreign Relations.

Delaney, C. 1991. *The Seed and the Soil: Gender and Cosmology in Turkish Village Society.* Berkeley: University of California Press.

Evans-Pritchard, E. E. 1940. *The Nuer: A Description of the Modes of Livelihood and Political Institutions of a Nilotic People.* Oxford: Clarendon Press.

Fernea, E. 1965. *Guests of the Sheik.* New York: Doubleday.

Fischer, M. and M. Abedi. 1990. *Debating Muslims: Cultural Dialogues in Postmodernity and Tradition.* Madison: University of Wisconsin Press.

Fortes, M. 1945. *The Dynamics of Clanship among the Tallensi.* London: Oxford University Press.

_____. 1949. *The Web of Kinship among the Tallensi.* London: Oxford University Press.

Foucault, M. 1979. *Discipline and Punish: The Birth of the Prison.* New York: Vintage Books.

_____. 1980. *The History of Sexuality.* New York: Vintage books.

Freeman, J. 1979. *Untouchable: An Indian Life History.* Stanford: Stanford University Press.

Friedl, E. 1989. *The Women of Deh Koh: Stories from Iran.* Washington: Smithsonian Institution.

Garner, C. B. 1994. "Out of Place: Gender, Public Place, and Situational Advantage," in *Nowhere: Space, Time and Modernity,* ed. R. Friedlander and D. Bord. Berkeley: University of California Press.

Gabriel, R. and A. S. MacDougall. 1983. "Jordan," in *Fighting Armies: Antagonists in the Middle East, A Combat Assessment,* ed. R. A. Gabriel. Westport, Connecticut: Greenwood Press.

Gage, A. 1994. "'Mezanmi, Kouman Nou Ye? My Friends, How Are You?': Musical Constructions of the Haitian Transnation." *Diaspora* 3: 253–272.

Geertz, C. 1973. "Ethos, World View and the Analysis of Sacred Symbols," in *The Interpretation of Cultures,* C. Geertz. New York: Basic Books.

Gellens, S. I. 1990. "The Search for Knowledge in Medieval Societies: A Comparative Approach," in *Muslim Travelers: Pilgrimage, Migration and the Religious Imagination,* ed. D. Eickelman and J. Piscatori. Berkeley: University of California Press.

Glazer, N. 1997. *We Are All Multiculturalists.* Cambridge: Harvard University Press.

Gluckman, M. 1955. *The Judicial Process among the Barotse of Northern Rhodesia.* Manchester: Manchester University Press.

_____. 1960. *Custom and Conflict in Africa.* Oxford: Basil Blackwell.

Goody, J. 1958. *The Developmental Cycle of Domestic Groups.* Cambridge: Cambridge University Press.

Gupta, A. and J. Ferguson. 1992. "Beyond 'Culture': Space, Identity and the Politics of Difference." *Current Anthropology* 7: 6–23.

Halliday, F. 1984. "Labor Migration in the Arab World." *MERIP Reports* 14: 3–10.

Hammarlund, A. 1994. "Migrancy and Syncretism: A Turkish Musician in Stockholm." *Diaspora* 3: 305–324.

Handler, R. and Linnekin, J. 1984. "Tradition Genuine or Spurious." *Journal of American Folklore* 97: 273–290.

Hefner, R. 1985. *Hindu-Javanese: Tengger Tradition and Islam.* Princeton: Princeton University Press.

Hegland, M. 1983. "Two Images of Husain: Accommodation and Revolution in an Iranian Village," in *Religion and Politics in Iran,* ed. N. Keddie. New Haven: Yale University Press.

_____. 1986. "Imam Khomeini's Village: Recruitment to Revolution." (Ph. D. dissertation, State University of New York at Binghamton).

_____. 1995. "Shia Women of Northwest Pakistan and Agency through Practice: Ritual, Resistance, Resilience." *Polar: Political and Legal Anthropology Review* 18: 65–80.

Humphrey, M. 1993. "Migrants, Workers and Refugees: The Political Economy of Population Movements in the Middle East." *Middle East Report* 23: 2–9.

Huntington, S. 1980. "Officership as a Profession," in *The Political Influence of the Military.* New Haven: Yale University Press.

_____. 1980. "The Professional Military Ethic," in *The Political Influence of the Military.* New Haven: Yale University Press.

Irons, W. 1974. "Nomadism as a Political Adaptation: The Case of the Yomut Turkmen." *American Ethnologist* 1: 635–658.

Isaacs, H. R. 1989. *Idols of the Tribe: Group Identity and Political Change.* Cambridge: Harvard University Press.

Izady, M. 1992. *A Concise Handbook of Kurds*. Washington: Taylor and Francis.

Jarvis, C. S. 1943. *The Arab Command: The Biography of Lieutenant-Colonel F. G. Peake Pasha*. London: Hutchinson and Company.

Jones, W. H. M. 1980. "Armed Forces and the State," in *The Political Influence of the Military*. New Haven: Yale University Press.

Joseph, S. 1978. "Women and the Neighborhood Street in Borj Hammoud, Lebanon," in *Women in the Muslim World*, ed. L. Beck. and N. Keddie. Cambridge: Harvard University Press.

_____. 1999. *Intimate Selving in Arab Families: Gender, Self, and Identity*. Syracuse: Syracuse University Press.

Jureidini, P. A. and McLaurin, R. D. 1984. *Jordan: The Impact of Social Change on the Role of the Tribes*. New York: Praeger.

Kapferer, B. 1976. *Transaction and Meaning: Directions in the Anthropology of Exchange and Symbolic Behavior*. Philadelphia: Ishi.

Keely, C. and Sacket B. 1984 "Jordanian Migrant Workers in the Arab Region: A Case Study of Consequences for Labor Supplying Countries." *The Middle East Journal* 30: 685–98.

Keyder, C. and A. Aksu-Koc. 1988. *External Labour Migration from Turkey and its Impact: An Evaluation of the Literature*. Ottowa: International Development Research Centre.

Khafagy, F. 1984. "Women in Labor Migration: One Village in Egypt." *MERIP Reports* 14: 17–21.

Khuri, F. "Modernizing Societies in the Middle East," in *Civil-Military Relations: Regional Perspectives*. ed. M. Janowitz. Beverly Hills: Sage.

_____ and G. Obermeyer. 1974. "The Social Bases for Military Intervention in the Middle East," in *Political-Military Systems: Comparative Perspectives*, ed. C. M. Kelleher. Beverly Hills: Sage.

Kluckhohn, C. 1936. "Some Reflections on the Method and Theory of the Kulturkreislehre." *American Anthropologist* 38: 157–196.

Langness, L. L. and G. Frank. 1981. *Lives: An Anthropological Approach to Biography*. Novato, California: Chandler and Sharp.

Layne, L. 1989. "The Dialogics of Tribal Self-Representation in Jordan." *American Ethnologist* 16: 24–39.

_____. 1994. *Home and Homeland: the Dialogics of Tribal and National Identities in Jordan*. Princeton: Princeton University Press.

_____, ed. 1987. *Elections in the Middle East: Implications of Recent Trends*. Boulder: Westview Press.

Latowsky, R. 1984. "Egyptian Labor Abroad: Mass Participation and Modest Returns." *MERIP Reports* 14: 11–18.

Lawrence, B. 1989. *Defenders of God: The Fundamentalist Revolt against the Modern Age*. San Francisco: Harper and Row.

Leach, E. "The Structural Implications of Matrilateral Cross-Cousin Marriage." *Journal of the Royal Anthropological Institute of Great Britain and Ireland* 81: 23–55.

Lewis, I. 1961. *A Pastoral Democracy: A Study of Pastoralism and Politics among the Northern Somali of the Horn of Africa*. London: Oxford University Press.

Linton, R. 1936. *The Study of Man.* New York: Appleton-Century-Crofts.

Malkki, L. 1992. "National Geographic: The Rooting of Peoples and the Territorialization of National Identity among Scholars and Refugees." *Cultural Anthropology* 7: 24–44.

Mandlebaum, D. 1973. "The Study of the Life History: Ghandi." *Current Anthropology* 14: 177–96.

Masud, M. K. 1990. "The Obligation to Migrate: The Doctrine of *hijra* in Islamic Law," in *Muslim Travelers: Pilgrimage, Migration and the Religious Imagination,* ed. D. Eickelman and J. Piscatori. Berkeley: University of California Press.

Merton, R. 1961. *Social Theory and Social Structure.* Glencoe, Illinois: The Free Press.

Michalak, L. 1988. "The Impact of Continuing and Return Migrants from Tunisia: Case Studies from the Tunisian Northwest." (Paper presented to Conference on International Migration of Middle Easterners and North Africans: Comparing Diasporas, UCLA).

Mumtaz, S. 1990. "The Dynamics of Changing Ethnic Boundaries: A Case Study of Karachi." *The Pakistan Development Review* 29: 223–248.

Nash, M. 1977. "Modernization: Cultural Meanings—the Widening Gap between the Intellectuals and the Process." *Economic Development and Cultural Change* 25: (Supplement 1977).

Peake, F. G. 1935. *The History of East Jordan.* Jerusalem.

———. 1958. *A History of Jordan and Its Tribes.* Coral Gables: Univeristy of Miami Press.

Peters, E. 1990. *The Bedouin of Cyrenaica: Studies in Personal and Corporate Power,* ed. J. Goody and E. Marx. Cambridge: Cambridge University Press.

Redfield, R. 1941. *The Folk Culture of Yucatan.* Chicago: University of Chicago Press.

Rosen, L. 1989. *The Anthropology of Justice: Law as Culture in Islamic Society.* Cambridge: Cambridge University Press.

Rothstein, F. A. 1992. "Conclusion: New Waves and Old—Industrialization, Labor and the Struggle for a New World Order," in *Anthropology and the Global Factory: Studies of the New Industrialization in the Late Twentieth Century,* ed. F. Rothstein and M. Blim. New York: Bergin and Garvey.

Rouse, R. 1991. "Mexican Migration and the Social Space of Postmodernism." *Diaspora* 1: 8–23.

Rubay'ah, A. 1982. *hijrat al-rifiyyin min al-aghwar al-shimalliya ila madinat irbid: dawafi'iha, mashakiliha, atharaha 'ala khatat al-tanmiyya (Rural Migration from the Northern Jordan Valley to the City of Irbid: Its Impact, Its problems, Its Consequences for Development Plans).* Amman: Jordan University Publication.

Ryan, C. 2002. *Jordan in Transition: From Hussein to Abdullah.* Boulder: Lynne Reinner.

Salzman, P. 1978. "Does Complementary Opposition Exist." *American Anthropologist* 80: 53–70.

Samha, M. 1987. "The Impact of Migration on Population Changes in Jordan." (Paper presented at a conference sponsored by the Southwest Asia and North Africa Program of the State University of New York at Binghamton, April 1987).

Sanjek, R. 1990. *Fieldnotes: The Makings of Anthropology.* Ithaca: Cornell University Press.

Satloff, R. B. 1986. *Troubles on the East Bank: Challenges to the Domestic Security of Jordan.* New York: Praeger.

Scott, J. 1976. *The Moral Economy of the Peasant: Rebellion and Subsistence in Southeast Asia.* New Haven: Yale University Press.

Seecombe, I. 1987. "Labour Migration and the Transformation of a Village Economy: A Case Study from Northwest Jordan," in *The Middle Eastern Village: Changing Economic and Social Relations,* ed. R. Lawless. London: Croom Helm.

Shami, S. 1990. *Women in Arab Society: Work Patterns and Gender Relations in Egypt, Jordan and Sudan.* New York: St. Martin's Press.

Shepard, W. E. 1987. "Islam and Ideology: Toward a Typology." *International Journal of Middle East Studies* 19: 307–336.

Shryock, A. 2000. "House Politics in Tribal Jordan: Reflections on Honor, Family and Nation in the Hashemite Kingdom," in *Tribu, Parentele et Etat en Pays d'Islam,* ed. E. Conte, P. Dresch, and L. Valensi. Paris: Laboratoire d'Anthropologie Sociale, College de France.

Singer, M. 1972. *When a Great Tradition Modernizes: An Anthropological Approach to Indian Civilization.* New York: Praeger.

Smith, D. E. 1970. *Religion in Political Development.* Boston: Little Brown.

Socknat, J., S. Birks and I. Serageldin. 1986. "International Labour Migration in the Middle East and North Africa: Current and Prospective Dimensions, 1978–85," in *Social Legislation in the Contemporary Middle East,* ed. L. Michalak and J. Salacuse. Berkeley: Institute of International Studies.

Stevenson, T. 1993. "Yemeni Workers Come Home: Reabsorbing One Million Migrants." *Middle East Report* 23: 15–24.

Teske, R. and B. Nelson. 1974. "Acculturation and Assimilation: A Clarification." *American Ethnologist* 1: 351–368.

Tololyan, K. 1991. "The Nation-State and its Others: In Lieu of a Preface." *Diaspora* 1: 3–7.

Tutwiler, R. 1987. "Tribe, Tribute and Trade: Social Class Formation in Highland Yemen." (Ph. D. Dissertation, State University of New York at Binghamton).

Vatikiotis, P. J. 1987. *Politics and the Military in Jordan: A Study of the Arab Legion 1921–1957.* London: Cass.

Wahlin, L. 1987. "Diffusion and Acceptance of Modern Schooling in Rural Jordan," in *The Middle Eastern Village: Changing Economic and Social Relations,* R. Lawless. London: Croom Helm.

_____. 1994. *Back to Settled Life? Rural Change in the 'Allan Area of Jordan, 1867–1980: Assessment of a Research Project.* Stockholm: Kulturgeografiska Institutionen.

_____. 1994. "Inheritance of Land in the Jordanian Hill Country." *British Journal of Middle Eastern Studies* 21: 1–27.

Zheng, S. 1994. "Music in Cultural Displacement: The Chinese-American Odyssey." *Diaspora* 3: 273–288.

INDEX

❦

321